WILLIAM M. FOWLER, JR.

REBELS UNDER SAIL

The American Navy during

the Revolution

CHARLES SCRIBNER'S SONS / *NEW YORK*

Copyright © 1976 William M. Fowler

Library of Congress Cataloging in Publication Data

Fowler, William M   1944–
  Rebels under sail.

  Bibliography: pp. 340–345
  Includes index.
  1.United States—History—Revolution, 1775–1783—
Naval operations.   2.United States. Navy—History—
Revolution, 1775–1783. I. Title.
E271.F68   973.3′5   75–38556
ISBN 0–684–14583–9

1 3 5 7 9 11 13 15 17 19 H/C 20 18 16 14 12 10 8 6 4 2

Printed in the United States of America

Organization Chart, page 62. Drawn by George
Robinson.

The Thirteen Colonies, page 92. Reprinted by
permission of Charles Scribner's Sons from *Atlas of
American History* by James Truslow Adams, plate
66. Copyright 1943 Charles Scribner's Sons.

Invasion of Canada, 1775–1776, page 172. Reprinted by
permission of Charles Scribner's Sons from *Atlas of
American History* by James Truslow Adams, plate
67. Copyright 1943 Charles Scribner's Sons.

REBELS UNDER SAIL

Also by William M. Fowler, Jr.

William Ellery: A Rhode Island Politico
and Lord of Admiralty

To Albert Everett Flygare,
for seven decades a Gloucester sailmaker

Contents

Introduction

Americans are great celebrators and memorialists. At very little urging, selectmen, mayors, governors and presidents are wont to declare on any given day the silver anniversary, golden anniversary, diamond jubilee, centennial, bicentennial or tercentenary of some momentous event. With equal abandon memorials in various and sundry shapes—plaques, statues and the like—are put up around the countryside and even on the moon so that visitors may be reminded of the historical significance of the spot where they stand. And so the commemorative bandwagon rolls along at a ponderable rate, but occasionally in a splurge of historical hoopla it runs away with itself. Such might well be the case during America's Bicentennial.

Each day marks the two hundredth anniversary of some event somewhere, and with the memory flows the rhetoric, laced unabashedly with immodest descriptions like "the first," "most important," "biggest" and "birth of." A few have a good claim to the superlative, others only a tenuous one and most none at all.

Naval historians should be especially aware of contracting Bicentennial fever with its alarming symptom of verbal inflation, for in the past one whiff of sea air has carried many away to an ethereal plane where all is glory, romance and John Paul Jones. Indeed, romance and glory are part of the tale and should rightfully be told, but the truth is not served when we allow them to be the whole story. As in all wars and as with all services, the real experience was a paradoxical combination of exceptional gallantry and shabby expediency, heroism and cowardice, all existing amid a world of boredom punctuated by occasional moments of excitement.

To be sure, the American Revolution was, as Alfred Thayer Mahan would quickly testify, a naval war. However, the great decisions at sea, off Ushant, the Saints or the Chesapeake, were made not by the Continental navy but by the wooden giants making up the fleets of England, France and Spain. It could hardly be otherwise, for despite all the hope and effort, the Americans were navigating in shoal water, full of unseen hazards that would block their course to naval greatness. Compared to the enemy's squadrons, the Continental navy was a puny force. Nevertheless, against overwhelming odds, they ventured to sea, and in their own way, both by victory and defeat, they helped to achieve independence. For that they deserve to be remembered.

A large crew helped me to put this book together, and in naming some I am sure to omit others. For that omission I ask their pardon.

Philip C. F. Smith of the Peabody Museum in Salem, Massachusetts, helped me obtain photographs of items in his museum. In addition, he was instrumental in securing permission to use the four pictures of *Hancock*'s capture.

Professor Marshall Smelser of the University of Notre Dame provided kind words and sage advice. Most importantly, though, he stands as an example of fine scholarship and devoted teaching. Professor Raymond Robinson, chairman of the History Department at Northeastern, and Nancy Borromey, departmental secretary, were extremely helpful in extending to me whatever resources were available. On the other side of the campus the personnel at Dodge Library always stood ready to provide cheerful assistance.

Dean Arthur Fitzgerald of Northeastern listened sympathetically to the cries of poverty from a young assistant professor and responded with an assistance grant. A grant from the National Endowment for the Humanities released me from my teaching duties during the summer of 1974 so that I could spend full time on my project.

As the Beatles tell us, we all get by with a little help from our friends, and no one knows that any better than someone who has just finished several years of research and writing. My thanks especially to Phil and Dyan, "the car pool," for providing humor, understanding and plain good sense.

Finally I must find some way to thank my wife, Marilyn, whose patience grows to match my cantankerousness. It is impossible, for she has given so much more than I can return.

Abbreviations

DAB   *Dictionary of American Biography*
DANFS *Dictionary of American Naval Fighting Ships*
DNB   *Dictionary of National Biography*
JCC   *Journals of the Continental Congress*
MHS   Massachusetts Historical Society
NDAR *Naval Documents of the American Revolution*
NYPL New York Public Library
PCC   Papers of the Continental Congress

Chapter One

A Sea-Minded Nation

Was it foolishness and naiveté that prompted the representatives of a weak, disunited, fragile coalition of thirteen states to embark upon the creation of a powerful navy? Certainly not to those men who supported the decision, for they saw nothing unreasonable in it. If they could draw upon the experience of the militia to build an army, then they could rely upon their years with the sea to launch a navy.

Americans were a sea-minded people who from the very first days of settlement had been drawn as much to the sea as to the land. They traveled by sea; they looked to the sea to provide their living; the sea was a barrier to their enemies and an avenue to the mother country.

It was cod, herring and halibut that drew Europeans to the western Atlantic, to fish along the rich grounds of Georges Banks and the Grand Banks. Fishermen had led the way to America and they were followed at first by men more interested in religion and land, but economic necessity and a stingy soil soon dictated that fishing would be one of the main pursuits of these people.

But if fishing turned these men to the sea, so too did the forests, for abutting thousands of inlets and streams along the jagged shore stood tall conifers, white pines whose height and girth made them eminently suitable to be stepped as masts on

His Majesty's vessels. These northern white pines provided a strategic reserve at a time when it was becoming more and more important to England to conform to the mercantilist doctrine of self-sufficiency, placing less reliance on the forests of the Baltic nations and more on those within the empire itself. The timber resources of the North American continent seemed limitless at a moment when the demand for such products was rising at an unprecedented rate. The discovery and colonization of vast new overseas territories meant a rapid increase in seaborne commerce requiring great numbers of ships. Improvements in design and size of merchantmen required more timber, as did the large number of warships necessary for the protection of the sea lanes linking the mother country and colonies.

In New England the timber business was essential to the local economy, especially in New Hampshire, where it far outranked any other endeavor. To a lesser extent the business prospered even in the colonies farther to the south. Wherever there were great rivers such as the Connecticut and the Hudson, men could roam far inland harvesting timber and floating it down to the coast. Below the Chesapeake in the Carolinas and Georgia, where the long-leaf and slash pines cover the countryside, the forests were prized for their yield of naval stores of tar, pitch and turpentine.

With these vast resources at their disposal and the sea so close at hand, it was inevitable that the American colonials would not only supply the needs of the mother country but begin to consider their own requirements as well. It would not be long before they would embark on their own shipbuilding enterprises.[1]

Building homes for shelter against a hostile environment was the first industry in America that joined the settlers in a cooperative venture. Shipbuilding was the second. At Sagadahoc, near the mouth of the Kennebec, the ill-fated settlers of the Virginia Company of Plymouth launched the first vessel

built in America. She was *Virginia*, thirty tons. Seven years
later the Dutch explorer Adrian Bloc launched his sixteen-ton
yacht *Onrest* at the future site of New York City. Shipwrights
were among the earliest settlers in both Virginia and Massachusetts Bay, but it was in the latter especially that the business thrived and spread until it touched nearly every coastal
community from Penobscot Bay to Cape Cod. By the mid-
seventeenth century oceangoing vessels were sliding down
the ways at Boston and Salem, as well as Ipswich and Salisbury, as shipwrights moved farther along the shore following
an ever receding timber supply. To further stimulate this
growing industry the Massachusetts General Court provided
tax incentives to shipbuilders by not taxing vessels while they
stood in the stocks. The Bay Colony was also the first to
provide for a system of quality control through the appointment of inspectors who were to ensure that only sound timber was being used.[2]

New England was earliest and had the initial advantage,
but whenever the necessary conjunction of skilled men and
tall timber occurred, shipbuilding got underway. The Navigation Acts, passed under the Cromwellian government,
created a shipbuilding boom within the empire. Carried forward under the royal governments, this legislation did more
to launch ships "than the fabled beauty of Helen of Troy."[3]
Even in New York, which had long lagged behind her northern neighbors, there were at least three active shipyards by
the early eighteenth century.[4] Farther to the south the Yan-
kees and Yorkers faced fierce competition from Philadelphia,
where the energetic Quakers had begun framing vessels as
early as 1683. The impressive economic growth of that city
was mirrored in its shipbuilding industry, until by the eve of
the Revolution more large ships were being launched there
than anywhere else in the colonies.[5] In the southern colonies
shipbuilding remained pretty much a business of constructing small, shallow-draft vessels suitable for sailing in among
the sandbars of Virginia and the Carolinas. Even the verses

of that Maryland poetaster Ebenezer Cooke could not persuade men to divert capital from the lucrative plantation industries to shipbuilding:

> Materials here, of every kind
> May soon be found, were Youth inclin'd,
> To practice the Ingenious Art
> Of sailing by Mercantor's Chart. . . .
>
> Nothing is wanting to compleat
> Fit for the Sea a trading Fleet
> But Industry and Resolution.[6]

The only southern area of sufficient population and wealth to
support a shipbuilding industry, Charleston, found herself
handicapped by a very limited demand and high wages. In
this lone southern port the few yards that did survive relied
almost entirely on refitting work and building some small
craft for coastal voyages.[7]

Having started well in the seventeenth century, the American merchant marine and shipbuilding industry enjoyed phenomenal growth in the eighteenth. Under the protection of
the Navigation Acts the colonials and British enjoyed a
monopoly over the carrying trade of the world's most pros-
perous empire.[8] The rising demand for hulls to carry this
trade, coupled with the abundant resources in the colonies,
made shipbuilding the largest single industry in the American colonies.

From 1700 to 1775 the colonies increased their output of
vessels from four thousand tons per year to thirty-five thousand, so that by the latter year one-third of all vessels operating in the empire had been built in America.[9] From Penobscot Bay to the Ashley and Cooper rivers vessels were being
framed, planked and launched in such numbers that the shipwrights of the Thames petitioned Parliament to restrict the
colonies so that great injury might not be done to shipyards
in England.[10] Despite the attempts by the English ship-

wrights to restrict the business, the fact remained that vessels could be built more cheaply in America than anywhere else in the empire and the resulting demand both at home and abroad pushed the industry steadily ahead.

For the most part, shipbuilding in America remained throughout the colonial period an industry dominated by the small firm whose location shifted according to the availability of resources. No great amount of technology was involved, and there was little difference between the craft of a ship-wright in 1775 and that of his grandfather in 1700; both relied on their hand tools, such as the axe and adze, and built their vessels wherever they could find sufficient timber and naviga-ble water.

Shipbuilding was an arduous, complex, time-consuming business. First, timber would have to be selected. Oak was ordinarily preferred for the hull since it was strong and dura-ble, and pine for the masts and spars because of its flexibility and ability to take stress.[11] Gangs of workmen were sent into the forests to cut the timber and bring it to the yard. Ideally the cutting would be done in winter, when the trees had less sap in them and could therefore season in less time. If the trees were close to a stream, the logs could be floated down to the yard, but if not, then great, tugging teams of oxen would drag the timber to the site. Once at the yard the logs were dragged across a deep pit. Here two men, one man below and another above, would begin the arduous task of sawing the timber into usable planks. While the timber was being prepared, shipwrights were busy erecting the ways and placing the stem and stern posts. In going about their work, they did much according to experience and the rule of thumb, but in many instances they had to draw and follow actual plans. Once the timber was ready, the workmen laid out the frame, beginning amidships and working fore and aft. After the frame was in place, strakes of planking were snugged together and fastened to the inside timbers with long trunnels (tree nails), wooden pegs driven into holes prepared with huge augers. Thousands of trunnels were used, and before they were trimmed off from the inside, the empty hull had the look of a huge inside out porcupine. Iron fastenings could be used, but they were expensive and, besides, they corroded after contact with salt water and the tannic acid of the oak. With the planking up, the carpenters stepped aside and let the caulkers go to work. They swung their mallets and pounded pieces of oakum (hemp treated with tar) into the seams. In every yard it was the same story—if the vessel leaked, the carpenters blamed the caulkers and the caulkers accused the carpenters. After the hull was fully formed and the decks were in place, the vessel was ready to be launched. If she was sizable, the whole community would turn out for the christening, even in Boston, where such proceedings came under the disapproving eye of the eminent divine and social critic Cotton Mather, who thought the idea of christening a vessel to be an impious affront. It was a festive occasion: "A man would sit astride the end of the bowsprit and as the vessel began to move, he would call out the name that had been given her at the same time breaking a bottle of rum over the bowsprit first drinking from the bottle."[12]

Once afloat, the new hull was taken to a nearby wharf where a swarm of local craftsmen came abroad to complete her for sea. Rigged, fitted and manned, she would soon be ready to take on cargo and begin her career as an American merchantman. The average time for construction was about one year, although in at least one instance at Philadelphia a vessel was completed in the remarkably short time of seventy-three days.[13] To complete a fair-sized vessel required the combined efforts of at least thirty different craftsmen, including riggers, coopers, carpenters, sail makers, rope makers and many others. "Thus," as Carl Bridenbaugh has said, "the construction of a large ship represents, as does nothing else, the supreme achievement of early American craftsman-ship."[14]

American craftsmen were capable of turning out vessels of considerable size. A New Haven yard launched a vessel of seven hundred tons in 1725, and half a century later *Maria Wilhelmina*, eight hundred tons, slid down the ways at New York.[15] But these monsters were unusual and unnecessary in American commerce. In the American trade the emphasis was not on size but on speed, maneuverability and ease of handling. Large ships were too costly to operate and ill suited to the needs of American merchants and fishermen, who were as much concerned with weatherliness as with cargo capacity.[16] As a result, American yards were more likely to launch sloops and schooners of fore and aft rig than the larger, more cumbersome, square-rigged vessels. The schooner was especially popular in American waters since it could be built to some size without sacrificing fine sailing qualities and ease of handling.[17] Many were built in New England, with those built for Marbleheaders having an especially fine reputation; in fact, the first vessel to be taken into the Continental service was the Marblehead schooner *Hannah*.

The proliferation of American-built vessels in the eighteenth century was only partially a result of good design; the major factor was their cheap cost. On a per-ton basis, vessels launched in the colonies were on an average about thirty to fifty percent cheaper.[18] High labor costs in the colonies were more than offset by cheap materials enabling Americans to easily undercut foreign competitors. But while American-built vessels had a great cost advantage, they likewise had a great handicap, namely, their reputation for poor quality. Contemporaries generally believed that American vessels were inferior to those built in Great Britain, and there does seem to be good evidence that American-built vessels did not last as long as their English counterparts. A common complaint was that the timber in American vessels rotted prematurely. This was probably due not to any innate inferiority of American materials but rather to an injudicious selection of timber as well as the American style of building. All wooden vessels suffer from rotting, but its progress can be retarded when the wood is properly seasoned. Ideally a vessel should "stand in frame" for a year before being planked over, to allow time for her timbers to season, becoming more resistant to rot. Such a procedure was possible in a large English or European yard, but in a small American one where a shipwright's entire capital might be tied up in a single vessel it was not economically feasible. Quite often in an American yard the seasoning process for timber might last only as long as it took for the trip from the forest to the yard. Unseasoned timber inevitably meant quick rotting, and throughout the eighteenth century American vessels had a well-earned reputation for being short-lived.[19]

In addition to the problem of the durability of the timber, American vessels also tended to be more slightly built; that is, the pieces making up the frame were widely spaced. This, too, might well have adversely affected the longevity of American vessels.

Despite the cost advantage, few warships of His Majesty's navy were ever built in American yards. When the Revolution broke out, American shipwrights knew a good deal about building vessels for the merchant and fishing fleets but much less about building warships. Constructing naval vessels was a far more complex task than building sloops, schooners and fishing smacks. Not only were they of greater size, but they also had to be more sturdily built to accommodate the weight of their armament and more heavily sparred to move their great bulk through the water. Unseasoned timber and slightly built frames were by no means suited to the needs of the Royal Navy.

Aside from small patrol and dispatch vessels, only four warships of any rate were completed in the colonies for service in the Royal Navy.[20] The first of these was *Falkland*, 637 tons, built at Portsmouth, New Hampshire, in 1695.[21] Shortly after her launching, the Admiralty asked the opinion of the Thames shipwrights about the quality of American timber used in the construction of His Majesty's ships such as *Falkland*. They replied that it was "of so infirm a nature as not to be fit for use in His Majesty's ships."[22] Nevertheless, six years later another warship was built at Portsmouth—*Bedford*, 372 tons.[23] *Falkland* and *Bedford* were exceptions, and the naval commissioners would not again consent to the building of large warships in America until more than fifty years later when, over their strong objections, two more vessels were built in American yards.[24] Pressure to authorize the construction of these vessels came from Admirals Knowles and Warren, who commanded on the North American station. When opposition was voiced to the plan, Knowles asserted that the construction should go forward as an experiment "to find whither the [colonial] Builders could improve upon those [ships] built in England."[25] The naval commissioners thought otherwise and strongly advised against the plan, arguing that New England timber was so inferior that it was sure to rot. However valid these technical points might have been, the fact was the New England colonies under Governor William Shirley had just conquered the French fortress Louisbourg at great expense to themselves and the contracts for these ships were intended as partial recompense for that considerable effort.[26] Two warships were built—*America*, at Portsmouth, and *Boston*, in Boston. Apparently the "experiment" only proved what the naval commissioners had alleged all along, for neither *Boston* nor *America* enjoyed a long life in the Royal Navy.[27] These were the last warships of any size to be built in America until the Revolution.

While the colonial shipyards were conspicuous in their failure to build large warships, they did manage to complete successfully a number of smaller vessels for service in the navy. These vessels were predominantly sloops and schooners generally of shoal draft and designed for work on lakes or for ferreting out and apprehending smugglers along the coasts. Most of them, like the four large warships, were probably built on designs supplied by the Admiralty which could be slightly modified according to local circumstances and preferences. An exception to this would be the schooners since they were of American origin and design and could be better drawn in the colonies than elsewhere. Schooner-rigged vessels proved to be admirably adapted for naval work along the American coasts. Their weatherliness and shoal draft gave them an inshore capability lacking in larger vessels, and unlike other small craft they could be well armed carrying from four to ten guns.

Although only four rated men-of-war were ever built in the colonies, it does not follow that American shipwrights were unfamiliar with warship construction. Indeed, as some of the designs of the Continental vessels clearly show, Americans could design warships along some of the best lines. A good amount of this technical knowledge came from years of experience in repairing and refitting ships on the North American station. Working on board these vessels, shipwrights could not help but notice how their construction differed from merchant ships. By the eve of the Revolution there were men in all the American ports whose knowledge of shipbuilding was nearly as good as the best shipwrights at any of His Majesty's yards in England.

An expanding merchant marine made extraordinary demands on manpower, and thousands of young men in the colonies were drawn by those forces that have always attracted men to the sea: treasure, excitement and escapism. Many who opted to leave the farm for the forecastle stayed only a few years at sea and then returned to the land. Others lingered, with a few rising from seaman to mate and perhaps even to captain. By 1775 some thirty thousand seamen were employed on American vessels in either fishing or the merchant marine. Most of these young men came from the northern colonies, with New England heavily represented.[28] It was a rugged and strenuous life but perhaps no more perilous than facing the dangers of an untracked frontier or trying to eke out a living on a subsistence farm in an isolated backwoods area. But while the degree of peril might be similar, in at least one regard the sailor's life was quite different from the landsman's, for whereas the latter might prize individualism and independence, the former was part of a crew whose very lives depended upon quick obedience enforced by harsh discipline. The captain's orders were to be obeyed, and those who faltered or failed to comply might find themselves on short rations, confined or flogged.

Despite the vast gulf between quarterdeck and forecastle on board ship, there was in the American merchant marine a rough kind of democracy and social mobility not found in the British service. It was possible for a man to move upward into the officer ranks, and some merchant captains had actually begun their careers as ordinary seamen or lower. Still, these men were in all probability the exception, and the romantic notion of the young boy running off to sea and rising to command his own vessel is more folktale than reality, as thousands of young men unhappily discovered once they had signed on board. The image of jolly Jack Tars dancing the hornpipe and singing sea chanties should more accurately be that of men engaged in a constant and deadly battle against boredom, disease and an awesome sea.

Sailors testified to the harshness of life at sea by their high rates of desertion. Desertion was a greater drain on manpower in peace and war to both the merchant marine and the navy than disease, shipwreck or enemy fire. As the sailors themselves sang:

> O the times are hard and the wages low,
> Leave her, John-ny, leave her;
> I'll pack my bag and go be-low;
> It's time for us to leave her.[29]

In wartime, as desertion reached epidemic proportions, commanders in the Royal Navy resorted to the age-old but detested practice of pressing to fill their complements. There was no quicker way to empty seaport taverns and brothels than the cry "Press gang!" This rather heavy-handed form of selective service grew more common in American waters during the colonial wars of the eighteenth century as increasing numbers of Royal Navy vessels were sent to the North

American station.[30] Even after the Treaty of Paris in 1763 pressing continued in North American waters as a large number of ships were kept on station patroling against smugglers. American sailors did not take meekly to being pressed, and many times their anger and resentment boiled over into violent rioting. On occasion when the activities of the press gang were particularly obnoxious, other citizens joined with the sailors in tumultuous demonstrations of protest. In Boston the press gang caused such a furor that an angry mob stormed the colony house, smashed windows, then forced their way into the lower floor and sent the governor fleeing out to Castle William in the harbor for protection.[31]

As the turbulent years of the sixties and early seventies rolled on, sailors could almost always be found among the mobs protesting the most recent parliamentary act. When the Americans moved to combat the injudicious acts of Parliament with boycotts and nonimportation, sailors found themselves on the beach and unemployed. Their resentment toward the royal government grew, and radical leaders found among these men a receptive audience for their programs of disruption and resistance. Yet they were not simply the tools of these radical leaders, for the seaman "had a mind of his own and genuine reasons to act, and . . . he did act—purposefully."[32] When war came, they responded in large numbers to serve against the British, partly out of a desire for gain but also impelled by the opportunity to strike a blow at an enemy they had known for so long.

Whether in the form of political mobs or just rowdy brawls, violence and sailors, to contemporary observers, seemed to go together. Nor was violence counted to be the least of a sailor's vices. According to many, sailors were equally addicted to swearing, whoring, drinking and gaming, to name only some of the most heinous. Whether the forecastle did actually harbor such blackened souls can only be guessed, but shore folk certainly thought so and sailors enjoyed a reputation for sin, violence and adventure.

In wartime they more than earned their fearsome reputations when by the thousands they abandoned the sober business of the merchant marine for the heady excitement of privateering. Privateering was the fitting out and arming of private vessels in wartime "to cruise against and among the enemy by taking, sinking or burning their shipping."[33] All nations took part in this legalized *guerre de course*, but American seamen seemed to have a particular relish for it. Enticing the sailor to the business was the promise of a certain share or lay in the voyage according to his rank, and there are sufficient instances in the eighteenth century of young men returning from a voyage with enough riches to retire to give some substance to the romantic aura and dreams of wealth that lured so many to sign on. But if the profits were high, so too were the risks. Privateers were ordinarily small, lightly armed vessels designed not so much to fight as to run. Their task was to take merchantmen while eluding the enemy's warships. In this they were not always successful, and eighteenth-century warfare is replete with tales of privateers that either through carelessness or misfortune were captured or destroyed. Nor were privateers an unmixed blessing, for despite their great success at destroying enemy commerce, they were, nevertheless, a disruptive element in planning naval strategy. The fierce independence and sometimes consuming greed of the men who were privateers made them reluctant to conform to a superior officer for any kind of coordinated operation. This was true in some of the operations undertaken during the colonial wars and remained to haunt the Continental navy in the Revolution. The privateersman's failure to follow conventional practice could frequently lead to senseless losses. In one instance a Royal Navy vessel engaged an unknown ship for an entire night, only to find in the morning that she was a friendly privateer whose crew was unaware of the proper recognition signals.[34]

In American waters privateers aggravated the always serious problem of finding sailors to man vessels on the North American station. Men deserted naval vessels in droves for the more attractive and lucrative career of privateering. In the ports of New York, Newport and Boston at least 230 privateers with more than five thousand men cleared during the French and Indian War. So enticing were the fruits of privateering that in 1757 several of His Majesty's warships were unable to leave New York harbor because so many of the crew had deserted to go privateering.[35]

Although the colonies remained preoccupied with wartime privateering, they did pay some attention to fitting out public warships to serve in colonial navies. In a manner similar to the one that they would follow in the Revolution, various colonies during the eighteenth century authorized the building or buying of armed vessels at public expense. Massachusetts Bay fitted out *Protector* to participate in the assault against Louisbourg, while South Carolina engaged a number of vessels to scout for Spanish intruders or possible runaway slaves.[36] Other colonies followed suit, but in every case these colonial navies were overshadowed and severely crippled by the activities of local privateers.

Strangely, despite the swarm of Americans who went to sea in both peace and war, very few ever voluntarily joined the Royal Navy. It would appear that only four officers in the Continental navy had ever shipped on board a royal man-of-war: Nicholas Biddle, Hector McNeill, John Manley and Samuel Tucker.[37] At least one other American officer of Revolutionary fame came very close to taking a commission in the Royal Navy: George Washington. His brother Lawrence offered to obtain a berth for him, and the young Washington, then fourteen, had his bags packed but the "earnest solicitations" of his mother dissuaded him from the sea.[38]

Privateering, the merchant marine, shipbuilding—these were all part of a sea habit that had grown to sizable proportions in the years between Sagadahoc and Lexington Green. To the more naval-minded members of the Continental Congress it seemed obvious that America had all the natural resources to build a navy, as well as the men to man it. Buoyed with optimism and dreams of naval glory, these men urged their reluctant colleagues to move boldly ahead to the creation of an American fleet. Yet even as this debate raged within Congress, far to the north the naval war of the Revolution had already begun.

Chapter Two

The Schooner Squadron

By the spring of 1775 Massachusetts was ready for rebellion. All the elements were present, wanting only an incident to fuse them together into a violent upheaval. Just such an incident came when General Thomas Gage, the royal governor, finding himself pressured by an impatient ministry and embarrassed by his own impotency, resolved to move and assert his authority by striking a blow at the seditious elements who had thus far so brazenly defied him. He decided to send a secret expedition to the town of Concord, where, he was reliably informed, the Massachusetts Provincial Congress had gathered a considerable store of arms and munitions. The supplies would be destroyed and, if possible, two of the radical leaders, John Hancock and Sam Adams, taken into custody. To accomplish the mission Gage assigned his elite grenadier and light-infantry units, nearly seven hundred men, and on the night of 18 April these troops, under the command of Lieutenant Colonel Francis Smith, assembled at the foot of Beacon Hill to begin their twenty-mile march into history. Within eighteen hours nearly one-third of these men were casualties in a defeat that shook the British army and launched the American Revolution. By dusk on the nineteenth the British were back in Boston after their day at Lexington and Concord, while outside the town thousands of

American militiamen had gathered to begin besieging the British.[1]

The news of Lexington and Concord spread rapidly. Newspapers and broadsides describing the "bloody butchery" appeared everywhere. Within a few days all New England was alerted and arming while Paul Revere, the "Patriot Express," carried the tale south to New York and Philadelphia.[2] Soon men from colonies outside New England arrived at the American lines to offer their services.

Even as the first entrenchments were being thrown up around Boston, the war at sea was beginning on the south side of Cape Cod in Buzzards Bay, where the first naval action of the Revolution took place. The exact circumstances are unclear, but apparently Captain John Linzee of His Majesty's sloop *Falcon* seized a small American vessel off Dartmouth, where it had recently arrived from the West Indies. After putting a prize crew aboard with orders to proceed to Boston in company with his tender, Linzee stood off to continue the patrol. The citizens of Dartmouth had other ideas, though, and they soon set about to retake the prize. They sent out their own vessels and intercepted the American vessel and tender escort at Martha's Vineyard. After a brief skirmish they managed to retake not only the prize but the tender as well, with fourteen prisoners who were immediately dispatched off to American headquarters at Cambridge.[3]

Since the action in Buzzards Bay was a case of smugglers versus the Royal Navy (hardly a new occurrence in eighteenth-century America), it can be argued that it does not legitimately belong to the naval history of the Revolution. The undisputed honor of being the first to attack and take a vessel of the Royal Navy goes to the patriots at Machias, a small fishing and lumbering port 316 miles northeast of Boston, in the district of Maine, then still part of Massachusetts.[4]

It was not until 9 May that the inhabitants of this tiny wilderness outpost learned of the outbreak of hostilities around Boston. But even then the reports were sketchy and incomplete, and while some of the local "Sons of Liberty" urged the town to action, most people there saw little need or reason for Machias to become involved in a conflict that was not of their making or immediate concern.

Machias's tranquillity was abruptly disturbed by the arrival of one Ichabod Jones with his two sloops under the escort of His Majesty's armed schooner *Margaretta*, commanded by Midshipman James Moore.[5] Jones, a Boston merchant, was a familiar face in Machias. In more peaceful times he had frequently come by to trade provisions and other goods for lumber. This time, though, he was on more than a private trading voyage. He had been dispatched by General Gage and Admiral Graves, the naval commander in Boston, to secure firewood and lumber, both of which were coming into short supply in Boston as a result of the tightening siege.[6]

The three vessels dropped anchor off Machias on Friday, 2 June, and Jones, apparently not anticipating any difficulties, stepped ashore to begin his trading. But his task would not be that easy, and a special town meeting was called to decide whether or not it was proper under the circumstances to deal with an agent of the British. After heated debate, the radicals, led by a fiery Irishman named Jeremiah O'Brien, lost, and the meeting agreed to do business with Jones. Jones, piqued at this rather cool reception and especially angry with those who had voted against him, announced that he would deal with only those who had favored his cause in the town meeting. Meanwhile, Moore had spied atop a nearby hill one of those obnoxious yet prolific symbols of the American cause, a liberty pole. He demanded that it be taken down or else he would open fire on the town. The midshipman, a bit young and impetuous, had obviously overstepped his bounds, and his impertinent behavior threatened to upset the increasingly delicate situation. He was persuaded by cooler heads to back down, but by now the townspeople had had enough and they agreed secretly that in the morning, Sunday, they would seize Moore and Jones while they were at church. On Sunday, 11 June, Moore and Jones arrived at church. During the service

Moore, while gazing through an open window, spotted a group of armed men making toward the church. Fearing the worst, he and Jones leaped out the window and made their escape, Moore to his schooner and Jones into the nearby woods. Moore successfully reached his vessel, while the unfortunate Jones spent the next few days in misery hiding in the woods until he finally gave up.

Although the Americans failed to capture the midshipman, they were able to take Jones's two sloops, and after a brief exchange of musketry Moore decided to take *Margaretta* farther down the bay out of range. That night the Americans made an unsuccessful attempt to board. At daybreak Moore decided to leave the area entirely and stand out to sea. As he headed out to sea, *Margaretta* accidentally jibed in a sudden gust of wind and Moore lost a gaff and boom. His vessel crippled, he hove to to repair the damage. The delay gave the Americans time to overtake the schooner, and Jones's two sloops, now under the command of O'Brien, came within hailing distance. Escape was impossible, so Moore swung his vessel round and gave the Americans a broadside. It was of little use. The American vessels grappled alongside *Margaretta* as Moore fell to the deck mortally wounded by a musket ball. The crew was quickly overpowered and the schooner struck. Flushed with victory, O'Brien and his men returned up the bay escorting their prize, the first vessel of the Royal Navy to surrender to an American force.[7]

The news from Machias elated the patriots surrounding Boston. O'Brien, the "Machias Admiral," became a hero, and the Massachusetts Provincial Congress voted their official thanks to him and "the other brave men" under his command.[8] Admiral Graves, on the other hand, while chagrined at having to report the loss to his superiors, took no action to punish the town or effectively prevent a recurrence. A few weeks later the Machias "pirates," by now somewhat experienced in these matters, took two more of His Majesty's vessels, the schooner *Diligent* and its shallop *Tatamagouche*. This time there was no bloodshed. O'Brien and his men enticed the British officers ashore, where they were seized by the waiting Americans. It was a subterfuge that should not have fooled the simplest-minded commander, but it worked, and the men at Machias added two more vessels to their growing fleet.[9]

The men of Machias and Dartmouth had done much to strengthen the cause of those in the Massachusetts Provincial Congress who were urging a naval armament. Even nearer to the Congress's meeting place in Watertown, there was action on the water, for by late May and early June the Americans were waging a vigorous whaleboat war in Boston harbor. Having scoured all the nearby creeks, inlets and beaches, the Americans had gathered several hundred of these open boats. Of shoal draft and fast over short distances with a few good men at the oars, these boats proved to be a great annoyance to the British. Darting out so quickly that the British barely had time to respond, they attacked the lighthouses in the harbor and landed on the islands to carry off foodstuffs and livestock. Even if Admiral Graves's warships had had time to slip their cables to pursue, they were still slaves to an undependable wind, and in any case their deep draft prevented an inshore chase. On one occasion the admiral's nephew, Lieutenant Thomas Graves, in command of the armed schooner *Diana*, did make an attempt to attack several whaleboats involved in removing livestock from Noddles Island. It was a full tide as the lieutenant brought his schooner around to a position between the island and the mainland where he could train his guns on the fleeing Americans. But as the tide receded, he found his keel stuck fast in the mud. Under heavy fire from American shore batteries, the lieutenant, his vessel by now on her beam ends, ordered his crew to abandon the schooner. As the British pulled away from their stranded vessel, the gleeful Americans slogged through the mud and knee-deep water with armloads of combustibles and set *Diana* ablaze.[10]

Thus far the naval activities of the Americans had taken

place with about as much planning as a spring frolic. Nevertheless, the Americans had acquitted themselves well, with four enemy vessels captured and one destroyed. They had clearly demonstrated that His Majesty's vessels were by no means invulnerable and that in certain circumstances there was real hope for doing damage to the British fleet. These lessons were not lost on General George Washington, the recently appointed commander in chief, as he rode into Cambridge to take command of the American forces.

In light of the situation around Boston, especially as it related to naval activities, the suggestion made by some historians that Washington somehow had to be convinced of the need to commission vessels seems out of place. He would have been a poor commander not to have employed the weapons at his disposal. He hardly needed to have it pointed out to him that the enemy was totally dependent upon their sea lanes for supplies and that this was their most vulnerable point. Thanks to an intelligence network active both in Boston and along the coast, Washington was reasonably well informed of all arrivals and departures at the port. He knew that the ministry, not expecting any trouble at sea, continued to send men and matériel for the most part in unarmed and unescorted transports. If he could arm and equip vessels along the North and South shores of Massachusetts Bay, he could intercept these ships and take their valuable cargoes to fill his own much depleted magazines.

Once having concluded that such action was possible, he did not have to look far for the men or the vessel to accomplish his purpose. Colonel John Glover of the Marblehead regiment, a sea captain and merchant himself, offered the charter of his schooner *Hannah*, while the men from his "Webfoot Regiment" eagerly volunteered to sign on.[11] *Hannah* was a typical New England fishing schooner of about seventy tons. Rigged with the usual sails main, fore and jib, she was probably manned by no more than six to eight men when engaged in her customary occupation of fishing and trading. To command her Washington appointed Nicholson Broughton, a

captain in Glover's regiment.[12] Upon receipt of his orders
Broughton proceeded to Beverly, where *Hannah* was berthed,
and oversaw the conversion of his new command from fisher-
man and trader to man-of-war. Her gunwales were pierced to
mount four four-pounders and her rigging strengthened to
spread topsails and a flying jib. On and below decks changes
were made, as much as possible, to accommodate a crew that
would be nearly four times as large as the usual complement;
nevertheless, it is hard to see how any amount of refitting
could have made *Hannah* anything but close and uncomfortable for her crew.[13] Considering the problems and delay encountered in fitting out later Continental vessels, *Hannah* got
to sea with remarkable dispatch. She hoisted sail on the morning of 5 September 1775 and stood out to sea in search of her
quarry.[14]

Broughton's instructions were detailed and restrictive.
Washington had no intention of turning the captain loose
simply to attack indiscriminately any vessel displaying the
Union Jack. It would be some time before a recognized state
of war would exist with Great Britain, and at this point it was
not altogether clear exactly who the enemy really was. According to his orders, Broughton was to attack only those
vessels "in the Service of the ministerial Army," and he was
strictly enjoined not to engage armed vessels, as "the Design
of this Enterprise . . . [is] to intercept the Supplies of the
Enemy, which will be defeated by your running into unnecessary Engagements." The crew were to receive their
regular pay in the army plus a one-third share of any legitimate capture excepting military and naval stores, which were
reserved entirely for the use of the Continent. If they should
retake a vessel "of any Friend to the American Cause," the
general promised he would recommend to the owner that a
suitable reward be paid but the captured vessel itself must be
returned to the owner and could not be treated as a rightful
prize.[15]

Washington's instructions were complete in all those areas
where he felt he had authority. But on one very critical point

he found that all he could do was entreat, suggest and cajole. The problem was in the adjudication of prizes. Before a captured vessel could be declared a legitimate prize and then disposed of, she had to be brought before a duly authorized court where she might be libeled by her captors and, if determined to be a lawful prize, condemned. Quite properly Washington looked to the civilian authorities for the establishment of such courts. He believed that cases of capture by vessels sailing under Continental commissions should be tried in courts erected by Congress for that purpose. Despite numerous dunning letters from the general on the need for the courts, the Congress delayed. Their procrastination caused him to endure a seemingly endless stream of difficulties that taxed his patience and time. Finally Massachusetts established its own admiralty courts, and it was to these that Washington's prizes were eventually sent for disposition.[16]

As *Hannah* tacked out of Beverly, bound east toward Cape Anne, great hopes for success went with her. They were soon disappointed. On 7 September she did manage to take a prize, the ship *Unity*, 260 tons. Unfortunately *Unity* turned out to be the property not of anyone in the service of the "ministerial Army" but rather of John Langdon of Portsmouth, New Hampshire, a "High Son of Liberty."[17] When Washington ordered her returned to Langdon, Broughton protested, but to no avail. His crew, though, were even more outraged, and the distressing prospect that they would not receive any prize money for their effort prompted them to stage a mutiny, and Washington found himself in the embarrassing situation of arresting men he had hoped to congratulate.[18] The unexpected departure of his crew to Cambridge to be tried for mutiny left Broughton and his schooner idle until the end of September when, after recruiting a new complement of men, he was able to put to sea again.[19] Never venturing much beyond Beverly, Broughton day sailed for about three weeks, putting in each night so that his men could avoid cramped quarters and cold food. On the morning of 10 October, shortly after getting under way on what looked to be another dull day of leisurely sailing, Broughton spied a vessel making toward him. It was His Majesty's sloop *Nautilus*, under the command of Captain John Collins. Broughton quickly came about and raced for the harbor. He had just made the entrance when he ran aground on the flats. With the tide ebbing, *Nautilus* dared not proceed farther in, so she dropped anchor within range of *Hannah* and opened fire. Soon the whole countryside was alarmed to what was happening in Beverly harbor, and while Broughton and his crew scrambled over the side and waded ashore, militia units from Salem and Beverly trained their batteries on the British sloop. After exchanging fire for a brief time with no effect, Collins gave orders to get *Nautilus* under way. As she tried to come about, the wind caught her and drove her to leeward into the mud where she "took the Ground." Stranded and exposed, *Nautilus* was in a precarious position; the fox now became the hare. For nearly four hours she was under fire until early in the evening when the tide lifted her free. Battered, *Nautilus* limped home to Boston, where the captain made his report of the damage to the Admiral: "In this Situation [we] received a great many Shot mostly in my Rigging and Sails, about 20 through the Hammacoes and Hull, One Gun dismounted, and a Swivel shot in two; one man has lost his Leg, and another wounded in the Side. 'tis very lucky they fired so high."[20]

On the American side the casualties were less severe. The only man who sustained an injury was Broughton, who caught a severe cold as a result of falling overboard.[21] Although *Hannah* survived her ordeal and was refloated, her naval career was fast drawing to a close. Other vessels with a "better fame for Sailing" were already being fitted out, and *Hannah* left the service of the Continent sometime in November 1775.[22]

Despite its inept execution, Washington remained convinced that his policy to establish a naval force was sound. On 4 October he instructed Stephen Moylan, the muster master general, and Colonel Glover to equip two more vessels for service on the Continental account.[23] He instructed Moylan and Glover to select suitable vessels, have them impartially appraised and then go about the business, as agents of the commander in chief, of obtaining supplies, armament and men. This was to be done at any one of several North Shore ports including Salem, Marblehead and Newburyport. In addition, they were to nominate reputable individuals to act as agents at the various ports to dispose of any prizes brought in by these Continental cruisers.[24] On 10 October the appraisers appointed by Glover and Moylan reported that two Marblehead schooners, *Speedwell* and *Eliza,* had been examined and found fit for the service intended.[25]

Thus far Washington had been proceeding without direction from the Congress. However, independent of the commander in chief, Congress had been considering naval action against the British. The day after Moylan and Glover made their report Washington received orders from Philadelphia that would require him to use his two new schooners, renamed *Franklin* and *Hancock,* on a special mission.[26]

The mission assigned to him by Congress was to intercept "Two North Country built Brigantines, of no force ... loaded with Six Thousand Stand of Arms, a large Quantity of Powder (and) other Stores for Quebec."[27] The prospect of replenishing his stores with the cargoes from these vessels delighted Washington, and he lost no time in assuring the president of Congress, John Hancock, that the orders would be "literally complied with" since the "Capture of an Ordinance Ship would give new life to the Camp and an immediate turn to the Issue of this Campaign."[28]

On 16 October Washington sent his orders to Captain Nicholson Broughton and John Selman, the men he had chosen to go in pursuit of the "North Country Brigantines." The orders were lengthy and quite specific. Once again Washington took special care to indicate to the captains that they were to attack only those vessels and men who were directly involved in supplying the ministerial army.[29] The orders were necessarily restrictive since both Washington and Congress were still not certain about the nature of the hostilities. The general and the men in Philadelphia moved with great caution lest they give any hint that what they were about was anything more that a simple act of self-defense against an unjust ministry and its rapacious servants.

With a favoring wind and a good tide Broughton and Selman passed Baker's Island and stood out to sea on the morning of 22 October, bound for their station in the Gulf of Saint Lawrence, where they planned to lie in wait for the unsuspecting brigantines.[30] After an uneventful and fruitless wait for the munitions vessels the two captains abandoned their passive mission and embarked upon a foray that was one of the silliest excursions of the Revolution.

Thus far in his short naval career Broughton, the senior captain, had yet to show a spark of initiative or daring. He had for the most part been a dull, uninspiring and rather plodding commander. Now having failed in his primary mission, he began another for which he had no authorization or justification. Far up in the Gulf of Saint Lawrence, away from any restraint from headquarters, save his orders, Broughton abandoned his yacht-club manners and embarked on a brief bit of pillaging and kidnapping. He and Selman descended on Charlottetown, the capital of what is today Prince Edward Island. After a short stay they left, carrying with them three of the most prominent citizens of the town. They arrived home in Beverly on 7 December and proceeded to Cambridge, where they expected to receive congratulations and praise from Washington.[31] Instead the happy warriors found a reception far colder than anything they might have experienced in the wintery North Atlantic. At a time when the Americans were looking to make friends anywhere they could, these captains had terrorized and alienated the residents of Prince Edward Island. Despite great hopes and a large expense, Broughton and Selman had accomplished almost nothing. In fact, their voyage was counterproductive. Piqued at their conduct and their wanton violation of orders, but not wishing to precipitate an open confrontation, Washington treated both gentlemen with the cool aloofness for which he was becoming famous. At the same time he encouraged Moylan to treat them with enough disdain and disrespect so that the full measure of his annoyance would be unmistakable. It was, and when their commissions expired on 31 December, "they [felt] sore, and decline[ed] serving longer."[32] No one tried to persuade them to change their minds.

Washington was disappointed with his navy but not disillusioned. Even the bad news from Broughton and Selman did not stop him from sending out more vessels. While *Hancock* and *Franklin* were still at sea, he ordered Moylan to fit out two more vessels at Beverly, the schooners *Lee* and *Warren*. While Moylan was busy on the North Shore, a young army captain, Ephraim Bowen, Jr., was carrying on a similar kind of work for the general south of Boston at Plymouth.[33]

After receiving his instructions on 13 October, Bowen had immediately left for Plymouth. Once in the town he consulted with a local merchant, William Watson, soon to be officially appointed Continental agent at Plymouth, and together they worked to enlarge Washington's fleet. Two vessels were fitted out: *Harrison* and *Washington*. *Harrison*, like her sister ships on the North Shore, was a topsail schooner, while *Washington* was a brigantine and the largest warship under Washington's command.[34]

Command of the brig was given to an experienced Rhode Island sea captain, Sion Martindale, of Newport and Providence. Martindale's promise far exceeded his performance, and much to his chagrin Washington soon discovered that the captain had ambitions and plans beyond anything he had in mind. Washington's aim was, and always had been, to intercept the enemy's supplies, thereby depriving them and equipping himself. The armament Martindale was putting aboard his brigantine clearly indicated that he intended to do more than simply intercept merchant vessels. At a time when both cannon and powder were scarce, Martindale was asking to be supplied with twelve carriage guns and sixteen to twenty swivels.[35] Washington entirely disapproved of this extravagant armament and through his secretary, Joseph Reed, told Bowen to "caution Capt. Martindale against a large Outset—The Design is to intercept the Enemy's Supplies, not to look for the Enemy's Armed Vessels."[36] Martindale's insistence on carrying such heavy armament helped to delay his departure, and only after what seemed to be an interminable time did he finally get to sea late in November 1775. The maiden voyage was short and ineffectual. Martindale returned to Plymouth with a small sloop taken in Massachusetts Bay and a crew close to mutiny. A discouraged William Watson blamed *Washington*'s ill fortune on her crew, who were in his eyes a "sett of the most unprincipiled abandoned fellows [I] ever saw." He had little faith in this motley assortment of "Fellows drawn promiscuously from the army for this Business."[37] Watson was correct in his assessment, for the next time out *Washington* ran afoul of H.M.S. *Fowey*. She struck without firing a shot and was carried into Boston, where after survey she was found to be "not fit for Sea."[38] Martindale was shipped off to England while his decrepit brigantine was left to rot at the dock, where she still sat four months later when the Americans took possession of the town. Washington, by now somewhat accustomed to bad news from the ports, received the tiding of Martindale's capture with what almost amounted to casual indifference as he wrote to the president of Congress that "we cannot expect to be allways successful."[39]

The other Plymouth captain, William Coit, proved himself to be a sharp-tongued salt with a penchant for humor and a knack for capturing ships. His command, *Harrison*, was a dull, lubberly schooner that, according to local wags, was near the same dimensions on the keel as the beam. Nevertheless, Coit had remarkable success with her despite her shortcomings. Shortly after taking two enemy provision vessels, Coit wrote to his friend Major Samuel Blachley Webb, Washington's aide-de-camp, describing his command. The letter is worth quoting at length to give the flavor of the man and the deficiencies of his command.

> She has a quarter-deck—Ah, and more than that too—4 four pounders, brought into this country by the company of Lords Say and Seal, to *Saybrook* when they first came. A pair of cohorns that Noah had in the Ark . . . Six swivels, the first that ever were landed at Plymouth, and never fired since.
>
> Now, that is my *plague;* but I can tell you somewhat of my *comfort.* My schooner is used to the business, for she was launched in the spring of 1761, and has served two regular apprenticeships to sailing, and sails quick, being *used to it.* Her accommodations are fine; five of us in the cabin, and when there, are obliged to stow spoon fashion. Besides, she has a chimney in it, and the smoke serves for bedding, victuals, drinking and choking. She has one mast too, which is her foremast; she had a mainmast, but it was put in so long ago, that it has rotted off in the hounds. She has a deck, too. When it was first made, it was new; and because it was ashamed of being old, the first time we made use of a clawed handspike, it broke a hole through; notwithstanding, the wench knew it was directly over the magazine. Upon the whole, if there comes peace, I would recommend her and her apparatus, to be sent to the Royal Society; and I dare eat a redhot gridiron if ever they have had, or will have, until the day of judgment, and curiosuty [*sic*] to her. I haven't time to give you her character in full, but in short, she is the devil. But while I can keep the sea and light only on unarmed vessels, she will do very well. But if obliged to fire both guns of a side at a time, it would split her open from her gunwale to her keelson.[40]

While Coit was better than most of the captains, to Washington they were all "rascally privateersmen."[41] That is, all except one, for amid this lackluster group there did emerge the first American naval hero of the Revolution, Captain John Manley. Manley, a Boston sea captain temporarily displaced by the war and living in Marblehead, was a man of long experience both in the merchant marine and in the Royal Navy.[42]

At Beverly, Manley took command of the schooner *Lee*, and after filling his complement of men and putting aboard four four-pounders, he hoisted sail on 28 October. The first cruise was brief and uneventful, and on 1 November *Lee* tacked into Plymouth to take on fresh water. This profitless voyage was hardly indicative of the great things to come, for in the next six months that he served under Washington, John Manley rose from obscurity to national fame by capturing more enemy ships than any other officer in the fleet.

His exploits were celebrated in ballads and poems, especially his capture of the brig *Nancy*. *Nancy* was an ordnance brig heavy laden with munitions consigned to the British forces in Boston. She was sailing unarmed and unescorted. Late in November when she became overdue, Admiral Graves, fearful that she might fall into rebel hands, ordered several of his vessels out either to convoy her into Boston or to destroy her if she had fallen into enemy hands.[43] News of the nervousness on board the admiral's flagship and the reason for it reached Washington's camp, and he immediately ordered his captains to be on the lookout for this rich prize. On 8 November *Nancy* was sighted by H.M.S. *Cerberus* off Nantasket and put under escort. For the next ten days *Cerberus* and her charge tried to work up into Boston harbor, but every time they were turned back by gale-force winds. Finally the weather grew so foul and heavy with snow and rain, *Cerberus* and *Nancy* stood out to sea to avoid being driven ashore.[44] When the storm finally abated, *Nancy* found herself alone and far to the north of her intended destination. She set her course to the south, and by dusk of 28 November she was off Cape Anne, smack in the middle of John Manley's cruising grounds. That evening Manley spotted the brig to windward. He immediately set a course to intercept her and cleared his decks for action.

The commander of the brig, Robert Hunter, was apparently unaware that he was in imminent danger, for when he saw the schooner, he took her to be a pilot boat out of Boston and he hove to to await instructions. He only realized his mistake when Manley and his men were scrambling over the gunwales with pistols and cutlasses at the ready. Hunter surrendered without a fight. Manley then went below to inventory his prize. The brig's hold was packed with 2500 stands of arms, mortars (including a fifteen-inch monster later named the "Congress"), a number of cannon, forty tons of shot and a great assortment of miscellaneous military stores.

Washington was elated at the news. This one capture provided him with more military supplies than the Congress could have accumulated with months of effort. Manley was the hero of the hour. *Nancy* was taken into Fresh Water Cove at Gloucester, where her cargo was quickly landed and carted on to Cambridge.

The capture of the ordnance brig was certainly the high point of Manley's activities that winter, but he had other victories as well. Altogether from early November until the end of December he took nine prizes. In recognition of his accomplishments, in January 1776 Washington named him commodore of the squadron, and Manley, now America's first flag officer, left *Lee* and transferred his command to the schooner *Hancock*. The commodore remained in command of the schooner fleet until spring, when he left Washington's staff to take charge of the new Continental frigate *Hancock*, then building at Newburyport.[45]

Even as Manley, Coit and the others were harassing the British in Boston, elsewhere along the coast other Americans cruising under local authority were causing no end of problems to enemy commanders.[46] With every set of dispatches received, Admiral Graves found himself swamped with requests for men, ships and supplies by officers from Pensacola to Halifax. Upon his shoulders rested the decision whether to comply or refuse, and in these early critical months of the war much depended upon the admiral's choice. He was not a wise man, and to him must be assigned a generous share of blame for the Royal Navy's lackluster performance during this early season of the Revolution.

Graves's mission was threefold: secure the approaches around Boston; blockade the entire American coast to prevent the landing of rebel supplies; and station vessels at strategic locations where they could be of aid to local commanders. Graves lacked the resources to accomplish any one of these tasks; to do all three was impossible. Of course, in this regard his problems were much the same as subsequent commanders on the North American station, but in one very important aspect Graves operated under a special handicap. For several months he had to operate in a quasi-war situation with little or no direction from the ministry or Admiralty on how to conduct himself in this uncertain state of belligerency. In fact, not until October 1775 did he receive orders authorizing him to seize American vessels.[47] If the admiral appeared at times to be unsure and vacillating, he was in great measure simply reflecting the indecision of those above him.

Graves's greatest annoyance was the problem closest to home, namely, how to deal with Washington's navy, whose attacks were both embarrassing and damaging. For all its vaunted power and illustrious history, the British navy found itself musclebound in Boston harbor, being pecked at by a mosquito fleet. Most of the large vessels riding at anchor in the harbor, including the admiral's flagship, *Preston*, were undermanned, having had men taken from their complement to replenish or reinforce other crews. *Preston*, like the other ships of the line in Boston, *Somerset* and *Boyne*, was an unwieldy dinosaur that consumed men and supplies to no good purpose. The ships were too large for the close inshore work required if the Americans were to be destroyed, and as a result they remained for the most part immobilized in the harbor, functioning only as floating barracks. The smaller fifth and sixth rates along with several schooners were sent along the coasts to protect the sea approaches to the harbor, but they too had their difficulties. First, they were too few in number to effectively cover such an extensive area, and second, without knowledgeable pilots and detailed charts, they ran great risks operating close inshore. Uncharted shoals, rocks and sandbars could easily ground a vessel and expose her to shore batteries or capture by a pack of rebel whale-boats.

A more aggressive commander might have taken the initiative and sent his vessels in squadron strength to attack and destroy the American bases, but Admiral Graves was a fretful and timid man in uncertain times. Some of his uncertainty was removed on 4 October when he received orders from the Admiralty "to carry on such operations upon the sea coasts of the four governmen[ts] in New England as he should judge most proper for suppressing the rebellion now openly avowed and supported in those colonies."[48] Graves, strengthened by the apparent resolve of the ministry, responded to these instructions and ordered out a small squadron under the command of Lieutenant Henry Mowatt. The lieutenant was to punish the New Englanders by burning and laying waste to certain miscreant towns north of Boston that had been the most perfidious and obnoxious in their rebellious behavior by daring to seize "several of his Majesty's Ships and Vessels." Now resolved to action, Graves ordered Mowat to take the full measure of retribution.

> My Design is to Chastize Marblehead, Salem, Newbury Port, Cape Anne Harbour, Portsmouth, Ipswich, Saco, Falmouth in Casco Bay, and particularly Mechias where the *Marguerrita* was taken . . . and where the *Diligent* Schooner was seized and the Officers and Crew carried Prisoners up the Country, And where preparations I am informed are now Making to invade the Province of Nova Scotia.
>
> You are to go to all or as many of the above named Places as you can, and make the most vigorous Efforts to burn the Towns, and destroy the Shipping in the Harbours.[49]

Mowatt left Boston with a small flotilla of five vessels, three schooners, a sloop and an armed transport. After several days of northerly gales that buffeted his force to and fro across Massachusetts Bay he finally drew up before the town of

Falmouth in Casco Bay (Portland, Maine). He announced to the startled citizenry that at nine the next morning, 18 October, he was going to open fire and destroy their town. All through the night the streets of Falmouth were alive with frightened townspeople, loading every cart and wagon they could find to carry their belongings into the countryside and beyond the range of the British guns. Repeated appeals to Mowatt failed to dissuade him from his mission, and at nine-thirty in the morning, true to his word, he signaled "commence fire." For nearly nine hours the British kept up a steady barrage "during which all the lower end and middle of the town was reduced to a heap of rubbish. Several houses in the back street and in the upper part, together with the church shared the same fate. The front of the Meeting house was torn to pieces by the bursting of a bomb, and the buildings which were left standing had their glass windows broken, and both walls and apartments terribly shattered."[50] Having finished his destruction, Mowatt ordered his fleet back to Boston.

The whole business was a terrible fiasco and blunder. In a military or naval sense it accomplished nothing. The foray left completely untouched the American bases at Beverly, Marblehead and Plymouth, where rebel vessels were being fitted out. As grist for the revolutionary propaganda mill it could not have been better planned if Sam Adams had done it himself. Everywhere along the seaboard the news of Falmouth was used by rebel propagandists as yet another example of the butchery and inhumanity of the ministerial forces. Instead of intimidating Americans, it only helped to push a lot of mugwumps off the fence and into the rebel camp.

Falmouth was the admiral's sole excursion into offensive warfare, and considering the results of that ill-timed and poorly executed mission, it was perhaps just as well. Elsewhere along the Atlantic coast his captains did occasionally exchange fire with the Americans, but nowhere was anything on the scale of Falmouth undertaken at his direction. The naval vessels in Narragansett Bay, in New York harbor, in the Chesapeake and along the southern coasts could sputter and fume and harass local shipping, but for the time being they were not strong enough to provide much more than an offshore haven for fleeing crown officers.

The approaching winter raised an unappealing spector for Graves and his fleet in Boston. Never before had a sizable contingent of the Royal Navy tried to winter on the North American station. The wooden ships were vulnerable to all the ravages of wind, ice and snow, and a winter in northern latitudes might well take a higher toll than any enemy fleet. In more conventional times Graves would have taken his fleet either home or to the Caribbean, where they could be refitted and victualed. In an age of wooden ships a year on station without extensive refitting and careening was about all a commander could expect of his vessels, and as the winter set in, many of Graves's ships were already showing menacing signs of deterioration.[51] It would be trouble enough surviving the winter just riding at anchor in Boston, but that would mean leaving the approaches into Boston unprotected. To be effective, Graves would have to aggressively patrol along the coast. If he planned to do that, he would have to overcome all the handicaps he had been suffering under since the outbreak of hostilities as well as some of the worst weather imaginable. One officer described what it was like to sail New England in winter: "Tis the Frost that makes the coasting Navigation so difficult, and almost impracticable to Ships. The running ropes freeze in the Blocks; the Sails are stiff like Sheets of Tin; and the men cannot expose their Hands long enough to the Cold, to do their Duty aloft; so that Topsails are not easily handled."[52]

Despite these difficulties, the winter months saw little abatement of activity, and the Americans and British continued to play their game of fox and hounds. The American schooners continued to seek out their prey, and many supplies that had been carefully stowed away at Cork, Woolwich or elsewhere found their way to the Americans at Cambridge rather than the British at Boston. On one occasion the intrepid Manley embarrassed the admiral by taking two prizes almost within sight of the flagship.[53] Although the biting weather chilled Washington's men as much as it did the British, they did nevertheless have at least one advantage in winter sailing. The Americans sailed vessels that, with one exception, were schooner rigged and therefore could be handled from the deck, while the British, although they had some schooners, depended for the most part on square-rigged vessels which could only be maneuvered by sending men aloft— a dangerous business in rough weather when the ratlines were likely to be covered with ice and one sudden lurch could send a man plunging to his death.

Graves's apparent incapacity, whether of his own making or not, had become the object of questioning, sarcasm and ridicule both among his own fellow officers in America and with his superiors in London.[54] Boston had already claimed the reputation of a general and it was only a matter of time before the admiral would follow. On 30 December *Chatham* dropped anchor near *Preston*, and Rear Admiral Molyneux Shuldham requested permission to come aboard. In the admiral's great cabin aboard *Preston* Shuldham announced to a surprised Graves that he had been relieved of command; Shuldham would be the new commander on the North American station.[55] Graves, embarrassed and angry at what seemed to be a peremptory replacement by a junior officer, returned home to fade into a neglect and obscurity from which he never again emerged. General Gage and Admiral Graves were the first British commanders to have their reputations buried in America. They were not the last.

Hampered by the same chronic shortage of men and ships as Graves, Shuldham found himself in a position little changed from that of his departed predecessor. It continued to be a war of besieged and besieger. This stalemate was abruptly broken on the morning of 5 March when the British awoke to see American cannons mounted on Dorchester Heights overlooking the town. These were the guns that had been captured at Fort Ticonderoga and then laboriously dragged overland to Cambridge. The British position was hopeless. Resistance was futile and on 7 March General William Howe, Gage's replacement as commander in chief, gave the order to prepare for evacuation. Ten days later Shuldham ordered his captains to fall down the harbor and prepare to take under convoy a motley assortment of vessels bound out of Boston for Halifax. Men scampered onto the yards, and amid the clatter of blocks and the crack of sails the fleet got under way. Shuldham did his job well and for the most part kept his convoy intact; only one vessel fell into American hands, the brig *Elizabeth* taken by John Manley.[56]

The evacuation of Boston and the subsequent shift of the theater of operations farther south left Washington's fleet in Massachusetts Bay isolated and ineffective. For a time after his departure to New York, Washington tried to direct his navy via remote control, but that proved extremely difficult, and gradually as their charters expired, the vessels were dropped from the list and their crews went on to other pursuits. But if the fleet faded away almost unnoticed, it had had its moments of glory. During its existence Washington's captains took fifty-five prizes, and despite their frequent mishaps and bunglings, they contributed materially to the American victory by bringing in much needed supplies. But perhaps most important of all they gave a boost to American morale by demonstrating the vulnerability of British sea power. If the ships of the Royal Navy could not even secure an area as limited as Massachusetts Bay, then how could they possibly hope to prevent American cruisers from striking at them from other areas along a seemingly endless American coast? Washington's captains had ably demonstrated that several years of neglect had dulled Britannia's trident. When engaged at the right time and location and with the proper tactics, the Royal Navy was not omnipotent, and although Washington might not always be pleased with his "rascally privateersmen," their failures paled in comparison to their successes. The activities in New England had helped to build a sense of pride and competence that would be infectious among some members of Congress as they pushed forward to create a fleet far more powerful than Washington's cockleshells.

Chapter Three

Congress Takes the Helm

The American colonies had a naval potential nearly unparalleled in history: thousands of men, generations of experience and an embarrassment of wealth in timber and naval stores. But resources alone, even if unlimited, were useless unless there were men with vision and energy able to shape promise into reality. The creation of an effective navy required a skillful and harmonious interplay among statesmen, seamen and bureaucrats taming these resources to build, deploy and engage a naval force adequate to the new nation's needs.[1]

It was the task of the Continental Congress to marshal these resources. To them fell the burden of selecting bureaucrats to administer the navy and captains to command its ships. They did not always choose wisely or well, but their sins were no greater here than in anything else they did. For the most part their authority rested on good will and voluntary compliance. As a result, if Lord Acton's aphorism concerning the corrosive influence of power is correct, this legislative body must be counted among the most virtuous ever assembled.

It was the Virginia House of Burgesses, reacting to the Intolerable Acts, that called for the convening of a Continental Congress, which first came to order on 5 September 1774 at Carpenters Hall in Philadelphia.[2] Fifty-six men assembled, arriving from every colony except Georgia. For the most part they represented the best political talent America had to offer, and for the next two months they met daily, mulling over their mutual grievances while trying to come up with a plan to express their discontent with the British ministry. It was all a moderate affair. They were men who, for the most part, were distressed but not yet rebellious, and while there were radical firebrands among them who would have liked a more violent and dramatic resistance to the acts of Parliament, they were quickly engulfed by the forces of conciliation and compromise.[3] The majority were content to petition and resolve. Only when Parliament and the crown turned a deaf ear to their complaints did they move to stronger action. They drew up a set of declarations condemning various acts of Parliament as unconstitutional, and on 20 October they signed the Continental Association pledging nonimportation, nonexportation and nonconsumption of British goods until they obtained a redress of their grievances. Economic boycott had served the Americans well before when it had been used to help bring about the repeal of the hated Stamp Tax and the Townshend Duties. The government might be oblivious to the justice of the American cause, but they could hardly afford to ignore a closure of the American market. Having accomplished the main business of the meeting, the delegates then drew up the usual address to His Majesty pleading their case while at the same time pledging continued loyalty. The agenda completed, they adjourned until 10 May 1775, when they would meet again unless their grievances were resolved.

During the two months in Philadelphia many friendships had been formed, and on the evening of adjournment all the members of the Congress met at their favorite watering place, the City Tavern, to bid farewell to one another, believing that in all likelihood they would never again meet in Philadelphia.[4] Two days later, John Adams, relieved at having finally escaped the "nibbling and quibbling" in Congress, wrote confidently in his diary, "It is not very likely that I shall ever see this part of the World again."[5] He could not have been more wrong.

It was one of those happy accidents in history that the Congress chose 10 May for reconvening. In September and October 1774 the radicals, impatient to push ahead, had tried and failed to move the Congress to action; now, only twenty-two days after Lexington and Concord, the whole country-side was alarmed and the delegates were coming together amid loud cries for resistance and retaliation. There were several new faces in this Congress, none of them conserva-tives and none of them seriously questioning the propriety of armed resistance; General Gage had seen to that. The issue now was independence. It would be more than a year before that would be officially debated; nevertheless, it was still much in the minds of the delegates as they assembled in Philadelphia. The moderates, although weakened by the events to the north as well as by the absence of some of their more influential members, were still a powerful force urging compromise and reconciliation but not disarmament.[6] Once assembled, the Congress stirred themselves and began to grope ahead. It was soon apparent that, despite their official assertions to the contrary, they were indeed behaving as if they were an independent power endowed with all the trap-pings of sovereignty. On 26 May they resolved that the colo-nies be put in a state of military readiness so that they might be able to defend their rights and liberties. On the twenty-ninth they called upon the people of Canada to join them in their common cause. By the end of June they had voted to raise and equip an army; appointed George Washington as commander in chief, and voted to issue two million dollars in bills of credit to finance their operations. In July they entered into negotiations with the Indians and elected Benjamin Franklin postmaster general.[7]

In less than one hundred days the Continental Congress had created an independent government and begun to wage war. Despite what they had done, these men in Philadelphia were still careful to couch all their actions as defensive measures undertaken only to protect their rights as freeborn Englishmen. To be sure, some were by now persuaded that independence was inevitable and in fact desirable, but many of their colleagues remained to be convinced. Independence would mean the trauma of war and the dissolution of old bonds. In less than a year events would leave these men no choice, but until then they preferred to remain at anchor while the storm swept in upon them.

Since the Congress was hesitant to declare independence and accept the war that would inevitably follow, it is no surprise that they were equally skeptical of creating a navy. It was one thing to appoint a commander in chief over a rabble in arms surrounding "ministerial butchers" in Boston. After all, that could be justified on strictly defensive grounds, but a navy was another matter, for the mobility and striking capability of armed vessels give them an inherent offensive character. This factor plus political problems and concern over the high cost of a navy prevented the Congress from acting on a naval program for several months.

Although the Congress sat on their haunches before committing themselves to a naval program, the matter was, from the very beginning, much in the minds of certain delegates, especially that irascible Yankee John Adams, who, despite his earlier prediction to the contrary, had returned as a delegate from Massachusetts. Adams, supported by others such as the South Carolina radical Christopher Gadsden and Silas Deane, a Connecticut merchant, led the naval lobby in these early sessions of the Second Continental Congress.

Adams's subsequent reputation as a strong navy man, coupled with his fame in other areas as well, has tended to blanket the very important contributions made by his colleagues in the formation of early naval policy. Not the least of these gentlemen was Christopher Gadsden, a man who had emerged as a radical leader in South Carolina during the Stamp Act crisis and since that time had been the leading political figure in his colony. It was Gadsden who urged

Adams, who by his own admission had "never thought much of old ocean, or the dimension of it," to consider the creation of an American fleet.[8] Earlier in his career Gadsden had served on one of His Majesty's men-of-war, and he was perhaps better acquainted with the men and officers of the Royal Navy than any other member of Congress.[9] He convinced Adams that, contrary to the conventional wisdom, the British fleet was not nearly so formidable as it had been made out to be. Others might stand in awe of the fleet as it bludgeoned and threatened along the coast, but Gadsden knew that behind all the bluster there was a serious weakness that could be exploited by the Americans if they were clever and skillful enough.

Gadsden's scheme was to entrap some of the smaller sloops, schooners or cutters while they were close to shore, out of the protective reach of the larger men-of-war. By themselves or even in company with one another, these lightly armed vessels would be easy prey for the Americans, who could swoop down in their own ships or open boats to board and overwhelm the unsuspecting British. Once having equipped themselves with these captured vessels, the Americans could, according to Gadsden, proceed up the naval chain of conquest and gradually take larger vessels. For the faint of heart who might think him a bit credulous about the ease of taking the larger ships, Gadsden pointed out that the best sailors were generally assigned to the smaller vessels and that the jacks who manned the line of battle ships were more than likely pressed men of uncertain loyalties. They were kept in line with harsh discipline and a healthy contingent of marines. They had no love for the men on the quarterdeck, and when the Americans came swinging over the gunwales, they were more likely to be greeted by huzzas than cutlasses. Impatient to the point of impetuousness, Gadsden thought it "of great Importance that Some Experiment should be made."[10] The majority of Congress did not share Gadsden's excitement over such a project, and his scheme was apparently not even brought to the floor.

Adams, now infected with naval enthusiasm, passed on Gadsden's suggestion to his friends in the Massachusetts Provincial Congress, where similar plans were also being proposed by a group of men led by James Warren of Plymouth. They had as little success with their congress as did Adams with his. The reason given for delaying action in Massachusetts was the lack of powder, but the fundamental cause was the same as it was in Philadelphia: caution, reinforced by uncertainty and unwillingness to venture ahead while there still remained a hope for reconciliation.[11]

As hopes for reconciliation dimmed, men in Massachusetts, Philadelphia and elsewhere in the colonies found themselves being edged forward by events into positions from which it would prove difficult to retreat. From June until their adjournment in early August the Congress came under mounting pressure to take action. By the middle of the summer Rhode Island and Connecticut had already engaged armed vessels and Massachusetts was in the final stages of debate on the issue. The triumph of O'Brien at Machias was touted as proof of British vulnerability and American prowess. In early July Josiah Quincy of Braintree, a neighbor and long-time associate of Adams, wrote to his old friend proposing that Congress should build a fleet of row galleys. These would be small open boats mounting cannon and propelled by oars that could be used along the coasts to fend off British raiders. Indeed, Quincy wrote, "why might not a Number of Vessels of War be fitted out, & judiciously stationed, so, as to intercept & prevent any supplies going to our Enemies?"[12] The same day that Quincy was writing from Braintree, Warren was suggesting an even bolder plan for Congress's consideration. Why not forty "good going sloops" of ten to sixteen guns? Such a force, Warren noted, would "make a good figure" in the journals of the Congress.[13]

It was hot and uncomfortable in Philadelphia that summer and especially so in the hall at the Pennsylvania State House on Chestnut Street where the Congress was meeting. But the sultry weather did not seem to lessen the spirits of the Congress, and besides, there were compensations to meeting in America's largest city. In spite of its Quaker origins, it was possessed of an elegant society much given to fine foods, wines and gracious living. Some of the more austere members of Congress, the "brace of Adams" among them, thought the people of Philadelphia too lavish in their style of living, but that did not seem to inhibit them from enjoying what they were so quick to criticize. After a long, tedious day in Congress the delegates often gathered at a tavern or private home for the evening meal and then hurried off to their lodgings, spending as little time as possible exposed to the warm night air, which was heavy with a miasma reputed to carry strange and debilitating fevers.

Every day more news arrived detailing events from Georgia to Nova Scotia. Some were true, most were exaggerated and a few blatantly false, but they were all received and read with a feeling of excitement and in a tense atmosphere. The usual number of eccentrics popped up to lay before the Congress the latest in craziness. One day a German hussar in full regalia appeared at the doors ready to raise a troop to ride to Boston. On another day Congress listened to a plan to capture or burn the entire British fleet.[14] Only a credulous body heady with optimism would have given such men a serious hearing. Buoyed with a faith in themselves and in their cause, the delegates in Congress went doggedly ahead, almost totally ignoring ominous storm warnings and the tremendous odds facing them.

While still not yet ready to move on their own account toward a naval armament, on 18 July the Congress resolved that "each colony, at their own expense, make such provisions by armed vessels or otherwise . . . for the protection of their harbours and navigation on their coasts."[15] This resolution was part of a greater scheme then being debated in the Congress: a plan, proposed by the radical members, to open up the ports of America to all nations in open defiance of the acts of Parliament and with the hopes of obtaining military supplies. If the ports were opened and trade renewed, the next requirement would be protection, and for this purpose on 12 July a committee was appointed to devise ways and means to protect the trade of the colonies. Whether or not such protection would be needed depended upon the action of Congress in opening its ports. When the Congress declined to open up trade, the need for protection became superfluous, and the best that the navy lobby could get was the feeble and evasive resolution of 18 July.

While the idea of an American navy lay in irons, the resolution of 18 July helped at least in giving additional impetus to a few of the states to launch their own navy. A committee of the Pennsylvania Assembly under the able guidance of Benjamin Franklin was engaged in fitting out row galleys to protect the shoreline along the Delaware.[16] In New England, Connecticut had had two vessels fitting out since the first of July and Rhode Island had employed the armed sloop *Katy* since 13 June.[17] The New England states and Pennsylvania had taken the lead, but they were not alone, and in late July the Council of Safety of South Carolina dispatched the sloop *Commerce* under the command of Clement Lempriere "to take such measures, as he shall think proper, to procure Gunpowder for the Public." Following these instructions, Lempriere ran afoul of the Royal Navy and South Carolina became the first southern state to engage the enemy at sea.[18]

Many men both in and out of Congress were anxious to do more, and they were growing weary at the desultory pace at which events were moving. In this, as in other matters, it was the radicals in the Congress who were most disenchanted. Franklin, certainly the most elderly if not the most influential of this group, wrote to his friend Silas Deane, a delegate from Connecticut, that he ardently wished America would have a navy but regrettably there was little that could be done until "we are no longer fascinated with the idea of a speedy Reconcilation."[19] Adams, impatient as usual with the dawdling Congress, wrote in exasperation to Warren, "We ought to have had in our Hands a month ago the whole Legislative, executive and judicial of the whole Continent, and have completely modeled a Constitution; to have raised a naval Power, and opened all our Ports wide."[20]

On 2 August the Congress recessed. Several members traveled to Boston to see first hand the two hostile armies confronting each other. Others returned home to sense the feelings of their constituents and to report to them what had gone on in Philadelphia. In retrospect it is apparent what had been done in Philadelphia; the Congress, despite some hesitancy, had moved irrevocably toward independence. It would be more than a year before that would be official, but the truth was that with every new assumption of power the Congress behaved more and more like a sovereign, independent government.

The congressional vacation was short. Early in September delegates began drifting back into Philadelphia, and on the thirteenth the president of the Congress, John Hancock, rapped his gavel and the session officially began.[21] During the recess nothing had happened to indicate that the ministry had mellowed or modified its stand; instead there was clear evidence to suggest exactly the opposite. It was necessary now more than ever that Congress take strong action, and no one was more determined to see that done than the two Rhode Island delegates, Stephen Hopkins and Samuel Ward. Ward and Hopkins, both former governors of Rhode Island, had spent most of their lives assailing each other in the spirited and scurrilous political battles of Rhode Island politics. They had always fought over spoils, not ideology, so now these two gentlemen temporarily called a halt to the scramble for offices and came together to the Congress in a show of unity. They arrived armed with instructions ordering them to lay before the Congress a resolution of the Rhode Island General Assembly. The resolution had grown out of the colony's recent rude awakening to its vulnerability by sea. For months Captain James Wallace, commander of His Majesty's Ship *Rose*, had been patrolling the waters of Narragansett Bay, stopping trade while harassing and threatening the local residents with all kinds of harm if they did not submit to his demands.[22]

Nearly helpless under the threat of Wallace's guns, the Rhode Islanders turned to the Congress for assistance, and on 26 August the Assembly resolved "that the building and equipping [of] an American fleet, as soon as possible, would greatly and essentially conduce to the preservation of the lives, liberty and property of the good people of these Colonies and therefore instruct their delegates to use their whole influence at the ensuing congress, for building at the Continental expense a fleet of sufficient force for the protection of these colonies."[23]

Although Hopkins and Ward arrived in Philadelphia about 12 September, they waited until early October to lay their resolution before Congress. Initially the delay was caused by the lack of a quorum, but once the members had assembled, the Congress turned its attention to other matters, chiefly the critical question of whether to open American ports to foreign trade. The debate on this issue left little time for discussion of other affairs, and it was not until 3 October that Hopkins and Ward had a chance to present their resolution. Much to their disappointment, once having brought it to the floor, the Rhode Islanders saw their project immediately tabled for future consideration while the delegates went on to continue the seemingly endless debate on trade.

For months Congress had been considering all sides of the trade question. Should American ports be closed entirely? Should they be open to all nations? How would Great Britain react to the opening of the ports? What harm could her navy do? If trade were opened, how would the Americans protect themselves against the Royal Navy? On numerous occasions during the debate it was pointed out how vulnerable the American coasts and shipping were to the British navy. No one really needed to be reminded how easily Lord Dunmore, the royal governor of Virginia, tacked back and forth across the Chesapeake, terrorizing the local inhabitants and harassing shipping, or with what unabashed arrogance Wallace plundered the shores along Narragansett Bay.[24] In fact, men on both sides of the issue eagerly cited these actions to illustrate America's exposed position. The conservatives, to prove how foolish it would be to open the ports in defiance of such armed might, and the radicals, to demonstrate how much work needed to be done to put American defenses in a proper state of readiness. While the debate on general policy and philosophy droned on, as it would for several months, the Congress was pressed from other quarters to make decisions on matters that demanded a quick remedy.

Thanks to the politicking of Ward and Hopkins, the Rhode Island resolution came to the floor again on 7 October, and this time, rather than being quickly shunted off and pigeonholed, it was given a hearing. Samuel Chase, a Maryland delegate, who was first to speak on the resolution after the Rhode Island sponsors had made their presentation, called it "the maddest Idea in the World to think of building an American Fleet." Chase urged his colleagues to forget the plan and get back to more sensible things such as defending New York and fortifying the Hudson.[25] There was a murmur of agreement as Chase took his seat, and Hopkins, no political novice, quickly sized up the opposition, realized the odds were against him and so rose to announce that Rhode Island would not object if their motion were put off to a future day. No one took him up on the offer, and since no official motion to table had been made, the debate continued. If Hopkins and Ward anticipated a surge of support for their proposal, they were soon disappointed. Even those who were inclined to favor a navy were not convinced by the Rhode Island plan. Indeed, one could not really even call it a plan. There was no substance to it. It was at the same time both vague and grandiose and almost certainly expensive. Even Christopher Gadsden expressed his opposition to the extensiveness of the plan, while his fellow South Carolina delegate, Edward Rutledge, asked to know how many ships were required and at what cost before he could form an opinion. The skirmishing went on for a good part of the afternoon until the resolution was once again laid aside for future consideration while Congress went on to other business.[26]

The naval lobby had suffered its first major defeat. While the proposal had not been rejected outright, the amount of scoffing it engendered and the indefinite postponement it received clearly indicated that Congress was not yet ready to embark on a naval program. Obviously in the future any naval proposal that came to Congress would have to possess at least two virtues before it would be seriously considered. It must be modest and it must be precise.

For the time being, Congress had refused to commit itself to a general program of naval armament, but it did not necessarily follow that Congress could avoid dealing with specific problems as they arose. Although they were always careful to keep the general and the particular problems strictly separate, nevertheless with each response they moved closer and closer to a full commitment until finally in December they were ready to authorize the construction of a powerful American fleet.[27]

The first leg in the course that would eventually bring the Congress round to building a fleet began on 5 October when John Barry, commander of the recently arrived merchantman *Black Prince*, gave to the Congress certain letters he had brought from England. These letters detailed the recent departure of two English brigs on 11 August laden with munitions and bound for Quebec. Quick dispatch of American vessels to intercept these brigs, which were unarmed and traveling without convoy, could bring to the American forces at Boston a windfall in arms and ammunition.

Spurred to action by such an alluring possibility, Congress temporarily gave up their discussion of trade and resolved, after some strong opposition, to appoint "a committee of three . . . to prepare a plan for intercepting two vessels which are on their way to Canada, laden with arms and powder, and that the committee proceed on this business immediately."[28] The committee—John Adams of Massachusetts, Silas Deane of Connecticut, and John Langdon of New Hampshire, all New Englanders and all ardent supporters of a navy—took their charge, left the room and a few minutes later returned with their report. In a body that was better known for delay than action such speed was truly remarkable. Since time was of the essence, the committee did not recommend that the Congress itself fit out vessels; rather, they suggested that the president ask the Massachusetts Provincial Congress to place its armed schooner and sloop (the ones taken by O'Brien at Machias) under the command of General Washington so that he might order them to intercept the incoming brigs.[29]

For further assistance in this mission the committee recommended that letters also be sent to Rhode Island and Connecticut to request that any ships they had in their service be sent to the north also to lie in wait for the brigs.[30] Although there were some who questioned the propriety of the measure, it was overwhelmingly approved, and that afternoon the president dispatched letters to Massachusetts, Connecticut and Rhode Island informing them of the situation and asking their aid. According to the letters the vessels were to be "on the continental risque and pay" and the men involved were to receive as an encouragement one-half of the prizes over and above any pay they might receive from their state.[31]

It might seem that with the dispatch of the letters to the New England governments the work of the committee was finished, but such was not to be the case. The next day, 6 October, this same committee brought in another report, far more general in nature, outlining a plan for the equipping by Congress of two vessels to sail to the eastward to intercept any ships bearing supplies to the ministerial army.[32] It was a modest proposal, but if adopted, it would have involved the Congress for the first time in a direct way with the establishment of a Continental navy. As might have been expected, Congress voted to let the plan "lie on the table for the perusal of the members."[33] Although the tabling might be interpreted as a defeat for the navy lobby, it was more likely a trade off, for immediately following the vote to table, Congress agreed to make the Rhode Island resolution, which had been hanging fire since 3 October, the first order of business in the morning. It was an arrangement satisfactory to both parties. If the

Rhode Island scheme was approved, the committee's modest plan would no longer be necessary, and if it was not approved, then Adams, Deane and Langdon could simply push on with their own proposal. The next morning, as promised, the Rhode Island plan was debated and, as already indicated, again postponed.[34] Having avoided the general issue, the Congress found that the most sensible thing to do was to come back to the committee's original specific proposal, and on Friday, 13 October, after a week of perusal, it took up the committee's recommendation.

For the opposition the timing could not have been worse because that morning a letter from General Washington was read in the Congress. Washington briefly described how he had recently taken under his command, at Continental expense, three schooners to cruise off Massachusetts to intercept enemy supply ships.[35] For some time Congress had been aware that some of the colonies were active in engaging warships for their own defense, but the news that they themselves were now engaged in such measures, via the authority of their commander in chief, came as a bit of a surprise to them. Although some members might continue to hem and haw about the propriety of such a measure, the fact was it was now a *fait accompli*, and this seriously undercut their position. Even though the status of the schooners was somewhat nebulous, they were nevertheless sailing, albeit in a loose fashion, under the general authority of the Continental Congress. With this in mind, but still refraining from any general commitment to a large naval force as Rhode Island had urged, Congress agreed to the committee's report and resolved "that a swift vessel to carry ten carriage guns and a proportional number of swivels, with eighty men, be fitted with all possible despatch for a cruise of three months, and that the commander be instructed to cruise eastward, for intercepting such transports as may be laden with warlike stores and other supplies for our enemies, and for such other purposes as the Congress shall direct."[36]

Once the main motion passed, a second resolution was of-

fered which called for an additional vessel to be fitted out for the same purpose. It also passed, and a committee of three was appointed to select the proper vessels and to bring in an estimate of the expense. The committee consisted of Deane, Langdon and Gadsden.[37] The replacement of Adams by Gadsden was probably an attempt to give a better sectional balance to the committee while not diluting its ardor.

Adams was delighted. He wrote to his friend Warren, with whom for months he had been commiserating over the melancholy state of affairs, that he now felt "a little of a Seafaring Inclination her."[38] He predicted great things to come and buoyantly prophesied, "We shall take some of the twenty Gun Ships before long. We must excite by Policy that kind of exhalted Courage, which is ever victorious by sea and land —which is irrestible. The Saracens had it—The Knights of Malta—The assassins—Cromwell's soldiers and sailors. Nay, N. England men have ever had it hitherto. They never yet failed in an Attempt of any kind."[39]

Adams was motivated by patriotic zeal and a desire to see New England men with their experience and traditions lead the nation in launching a navy. As a statesman he was anxious to see America fully utilize her vast naval potential. Few men then or now questioned the sincerity of his motives. He could be, and often was, stubborn, querulous and intolerant, but he was never base. Unhappily the same cannot be said with equal certainty about at least one of his other New England colleagues, Silas Deane. Deane was an "avoricious" and "Sottish" man driven by boundless ambition.[40] He was later to gain some notoriety as an alleged profiteer and scoundrel while representing the United States in Paris, but now he was concerned in pushing an American fleet so that he might advance his interests and those of his friends and relatives. He wrote to his friend Thomas Mumford, a Connecticut merchant and ship owner, boasting that as a member of the committee that had prepared the plan for intercepting the English brigs, he had been instrumental in persuading the Congress to agree to foot the bills for sending vessels to the north.

Having accomplished that, he reported to Mumford, he was now serving on the committee responsible for bringing in an estimate for arming the two vessels agreed to on 13 October.[41] Anticipating favorable action on the report and hoping that it would be a prelude to bigger things, Deane alerted Mumford to the opportunities for business and profit that lay ahead if they moved quickly. He pointed out how admirably situated their home town of New London was to receive an American fleet and how "worth while it would be for New London to labor to obtain the advantages of such a Collection of Navigation expending their Money there."[42]

Deane's ambition and avarice were perhaps greater than most men's, but it certainly was no secret that of all the colonies in America the New England ones would profit most from a navy. If warships were to be built, then undoubtedly a goodly number of them would slide down New England ways to be manned by Yankee seamen. The prospect of a New England navy at Continental expense troubled many of the delegates from the middle and southern states. They had been similarly bothered back in June when the Congress had been asked to adopt the army at Cambridge composed almost entirely of New Englanders, but that problem had been alleviated with the selection of a southerner to be commander in chief. It remained to be seen if a similar arrangement could be worked out with the navy. This brand of sectional suspicion, along with some very reasonable questions concerning the wisdom of such a course, promised stormy weather ahead.

On 17 October the committee made its report. Apparently with little debate the report was considered very briefly and then recommitted to the committee. In all probability this was done to allow the committee additional time to prepare a more detailed cost estimate. Two weeks later they returned with their plan. It went far beyond what the committee had been charged to do. Principally the work of Deane, it called for a fleet of ten warships—four thirty-six-gun ships, two twenty-fours, two eighteens and two fourteens—to be fitted out at an estimated cost of $166,710.43.[43] It was a princely sum

of money to ask an impecunious Congress, totally dependent upon the largesse of thirteen parsimonious colonies, to appropriate. The justification was that such a force would compel the British navy to abandon their tactic of sending out single ships or small squadrons to patrol and harass the coast. Assuming that the Congress would be able to build such a fleet and that the British would have difficulty responding, Deane presented his arguments to a skeptical Congress.

> The Enemy have not a Naval force Now on this Coast equall to the foregoing, if the *Asia, Somerset,* & *Boyne* be put out of the Question—These Three Shipps are ordered home and Forty Gunn Shipps and downward are to be employed on the American Station for the future—it is evident if they cruize in a Fleet they will not be formidable to Trade, and if single they will be liable to be attacked by an equall if not superior force of the Continental fleet—Connecticut has fitted out Two & Rhode Island Two, these joining with the Two from Massachusetts and those which other Colonies & Individuals will fix for the Sea will go near, to form a Naval force equall if not Superior to what the Ministry will think of sending to America the Next season for they dream as little of Our meeting them, on the Sea as of Our invading Canada, and though their Naval power, & resources be ever so great in Brittain, they must inevitably be defeated the Next Campaign in America if We get early to Sea, these Shipps, and with them surprize, & intercept their Transports, or any considerable part of them.[44]

It was too bold a plan for the temper of Congress, and instead of ten ships they authorized only four: one of fourteen guns, one of ten, one not to exceed twenty guns and one not to exceed thirty-six.[45] The committee had gotten less than half of what they had requested, but on the other hand, they managed to extract from Congress a commitment for a naval force more than twice the size of the one for which they had originally been asked to estimate. To administer this infant fleet Congress voted to add four new members to the committee so that it might have broader representation. They selected Stephen Hopkins, Joseph Hewes of North Carolina, Richard Henry Lee of Virginia and John Adams. It was this enlarged committee that became known as the Naval Committee. Over the next three months they oversaw the equipping, manning and dispatch of this fleet. Significantly, the wording of the resolution outlining the committee's functions directed them to use the ships "for the protection and defense of the united Colonies."[46] No longer was the Congress merely thinking in terms of privateering expeditions to intercept incoming supply vessels; now they were building a navy that would cruise over a broader area with an enlarged mission.

Eager to get under way, the committee arranged for quarters in a local tavern and agreed to meet every evening at six to conduct their business. The meetings were productive, lively and convivial. John Adams remembered his service on the committee as "the pleasantest part of my labors . . . in Congress.[47] With unusual nostalgia he recalled the men he had met with during those fall and winter evenings of 1775, especially Stephen Hopkins, "Old Grape and Guts" as some called him. Hopkins, always attired in simple Quaker-like dress with a large broad-brimmed hat, was as astute and experienced a politician as eighteenth-century America ever produced. For more than forty years he had been a key figure in the rough-and-tumble politics of Rhode Island, where he had earned a reputation for wit, wisdom and drinking. According to Adams, the old gentleman greatly enlivened the meetings, and after adjournment many remained behind with him until very late, smoking, drinking and swapping stories in a room swimming with the heavy, warm odor of port and rum.[48]

For Adams and the others the Naval Committee assignment proved to be both pleasant and rewarding as they carefully charted their course and plowed ahead. On 2 November the Congress appropriated $100,000 for the committee to fit out four vessels and at the same time authorized them "to agree with such officers as seamen, as are proper to man and command said vessels."[49] To encourage enlistments Congress offered the crews one-half of all ships of war captured and one-third of all merchant ships.[50] *Black Prince* was the first ship bought by the committee. She was renamed *Alfred*, in honor of the founder of the British navy. Three other vessels were then bought in quick succession and renamed *Columbus, Andrew Doria* and *Cabot*.[51]

It was a remarkable coming about for the Congress. Scarcely a voice was heard to oppose these measures where only a few weeks earlier such action would have raised a howl of protest. But over the past months the Congress had become more testy toward the ministry, and even more importantly they had recently received eminent testimony to the effectiveness of an American naval force.

The testimony came from the recently returned Committee to Headquarters, Benjamin Franklin, Benjamin Harrison and Thomas Lynch.[52] These gentlemen had been sent by Congress to confer with General Washington at his headquarters in Cambridge. Their discussions with the general ran over a wide range of topics including his commissioning of armed vessels. The committee was favorably impressed with the fleet, an opinion undoubtedly reinforced when Washington announced that three of the vessels would be named *Franklin, Harrison* and *Lynch* in honor of the distinguished visitors.[53] The combination of proven success and flattery worked much to the advantage of the naval lobby, and the glad tidings carried to Congress by the committee helped to strengthen the case for a navy. Adams could feel the wind shifting, and on 5 November he wrote to Warren that there was "a Disposition . . . in Congress to spare no Pains or Expence, in the necessary Defence of our Rights by sea or Land."[54]

As the Naval Committee obtained vessels, they also began to scout for commanders. It turned out to be a family affair as the jovial storyteller Stephen Hopkins displayed all his political dexterity. His younger brother, Esek, was made commander in chief of the fleet. Esek's son, John Burroughs

Hopkins, was given command of *Cabot*. Abraham Whipple, commodore of the Rhode Island navy, became captain of *Columbus*, and Silas Deane's brother-in-law, Dudley Saltonstall, ended up commanding *Alfred*. The only outsider to enter this circle of friends and relatives was the Pennsylvania captain Nicholas Biddle, who took charge of *Andrew Doria*. Although Biddle was well qualified for the position and indeed later distinguished himself in the service, it seems likely that his appointment owed more to Pennsylvania's political influence than to his credentials. It is hard to avoid the conclusion that the committee was more interested in familial ties and sectionalism than in seamanship, but in all fairness there were other factors at work that should be pointed out. The committee was working within tight time constraints. The four vessels were all at Philadelphia, and if they were to be readied for sea quickly, someone needed to take command as soon as possible to oversee their fitting out. Having no time to solicit applications, the committee simply relied upon men personally known to them who they felt were both reliable and available. Later when delegates from the middle and southern states became concerned over the New England domination, there would be an attempt to balance the command posts according to sections, but no matter where the men came from, throughout the Revolution kinship, friendship and politics would always be more important than competence. Fortunately the first three criteria did not necessarily exclude the fourth, and many good officers, badly chosen, served aboard Continental ships.

Fitting out the four warships proved to be more difficult than anticipated. At least seventy cannon were needed, and they were scarce. The arrival in late November of the fleet's commander in chief helped to expedite matters, but the fitting out still went slowly. Recruiting quotas were far from being met, and only when Pennsylvania signed over one hundred sailors were the Continental ships fully manned. Aside from the cannon and men, there was a long inventory of other items needed for the fleet. Many of these were eventually obtained through the generosity of the Pennsylvania Committee of Safety, but in other cases the Naval Committee had to fall back on its own slender resources.

Having gone a long way toward accumulating the substance of a navy, the committee soon turned its attention to the problem of shaping this collection of men and ships into a well-disciplined force. It was essential to have a body of rules and regulations. Toward the middle of November the members of the committee discussed this need, and after some consideration they decided to give the job of writing the rules and regulations of the American navy to John Adams.[55] We can only speculate why Adams was chosen. He had no naval experience, but as a well-known lawyer practicing in a seaport, he had considerable experience in Admiralty matters. At any rate he entered into the business with his usual zeal and singlemindedness. He made his report on 25 November, and on 28 November Congress approved Adams's "Rules for the Regulation of the Navy of the United Colonies."[56] In general they followed the pattern of their British counterpart but tended to be less severe.[57]

Gradually the ships in the river at Philadelphia were taking on the appearance of naval vessels. As officers barked orders, cannons were run out in drill and men scurried about the decks and up the ratlines. All through the cold, bitter months of December preparations continued, but for what purpose? Where would the fleet go? Sailing north into New England waters was too dangerous as long as the British fleet was at Boston. A more promising area was in the vicinity of the Chesapeake and northern Virginia. Lord Dunmore, former royal governor turned pirate (at least, according to the Virginians), had been raiding and prowling the area for months. His fleet was not too formidable, and if the Americans were well led, they could rid the area of this dangerous nuisance. As they talked about where to send their fleet, the committee moved to augment it with additional vessels. By early January they could count eight vessels under their authority, the original four plus the sloops *Hornet* and *Providence* and the schooners *Fly* and *Wasp*.[58]

On 5 January, after carefully considering all their options, the committee dispatched orders to Commodore Hopkins. He was told to sail to the Chesapeake and destroy Dunmore's flotilla. When that was successfully accomplished, he was to cruise along the southern colonies, ridding the coasts of the enemy. After completing those two missions, he was to lay a course for Rhode Island and clear those waters as well.[59]

Hopkins fell down the river immediately and rendezvoused in the Delaware with *Hornet, Wasp* and *Fly*, and after some delay because of ice the fleet finally worked its way to sea by the middle of February.[60]

Hopkins's departure was a great moment for the Naval Committee. Despite all the opposition and handicaps facing them, they had managed to put to sea a fleet of eight ships in the remarkably short period of only three months. With the sailing of the fleet their job was done, and the committee could sit back with a feeling of satisfaction and pleasure. They had laid the cradle for the navy; now it was up to the Congress to find a way to carry on the business.

Chapter Four

The Marine Committee
and Friends

Despite the cold temperature and blustery winds, hundreds of people braved the weather to go down to the Philadelphia waterfront to wish Hopkins and his men fair winds and good hunting. City officials, members of Congress, the Naval Committee—they were all there crowded on the docks, craning for a look at the American squadron as it hoisted its ensign and stood quietly down the river.[1] For the uninitiated who had never seen anything more than an occasional privateer or patrol vessel it was an impressive sight. Others more experienced and critical, though, viewed the ships in a different light. To them they were a hodgepodge assortment of lumbering merchantmen built and rigged for trading, not for fighting. Although they had been refitted and armed, from stem to stern they were still merchantmen, and it would take more than a few weeks in a shipyard to remedy that failing. Hopkins's fleet would suffice for a start, but to many men who stood gazing at the American ships it seemed that the Congress could and should do more. Indeed, even as the tide carried the ships beyond view, the Congress had already moved to vastly augment their naval armament.

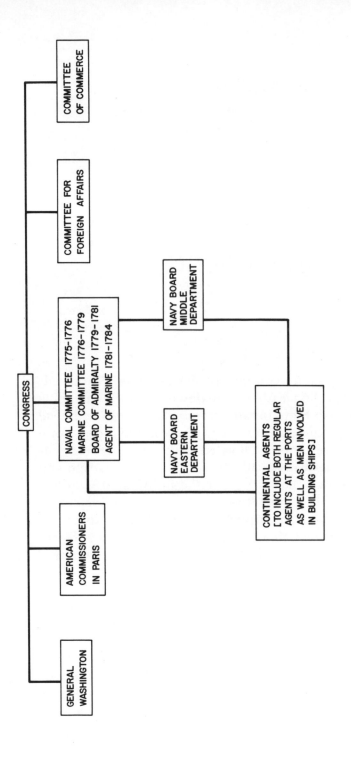

THE ADMINISTRATIVE STRUCTURE OF THE CONTINENTAL NAVY

"QUITE OFTEN SPINNING RANDOMLY IN THEIR OWN ORBIT WITH SCANT REGARD FOR THEIR NEIGHBOR"

On 11 December, after lying in limbo for nearly four months, the Rhode Island resolution calling for a Continental navy came to the floor again. This time it would not be pigeonholed and ignored. Many delegates, especially those on the Naval Committee, were primed for action and ready to reach out on a far more venturesome tack than simply buying and arming merchant ships. To them it was a scandal that America should have to depend on vessels that could never be anything better than second rate when it was within their power to build warships that would be able to match gun for gun anything the Royal Navy could throw against them. After some debate they carried the issue and Congress resolved "that a Committee be appointed to devise ways and means for furnishing these colonies with a naval armament."[2]

The nucleus of the committee was the five members of the Naval Committee to which were added seven new members.[3] This ensured continuity, although it did cause some overlap. It was a large and cumbersome committee, but politics made it so; if it was to have sufficient clout to get a building program through, it had to be endowed with wide representation and broad support.

Two days later, 13 December, the committee presented a report. It was not new and it was not really theirs. What they had done in their two brief days of deliberation was to refurbish and enlarge Silas Deane's plan which had been drawn up back in November at a time when that gentleman was intoxicated with excitement over the delightful prospects of parceling out construction contracts to his associates.[4] The proposal called for building thirteen frigates: five thirty-twos, five twenty-eights and three twenty-fours.[5] There must have been some hard bargaining in committee as the delegates haggled about where these ships would be built. None of the surviving evidence is clear on what went on, but it's likely that the New Englanders pushed hard for the lion's share. An abundance of good harbors and plentiful timber plus thousands of idle shipwrights and sailors helped make a good case for concentrating the work there. But there were stronger arguments against centering the building in any one area. Building several frigates close to one another would give the Royal Navy a chance to strike a capital blow by swooping down on these locations and in one raid delivering a mortal blow. Logistics would also be a problem if a great number of the ships were built in one location since it would put an intolerable strain on local resources. A final argument to be made, and certainly the strongest and most easily understood, was that if the Congress was going to spend large sums of money, it was only fair that the disbursements be over as wide an area as possible. At any rate, the committee recommended and the Congress agreed that the frigates should be built in the following areas: "in New Hampshire one, in Massachusetts Bay two, in Rhode Island two, in Connecticut one, in New York two, in Pennsylvania four, and in Maryland one."[6]

The whole program was to cost not more than $866,666 2/3, or $66,666 2/3 per ship. Time and paper money would soon show what an incredibly low estimate this was, and by the time of their launching these ships would come to represent one of the greatest cost overruns in American history.

Almost all the materials for construction were available in the states. The only items wanting domestically were powder —at least one hundred tons would be needed—and canvas, about 7500 pieces, for the two suits of sails to be carried by each frigate.[7] The Secret Committee, whose function was to obtain military supplies from abroad, was ordered to procure the canvas and powder at the earliest opportunity. Although all this procurement and construction promised to be a difficult undertaking, the Congress in its usual sanguine manner thought the ships should be built and ready to sail within four months so that the fleet would see action by the end of March 1776.

Having fathered the navy, it remained for the Congress to give it direction, for which they turned to their customary, if inadequate, tool of administration, the committee. On 14 December a committee of thirteen, nearly identical in membership with the one of 11 December, was elected to act as a body to carry "into execution the resolutions of Congress for fitting out armed vessels."[8] With the demise of the old Naval Committee in early 1776, this body, known as the Marine Committee, took direction of the Continental navy and for the next three years would try to steer the navy through troubled waters littered with a swarm of obstacles.

The first bit of business before the committee was getting the frigates off the drawing boards and down the ways. They quickly took up the task, chose the esteemed, if vain and pompous, John Hancock as their chairman and resolved to meet regularly every evening at six.[9] Impatient with delay, these men were, at the beginning at least, filled with enthusiasm and eager to get the job done. But as the days dragged into weeks, months and years, their zeal diminished until finally not enough members could be found to make a quorum. However, this would come only after they learned in what shoal waters they were navigating. For the time being, at least, in late 1775 and early 1776 the prospects for naval success looked bright.

In its deliberations and planning the committee had few precedents to fall back on. No building program of this size, on land or sea, had ever before been attempted in America, nor were there any government shipyards to which the work could be consigned. The committee would have to depend upon private individuals, and they turned, as they would in so many other instances, to the example of the Royal Navy. It had long been the practice of the British government that, while preferring to use public shipyards for construction, during the exigencies of wartime they would contract out to private yards for vessels of less than fifty guns. The ships would be built according to Admiralty specifications, often with government supplies and always under the close eye of a resident government agent.[10] For the Admiralty the system had worked reasonably well, and the Marine Committee hoped that, by working along parallel lines, they would be equally successful in getting ships to sea.

Over the next three years the Marine Committee learned a

great deal, and not least important of the lessons was the fact that a navy's success depends as much upon clerks and bureaucrats behind desks as upon the men in the forecastle and on the quarterdeck. What truly makes the difference in naval warfare is not so much the dramatic and romantic victories of a Drake, Hawkins or Jones but rather the careful, sustained and often tedious attention to detail. Any one of these details might seem trivial and unimportant, but taken together they provide the very sinews of the fleet. This kind of scrupulous concern is necessary both on land and on sea. The British Admiralty had had the luxury of nearly two hundred years to recognize this, but even so they encountered difficult and perplexing problems during the Revolution that strained even their capabilities and experience.[11]

A similar set of hazards and obstacles, albeit reduced in size and scope, faced the Marine Committee of the Congress. In normal times with the nation at peace such a task would have been difficult enough, but the Revolution made it horrendous.[12] The wonder is not that they so often failed but that they managed to accomplish as much as they did.

One of the initial concerns was in finding willing and experienced men to serve on the committee itself. Since so many members of Congress were associated in one way or another with trade and shipping, they had at least a nodding acquaintance with marine matters. Experience, while in short supply, was not so much a handicap to the committee as was the instability of membership and the inability of those who did serve to devote an adequate amount of time. Committee members came and went with unparalleled frequency. Indeed, not only the Marine Committee but all the committees of Congress suffered from this malady. The Marine Committee of 1776 was almost entirely different from the one of 1777, and the following year, 1778, saw an even greater turnover. In all it has been estimated that during the four agonizing years of its existence at least sixty men sat on the committee.[13] Those few men who stayed around long enough to appreciate the situation lamented the effect of this constant change of faces. But what could they do? The problem was rife throughout the entire Congress, to the point where experienced committeemen were as rare as specie in the treasury. Further contributing to this problem was the fact that there were so many committees in Congress. No matter how trivial an issue, a committee would be formed to consider it. During the course of the war the Congress created, in addition to its regular standing committees, literally hundreds of special committees to consider everything from writing a declaration of independence to paying for a dead mule. The staffing of all these committees threw a heavy burden on the members of Congress and created a strong centrifugal force that kept them always on the periphery of problems, never leaving them with sufficient time or energy to really come to grips with the issues.

The experience of William Ellery, a Rhode Island delegate and regular member of the Marine Committee, provides a good example of the kind of difficulties haunting the Congress. Ellery served on the committee for three years. As a Rhode Islander he was very much interested in the navy and devoted as much of his time as possible to its administration. During the course of his service he became one of the most knowledgeable members of Congress in naval affairs. Yet, despite his ability and desire to be of service, he was constantly frustrated by the demands being made on him from other quarters. From 1776 to 1779 he served on at least thirty-three special committees and six standing ones.[14] In addition, he was quite often the only Rhode Island representative attending, which in itself gave him a full-time job. As a result of all of these official demands, not to speak of his own personal difficulties, such as keeping up with a peripatetic Congress as it moved to Baltimore and York or attending to his family, Ellery was simply not able to allot his time as he wished. His plight was a common one shared by all his colleagues.[15] The fear of concentrating power in anything smacking of centralized or executive power had brought the Congress to this state of affairs. Every department—army, navy, treasury, foreign affairs—was run by committees.

This "town meeting" type of approach to government was a natural product of the forces that caused the Revolution. The Americans were struggling for home rule and against the centralizing tendencies of an imperial government, and so they were not about to exchange a strong government in London for one in Philadelphia. Nevertheless, whatever the philosophy behind it, the plain fact was the system did not work. It was an unhappy predicament for the Marine Committee but it would take some time before they would realize the full depth of their plight. For the present, at least, they went buoyantly about their business.

To oversee the construction program that was spread out from Portsmouth to Baltimore, the committee decided to appoint local men to act as agents handling naval affairs at their port in the name of the committee. These men, usually local merchants, were responsible for the myriad details involved in getting the frigates to sea. For their troubles they were paid a commission of five percent on all the Continental funds that passed through their hands.[16] As American naval activity increased, more agents became necessary, and their duties were gradually expanded, as indicated in the instructions sent to the agent for New Jersey, Okey Hoaglandt.

> It will fall to your share, to supply all Continental Cruisers or other Vessels in the Continental service, with Provisions Stores & necessarys to assist the Captains and Officers in whatever may be needful to advance them monies necessary for their supply, give them advice and in all things take care of the interests of the United States. If any Prizes are sent into New Jersey by the Continental Cruisers you are to receive them, libel and prosecute them to condemnation—then, make public sale of vessels cargoes and all effects that are condemned (unless ordered otherwise) and for your guidance we send you a Pamphlet containing the Rules and Regulations in these respects. You are duely to transmit to this Committee Inventories of All Prizes and their Cargoes taken by the Continental Vessels of war and sent into your State, and such parts of the

Cargoes as we may order to be kept for the Public use, are not to be sold but valued and reserved agreeable to our Orders. You are regularly to transmit to this Committee sales of all Prizes by you disposed of, which Sales are to correspond with the Inventories first taken, and hold the Proceeds ready to be paid agreeable to our orders.[17]

In general the agents exercised a powerful office, particularly those located in the major ports. The slow and unreliable nature of eighteenth-century communications coupled with the sometimes vague instructions from Philadelphia meant that these gentlemen exercised considerable leeway in making their judgments. An overly ambitious agent or an incompetent one could cause their congressional superiors much anxiety, and they often did.[18]

The disputes that arose between the committee and the agents more often than not involved the question of money. When the navy was first established, it was hoped that a good part of the expense would be defrayed by the sale of prizes taken by Continental cruisers. Although this was an optimistic view, it was not an entirely unreasonable one. In previous wars many American privateers had returned handsome profits, and there was good reason to believe that as much might be expected of the navy. In fact, many people looked upon the navy as nothing more than a glorified privateering fleet whose mission was not to engage the enemy's warships but to raid their commerce and return a profit. During the war the navy did capture between two hundred and two hundred and fifty prizes. Most of them were carried into American or friendly ports, where they and their cargoes would be libeled, condemned and sold. It was the responsibility of the agent to ensure that the process was carried out fairly and equitably and to be especially vigilant that the Continent received its due share. Rarely did it work as easily as it sounds. On one side the committee continually dunned the agents to account for monies supposedly in their possession, while on the other, local suppliers and builders besieged them to use their monies to pay them. As costs rapidly out-stripped income, the agents found themselves in the uncomfortable position of pleading poverty to everyone, and instead of being suppliers of cash, they became heavy consumers dependent upon a querulous Congress. In less than four years John Bradford, the agent in Boston, furnished over half a million dollars to the navy from prizes brought into this port, but even that was not enough, and the flow of cash was always to Boston rather than from it.[19]

Amid charges and countercharges about who had what monies it was impossible to come to any precise conclusion. Depreciation was wreaking havoc on what passed as a monetary system. As an example of how severe this problem alone had become, in 1775 Congress estimated that it would cost less than $700,000 to build and equip thirteen frigates. By 1780 Congress was asked to supply nearly one million dollars, not for a fleet, but merely to refit and supply one frigate![20]

The financial woes of the Marine Committee were only a small part of what was a very bleak picture. The Congress, teetering on the edge of bankruptcy, tried to solve its problems by printing more money, until the expression "not worth a Continental" became a catch phrase to describe anything that was worthless.[21] Altogether between 1775 and 1783 the Congress allotted in the neighborhood of eight percent of its total budget for naval expenditures, or somewhere between $12,500,000 and $13,500,000.[22]

It was a princely sum of money for the eighteenth century, and the Marine Committee tried, as best it could, to keep track of it. Repeatedly they asked their subordinates for an accounting. Often such requests were ignored, or if a response was forthcoming, it most generally was an excuse for not sending such accounts. No one really knew where all the money went, and the Marine Committee, despite its pious admonitions, hardly set the example for orderly bookkeeping and efficient administration. At the end of the war, when the auditors replaced the generals, they reported that the marine records were in a shambles. The Naval Committee, which had been defunct for nearly eight years, had still to account for funds, and as for the Marine Committee, all Joseph Pennell, the harried accountant, could state was that "the Marine Committee have kept no Books of Accounts during their Management of the Business and their Minutes of Money matters are not sufficiently expressive to direct the making of necessary Entries."[23]

Correspondence between the various marine agencies was frequently laced with accusations and innuendo about malfeasance and misappropriated funds. The Marine Committee devoted sheaves of paper and gallons of ink to inquiring about that last bit of money sent or the proceeds from a recent prize sale or why so much was being spent for cordage and cannon or whatever. Allegations of wrongdoing were plentiful but facts were scarce, and the records, such as they were, were insufficient for indictment.

A good many of the headaches the Congress experienced with the navy could have been avoided if they had been less smitten with dreams of naval glory. The business of building thirteen frigates and handling what was left of the old Naval Committee fleet severely taxed the Congress and the Marine Committee. Undaunted by their difficulties and flushed by some naval victories, Congress resolved late in 1776 to put on a full press of canvas and expand their new fleet. It was agreed

That there be immediately undertaken:

In New Hampshire,	1 ship of 74 guns
In Massachusetts Bay,	1 ship of 74 guns and 1 ship of 36 guns
In Pennsylvania,	1 ship of 74 guns
	1 brig of 18 guns and a packet-boat;
In Virginia,	2 frigates of 36 guns, each;
In Maryland	2 frigates of 36 guns each.[24]

With this action Congress was off on a new tack. They were now committing themselves to build not just frigates and auxiliary vessels but great seventy-four-gun ships of the line. This resolution marked the high tide of naval enthusiasm in the Continental Congress. In a little over a year the naval lobby had succeeded in carrying the Congress from commissioning schooners to building frigates and finally to the most ambitious task of all: launching ships of the line. It had all been accomplished with relative harmony, which would soon change as certain rifts appeared to mark the beginning of some deep divisions within the Congress.

The seventy-fours became the first issue to cause friction. Although they had been approved by the Marine Committee and the Congress, many men questioned the wisdom of allocating such vast resources as would be necessary for the construction of these behemoths. When construction got under way and the problems mounted, it became obvious that the project had become an expensive and troublesome burden. Only one of three ever got beyond framing, and it evolved into a seemingly endless project with an insatiable appetite for money and supplies. As a symbol the project came to represent the hopes of some for a powerful American fleet, while to others it simply epitomized folly and poor judgment. The question was whether the Congress should attempt to build a strategic force capable of engaging the Royal Navy or whether they should stick with what amounted to a privateering navy harassing and destroying British commerce. On this issue the Congress always vacillated. They tended to lean toward the concept of a privateering fleet, yet they never abandoned the seventy-four project; it dragged on for years, remaining a controversial burden despite several attempts to scrap it.

If the Marine Committee and Congress had troubles determining what ships to build, they also had their problems deciding what they should do with the ones they already had. As early as the spring of 1776 the question of how the American ships were being used had caused much unhappiness, especially among some of the southern delegates who had been initially persuaded to go along with the creation of a fleet out of a belief that its first mission would be to clear their coasts of British raiders.[25] This had been Esek Hopkins's mission when he left Philadelphia in January 1776. For his own reasons the commodore ignored his orders, bypassed the coast entirely and lay straight for the Bahamas. However sound the military reasoning for his action might have been, it was a colossal political blunder. The southerners, still pestered by British raiders, were thoroughly annoyed at the slight. The whole business left them harboring a considerable amount of ill will and suspicion toward Hopkins and New Englanders in general, who they felt had an inordinate degree of influence over the navy.[26]

The Hopkins cruise was the first but certainly not the last time that southerners felt neglected by the navy. In the fall of 1779 Henry Laurens, a delegate from South Carolina and former president of the Continental Congress, complained to his son that he had tried for more than a year to get American frigates sent south to cruise along the Virginia and Carolina coasts. Laurens said that every time he had tried he had failed, not for any tactical or logistical reason but rather because of the intervention of the New Englanders. It was the New Englanders, especially the Bostonians, who blocked such action so that they could keep the frigates coming into Boston with their valuable prizes and cargoes. Laurens could not have been alone in his suspicions, and his observation that Boston seemed to get the lion's share of the Continental prizes was accurate. However, the reasons were not so much conspiratorial, as Laurens tended to think, as geographic and military.

Criticism of the Marine Committee was rife everywhere. Nevertheless, they labored along, trying to build an imposing navy on what was really a preposterous foundation. A dearth of supplies and an empty treasury were handicaps that were difficult to overcome. But even if the financial and material resources had been adequate, the administrative structure was still not equal to the task. As long as departments were run by legislative committees, they would lack good administration. Eventually the Congress would come around 180 degrees and abolish the committees in favor of executive offices, but in the meantime half measures at reform would have to do.

Administrative reform for the navy entailed establishing regional navy boards. The first one was established at Philadelphia in October 1776.[27] It was officially titled the Navy Board of the Middle Department and was composed of three commissioners appointed by Congress. These gentlemen were to take jurisdiction over all naval activities within the area of the Middle Department, that is, Maryland to New York.

They had an impressive set of instructions and on paper they exercised considerable authority, but as was so often the case, appearance and reality were not the same and for both military and political reasons their power was actually quite circumscribed. The military reasons were obvious. Philadelphia was not a good naval base. Its vulnerability by land was dramatically demonstrated when the British marched in and occupied it during the fall and winter of 1777 and 1778. Even after their departure its usefulness remained impaired by the fact that the only way to get to sea from the port was to run the British gauntlet through the Delaware and round the capes. With these liabilities it is no surprise that many of the commanders who would otherwise have put in to Philadelphia preferred instead to head north to Boston and out of the board's jurisdiction.

For political reasons as well the Board of the Middle Department found itself to be not much more than an empty square on an organizational chart. Living cheek by jowl with the Marine Committee, they were constantly overshadowed by their parent. People having business with the board would often ignore it and take their affairs directly to the committee. The board was a cipher, and in an administrative sense it was probably superfluous, which helps to explain why it was so difficult to get anyone to serve on it.[28]

While Philadelphia had a board and no business, Boston had the business but no board. It was in the north that administration needed to be tightened up, but Congress seemed to shy away from tackling the obvious. The reason was simple. The Congress and the committee were jealous of their authority and had no inclination to see any portion of it delegated to men hundreds of miles distant. However, this reluctance gradually weakened as reports of maladministration, inefficiency and even peculation came to the Congress with disturbing regularity. The agent at Boston, John Bradford, was accused of "incapacity," while at Providence the situation was characterized by "selfishness."[29] Remedy was needed, and no matter how skeptical some members might be, especially southerners who viewed the rising naval hegemony of the New Englanders with grave misgivings, action had to be taken. On 19 April 1777 (an anniversary date that passed without official recognition) Congress resolved to appoint three commissioners who would constitute the Navy Board for the Eastern Department. They were to reside in or near Boston and receive a salary of fifteen hundred dollars for superintending "all naval and marine affairs of these United States with the four eastern states under the direction of the Marine Committee."[30]

In contrast to the Middle Department, where men had to be persuaded to serve and cajoled to stay, the establishment of the Eastern Department brought on political maneuvering and dealing for the three posts. The competition for the jobs indicated that people were aware how important and active this board would be. The New England delegates began to lobby for their favorite sons. The Massachusetts representatives felt that since the board was in Boston, the three commissioners should all be from that state. The other New Englanders did not agree and urged their own candidates. New Hampshire's nominee was the Continental agent at Portsmouth, John Langdon, whose name was entered but not seriously pushed.[31] New Hampshire's *de facto* withdrawal left it a three-way contest between Massachusetts, Connecticut and Rhode Island. Connecticut nominated a New London sea captain, John Deshon, an obscure individual known "to no one."[32] From Rhode Island the candidate was a former Newport merchant, William Vernon.

The Massachusetts delegates tried for all three seats on the board, but they soon discovered that the "Gentlemen of Connecticut and Rhode Island were urgent."[33] Under the circumstances it seemed prudent to compromise, and each state got one seat. Deshon, Vernon and James Warren of Plymouth became the new commissioners.[34]

Warren's selection came only after some political scuffling among the Massachusetts men. His selection was fortunate. He brought to the board one of the best-known names in New England. His brother was the famous Dr. Joseph Warren who had been killed at Bunker Hill, and his wife was Mercy Otis, the sister of James. In an age that valued women more for their domestic skills and docility than for any intellectual achievements, she achieved considerable fame as a writer and historian. She and Abigail Adams are the two greatest women to emerge from the Revolutionary era.

It took the new commissioners several weeks to get their personal affairs in order, and it was not until sometime between 25 August and 4 September 1777 that they first assembled as the Navy Board of the Eastern Department. They immediately went about organizing their office and hired William Story to be their clerk.

No matter what one may think about the role of the American navy in the Revolution, whatever was accomplished by that service was due in no small measure to these three commissioners in Boston. Poorly paid and sometimes shabbily treated, these men displayed a better grasp of naval problems than any of their superiors. They were diligent, honest and devoted public servants at a time when such qualities were in scarce supply. The board functioned for four years, and during that time, in contrast to what went on elsewhere in the government, the personnel remained the same. Warren seems to have acted as the senior member of the board, with Vernon next in line, while Deshon was the most junior commissioner.[35]

As was intended, the board handled a plethora of detail and decisions that otherwise either would have gone unattended or would have been forwarded to Philadelphia. The vast bulk of their work involved building new ships and refitting those already in the service as they came into port. However, they were by no means confined to victualing, and early in their career they began to assert themselves vigorously in matters of naval policy and strategy. It is likely that few had originally thought of the board as an initiator of policy, but as the Marine Committee and Congress grew less effective, the commissioners moved to fill in the gap.[36] This assertiveness was not always appreciated or understood in Philadelphia, and it occasionally resulted in some gruff exchanges of correspondence.

The board never completely disregarded or ignored any order from the Marine Committee. However, if a situation arose for which they had no instructions, the board assumed they were free to act in any manner they thought best, after which they would notify the committee of what they had done. In practice this meant that the board exercised considerable authority not only over activities in port but also in the disposition and assignment of the American ships at sea.

The most important and by far the most interesting area in which the board moved was on those occasions when they suggested and planned operations for the American navy. In this capacity the board helped to plan several voyages, including one of the most successful of the entire war: the interception of the Jamaica fleet.[37]

In comparing the activities of the Marine Committee with those of the Eastern Department, the inescapable conclusion is that the navy probably could have been run better from Boston than from Philadelphia. The three men on the board had more and better ideas than the dozens of men who served on the Marine Committee.

If this tendency for control to dissipate over distance was apparent in the case of the navy board in Boston, it was even more glaring in the area of overseas operations. The American commissioners in Paris were heavily involved with naval affairs, especially Benjamin Franklin, who, although he never cared for the business and viewed it as a distraction from his principal diplomatic duties, found himself drawn into a vortex from which escape was impossible. American ships kept popping up with captains who came to him seeking men, money and a friendly prize court. He could not possibly turn them away.

Although the Marine Committee in Philadelphia was ostensibly in charge of naval affairs, Franklin and his associates in Paris rarely felt responsible to them when they conducted naval business. They did correspond with one another, but it was all rather informal, and for all intents and purposes the Americans in Paris, when lacking orders to the contrary, ran their own naval show.

Chapter Five

Reorganization and Failure

The navy was light at the head. After three years of trying, the Marine Committee's position had eroded to the point where it was little more than a cipher. It had virtually no control over its ships in European waters, and those closer to home seemed always drawn toward Boston and the Navy Board of the Eastern Department. It was a depressing situation. The New York delegate and future chief justice, John Jay, diagnosed the malady for his friend General Washington.

> While the maritime Affairs of the Continent continue under the Direction of a Committee they will be exposed to all the Consequences of Want of System Attention and Knowledge. The Marine Committee consists of a Delegate from each State. It fluctuates, new Members constantly coming in and old ones going out. Three or four indeed have remained in it from the Beginning, and have a proportionate Influence or more properly Interest in it. Very few of the Members understand even the State of our Naval Affairs or have time or Inclination to attend to them.[1]

The turning point arrived in the spring of 1779 when, much to the chagrin of the committee, on three consecutive occasions they could not round up enough members (five) to make a quorum. It was not for want of business that the members stayed away—of that there was plenty—it was for lack of interest. There had to be a better way, and after the summer doldrums had passed, Congress took up the issue in the fall of 1779.

It was a touchy business. Not everyone was enthusiastic about streamlining the marine department. According to some men, Jay among them, there were several people in the Congress who were very much opposed to any change in the system because they controlled it and bent it to their own purposes.[2] He and others were especially suspicious of the so-called Family Compact, an informal political alignment between the Virginia delegates and some of the New Englanders.[3] Through this alliance—or so it was alleged—Virginia and the New England states had been able pretty much to control the Marine Committee, seeing to it that every chairman of the committee was either a Virginian or a New Englander.

Although self-interest was an undeniable motive for some, there were other more philosophical and high-minded reasons for opposing change. Whatever the flaws of the present system, they were far preferable to some new evil masquerading as reform, especially if, as the talk in Congress seemed to indicate, a new system might abolish the committee and set up an executive department. This suggestion was anathema to the old radicals, many of them New Englanders, who still clung tenaciously to their republican ideals. To these men, chief among them the fractious delegate from Boston, Sam Adams, the Congress was a grand town meeting where all things were everyone's business and where no man would have any rank or power above another.

Unhappily, the experience over the past few years belied Adams's fine-sounding republican rhetoric. The plain fact was that when everything became everyone's business it soon degenerated to being no one's business. Adams and his "town-meetingites"[4] found themselves facing an opposition composed of men who were willing to sacrifice any real or imagined benefit from republican simplicity in order to concentrate authority in the hands of a few men who could get things done.

In a deft piece of navigation the Congress managed to pass between the Scylla of dispersing power among many and the Charybdis of giving it to too few. They succeeded by striking a compromise that lay somewhere between a committee and an executive. They created a board.

It was to be composed of five men, three from outside Congress and two congressmen, with no two members coming from the same state. The three noncongressional commissioners were to be paid $14,000 per year. The congressional members would receive no compensation, and there would be a permanent secretary at $10,000 per year.[5]

This Board of Admiralty, as it was called, was by no means a new or different approach to naval administration. As in so many other areas of the navy, the Americans were copying the British example, for at least since the reign of William and Mary there had been an Admiralty Board conducting the affairs of the navy.[6] The British board had worked well, and now at the instigation of several congressmen the Americans established their own board composed of American "Lords of Admiralty."

The resolution creating the board was adopted on 28 October, but it would be well after Christmas before the fledgling "Lords of Admiralty" took command of their navy. From late October till early December time was consumed as Congress searched for men to fill the new positions. As noncongressional members the Congress chose three men who could bring a good sectional balance: William Whipple of New Hampshire, George Bryan of Pennsylvania and Thomas Waring of South Carolina. When notified of their election, all three gentlemen replied with a resounding "no." Who could blame them? The board's prospects at best looked bleak, and no one was eager to tie his career and reputation to a foundering navy. Furthermore, the job carried with it a double curse: living in Philadelphia and a congressional salary. The City of

Brotherly Love had become the most expensive place in America. It was, according to a French traveler, "the great sink wherein all the speculation of America terminates and mingles."[7] Living in this "sink" was a financial burden that pressed hard upon everyone but was especially severe on the salaried civil servants of the Congress, who, living on a fixed income, could not easily adjust to skyrocketing prices. By early 1780 some congressmen were paying $1200 and more per month for just a room, and there was no end in sight. Under these circumstances it is no wonder all three men declined the burden of the Admiralty. Whipple, a former congressman himself and a person whose knowledge of maritime affairs would have made him a valuable member, bluntly replied that he did "not suppose any man who has lived a month in Philadelphia can think that the sum is by any means equal to the necessary expenses that a man in that Character must be at."[8] The two congressional members, James Forbes of Maryland and William Floyd of New York, said nothing and apparently with little feeling either way simply accepted this appointment along with all their others.

In early December Congress at last found a man to be a noncongressional member: Francis Lewis, a wealthy merchant and former member from New York. His acceptance forced the resignation of his fellow New Yorker, Floyd, and in his stead William Ellery, the spectacled and balding Rhode Island delegate, was elected. With three members, a quorum, present, they pressed forward. For the next year and a half this Continental Board of Admiralty would try to bring sense and effectiveness to the navy. The membership of the board, like that of its predecessors, fluctuated, but there were two men who remained to stand watch for the full time—Lewis and Ellery—Lewis as the noncongressional member and chairman and Ellery first as a congressional member and later, after an unsuccessful bid for reelection to Congress, as a noncongressional member. After Ellery joined the board in June 1780, he and Lewis handled all the naval administration in Philadelphia, so for all intents and purposes these two men were the Board of Admiralty.

The first order of business for the new board was to establish authority over their subordinates and to collect enough data from them so that they could at least sketch out the status of the navy. It was no easy task.

The agents proved to be as independent as ever. It might have been different if the board had been able to sweep through with a broom and do a general housekeeping. But that was impossible, and the new commissioners found themselves the ostensible heads of an administrative structure they had had no part in creating and had little hope of changing.

At one time or another the board would have harsh words for every one of their subordinates, but their severest censure was reserved for John Bradford in Boston and John Wharton in Philadelphia. When it came to rendering accounts of the money they had spent or answering questions put to them by the board, these two gentlemen were as independent as a hog on ice. Bradford dallied with his accounts, and suspicion grew that he might have something to hide, while Wharton just flatly refused to forward his records, maintaining that it was not his job to be a clerk and that if the board wanted that kind of work done they had best send their own man.[9]

Wharton's truculence was an irksome but not critical blow to the board. His post was not an essential cog in the marine department, and in the summer of 1780 the board and Congress, fed up with his obstreperous behavior, abolished the Navy Board of the Middle Department.[10] Matters could not be so easily handled in the north, though, for it was in that area that most of the important naval activity was taking place.

Bradford and his fellow agents in New England, especially John Langdon at Portsmouth and Nathaniel Shaw in New London, were vital to the Board of Admiralty. They were important not only because they supervised naval activities at their ports but also because they had become the chief source of cash for the navy. By early 1780 the Continental treasury was nearly exhausted. What little money was available was diverted to the greater needs of the army, and the Board of Admiralty found itself embarrassed and broke. When pressed by creditors, as was often the case, they counseled patience but could offer little hope. With the congressional wells run dry, their only hope was to draw on their agents, who they believed had cash and supplies that had been turned over to them as Continental prizes. The board was desperate for money to refit ships and to finish those under construction, especially the frigates in Connecticut and Massachusetts and the seventy-four at Portsmouth.[11] They dunned Shaw, Bradford and Langdon to forward money. Shaw replied he had not seen any significant prizes in his port since 1776.[12] Langdon was no help since he needed money for the seventy-four. And as for Bradford, however little the board might have thought of his bookkeeping, they always erred in the opposite direction when estimating his revenues. Whatever Bradford's faults, there is no evidence to suggest that he was hoarding money or supplies, and he must have greatly tired of the board's repeated requests for funds that he simply did not have.

The board might have survived their financial maladies—after all, the Congress was not much better off and it managed to win a war—but what finally did the Board of Admiralty in was the general deterioration of the entire American navy. Both 1779 and 1780 were bad years for the navy and the board. They lost at least a half-dozen ships to the enemy.[13] Added to the simple material losses represented by these humiliations were a host of concomitant problems that settled on the board. Chief among them were questions of personnel and morale.

It was a standing policy that whenever a ship was lost or wrongdoing suspected, an official inquiry would be made to determine possible culpability and ascertain whether or not there were grounds for a court-martial. Such proceedings were never pleasant, and on those occasions when they

(84)

reached an actual trial, they could be especially painful. In its short tenure the board had the misfortune to be in charge during some of the messiest trials of the war. It was a costly way to be rid of fools and incompetents, for the public airing that these courts-martial required simply highlighted the poor relations the board had with its officers corps. The loss of so many ships was not accompanied by a corresponding decrease in officers, so that by the summer of 1780 the Board of Admiralty found itself with a surfeit of officers and a shortage of ships. Nothing is more troublesome to naval administration than beached captains, and the board found itself in the uneasy position of trying to mollify and deal fairly with a group of men obdurate by nature but now made even more impatient and irascible by unemployment. They were sensitive to every slight, real or imagined, and they were not the least hesitant to let the board, or anyone else for that matter, know about their displeasure.

Buffeted on all sides, the board lumbered on, trying to make headway. Their fleet was small. By summer 1780 there were only five warships left: the frigates *Alliance, Confederacy, Deane* and *Trumbull* and the sloop of war *Saratoga*.[14] But whatever its size, at least it was an independent naval force, and as long as it remained so, Ellery and Lewis could pride themselves "Lords of Admiralty." Such pride though was to be short-lived.

On 25 July 1780 Congress received a request from the Chevalier de La Luzerne, the French minister at Philadelphia. Because he represented the French crown, upon whose armories and treasury they had become so dependent, Congress paid special heed to whatever the chevalier said. Indeed, his influence was so great "that he may almost be considered one of the heads of the American government."[15] This time his request concerned the American navy. He asked that the American ships be put under the command of Admiral de Ternay, who had recently arrived at Newport escorting the expeditionary force of General Rochambeau.[16] The Congress rushed to comply, and the next day, 26 July, over the loud objections of the board, they ordered that the American ships be removed from the jurisdiction of Lewis and Ellery and be given over to the command of General Washington, to be "employed in cooperating with the fleet of his Most Christian Majesty."[17] Putting them under Washington's command was nothing more than a technicality that would preserve the appearance of American ships under American command. If the intentions of the Congress were carried out, the American vessels might just as well have hauled down the Stars and Stripes and hoisted the fleur-de-lis in its stead. It was a sad time for the navy. Defeat, neglect and poverty had left it badly weakened, with little hope for the future. With the French men-of-war swinging at anchor in Newport, many questioned the value of an American fleet at all. What needed to be done at sea could be better done by the French, and it was ludicrous and wasteful for the Congress to go on supporting this Lilliputian force.

Naturally Lewis and Ellery did not agree, and they tried their best to salvage something out of the remnants of the fleet. Confusion over who was in charge of the American ships and the subsequent bottling up of de Ternay's second division at Brest by the British gave the board some time during which they wanted to try a scheme. The board couched their plan in a way they thought could not help but entice Congress; they promised to make money. The plan as presented to Congress was prefaced with some remarks about the "embarrassments in which the public treasury and public boards" operated.[18] The board, Congress was assured, had not been unmindful of this distressful situation, and indeed they had put themselves "to the torture to find ways and means" to make money.[19] After some further hyperbole they finally came to the point. They wanted Congress to put up $200,000 to ready the Continental vessels for an offshore cruise between Sandy Hook and Charleston, South Carolina. Such a cruise might yield enough in prizes to "relieve not only this board but even the treasury from its difficulties."[20] Although the board might have thought its proposition a tantalizing one, the Congress felt otherwise. The letter was received, read and forgotten. It was not even assigned to a committee for further consideration. Nevertheless, somehow the board managed to scrape together enough men, money and supplies to fit *Trumbull* and *Deane* for a short cruise.[21] After three weeks at sea they returned "without taking anything worth naming."[22] The board was worse off than ever. The frigates *Confederacy*, *Trumbull* and *Deane* were lying in the Delaware in need of refitting. *Alliance* had arrived at Boston and was in need of attention, while the frigate *Bourbon* and the seventy-four-gun ship were still on the stocks. The only Continental vessel at sea and cruising was the sloop of war *Saratoga*.[23]

Tired and frustrated, half of the board, William Ellery, requested leave to go home to Rhode Island in early September. His request was granted, but his trip was to be more than personal; it became a quest in search of funds. He inquired of Nathaniel Shaw, the local agent at New London, if he had any funds. He made similar requests in Rhode Island and even went up to Boston to check on Bradford. Everywhere the answer was the same: no. In fact the local agents wanted to know if Ellery had any money to give to them. After an unsuccessful road trip he returned to Philadelphia in early November with his pockets just as empty as when he had left.[24]

Things did not improve in 1781. It would have been easier to roll Sisyphus's stone than to run a navy with the materials at hand. The most essential commodity, money, was also the rarest, and as the financial condition of the Congress continued its downward plunge in 1781, so too did the navy's. By early summer 1781 a great gloom blanketed the board. Their already emaciated fleet had been even further thinned during the spring. *Confederacy*, which had finally gotten to sea after much delay and expense, was captured in mid-April, while her consort, *Saratoga*, disappeared at sea with all hands lost.[25]

Through the spring and early summer Lewis and Ellery

remained at the board attending to their dwindling business. Discouraged and disillusioned, in early June Ellery wrote to his friend Vernon at the navy board in Boston.

> The next time America goes to war I hope she will have a respectable navy. Our few little ships remaining don't deserve that name. I expect your board will be dissolved soon and both the boards in this district. Indeed if they should not be dissolved by an Act of Congress, they must for a good reason, dissolve themselves. I shall not continue long at the board of Admiralty.[26]

Ellery was right. One month later he resigned his post and went home to Newport. In less than a week Lewis followed suit.[27] With the board out of business, the Admiralty seal was temporarily deposited with Charles Thomson, the secretary of Congress. Two months later the seal and the remnants of the navy were given over to the control of Robert Morris, the superintendent of finance.[28]

Although Morris's title hardly suggests naval activity, his office had become the great pit into which the Congress tossed nearly every difficult and perplexing problem, including the navy. At the point of despair they had given to Morris, in the eyes of some, dictatorial power over financial affairs of the Continent. To that awesome responsibility had now been added the less weighty but nevertheless irksome problem of the Continental navy.[29]

The superintendent's overriding commitment was to regularize and stabilize Continental finances by instituting the most rigorous controls and economies possible. He and his staff exercised exclusive control over the navy. In one fell swoop Congress had abolished the entire administrative structure, including the Navy Board of the Eastern Department and all the Continental agents. Everyone was immediately to forward their accounts to Morris, where they would be settled and, if need be, investigated.[30] In Morris's scheme of things the navy had a low priority, and indeed after Yorktown it is likely it had no priority at all. At the end of 1781 the entire American navy in commission consisted of two frigates, *Alliance* and *Deane*. The frigate *Bourbon* and the seventy-four at Portsmouth were still on the stocks.

By 1783 it was apparent that neither Morris nor Congress had much need for the navy. As far as the superintendent was concerned, the ships were useful primarily as transports to move money and supplies, but that was hardly reason enough to justify the current expenditure of over $160,000 per year.[31] Gradually the remaining ships disappeared from the lists. *America*, the name given to the seventy-four at Portsmouth, was presented as a gift to the French to replace a ship of the line run aground in Boston harbor.[32] *Bourbon* slid down the ways in July 1783 and was sold in September.[33] *Deane*, renamed *Hague*, was put up for auction that same summer.[34] The ship *Duc de Lauzun*, bought by Morris as a packet, found a buyer in France, while *General Washington*, another Morris purchase, ended up in private hands in the summer of 1784.[35]

The last ship left was the frigate *Alliance*. She had once been the pride of the American navy; now she was the navy. But her days were numbered as well. In August 1783, while outward bound from the Rappahannock with a cargo of tobacco, she began to leak badly. She was taking about nineteen inches an hour in calm water. The men strained and sweated at the pumps to keep her afloat, but toward evening the wind picked up and the rough seas battered the leaky hull until she was taking nearly an inch per minute. Luckily she was not far off the Delaware capes, and her captain, John Barry, ordered her about and headed for safe water.[36] She was brought up to Philadelphia, and in October a committee inspected her and reported that although the frigate showed some signs of rot, she was fundamentally sound and could be put back into service for about $22,000.[37] For the next year and a half *Alliance*'s fate hung in limbo while the Congress debated her future. Some felt that the national honor required she be kept in service.[38] Others did not agree, including Robert Morris. In March 1784 he reported that *Alliance* was "a mere Bill of

Costs" and that if it were up to him, he would immediately advertise her for sale.[39] For another year Congress toyed with the idea of keeping the frigate, but finally economy prevailed and she went on the auction block in August 1785.[40] When the gavel came down, she was the property of none other than Morris himself. He used her to carry tobacco to Bordeaux, and two years later *Alliance* dropped anchor at Canton, one of the first American vessels to call at a Chinese port. In 1790 she was sold again, but this time her sailing days were over. Stripped of everything movable, she was abandoned and left stuck in the mud of Petty's Island off Philadelphia. She lay there as late as the 1880s as a visible and sad monument to the Continental navy.

From the commissioning of the schooner *Hannah* to the sale of *Alliance* was almost ten years to the day—ten years during which the Congress had sought to find a proper way to administer their navy. The search had led them from committees to a board and finally to an executive. The first was totally inadequate, but the last two were reasonable alternatives whose failure may be attributed not so much to internal flaws as to congressional insolvency and neglect. A decade later, under a new, more powerful government, another American navy would be created—one boasting ships far more powerful than anything the Continental Congress had floated and run not by a mishmash of committees but by an efficient executive department. That much at least had been learned in the Revolution.

Chapter Six

The War at Sea:
The American Theater

John Adams, Robert Morris and a few other members of Congress hardly needed an Alfred Thayer Mahan to lay out for them the significance of sea power to the American Revolution. The opportunities for important naval action were great, but the probability that the Continental fleet might play a decisive role was slim. Nevertheless, keenly aware of the strategic implications of the war at sea, Congress went on dreaming and scheming. Some of their plans became hopelessly ensnarled in a web of congressional politics that quickly snuffed out any hope for success. Others passed the political tests and then died for want of men and ships. Through it all, though, a few hearty souls held to the belief that the Continental navy could accomplish something more than conducting a *guerre de course* and running a dispatch service.

In the very simplest terms, there were two ways in which the American rebels could use their navy: as either a defensive or an offensive weapon. From a defensive outlook the overriding goal was the safeguarding of the coasts and protection of commerce. At one time or another nearly every delegate in Congress and certainly every state called for this type of utili-

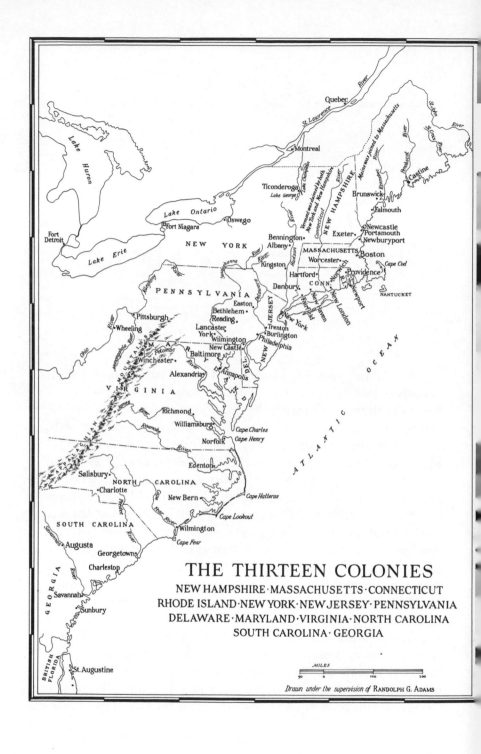

THE THIRTEEN COLONIES

NEW HAMPSHIRE · MASSACHUSETTS · CONNECTICUT
RHODE ISLAND · NEW YORK · NEW JERSEY · PENNSYLVANIA
DELAWARE · MARYLAND · VIRGINIA · NORTH CAROLINA
SOUTH CAROLINA · GEORGIA

MILES

Drawn under the supervision of RANDOLPH G. ADAMS

zation. Massachusetts thought *Hancock* and *Boston* and *Raleigh* should be used to rid their bay of the ubiquitous *Milford*; Connecticut urged the navy to clear Long Island Sound, while the middle and southern states were always urgent in their appeals for protection. People along every part of the coast, from Machias to Savannah, felt that they were entitled to naval protection, just as every state thought it had a right to expect the presence of Continental troops for its defense. But the sad fact was that even in its best hours there was no way the Continental navy could effectively defend the American coast. The navy did manage, with the help of state and privateering forces, to restrain and hinder Loyalist raiders and they even dissuaded a few British vessels from ranging too close to shore; nevertheless, whenever the Royal Navy decided to attack in force, as at Philadelphia in 1777 or Charleston in 1780, they always came with such superior fire power that American naval resistance was pitiful and futile.

A second type of defensive task assigned to the navy was convoy duty. This might involve giving merchant ships a "good offing," that is, escorting them far enough out to sea so that they were out of reach of blockading squadrons, or it could well mean providing continuous protection from port to port. Generally the latter situation involved fleets of merchantmen traveling to and from the West Indies. Convoys to Europe were considered dangerous and unnecessary since most of the goods the Americans needed—arms, munitions and clothing—were brought safely across the Atlantic in neutral bottoms to West Indian ports where they were exchanged for American tobacco and cash. The gunrunning and contraband trade were active throughout the war. The French connived at it and participated from Martinique until they officially joined the Americans in 1778 and then did openly what they had been doing clandestinely for two years.[1]

The biggest mart and rendezvous for American ships was the tiny isle of Saint Eustatius.[2] Under Dutch rule, this small link in the chain of Leeward Islands, lying about midway between Guadeloupe and Puerto Rico, was the busiest and richest port in the Western Hemisphere. In just over one year 3182 vessels cleared this port. Admiral Lord Rodney, who in 1781 descended upon " 'Statius" and abruptly ended its thriving career, said of the island, "This rock of only six miles in length and three in breadth has done England more harm than all the arms of her most potent enemies, and alone supported the infamous American rebellion."[3]

It was to and from 'Statius and Martinique that American warships sometimes escorted merchantmen.[4] Although they could never have fended off large enemy warships or squadrons, these escorts did on occasion thrust off the approaches of privateers and keep hostile warships occupied long enough to allow merchantmen to scatter and scurry away.

In a third type of activity, which in a general sense can be classed under a defensive or passive heading, ships of the Continental navy themselves undertook mercantile and packet voyages. Many times American warships were dispatched specifically for the purpose of carrying messages and cargo. *Andrew Doria* went to 'Statius to carry home a load of uniforms. *Virginia* on her maiden cruise carried a cargo of tobacco and letters to Martinique.[5] The Marine Committee never liked to send their ships on this kind of mission, which from their point of view accomplished next to nothing for the navy and had a negative impact on recruiting; after all, what seaman wanted to enlist for a voyage on which there was so little promise of loot? The Congress did have some vessels designed and built especially for packet service—*Mercury* and *Phoenix*, for example—and there was talk about establishing a regular sailing schedule, but little came of it and American warships quite often found themselves relegated to messenger service.[6]

Defending a seemingly endless coastline, acting as mother hen to flocks of merchantmen and ferrying cargo and letters were important jobs that under the circumstances the Continental navy fulfilled reasonably well. However, that brand of yeoman service was not what the more energetic and strategically minded congressmen and naval officers had in mind. By its very nature a navy is an offensive weapon, and that was how they fully intended to use it.

It made eminent good sense for the Americans to get out into deep water and attack. The British were strung out across three thousand miles of Atlantic Ocean and along a coast offering so many hiding places that not even the mighty Royal Navy could watch more than a fraction of it. With the British navy occupied in so many places, a plethora of relatively undefended targets were available to the Americans, if they could only put together squadrons and take the initiative.

To be effective as a strategic force, the navy had to operate as a navy, that is, a coordinated entity with an overall plan and goals, not as maverick privateersmen sailing about looking for targets of opportunity, attacking and plundering merchantmen. Privateering had its place, but not necessarily with the navy; it only tended to fragmentize and dilute naval strength. Privateering was better left to the privateers. Robert Morris best summed up this point of view when he told John Paul Jones:

> Destroying their settlements—spreading alarms, showing and keeping up a spirit of enterprise that will oblige them to defend their extensive possessions at all points, is of infinitely more consequence to the United States of America than all the Plunder that can be taken. If they divide their force we shall have elbow room and that gained we shall turn about and play our parts to the best advantage which we cannot do now being constantly cramped in one part or another. It has long been clear to me that our Infant fleet cannot protect our own Coasts; and the only effectual relief it can afford us is to attack the enemies defenceless places and thereby oblige them to station more of their ships in their own Countries, or to keep them employed in following ours, and either way we are relieved so far as they do it.[7]

Morris was right, but it is one of the ironies of the Revolution that those methods of operation he and others thought so little of—single ship voyages and privateering—because of their drama and romance, have become the glory of the American Revolutionary navy and have given to American naval history a bias it has never overcome.

The navy's first important venture in American waters was one of its most successful: Esek Hopkins's attack on Nassau early in 1776. As jagged chunks of ice brushed past *Alfred*, she slid out to sea under a drab sky of clouds. Hopkins was down below in his cabin poring over his charts. His mission was to clear the southern coasts and then sail north to do the same in Narragansett Bay. Those were his orders, but that was not his intention. Instead he bypassed the coast entirely and laid out a course for New Providence in the Bahamas.[8] He took with him eight vessels. The commodore himself was aboard the flagship *Alfred*, commanded by Dudley Saltonstall. Close by was *Columbus*, with the famous Rhode Island captain Abraham Whipple in command. They were the two largest vessels, both mounting twenty-four guns. The other six were considerably smaller. John B. Hopkins, the eldest of the commodore's ten children, had charge of *Cabot*. Another Rhode Islander, Hoysted Hacker, took over the schooner *Fly*. Not all the captains were New Englanders. John Hazard from New York got to command the sloop *Providence*, and Nicholas Biddle, a well-known Philadelphian, went aboard *Andrew Doria*. Rounding out the squadron were *Hornet*, with William Stone, and *Wasp*, under William Hallock. Altogether the squadron mounted 114 guns and carried nearly 700 sailors and more than 200 marines under the command of Captain Samuel Nicholas.[9]

Two days out of Delaware Bay the squadron was in "hard gales and thick weather." *Hornet* and *Fly* collided, forcing both to drop out and return home. The weather cleared, and for the remaining six ships it was, in the words of Captain Nicholas, "a very pleasant passage of fifteen days."[10] On Friday, 1 March, they dropped anchor off the island of Abaco, about seventeen leagues north of their target, the town of Nassau on the island of New Providence. Foolishly Hopkins made no attempt to hide his presence or to take advantage of the speed and surprise that were his; instead he lingered at Abaco until late Saturday, all the while giving the Bahamians at Nassau ample opportunity to prepare him a proper reception. Happily for the Americans, the governor at Nassau, Montfort Browne, turned out to be just as lackadaisical as the commodore, and although he knew the Americans were on their way, he made no attempt to prepare a defense.

On Sunday morning Hopkins was off Nassau. The rest was *opéra buffe*. The marines, 270 strong, "stormed" ashore in America's first amphibious landing. After firing off three twelve-pounders as a symbolic gesture, the defenders of the easternmost fort abandoned their positions to the Americans. That was enough for one day, and the marines spent the rest of Sunday relaxing in the captured fort. The next morning, with Nicholas at their head, they marched into town and demanded the keys to the remaining fort. Without protest or a semblance of resistance, Browne obligingly turned them over. Hopkins was now master of Nassau. As one historian has put it, "The Americans had conquered merely by coming."[11]

An inventory of the captures showed an impressive amount of stores: fifteen brass mortars along with a great number of cannon and shot. One item was conspicuously missing—powder. Because Hopkins had dallied so long and because he had failed to seal off the island, Governor Browne had been able to spirit away at least 150 barrels of powder to the safety of Saint Augustine.[12]

For two weeks Hopkins stayed at Nassau loading captured stores and resting his crews. On 17 March, the same day the British evacuated Boston, Hopkins took leave of Nassau. The voyage home was as dull as the voyage down until the squadron reached the waters off Block Island. It was here that they ran afoul of H.M.S. *Glasgow*.

On the orders of Vice Admiral Molyneux Shuldham, *Glasgow*, commanded by Captain Tyringham Howe, was carrying dispatches from Boston south to New York and Virginia alerting British forces in those areas about the evacuation and British plans for the summer.[13] It was early on Saturday morning, 6 April. The weather was clear with moderate seas as *Glasgow* was running south about fifteen leagues southeast of Point Judith. Although there were lookouts aloft, it was still dark, and almost before Howe knew what was happening, he found himself practically in the middle of the American squadron. *Cabot* was in the van, and as soon as he saw her, Howe came about on a port tack, cut across her bow and called for her to identify herself. Flames and smoke shot out of *Cabot*'s six-pounders as she answered with a broadside. It had little effect, and when Howe ordered his nine-pounders to reply, *Cabot* was severely crippled and had to fall off. *Alfred,* second in line, came up to engage. By now every sailor was at his station. For most it was their baptism in battle and the first time they had ever faced the guns of the Royal Navy. *Alfred* was more of a match for *Glasgow* than *Cabot,* but she fared little better. A British ball tore through her aft section, taking out the wheel block and the lines to the tiller. Out of control, the ship came up into the wind, giving *Glasgow* a chance to rake her fore and aft. It took several minutes for *Alfred*'s crew to repair the damage and regain control. In the meantime *Andrew Doria* and *Columbus* joined in the fray. The Americans knew what they wanted to do: close in, grapple and board. The problem was they were up against a skilled commander who knew their intentions and was able to frustrate them.

The Americans were never to take advantage of their overwhelming superiority. Instead of acting together, they fought piecemeal in a pell-mell style that allowed Howe to fend them off one by one. Finally Howe decided to break contact and make a run for it. He bore off for Newport with *Alfred, Andrew Doria* and *Columbus* in hot pursuit. The chase lasted only a few hours, and by daybreak the British ship was close enough to Newport that Hopkins decided to give up the pursuit before he ran into more British vessels.

Although there had been a hot and heavy exchange of fire,

casualties on both sides were relatively light. *Glasgow* had one man dead and three men wounded, all by musket fire, which was a rather sad commentary on American naval gunnery. It was worse for the Americans. *Alfred* had six dead and six wounded; *Cabot*, four dead and seven wounded; *Columbus* had one man wounded. *Andrew Doria* escaped without injury, and *Providence* had never been engaged. Somewhat chagrined but with his fleet at least still intact, Hopkins dropped anchor in New London on 8 April.

Despite their amateurish performance against *Glasgow*, Hopkins's squadron had succeeded in taking a conflict that up until now had been primarily local and broadening it to a much larger scope. The commodore's swipe at the Bahamas had shown how woefully inadequate British defenses were in the western Atlantic. One naval officer who saw this quite clearly was John Paul Jones, the senior lieutenant aboard *Alfred*.

The memory of Nassau and the fight with *Glasgow* was still fresh in Jones's mind when he thought of a plan to strike at the British in higher latitudes. In the fall of 1776, with time on his hands and the American fleet lying idle in Providence, he recommended taking *Alfred*, *Columbus* and the sloop *Providence* on a cruise to the west coast of Africa. It was an area, according to Jones, lightly defended and bristling with targets ashore and afloat. In a comment interesting for what it said about the physical condition of the American ships, he noted that the three vessels he mentioned would probably not be able to survive another winter in North American waters anyway, so they might as well be sent to the warmer latitudes of the south Atlantic.[14] Samuel Eliot Morison has suggested that Jones had his eye on more than just ravaging the African coast—that he planned to occupy the island of Saint Helena and lie in wait there for the homeward-bound East India fleet, which always put in to the island for water and supplies. What a rich prize that would have been![15]

Morris was sympathetic. The idea joined nicely with his

own concept of how the navy should be used. However, there were some problems that he pointed out to the captain. Africa was thousands of miles away, and any American ships on that station would be alone and isolated, with no friendly port in which to run for safety and no facilities for repair and refitting. Secondly, if his intelligence was accurate, all the British ships in the area were of greater force than anything the Americans could send. In case of an encounter, the odds would be against Jones. Despite the perils, Morris, who at the time was acting for the whole Congress, since he remained in Philadelphia while everyone else had gone to Baltimore, did not veto the plan. Instead he provided Jones with an alternative and left it up to the captain to decide. Morris's suggestion was that Jones should take five ships—*Alfred, Columbus, Cabot, Hampden* and the sloop *Providence*—on a cruise into the Caribbean. They would first swoop down on Saint Kitts at the northern end of the Leeward Islands. After plundering the island, they would set out for Pensacola, sailing by way of the south shore of Hispaniola and the north side of Jamaica, harassing and destroying along the way. From Jamaica, Morris suggested laying a course through the windward passage and then running along the Cuban shore until Jones could steer north to bear down on Pensacola, the capital of the British colony of West Florida. Then as a parting blow at the British before he returned home, Jones would spend a few days at the mouth of the Mississippi. It was a voyage worthy of Sir Francis Drake and would have led the British a merry chase. If Jones had been able to carry it off, he and his men would have shared great wealth and fame. Morris asserted that it was not plunder that drew him to this daring plan but rather the chance to draw British ships away from the American coast and force the British to strain their resources to their limit and beyond.[16]

It is not clear what Jones's reaction was to all this, but his commander, Esek Hopkins, was cool to the idea. Even though the plan might have been strategically sound, it was impossible to execute. Hopkins and his fleet were in dire straits. He had little money, too few men, many of those sick, and his ships needed work. Congress was deaf to the plan since it was busy worrying over the whereabouts of the British army and its own safety, and it did not seem to make a great deal of sense to be talking about Africa and the Caribbean when Philadelphia was about to fall.

If sending squadrons to Africa and the West Indies was too ambitious, there was always a more modest third alternative. It was an operation that the Marine Committee had first asked Hopkins to undertake back in August 1776. The mission was to attack and destroy the British fisheries in Newfoundland and then cruise for as long as possible in the Gulf of Saint Lawrence with the hope of encountering and taking the Hudson Bay fleet. Four vessels—*Alfred, Columbus, Cabot* and *Hampden*—were to stay at sea for six months. The committee readily acknowledged to Hopkins that there were enemy warships in the area, but they did not think the American captains would have any difficulty avoiding them.[17] The committee failed to mention a far more potent adversary than enemy ships—the weather. They sent their orders in August and apparently expected Hopkins to sail as soon as possible. That would mean a winter cruise in some of the iciest, foggiest and most dangerous waters in the world. It would be a perilous undertaking made even more dangerous by the leaky, decrepit condition of the ships.

This was neither the first nor the last time that a northern foray against British fisheries and the Hudson Bay fleet was suggested. Broughton and Selman's voyage a year before under Washington's direction had been along these lines, and in fact Jones himself had just returned from a very successful late summer cruise in those waters during which he had taken sixteen prizes. If one could ignore the dangers of the weather and enemy cruisers, then these hunting grounds had much to recommend them. They were close and familiar waters for thousands of Yankee fishermen and sailors who had made their living in them during the prewar years. These men knew where to find the British fishing fleets and where to hide if discovered. In addition to the fishing fleets there were now numbers of army supply vessels coming in and out of the Saint Lawrence. These were also tempting targets.

Hopkins decided not to go himself, and instead he gave the task of a northern cruise to John Paul Jones. Jones was assigned not four but two vessels, *Alfred* and *Hampden*. He tried to take *Providence* also but could not get enough men to go aboard. The ships sailed late in October, but before they even hit the open sea, trouble struck. An incompetent pilot ran *Hampden* up on a submerged ledge, and she had to return to Providence, where she was judged to be too badly injured to make the voyage. Her crew was transferred to *Providence*, and on 1 November she and *Alfred* fell down Narragansett Bay bound for the area of Cape Breton Island.

This was only Jones's second independent command. His orders from the commodore were to sail directly north to Sydney, Nova Scotia, where it was reliably reported that captured American seamen were being used in the coal mines. Jones was ordered to attack and free them, while at the same time destroying any colliers in the harbor that might be loading coal for the British garrison in New York. If all went well, the American navy would be richer by several dozen seamen and the British would be having a cold winter in New York.

The weather was predictable—bad. In a rough sea *Providence* started to leak so much that her crew grumbled to the captain, Hoysted Hacker, and demanded that he put back. Hacker agreed and *Providence*, with men at her pumps night and day, returned to Rhode Island. Jones, annoyed at what he viewed as desertion, continued cruising off Nova Scotia. He attacked the town of Canso and took several prizes, including the transport *Mellish* with a large cargo of uniforms for Burgoyne's army. From prisoners Jones learned that there was no need to go to Sydney. The Americans there had gained their freedom by enlisting in the Royal Navy. By the end of November Jones had on board more than 140 prisoners. His own crew had been depleted manning the prizes and probably numbered fewer than the men they were guarding. Under the circumstances he decided it would be best to head home, and after a run-in with the ubiquitous *Milford, Alfred* dropped anchor in Boston harbor in mid-December. Altogether Jones had taken seven prizes, and even though four of them had been recaptured, the voyage was still highly successful for the young commander.

Since northern cruises seemed to be especially productive, the Marine Committee and later the Board of Admiralty would have liked to plan more of them. In 1779 the Navy Board of the Eastern Department tried to organize a northern squadron to intercept the Hudson Bay fleet, but after raising a good deal of hope, they had to abandon the project.[18] One of the principal reasons it was so difficult for them to get ships to the northward was the urgent demands for protection that came from local governments south of the Mason-Dixon line. The problem was related to politics more than strategy. These states wielded great influence, and Congress could ignore their complaints only at great peril. They were being pestered by Tory privateers, many operating out of Bermuda, as well as Royal Navy warships patrolling the coast. The complaints were loud and urgent enough that in 1779, in order to please the southerners, the Marine Committee made some important alterations in a plan proposed by the Navy Board of the Eastern Department.

The board's plan called for a powerful squadron of four Continental ships—the frigates *Warren, Queen of France* and *Confederacy* and the sloop *Ranger*—to rendezvous at New London. From there they were to set out on an odyssey that would take them into latitudes from Jamaica to Newfoundland. Their immediate goal out of New London was to clear Long Island Sound of the cruisers and privateers that were bedeviling the Connecticut and New York shores. The maximum amount of time allotted for this segment of the mission was fourteen days. If the ships lingered longer, they would be running a high risk of entrapment by an aroused British navy coming out of New York.

Long Island Sound was only one-fourth of the operation. If the squadron survived these perilous waters, they were to sail express to Cape Henlopen and sweep the coast from there all the way to South Carolina. At those latitudes they were to pick up the westerlies and descend on Bermuda to "take or destroy all the British ships and property" on the island. Apparently the board was confident the ships would be leading a charmed life, because from Bermuda the quartet was to break up; two were to lay a course for the West Indies to harass and destroy, and the others were to pair off toward Newfoundland to lie in wait for Indiamen and transports heading for New York.[19] It was a plan designed to please Connecticut, please New York, please the South, attack Bermuda and interdict supply lines all in one fell swoop. It was a political and naval potpourri.

To the Marine Committee in Philadelphia it must have seemed like a smorgasbord operation with a little bit for everyone. The political motivation was obvious, and no one was fooled by it, least of all Congress. The navy board was trying a bit of logrolling. From experience they knew how difficult it was to get the committee and Congress to support naval operations. Perhaps if they put forth a plan as wide ranging as this, they could get enough support to push it through. The committee discussed the plan during its regular evening sessions and trimmed it down. The cut version showed quite clearly just how strong southern influence was in the committee.

Instead of four vessels in Long Island Sound there would be only one, the frigate *Confederacy* under Captain Seth Harding. She might be joined by state ships if Connecticut's Governor Trumbull would furnish them; according to the Marine Committee, there were no other Continental ships available. The other three—*Warren, Queen of France,* and *Ranger*—would sail directly from Boston to Cape May under the command of Captain Joseph Olney, the senior officer and commander of

Queen of France. These three—hopefully five if *Deane*, then being refitted, and *Confederacy*, which was to remain in Long Island Sound only briefly, joined them—would then proceed from Cape May down the coast "to the Bar of Charles Town, and afterwards . . . Cruise in such Latitudes and Longitudes which are best calculated to give the greatest aid and protection to the Trade of Delaware, Chesapeake and Charles Town, and as often as circumstances and the safety of your ships will admit of it you are to enter the mouths of Delaware and Chesapeake for the purpose of destroying the small armed Vessels from New York that lurk about the Capes to the certain destruction of almost every Merchantman that sails."[20] Gone were the plans to go to Bermuda; gone were the expeditions to the West Indies and Newfoundland. Under political pressure the Marine Committee had opted to placate local governments rather than pursue strategic objectives. Robert Morris was disappointed.

On the morning tide of 13 March 1779, amid the sound of cracking canvas and creaking rigging, *Warren*, *Ranger* and *Queen of France* slipped down Boston harbor, past the castle and out beyond Thompson's Island into Massachusetts Bay.[21] Out in the bay Olney called his captains aboard the flagship for a conference. John B. Hopkins came over from *Warren*. He was not altogether happy about being called to Olney's ship. According to the listing of captains, he was senior to Olney and by right ought to be in command, yet for some reason the Marine Committee had seen fit to bypass him. From *Ranger* came Thomas Simpson, brother-in-law to John Langdon and an independent man who did not mind telling people what he thought of the politicians who ran the navy Olney brought out the signal book and they discussed recognition procedures, battle plans and possible rendezvous in case of separation. It was a brief meeting and the men returned to their ships, laying a course east to bring them out beyond Cape Cod and then south to Cape May.

The weather was unusually good for that time of year, and for three weeks the squadron plowed south in what was turning out to be a dull and unproductive voyage. In the early gray dawn hours of 6 April, when the squadron was about fifteen miles off Cape Henry, the lookout aloft on *Ranger* called to the watch below that he had spotted two sail to windward. Simpson alerted Olney, and the commodore signaled for the squadron to raise British colors and close. As they bore down on the strangers, they fired guns to leeward as a signal to heave to. Apparently believing that the ships were flying their true colors, one of the vessels, a schooner, complied. She was *Hibernia*, of eight guns, a privateer schooner out of New York with forty-five men on board. By the time the captain realized he had been bamboozled, it was too late and he quickly lowered his colors as a prize crew came on board. After an eventful beginning the rest of the day passed quietly. The next morning the lookouts made another sighting, a fleet of nine sail off the northeast. Signals were made and the chase was on. The pursuit lasted all day, with *Warren* crowding every bit of sail and outdistancing her consorts. By four in the afternoon they were within range, and in a few hours the Americans were able to take seven of the nine. The biggest of the lot was the ship *Jason*, twenty guns and 150 men. *Jason* and the other eight were en route to Georgia from New York with provisions, dry goods and enough gear for a regiment of dragoons. Also aboard were two colonels, one a Hessian and the other a Scot. It was a rich haul.

The American captains, more interested in protecting their catch than in guarding the coast, decided that they should abandon the rest of the cruise and put about to escort their prizes back to Boston. This was in blatant disregard of their orders, and what might have been only the beginning of a successful naval cruise now turned out to be a short-lived privateering venture geared more to greed than strategy. If the captains expected a hero's welcome in Boston, they were sadly mistaken. The navy board was outraged at their conduct. They had strained every nerve to get men and money for what they hoped would be a long and fruitful voyage. Now in little more than a month the squadron was back. As soon as they touched land, the crews disappeared and once again the Continental ships lay idle while the board went through another arduous round of searching for men and money. Nor did the personal conduct of Olney and Hopkins do much to endear them to the local authorities. Not only were they openly contemptuous of the board, but apparently while at sea these captains had been busy buying up crewmen's shares of the prizes. It often took a long time for the prizes to be adjudicated, and in order to get cash, men would sell their shares at ridiculously low prices. Olney and Hopkins took advantage of this and went among their men offering to buy up shares at about one-fourth of their value.[22] All of this, of course, was reported to the Marine Committee, which decided to air these matters in a formal court-martial. Olney and Hopkins were suspended from the navy, and neither ever again held a Continental command. Simpson, although he was equally guilty of disobeying orders, escaped censure since his name was never linked to the venal schemes associated with Olney and Hopkins.

Dismayed but undaunted, the Marine Committee continued to hope for a cruise in southern waters, and in late May 1779 they planned a voyage for *Deane*, *Boston* and *Confederacy*, all recently arrived in Delaware Bay. They were going to cruise offshore in the latitudes of thirty-five to forty degrees —Albemarle Sound to Philadelphia. Only *Boston* and *Confederacy* sailed, and it was hardly worth the effort. On 6 June they took the privateer *Pole*, mounting twenty-four guns, along with a small schooner and sloop. That was the full extent of the voyage.[23]

The busiest year of the war for the Continental navy was 1779. Not long after *Boston* and *Confederacy* returned with their prizes, the Marine Committee received some good news from the north. Abraham Whipple, commander of the frigate *Providence*, was one of the most able captains to serve in the Continental navy. It was Whipple who had led the Providence Sons of Liberty down Narragansett Bay back in June 1772 when they boarded and burned His Majesty's schooner *Gaspee*. Partly for that exploit and his reputation as a patriot and partly because he was Esek Hopkins's brother-in-law, Whipple was placed number twelve in the list of captains. He had commanded *Columbus* on the voyage to Nassau in 1776, and upon his return he was named to command the frigate *Providence*, then building in Rhode Island. He had taken her to Europe in 1778, captured a few prizes and been presented to the king of France. It was now mid-July 1779 and Whipple was aboard his frigate off Newfoundland. He was in command of a squadron composed of *Providence*, *Queen of France*, under Captain John Peck Rathbun, a fellow Rhode Islander, and *Ranger*, under Captain Thomas Simpson. As is so often the case in those waters, there was a thick pea-soup fog accompanied by a damp, penetrating chill and calm seas. The Americans, blind but not deaf, began to pick up the sounds of signal guns and bells in the distance. The sounds came closer until finally the squadron was surrounded by unseen ships. Whipple and his men had stumbled right into the middle of a Jamaica fleet, some sixty sail, all of them lying low in the water bound home for England with rich cargoes of cotton, sugar, woods and other tropical products. Toward noon, as the fog began to burn off, Rathbun discovered he was close by a lumbering merchantman. By feigning the role of an escort frigate, his ship was able to get close enough to lower away a boat with a boarding party that was able to take the merchantman without a shot. Whipple and Simpson quickly followed suit, and before long they had plucked eleven prizes with little or no difficulty. With prize crews aboard the merchantmen, the Americans set sail for Boston. On the voyage home three of the prizes were retaken, but even so Whipple had made one of the greatest hauls of the Revolution and he and his men shared more than one million dollars in prize money. Whipple, triumphant and wealthy, received the accolades of the navy board and the Marine Committee while men in Boston and elsewhere began to sing ballads celebrating the frigate *Providence* and her brave captain.

Come listen and I'll tell you how first I went to sea,
To fight against the British and win our liberty.
We shipped with Captain Whipple who never knew a fear,
The Captain of the Providence, the Yankee privateer.*

Chorus:
We sailed and we sailed and kept good cheer
For not a British frigate could o'ercome the privateer.

We sailed to the southard and suddenly did meet,
Three British frigates—convoy to a West Indian fleet,
Old Whipple put our lights out and crawled upon their rear
And not a soul suspected the Yankee privateer.

So slowly did we sail along, so silently we ran,
With no alarm we boarded the biggest merchantman,
We knocked the watch down easily, the lubbers shook for fear,
We took her prize without a shot for the Yankee privateer.

Chorus

For ten long nights we followed and ere the moon arose,
Each night a prize we captured beneath the Lions nose,**
And when the British looked to see why ships should disappear,
They found they had in convoy the Yankee privateer.

Chorus

The biggest British frigate bore round to give us chase,
But though we were the fleeter, Old Whipple didn't race,
Until he'd raked her fore and aft, for the lubbers couldn't steer,
And then he showed the foe the heels of the Yankee Privateer.

Chorus

Then northward sailed our gallant ship to a town that we all
    know,
And there we lay our prizes all anchored in a row,

*An error, of course.
**Another error.

And welcome was our victim, to our friends and family dear,
For we shared a million dollars on the Yankee privateer.[24]

The men in Philadelphia knew that in Abraham Whipple
they had found a fighting captain, and they had ample business for such a man. After a period of resting and refitting,
on 20 November 1779 the navy board, in compliance with
the wishes of the Marine Committee, ordered *Providence,
Boston, Queen of France* and *Ranger* to cruise south to Charleston to assist in the defense of that city from an expected
British assault. Whipple was again named commodore, and
his squadron hoisted sail on 23 November.[25] For Whipple,
the four ships and most of his men this was to be their last
venture under Continental colors. They were sailing into a
trap. After a very routine voyage of exactly one month the
squadron arrived at Charleston and took up positions from
which they could best defend the harbor. Less than two
months later a powerful British force under the command
of General Sir Henry Clinton and Vice Admiral Marriot
Arbuthnot arrived and laid siege to the town. The Americans sank *Queen of France* and several South Carolina ships
in the channel of the Cooper River to block passage. Un-
deterred, the British conducted a near textbook siege until
finally on 12 May 1780 Charleston surrendered. The British
bagged 5500 Continental soldiers along with the remaining
three ships of the American squadron. Whipple was taken
prisoner and later allowed to go on parole to Chester, Pennsylvania, where he remained in retirement for the rest of the
war. The surrender of Charleston was the worst American
defeat of the Revolution, and it still ranks behind the Union
capitulation at Harpers Ferry in 1862 and the fall of Bataan
as one of the largest surrenders of troops in American history.[26] It also pointed out the folly of using ships, whose
greatest asset is mobility, as stationary gun platforms. The
American navy lost four ships at Charleston for no good
reason.

In the north an American fleet at Penobscot Bay fared even worse than the one at Charleston. On a direct line Penobscot Bay lies about 150 miles northeast of Boston, midway along the coast of Maine. The entrance of the bay is about thirty miles across, and the distance from the sea to its head, where the Penobscot River empties, is about the same. The river is wide and deep enough to be navigable for almost sixty miles, all the way to the present site of the city of Bangor. Along the northeast shore of the bay, ten miles from the river, there is a small, rocky finger of land, one and a half miles long and three quarters of a mile wide, that juts out on an east-west axis into the water. It was then called Bagaduce; today it is known as Castine. This small spit of land was the key to control of the entire bay.

British interest in the area was first aroused early in the war by William Knox, the colonial undersecretary. Knox thought a naval base at Bagaduce would help secure the line of communication between British forces at Halifax and at New York; the line was then being harassed by Yankee privateers out of Massachusetts and New Hampshire. Furthermore, the secretary argued, a base at Bagaduce would help protect the outlying fringes of New Brunswick and Nova Scotia from American attack. It was an interesting idea, but at the time Knox suggested it, the government had other plans in mind; for the present, at least, Penobscot would have to wait. As the war dragged on, though, and the optimistic predictions of quick victory failed to materialize, the ministry took a second look at Knox's scheme and saw in it benefits other than those mentioned by the undersecretary.

The area could be taken over for the Loyalists. Thousands of them had been displaced, and the prospects of their ever returning home grew dimmer with each passing day of the war. If the area were secured, they could settle in the Penobscot region. That would help the British government fulfill a debt they owed to the Loyalists, who had gambled and lost for the crown while at the same time providing an occupied buffer zone between the Americans and Canada. The proposal received strong support from exiled Loyalists in England, and they lobbied vigorously in its support.[27]

Another reason, newly advanced, for securing the area had to do with the supply requirements of the Royal Navy. For some time the naval base at Halifax had been sending mast ships to Penobscot to bring back timber needed to repair and refit ships putting in at Halifax. Without firm control of the area, though, shipping the timber was a risky proposition, subject to constant harassment and attack by the Americans. As the need for timber at Halifax grew, this became an increasing concern. In 1779 the British decided to occupy Penobscot.

The expedition was organized from Halifax. With a small naval escort under the command of Captain Henry Mowatt, the man who had burned Falmouth, transports with about seven hundred Highland troops aboard headed for Penobscot in early June. On the seventeenth they arrived at Bagaduce and, despite the presence of several hundred American civilians in the area, landed with no opposition. The commander of the force, General Francis MacLean, immediately ordered his men to dig in and prepare fortifications.

In Boston the news was received with great alarm. For the first time in more than three years part of Massachusetts was in enemy hands. Ever since late 1776 Newport, Rhode Island, to the south had been in British possession, and now with the enemy pressing in from the north, the people of Boston felt trapped in a tightening vise. They feared that they might well be the next target. That was the worst possibility, but even short of actual attack there were other possibilities equally distressing. With bases barely three hundred miles apart, the Royal Navy could easily sweep along the New England coast, raiding and pillaging and closing down the very lucrative Yankee privateering operations.

The real and potential danger was too great to be ignored and too immediate to wait for congressional action. On 26 June the general court ordered the Massachusetts Board of War to lay plans for dislodging the enemy and:

to engage or employ such armed vessels, State or National, as could be prepared and procured to sail in 6 days, to charter, or if necessary, to impress in the harbors of Boston, Salem, Beverly and Newburyport, a number of private armed vessels, belonging to individuals competent, when joined with the others, for the enterprise; to promise the owners a fair compensation for all losses and damages they might sustain; to give seamen the pay and rations of those in the continental service; and to procure the necessary outfits and provisions as quickly as possible.[28]

Speed was essential. They had to attack before the British had enough time to strengthen and reinforce their position. Boston came alive as preparations for the biggest naval operation since the Louisburg expedition got under way. The narrow isthmus leading into the town was clogged with wagons and carts bringing in supplies. Down on the docks teamsters yelled and cursed as they skillfully threaded their way through the piles of equipment being loaded aboard vessels. Everywhere the creak of block and tackle could be heard as seamen strained on the lines to hoist cannon and ammunition on board. The harbor was thick with ships making up the largest American fleet ever assembled during the war.

The Massachusetts state navy sent their entire fleet, which then consisted of two brigantines, *Active* and *Tyrannicide*, while New Hampshire lent her state ship *Hampden*. Through the navy board the Massachusetts council asked what the Continent would contribute. Vernon and Warren offered, on their own authority, to attach three vessels: Dudley Saltonstall's frigate *Warren* along with two smaller vessels, the sloop *Providence* under Hoysted Hacker and a newly captured prize, the fast brig *Diligent*.[29] Augmenting the state and Continental ships were about sixteen privateers mounting in the range of sixteen to twenty guns each. This fleet of twenty-two armed vessels was ostensibly placed under Saltonstall's command, but as was usually the case whenever privateers teamed up with public ships, there was serious question of how amenable the former would be to orders from Continental officers. The Marine Committee always looked askance at such joint ventures, and the events at Penobscot fully justified their misgivings. Saltonstall's orders were to take these ships and escort twenty transports loaded with militia safely to Bagaduce. After landing his cargo, he was to remain at Penobscot and assist in taking the place from the British.

This was not only the Americans' biggest naval undertaking of the war; it was also their largest amphibious operation until General Winfield Scott went ashore at Vera Cruz in the Mexican War. The whole business turned out to be a classic example of how not to conduct a joint army-navy attack. Such operations require the utmost in cooperation, experience and precise planning, but the Americans neglected every one of these requirements. Saltonstall did not have the vaguest notion of how to support a land operation. His counterpart on land, Brigadier General Solomon Lovell, was a well-meaning and relatively competent militia commander, but his experience did not go much beyond the local common on muster day. As usual, the lines of authority and responsibility among commanders were fuzzy, resulting in squabbles over picayune issues that made joint planning an unpleasant and unproductive chore.

On 19 July, after less than a month of preparation, Commodore Saltonstall gave the signal, and his fleet got under way for Penobscot. It was a pleasant summer sail down east with a short stop at Townsend (Boothbay) to pick up additional militia.

No operation of this size could be kept under wraps for very long, and from Loyalist informants the British at Bagaduce knew well in advance that the Americans were coming. They worked day and night digging in and improving their positions while artillery was shifted to take advantage of greater fields of fire. In the harbor Captain Mowatt ordered his three sloops, *North*, *Nautilus* and *Albany*, brought up to cover the mouth of the harbor. Behind them he placed four small transports that, if necessity required, he was prepared to set afire and send into the American fleet.

Six days after leaving Boston the American fleet came to off the Bagaduce peninsula, well out of reach of British guns. After surveying the situation, Saltonstall ordered nine of his ships ahead in three divisions to engage Mowatt's sloops. With *Warren* in the van, the Americans advanced toward the British, but Saltonstall, cautious and not eager to get too close, kept his ships at a respectful distance. At that range there was little danger, and for a couple of hours the two sides exchanged shots with only slight damage inflicted. Despite their overwhelming advantages, the Americans had not begun well. Ashore, the British watched the confused evolutions and poor gunnery of the American fleet and rightly concluded that their attackers were not nearly so formidable as they first appeared. Lovell ordered his troops ashore, and within a few days the main fort, Saint George, was under siege. The British held out, though, and Lovell, just as timid as Saltonstall, was unwilling to make an assault. While Lovell paused outside the fort, Saltonstall moved again to attack Mowatt. Led by *Warren*, three ships moved in, but once again Saltonstall came about before they could get close enough to do any real damage. The British gunners, with a better eye, more experience and a good deal of luck, managed to put two shots into *Warren*'s mainmast, a shot into her bowsprit and one that parted the forestay. *Warren* withdrew and spent the next two days repairing her damage.

Inside Fort Saint George things were beginning to look up. MacLean stripped his transports of cannon and mounted them on the ramparts, and at the same time he ordered sailors from the same ships into the fort to man the breastworks. Lovell's delay allowed MacLean time to improve and strengthen his position. The campaign was settling into a pattern that gave every advantage to the British. It was a siege that promised to be a long, drawn-out affair of desultory firing accompanied by a lot of digging and waiting. It was not the kind of operation that the militia and privateers had bargained for. They had expected a quick victory and an equally quick return home. Under these circumstances, just how long Saltonstall and Lovell could hold their people at Penobscot was uncertain.

Saltonstall was not inclined to risk all in an attack. He had no stomach for pushing up the harbor after Mowatt as long as the guns at Fort Saint George could bear down on him. The privateers, who thus far had been of no help at all, agreed. Saltonstall, Lovell and their officers spent endless hours together arguing about what the others should do. Lovell wanted Saltonstall to take the enemy sloops first, but Saltonstall wanted Lovell to take the fort first. The general would not budge. He told Saltonstall bluntly that "the alternative now remains, to destroy the ships, or raise the siege."[30] Other militia officers felt the same way. Colonel John Brewer, a Penobscot native, urged the commodore to attack; Saltonstall responded angrily to Brewer, "You seem to be d——d knowing about this matter! I am not going to risk my shipping in that d——d hole."[31] Like many American naval commanders, Dudley Saltonstall had the heart of a privateersman. His overriding concerns were the preservation of his ships and the avoidance of risks. He could never quite accept the doctrine that under certain circumstances it might be wise to risk all in order to achieve victory. On the other side, of course, Lovell and Brewer knew their men, and they were none too anxious to lead raw militia against entrenched veteran troops.

Saltonstall tried to maintain his position, but it was difficult. In early August a dispatch boat from Boston arrived with intelligence from the navy board. They had information that a British relief force was on its way. They told Saltonstall that all would be lost unless he hurried. Under pressure from all sides, he relented, and plans were laid for a full-scale land and sea assault to take place on 13 August.

All through the night of the twelfth militia officers moved among their men, checking equipment and giving last-minute instructions. Offshore, Saltonstall was watching as his ships, according to plan, began to move silently into position. In the gray dawn hours Lovell moved his men close to the fort. Everything was ready. A morning fog delayed the attack a few more hours. As it began to lift, the Americans stood by their guns, but before the firing commenced, *Diligent* drew alongside the flagship with an urgent message. She had been on picket duty off the coast and came to report that she had sighted several sail bearing up toward Bagaduce. The attack was called off and a hasty conference called. What *Diligent* had spotted was a British squadron, ten days out of Sandy Hook, sent to reinforce MacLean and Mowatt. It consisted of the sixty-four-gun ship of the line *Raisonable* accompanied by three frigates, *Blonde, Virginia* and *Greyhound*, along with three sloops, *Camilla, Galatea* and *Otter*. George Collier was in command. At first Saltonstall thought about defending and trying to hold the British while the transports evacuated the troops to safety farther up the bay. That plan disintegrated as the British ships drew closer and the privateersmen saw their sides bristling with open gun ports. Saltonstall knew that he could never get his nervous privateersmen to join in a straightforward battle, and even if he could, it was doubtful how much help they would be against disciplined and well-trained British crews. Under the circumstances Saltonstall could do nothing but signal to his ships to scatter and seek safety as best they could. It was a Donnybrook. Vessels ran aground. Some, including *Warren*, were blown up by their crews. Others tried to run to safety up the Penobscot River. That was futile, and they also ran hard aground. Everywhere sailors and soldiers were scrambling through brush and woods trying desperately to get away.

When it was all over, the Americans could count fourteen vessels blown up or burned by their crews and twenty-eight captured. Five hundred Americans were either dead or taken prisoner, and more than seven million dollars had been wasted.[32]

News of the catastrophe got back to Boston before most of the survivors. Someone needed to be blamed, and Saltonstall was the logical choice. He was, after all, the senior officer, but there was another possible reason as well. The state of Massachusetts was saddled with nearly all the bills for the unfortunate expedition. If they could, the men in Boston were eager to find someone to share the burden. Fixing the blame on Saltonstall, a Connecticut man, would provide a strong argument in favor of the Continent's splitting the cost. A committee of inquiry from the General Court found that Lovell had not been properly supported by Saltonstall and that the principal reason for the failure was the failure of the commodore to display "proper spirit and energy." Shortly after that, Saltonstall was court-martialed and dismissed from the service. Some thought he got off lightly and should have been shot for presiding over one of the saddest spectacles in American naval history.[33]

The disaster down east was the greatest and last attempt by the Americans to do anything by way of naval squadrons. It had helped to make a shambles of an already weakened navy, a job that was practically completed a few months later at Charleston. In December the new Continental Board of Admiralty took over. There was little left in the way of ships or spirit in the navy. Nearly five years earlier there had been no end to the great visions and hoopla surrounding the navy, but all that had faded now. Nevertheless, there had been some significant accomplishments, and as the old Marine Committee passed from the scene, it could look back with some pride on the activities of the Continental navy in American waters. The Hopkins voyage and the Jamaica fleet were two important victories, and there were many smaller ones as well. Nor had the committee been lacking in suggesting major operations, such as raiding the Hudson Bay fleet, sweeping the coast and attacking Bermuda and sailing to West Africa. These movements might have accomplished something truly significant, but a surfeit of politics and a shortage of money had thwarted them.

Although the Marine Committee and Board of Admiralty were convinced that American warships should always avoid sailing alone or with privateers and state ships, for practical reasons of manning and supply they were often forced to relent in this policy and allow exceptions. In most cases this meant solo cruises. The results of these were generally disappointing, but there were some rollicking engagements off the Atlantic coast and in the Caribbean in which ships and captains gained fame for their glorious exploits and conspicuous bravery.

Nicholas Biddle, captain of the frigate *Randolph,* was such an officer. He was a member of a prominent Philadelphia family and had briefly served in the Royal Navy. He was among the first captains commissioned by Congress and had commanded *Andrew Doria* on the Nassau cruise. After that, he had been appointed to the new frigate *Randolph* and had been sailing with her since February 1777. Early in 1778 he departed Charleston in company with four ships of the South Carolina navy, *General Moultrie, Notre Dame, Polly* and *Fair American.*

For nearly a month they cruised the West Indies with virtually nothing to show for their efforts. About mid-afternoon on 7 March they were cruising sixty leagues due east of Barbados when the lookout aloft on *Randolph* eyed a sail to windward. From his quarterdeck Biddle could barely make her out through his glass, but there was no mistake that she had spotted *Randolph* and was bearing directly for her. The captain brought *Randolph* on a new course to close with the stranger and ordered the others to follow. Because of the angle at which they approached one another, it was impossible for the Americans to make out the size of the ship. According to Captain Blake, the marine commander aboard one of the state ships, the stranger had her topgallant and topsails furled and she looked to him to be a "large sloop with only a squaresail set."[34]

For nearly four hours Biddle kept his head on course. By then it was dark and the stranger was closing rapidly. When she was within range, she fired a shot across *Randolph*, and only at that moment did Biddle realize what he had on his hands. It was the sixty-four-gun ship of the line *Yarmouth*, under the command of Captain Nicholas Vincent.[35] In the darkness the British could not identify the American, so they drew closer to get a better look. When they were within hailing distance, Vincent called to Biddle to identify himself and hoist his colors. Almost immediately the Grand Union flag was broken out and *Randolph* let loose with a broadside. *Yarmouth* seemed stunned and slow to respond. The gun crews aboard *Randolph* fired three and four times as fast as the British. Biddle had trained them well. The two ships passed each other, but before they could come about to engage again, *Randolph*, with a thunderous roar and a blinding flash, blew up. Debris came down for hundreds of feet in every direction, splashing into the water and clàttering onto the deck of *Yarmouth*. The men aboard *Yarmouth* and the state ships stood agape, watching as the smoke cleared to reveal nothing but emptiness and obsidian darkness where *Randolph* had once been. Everything had happened so quickly that the South Carolina ships had never had a chance to engage, so now they scurried off into the night.

Four days later *Yarmouth*, still patrolling off Barbados, spotted some wreckage in the water. It was a makeshift raft with four men clinging to it. They were the crew from one of the aft guns on *Randolph*. Somehow they had been blown over the side and managed to keep afloat long enough to lash together some timbers. Vincent took them aboard. Out of a crew of 315 men they were the only survivors. It was the Continental navy's single largest loss of the war.[36]

It is not altogether clear why Biddle took such a desperate gamble with *Yarmouth*. One historian has suggested that he thought he could get close enough to grapple and take her by boarding. His brother, though, wrote that Biddle had taken on *Yarmouth* in order to protect one of the state ships. Whatever the reason, he showed extraordinary courage, and his death at age twenty-seven deprived the Continental navy of one of its finest captains.

Ironically, the laurels for the hardest-fought and bloodiest engagement of a Continental ship must go to Captain James Nicholson, the man who as long as he was in the service never captured or defeated a single enemy. After running aground and surrendering *Virginia* in 1778, Nicholson was put ashore for a while and spent the next year and a half waiting out a possible court-martial that never came. In September 1779 he was given command of the frigate *Trumbull*, which had been launched and was then fitting out in New London. Plagued by countless delays, she was at last, and to the great relief of the Marine Committee, finally ready for sea in the spring of 1780.

As usual there was trouble getting enough hands (it could not have been easy for Nicholson, a southerner, to recruit in a Yankee port), and as a result the captain had to take on a lot of "green country lads." In mid-May *Trumbull* was at sea. She was the last surviving frigate of the original thirteen. The other twelve had all been either captured or destroyed.

On 1 June *Trumbull* was about 250 miles north of Bermuda. The wind was from the south and the frigate was heading in a northeasterly direction, apparently hoping to pick off some British vessels as they approached or left New York. After two weeks at sea Nicholson was still empty-handed, but the weather was good and his "country lads" had been kept busy drilling and exercising the guns. Shortly after nine in the morning the lookout saw a sail directly to windward. As soon as she saw *Trumbull*, the stranger altered course to bear down on the American. By one o'clock the ships were close enough that Nicholson ordered *Trumbull* cleared for action. Hammocks were brought up and stuffed in the nettings above the bulwarks. The decks were wetted and sanded while gun crews cast off lines securing the cannons and removed the tampions from the muzzles. As Nicholson watched from the quarterdeck, the other vessel kept coming on. Within a few minutes *Trumbull*'s cannons were loaded and the gun captains were standing by with lighted matches. The approaching ship was close enough now for Nicholson to recognize her as British. She was *Watt*, a thirty-two-gun letter of marque out of Liverpool, under the command of John Coulthard. When the ships were parallel and within pistol range, Nicholson ran up the American flag and gave a broadside. *Watt* replied in kind. For two and a half hours the ships bombarded each other, enshrouded in a thick pall of smoke from the black powder. Above the noise of the battle, gun captains could be heard shouting their commands. "Load." "Run out." "Fire." Sharpshooters high in the rigging sighted down their weapons, looking for officers or anyone who popped his head above the bulwarks. At Nicholson's orders the gunners on *Trumbull* aimed low and battered away at *Watt*'s hull. Coulthard preferred to fire high into *Trumbull*'s rigging. The two ships, closely matched, gave each other a severe drubbing. By all accounts it was one of the hardest fought and most sanguinary naval engagements of the war. *Trumbull* had six men killed and thirty-two wounded. *Watt* took upwards of ninety casualties. Hulled in several places and taking in water, *Watt* withdrew from the battle. For eight hours Nicholson pursued but it was no use. Parts of his masts had been shot away, shrouds were severed and his sails could barely hold the wind. He gave up the chase and bore off toward Boston. The next day a gale came up and *Trumbull* lost her main and mizzenmast. Twelve days later *Trumbull* limped into Boston harbor under a jury rig.[37]

There were high words of praise for James Nicholson. Gilbert Saltonstall, captain of marines aboard *Trumbull*, wrote to his brother: "Upon the whole there has not been a more close, obstinate and bloody engagement since the war [began]. I hope it won't be treason if I don't except even Paul Jones—all things considered we may dispute titles with him."[38] The captain deserved the accolades. He had taken a green crew of only 199 men and whipped them into a unit capable of taking on and holding their own against a superior enemy. But Coulthard also deserves praise, for he displayed great bravery and fine seamanship, and with his men straining at the pumps, he managed to get *Watt* safely into New York, where he received a hero's welcome.[39]

Nicholson stayed in Boston long enough to repair *Trumbull*. He then took her down to the Delaware capes, where for the next year he made a series of thoroughly undistinguished cruises. In July 1781 Robert Morris, the man now in charge of the navy, ordered Nicholson to take *Trumbull* to Havana with a cargo of flour and some dispatches. *Trumbull* departed early in August, taking under her wing a convoy of twenty-eight merchantmen bound for the West Indies. They had barely gotten to sea when they were spotted by three British cruisers who immediately gave chase. The merchantmen scattered, and *Trumbull* crowded on every inch of sail, making her bid to escape. As she was surging ahead, a sudden squall came up, and in an instant *Trumbull* had lost her fore-topmast and main-topgallant mast. Sails and rigging came crashing down on deck. One arm of the fore-topsail yard tore through the foresail. The whole forward part of the deck was a tangle of sails, rigging and timber resembling a cat's cradle gone wild. The crew tried to clear the mess, but with the ship lurching in the squall it was impossible. Escape was now hopeless. Nicholson ordered his crew to stand by their guns. Fully three-fourths of his crew ignored the command and refused to come on deck. Some were cowards, but most were British prisoners of war forced into the service who now saw a chance to strike at their captors and perhaps gain freedom. The lead British frigate came within range. She was *Iris*, the former Continental frigate *Hancock*, which had been captured back in 1777 off New England. Joined by a few loyal seamen, petty officers and officers, Nicholson put up a fight. He might have held off *Iris*, but then the second ship, *General Monk*, the former American privateer *General Washington*, came along and joined in the fray. It was pointless to continue. Nicholson struck. *Trumbull,* by now completely dismasted, was towed into New York, where she was condemned, stripped and left to rot in the mud flats.[40]

It was an ironic twist of fate that brought *Trumbull* and *Hancock* together, for it meant that the first of the thirteen American frigates built by Congress had captured the last. Turn about is fair play, though, and later in the war *Hancock (Iris)* was captured in the West Indies by the French. She ended her days as a powder hulk at the French naval base in Toulon. It was there that in 1793 she was blown up by a British naval force.[41]

The Continental navy's last battles in American waters were fought by an Irishman, John Barry, commanding the Continental frigate *Alliance.* It was May 1781 and Barry was bound home to Boston, from France. It had not been a pleasant voyage. A number of sailors, many former prisoners of war, had conspired to mutiny. They had been discovered, and Barry, a man known for his violent temper as well as his size (he was six feet four inches tall), was determined to deal with them in a manner sure to discourage any others who might have thoughts along these lines. The mutineers were hung from a yardarm by their thumbs while, with all hands watching, the bosun applied the cat. That done, *Alliance* continued on her way.[42]

Toward dark on 28 May, about four hundred miles east of Sandy Hook, Barry discovered he was being stalked by two vessels coming for him off the weather bow. During the night the two ships kept their distance. At sunrise, when they were still a league off, they hoisted the Union Jack and beat to quarters. By this time the wind had died. At eleven they were close enough to give battle. With no wind, *Alliance* lost steerage and drifted. The two British vessels—*Atalanta,* under Captain S. Edwards, and *Trepassy,* under Captain J. Smyth— had all the advantages. Being lighter than *Alliance,* they could put out sweeps and maneuver their ships around the American. Using this technique for nearly two hours, they kept a position across *Alliance*'s stern and quarter. Barry was wounded and had to be carried below to the cockpit. Toward mid-afternoon a light breeze started to blow, and *Alliance* was able to swing around and deliver a series of devastating broadsides. *Atalanta* was disabled and surrendered. *Trepassy* tried unsuccessfully to get away but then had to give up also. Barry ordered all his prisoners, some 250, on board *Trepassy* and sent her as a cartel vessel to Halifax. *Atalanta* was put in charge of a prize crew and sent on to Boston but was retaken en route. Barry, wounded but still very much in charge, took his own command, *Alliance*, on to Boston and arrived there on 6 June.[43]

By the fall of 1781 the frigates *Deane* and *Alliance* were the only Continental ships still in commission. For all intents and purposes, the war was over for the Continental navy even before Yorktown. Its last battle, appropriately enough, was fought by Barry. It was in March 1783, while he was sailing on *Alliance* in company with *Duc de Lauzun*, a recent purchase from France. The two vessels were northbound off the coast of Florida, carrying 100,000 Spanish-milled dollars destined for Philadelphia to replenish the Continental treasury. Eager to get home and equally eager to avoid British cruisers, Barry ordered every available sail hoisted. At dawn on 10 March he was spotted by three British ships, the frigates *Alarm* and *Sybil* and the sloop *Tobago*. *Alliance*, the only American frigate with copper sheathing, was fast, and she could easily have escaped the British. However, *Lauzun* was a dull sailer and quickly fell behind. To protect her, Barry fell back and dropped between the lead British frigate, *Sybil*, and *Lauzun*. While all this was going on, the lookout reported that a French ship of fifty guns was approaching. If the Frenchman hurried, Barry could turn the tables and perhaps bag the three British ships. Quite the opposite happened. Instead of hurrying, the French ship shortened sail and stood off while *Alliance* and *Sybil* engaged. The American gun crews worked with speed and precision, and in less than an hour *Sybil* was a silent floating wreck barely able to break off the fight. This is the battle that was made into legend by the poet Philip Freneau. According to Freneau, when *Sybil* challenged *Alliance* to identify herself Barry shouted, "This is the United States ship Alliance, saucy Jack Barry, half Irishman, half Yankee, Who are you?"

Having saved *Lauzun*, Barry headed home, but not before he exchanged some bitter words with the French captain who had done nothing but provide an audience. *Alliance* and *Sybil* fought their duel more than one month after hostilities had officially ended. It was the last time a Continental ship fired in anger.

A typical merchant ship of the mid-eighteenth century, this model, ca. 1750, is reputed to be the oldest ship model in America. COURTESY OF THE PEABODY MUSEUM, SALEM.

Model of the schooner *Hannah*. COURTESY OF THE SMITHSONIAN INSTITUTION, WASHINGTON, D.C.

Contemporary sketch of the schooner *Royal Savage* from the Schuyler Papers. COURTESY OF THE NEW YORK PUBLIC LIBRARY.

The gundalow *Philadelphia*, raised from Lake Champlain in 1935 and now on exhibit at the Smithsonian Institution. COURTESY OF THE SMITHSONIAN INSTITUTION, WASHINGTON, D.C.

Model of the Continental frigate *Raleigh*. COURTESY OF THE PEABODY MUSEUM, SALEM.

Admiral Lord Richard Howe. Painting by J. S. Copley.
COURTESY OF THE NATIONAL MARITIME MUSEUM, LONDON.

Vice Admiral Molyneux Shuldham. By William Dickinson.

Commodore Esek Hopkins. Engraving by J. C. Buttre.
FROM AUTHOR'S COLLECTION.

John Paul Jones. Bust by Jean Antoine Houdon.

John Barry. Engraving from a painting by Alonzo Chappel.

Benedict Arnold. Etching by H. B. Hall.

Robert Morris. Painting by C. W. Peale.

G R E A T
ENCOURAGEMENT
F O R
SEAMEN.

ALL GENTLEMEN SEAMEN and able-bodied LANDSMEN who have a Mind to diftinguifh themfelves in the GLORIOUS CAUSE of their COUNTRY, and make their Fortunes, an Opportunity now offers on board the Ship RANGER, of Twenty Guns, (for FRANCE) now laying in PORTSMOUTH, in the State of NEW-HAMP-SHIRE, commanded by JOHN PAUL JONES Efq; let them repair to the Ship's Rendez-vous in PORTSMOUTH, or at the Sign of Commodore MANLEY, in SALEM, where they will be kind-ly entertained, and receive the greateft Encouragement.---The Ship RANGER, in the Opinion of every Perfon who has feen her is looked upon to be one of the beft Cruizers in AMERICA.----She will be always able to Fight her Guns under a moft excellent Cover ; and no Veffel yet built was ever calculated for failing fafter, and making good Weather.

Any GENTLEMEN VOLUNTEERS who have a Mind to take an agreable Voyage in this pleafant Seafon of the Year, may, by entering on board the above Ship RANGER, meet with every Civility they can poffibly expect, and for a further Encouragement depend on the firft Opportunity being embraced to reward each one agreable to his Merit.

All reafonable Travelling Expences will be allowed, and the Advance-Money be paid on their Appearance on Board.

IN CONGRESS, MARCH 29, 1777.

RESOLVED,

THAT the MARINE COMMITTEE be authorifed to advance to every able Seaman, that enters into the CONTINENTAL SERVICE, any Sum not exceeding FORTY DOL-LARS, and to every ordinary Seaman or Landfman, any Sum not exceeding TWEN-TY DOLLARS, to be deducted from their future Prize-Money.

By Order of CONGRESS,

JOHN-HANCOCK, PRESIDENT.

DANVERS: Printed by E. RUSSELL, at the Houfe late the Bell-Tavern.

Recruiting broadside for *Ranger.* COURTESY OF THE ESSEX INSTITUTE, SALEM.

John Paul Jones capturing *Serapis*. Engraving from a painting by Alonzo Chappel. COURTESY OF THE UNITED STATES MARINE CORPS.

Bonhomme Richard (left) and *Serapis* (right). Painting by Joseph Roux.

OVERLEAF. These four privately owned paintings depict the capture of the frigate *Hancock*, 6–7 July 1777. They were painted by Francis Holman and are reproduced here throught the good offices of Philip C. F. Smith of the Peabody Museum, Salem.

LEFT TO RIGHT: American frigate *Hancock*, prize ship *Fox*, American frigate *Boston*, H. M. S. *Flora*, prize sloop, H. M. S. *Rainbow*. In an attempt to escape the approaching British, the Americans have set fire to their prize sloop. *Flora*, in the van, has already begun to exchange fire with *Boston*.

LEFT TO RIGHT: *Fox*, *Hancock*, *Flora*, *Boston*, and *Rainbow*. After his exchange with *Flora*, Captain Hector McNeill reported that the British shots were "so well aim'd that some of them pass'd through our Ship. . . ." In this picture, *Boston* is falling off to make repairs while *Hancock* and *Flora* slug it out. *Rainbow* is coming up on the right.

LEFT TO RIGHT: *Hancock, Rainbow, Flora, Boston*, and *Fox*. The Americans scatter, *Boston* to northward, *Fox* to the east, and *Hancock* to the south with *Rainbow* giving chase.

LEFT TO RIGHT: *Hancock, Rainbow, Flora, Fox*, and *Boston*. After a thirty-nine-hour chase, *Rainbow* overtook and captured *Hancock*. *Flora* took *Fox*. *Boston*, on the far right, was the only one of the three to escape.

The Seal of the Board of Admiralty. It is described in
the *Journals* as "thirteen bars mutually supporting each
other, alternate red and white, in a blue field, and sur-
mounting an anchor proper. The crest a ship under sail.
The motto Sustentans Et Sustentatum. The legend
U. S. A. Sigil Naval."

Chapter Seven

The War at Sea:
The European Theater
Before the Alliance

Revolutions characteristically develop a dynamism and outward thrust leading them to expand and export their product. The American experience is a paradigm in this regard, and even before the bloodshed at North Bridge men in and out of the Congress were talking about finding friends and allies abroad who would join in their cause. The invasion of Canada, the courtship of Bermuda, even the attack on Nassau were all manifestations of this sometimes fervent but always naive dream.

This appeal to the hearts and minds of other men was conspicuous for its failure, for few people shared the conviction of the Continental Congress that the king was a tyrant and "unfit to be the ruler of a free People," and even many who did, put discretion ahead of valor and preferred the safety of silent submission to danger from open rebellion.

As the hopes for neighborly assistance withered, the prospects abroad began to brighten. The great powers in Europe, especially the French, viewed the growing American war with the practiced and cynical eyes of losers out for revenge. France and Britain had been rivals for as long as anyone alive could remember. In their most recent encounter, the Great War for the Empire (1754–63), France had lost, and since that time she had been nursing a grudge and looking for ways to get even. The American Revolution fitted very nicely into this background of international ax grinding, and it would soon become another act in the long drama being played out between Britain and France. France's sympathetic attitude toward the Americans, or more correctly her hostility toward the British, and later their open alliance enabled the ships of the Continental navy to bring the Revolution right up and into the chops of the English Channel.

Although American privateers were visiting in European waters almost immediately after Congress legalized their activities in March 1776 and maybe even earlier, it was not until the fall of the year that a Continental vessel poked her nose into British home waters. She was *Reprisal*, a sixteen-gun brig under the command of Lambert Wickes. Wickes, a thirty-four-year-old native of Maryland and a good friend of Robert Morris, had been in command of *Reprisal* since April.[1] He had been cruising and skirmishing with the British around Delaware Bay, testing their mettle and giving his crew a taste of combat. Not much was really accomplished in these forays, which must have made it all the more difficult for him when his brother, a lieutenant in the Continental navy, was killed during one of them.

In June Wickes was ordered to carry William Bingham, a newly appointed American agent, to his post on the French island of Martinique. He sailed in early July and arrived off Saint Pierre on the twenty-seventh. As he made for the harbor, H.M.S. *Shark* came out to challenge him. The captain hailed Wickes and told him to lower a boat. Wickes shouted back that they could bloody well come over and do it themselves. The battle was on, and after a brief exchange *Shark* withdrew. It was not a particularly glorious or fierce engagement, but it was clever and it did impress Bingham, whose glowing report back to the Congress undoubtedly helped Wickes get a new and more important assignment.[2]

In October 1776 the Continental Congress voted to appoint three commissioners to represent them in Paris. Their immediate job was to wheedle and coax the French out of supplies, while their long-run objective was to secure a treaty and open alliance. Thomas Jefferson, Benjamin Franklin and Silas Deane, who was already in France as an agent of the Secret Committee, were elected. Jefferson declined, and his place was filled by another Virginian, Arthur Lee.[3] Lambert Wickes was given the assignment of carrying these gentlemen to their post. However, he was to be more than simply a conveyor, for the Committee of Secret Correspondence, under whose authority he had been temporarily placed, told him that after he had safely delivered the commissioners, he was to cruise European waters and send his prizes into French ports.[4] The orders were a closely guarded secret. If the British discovered the mission, they might well be able to capture America's most famous citizen and expose the plans of the Congress for violating international law.

About 1 November Franklin came aboard *Reprisal* at Philadelphia. He had brought a considerable amount of baggage, and the captain wasted no time in getting it below so that they could quickly shove off. Along with the luggage, Franklin brought with him two of his grandsons, Temple and Benjamin Franklin Bache. Despite Wickes's best efforts, the voyage was an ordeal, for *Reprisal* was a tiny vessel and quarters were anything but spacious. It was dark, cold and damp down below, so Franklin took every opportunity to go on deck, but even that brief exercise had to be frequently curtailed because of dirty weather and high seas. Although they ate at the captain's table, the food was no joy either, and Franklin complained that he had to live on salt pork alone. Occasionally the cook served fresh-killed fowl from those carried on board, but the old man had to pass; the meat was too tough for his teeth.[5]

Whatever *Reprisal*'s handicaps as a passenger liner, she was fast, and thirty days after clearing the Delaware capes, she entered Quiberon Bay. Franklin, thankful that his misery had come to an end, went ashore at Nantes, rented a carriage and rode to Paris, where he met Deane and was later joined by Lee.[6]

While the commissioners were going through the formalities at Versailles, Wickes was in Nantes working hurriedly to get *Reprisal* ready for sea again.[7] One afternoon in the middle of his work he was visited by Samuel Nicholson, James Nicholson's younger brother, who was looking for employment. He had been in London when he heard of the arrival of Wickes and Franklin, whereupon he decided to come over and offer his services. Ironically, whether he knew it or not, Samuel Nicholson was already in the Continental service. Congress had appointed him a captain on 10 December 1776.[8] He seems to have been unaware of his appointment when he first arrived, but once informed, he was pleased by the honor. Together the two captains began to hatch plans to cruise against the British, but first Nicholson needed a ship, and for that Wickes sent him off to see Franklin in Paris.

Nicholson's unexpected and unannounced arrival put Franklin on the spot. He wanted to do everything he could to help Nicholson and Wickes, but he had to be cautious. The French government was willing to wink at a good deal—they even went so far as to help set up dummy companies to ship arms to America—but there was a limit, and as long as they were officially at peace with Britain, they could never tolerate the open arming of warships in their ports. Franklin explained the delicacy of the situation to Nicholson and then ordered him to ride to Boulogne, where he was quietly to purchase a cutter for carrying dispatches to America. If he could not find anything suitable, he was to go to Calais, and finally if nothing turned up in that port, he could cross the Channel and shop in Dover.[9] No mention was made of arming vessels, and nothing was said about cruising; nevertheless, from Nicholson's subsequent behavior it seems safe to say that in their conversations Nicholson, Wickes and Franklin discussed far more than proper ways to get the mail home and that together they were conniving to cause quite a ruckus in British home waters.

Whether or not the French, and the British for that matter, whose spies kept them better informed than the commissioners kept Congress, really believed that Nicholson would just buy a cutter and go home is an open question. At any rate his search finally took him to Dover, England, where he made contact with Captain Joseph Hynson. Hynson was Wickes's stepbrother and supposedly a man who could be trusted. Through him Nicholson bought a cutter, *Dolphin*, and took her to Calais. Hynson stayed behind to finish up some personal business, or so he told Nicholson. He was being at least partially truthful, but the part he left out was that his business was with the British secret service, to whom he reported Nicholson's every move.[10]

While Nicholson and Hynson were negotiating in Dover, Wickes pushed his men to finish the repairs and alterations on *Reprisal* and got her to sea. For three weeks he sailed the Channel and managed to take five prizes. Four of them struck at the first sight of *Reprisal*'s open gun ports, but the fifth, the snow *Swallow*, resisted in a forty-five-minute battle that cost Wickes one man killed and two wounded.[11] None of the prizes were of much value, and Wickes did not think that any of them were worth the risk of sending all the way to America, so instead he took the safer course and dispatched them into the French port of Lorient. It was a brazen and somewhat foolish move, for it put the French in the position of hosting a belligerent warship with her prizes while they were at peace. Under the circumstances there was little else the French could do, so they made a show of delivering a twenty-four-hour ultimatum to Wickes. He must be gone in that time or suffer the consequences. The pre-emptive tone of the order undoubtedly pleased the British, who, through their ambassador to Versailles, Lord Stormont, were howling their heads off at this breach of international law. But Wickes was no fool, and he had learned a little about this diplomatic game. As soon as the French decree was delivered to him, he begged an extension because, he said, his vessel was leaky and he could go to sea only at great risk to the vessel and crew. With unbecoming speed, the French agreed, and Wickes was allowed time to heave down and caulk *Reprisal*.[12]

Wickes had gotten the Continental navy off to a promising start in European waters, and despite what they might have said in public, the commissioners were pleased with his adventures. In fact, even while *Reprisal* lay over on her side in Lorient, Wickes and Franklin were already discussing the next voyage.

The Americans in Paris thought that Wickes ought to sail north into the Baltic, where he could wreak havoc on the British trade and deal a heavy blow to the Royal Navy by interdicting the vital flow of naval stores from Russia and Sweden. It was an intriguing but impractical idea. Wickes pointed out that just getting into the Baltic was a tricky business since the only entrance was through the Skagerrak, a narrow passage between Denmark and Norway that could easily be watched. Even if he were lucky enough to get in and take some prizes, what would he do with them? Once alerted, the British would surely block the exit, and no Baltic country would risk receiving American prizes. Finally, how would *Reprisal* herself ever get free? Wickes's objections were well taken.[13] Later the commissioners did send Arthur Lee to Berlin for the purpose of trying to negotiate an agreement so that American ships could bring prizes into Prussian ports, but he failed, and for the duration of the war American ships were unable to operate in what might have been very rich hunting grounds.[14]

Tight and dry, *Reprisal* was ready for sea by late May 1777. Under some kind of pretext that apparently satisfied the French authorities, Wickes took her out of Lorient and down the coast a short distance to Nantes, where he rendezvoused with the newly fitted-out *Dolphin*, which had been given to Captain Samuel Nicholson, and the recently arrived brigantine *Lexington* under Captain Henry Johnson. Since the Baltic cruise had been vetoed, the commissioners in Paris decided to send this small squadron to another part of Europe where they could harass, capture and destroy British shipping. For the first time in the war the Continental navy was actually going to stalk vessels along the coast of Britain. *Reprisal, Lexington* and *Dolphin* were headed for the Irish Sea.[15]

As senior officer Wickes took command, and on 23 May he issued his instructions to Nicholson and Johnson. It was a bold venture. On 28 May they cast off and fell down the Loire to open water and headed out on a northwesterly course that took them around the Scilly Isles and then north into the Irish Sea, where they hoped to be able to intercept linen ships. Wickes told his captains that they were not to separate unless they were discovered and had to make a run for it. If that should happen, they would regroup to the north of Ireland off the Orkney Islands.[16]

The disposal of prizes would be a problem. They had gotten out of France only because the authorities, either through laxity or sympathy, had allowed them to pass, but they could never hope to go back with that ease. Everyone, including the British, knew what was going on, and while the French might feign surprise and find an excuse to explain how the three American ships got out, they could never justify letting them come back with their prizes. To get around this difficulty, Wickes told his officers that whenever they took a prize, the entire crew was to be taken off and replaced by their own men. Phony papers would then be provided so that the vessel, documented as a peaceful American merchant ship, could be sent into a neutral port. It was a clumsy subterfuge and fooled no one, but it did provide enough cover and confusion so that the Americans had time to get rid of their prizes in hastily arranged blackmarket sales.[17]

The cruise was successful but not spectacular. According to different sources, the three Americans took either fourteen, seventeen, eighteen or twenty-five prizes.[18] By themselves none of the prizes were especially valuable, and no one retired from the sea with the proceeds.

On 27 June Wickes and his two companions were off the coast of Brittany bearing south, apparently with the intention of going into Lorient or Nantes. They saw a large sail, and

Wickes signaled the squadron to stand toward her in the hope
that they could take another prize. This was one they should
have left alone, for to their great surprise she turned out to
be a large British man-of-war. The hounds were now the
foxes, and *Reprisal, Lexington* and *Dolphin* crowded on every
bit of sail they could to escape. For a time it looked as if the
stranger might overtake Wickes, and in a last-minute, desperate move he ordered his cannon dumped overboard to lighten
the vessel. It worked. *Reprisal* and *Dolphin* made it to Saint-
Malo, while *Lexington* took refuge at Morlaix. Angry that the
Britisher had pursued him so close to French shores, Wickes,
who had violated a host of laws himself, had the gall to com-
plain that the English "pay very little regard to the laws of
neutrality."[19]

Wickes's brazenness infuriated the British. For the first
time in more than a dozen years their ships were actually
being threatened in home waters. Insurance rates climbed,
and the Admiralty ordered four frigates onto station in the
Irish Sea. Despite all the scare talk, though, and the Cassandra-
like notices in the newspapers of London and elsewhere,
Wickes and his men had not done all that much damage.
People then and historians later have tended to exaggerate the
role of men like Lambert Wickes whose exciting and daring
raids were far more romantic than menacing. It is true, of
course, that marine insurance rates did go up in 1777 and later,
but this increase is attributable more to action in the Atlantic
and West Indies and, of course, after the spring of 1778 the
entrance of France into the war, than it is to Wickes and the
men who followed in his wake.[20]

Generations of carefully nurtured Anglophobia practically
guaranteed that anyone who smited the British would receive
a warm welcome in a French port, and Wickes was con-
gratulated and feted by the locals. However, whatever the
private feelings of the nation, France was officially neutral,
and a furious and sputtering Lord Stormont was again demanding action. The French and Americans sought loopholes
for the Americans to slip through, but none could be found

and Wickes was descended upon by a covey of French officers. It was obvious to him and to the commissioners that, for the time being, *Reprisal, Lexington* and *Dolphin* should leave France. Wickes agreed and on 14 September *Reprisal* and *Dolphin* quietly slipped out to sea. The plan was for *Dolphin* to go into Nantes under French colors, claiming to be from Saint Eustatius. *Reprisal* would stay off Morlaix and pick up *Lexington* so that the two of them could sail together to America. Nicholson did as he was told, and *Dolphin* went up the Loire to Nantes, where she was seized by the authorities, ending her career. *Reprisal* and *Lexington* never did meet, so the two sailed west, each on her own course. On 19 September *Lexington* was taken by the British cutter *Alert*. With two of the three gone, only *Reprisal* was left and she had the saddest fate of all awaiting her. On her homeward-bound voyage, somewhere off the Newfoundland banks, *Reprisal* foundered and went down with all hands save one, the cook. One hundred twenty-nine men were lost, including one of the most able captains in the Continental navy.[21]

In less than nine months Wickes and company brought the American Revolution to Europe, and by the time they bade farewell to France, the family spat between Great Britain and her colonies was well on its way to becoming an international affair.

In his role as a John the Baptist for the Continental navy Wickes had done well; in fact, even as he was having his troubles down in Brittany, farther to the north in Dunkirk another captain had already arrived and was doing his best to keep the waters boiling. He was Gustavus Conyngham.

If a contemporary drawing is to be believed, Conyngham was a rather rakish and tough-looking Irishman with a very pronounced hook nose. He had a reputation for a fierce temper, and the drawing shows him standing on a burning deck, sword in hand and with a sash full of pistols, ready to give the command to board some unlucky victim.

Conyngham was born into a landed Irish family in County

Donegal. At age eighteen he left his homeland and came to Philadelphia to work for his cousin in the trading house of Cunningham and Nesbit.[22] He went to sea for the firm, learned navigation and was given his own command. When the war broke out, the Secret Committee of the Continental Congress dispatched him to France to load "powder, saltpeter, arms, medicines, and every thing necessary for War."[23] He sailed aboard *Charming Peggy*, a small vessel of about 120 tons, and laid a course for France. After a brief stop at Londonderry—apparently a ploy to fool the British about his real destination—he slipped quietly into Dunkirk harbor on 3 December 1775.[24]

The French denied it, but it was an open secret that Conyngham was loading military supplies, and when *Charming Peggy* left Dunkirk, the British were waiting. She was easily taken and a prize crew put aboard to take her into port. Conyngham's career might well have come to an end right then, but the British were careless, and in a surprise move Conyngham and his men retook their ship. At this point the record becomes a bit blurred, but it seems likely that after retaking her, Conyngham brought *Charming Peggy* into a Dutch port where she was immediately interned. After his narrow escape Conyngham was left stranded without a command, and for at least a year he seems to have done very little other than spend his time shuttling back and forth between England and the Continent in the hope that somewhere and somehow he could find a command. Early in 1777, after hearing of Wickes's success, Conyngham came over to Paris and offered his services to Franklin. Obligingly Franklin took a blank commission out of the bundle sent him by the Congress, filled it out and made Conyngham a captain in the Continental navy.[25] He then sent him to Dunkirk, where in a very discreet fashion so as not to embarrass the French he was to meet an American agent, William Hodge, and go shopping for a ship.

William Hodge was a businessman, government agent, intriguer and friend of Robert Morris who had made his way

to Dunkirk via Martinique and Paris. What he and Conyngham were planning to do was quite illegal, but in Dunkirk
illegality was a way of life. In almost every way Dunkirk was
an unusual place. It was a haven and home for pirates, privateers, smugglers and all kinds of flotsam and jetsam that rode
in on each tide. The famous privateers Jean Bart and Thurot,
who had earned their reputations at the expense of the British, were Dunkirkers, as were many other French naval
heroes. The role of the port as a lair for sea raiders and its
proximity to England had prompted the British at the conclusion of the Seven Years War to insist that the peace treaty
contain a clause neutralizing the port by prohibiting any
fortifications and allowing a British agent to reside there to
see that none were built.[26] During the early years of the
Revolution the resident agent was Major Andrew Frazer, and
thanks to him Lord Stormont was kept well informed of the
activities in the town. However, Frazer's presence in Dunkirk was not always a plus for the British since his scarlet
uniform was a constant reminder of arrogance and an encouragement to the Dunkirkers to find new ways to annoy the
English. Their principal trade was smuggling, and if they
could do that and at the same time hurt the British, so much
the better.[27]

Early in April Conyngham and Hodge walked down to the
Dunkirk waterfront to take a look at an English-built cutter,
Admiral Pocock. The cutter was not very large, but she looked
well founded and fast. Speed would be important where she
was going, so they offered twelve thousand livres. The owner
accepted, and Conyngham and Hodge took possession, renamed her *Surprise* and told everyone they were going to use
her for smuggling, knowing that in a place like Dunkirk one
more smuggler would never be noticed. Conyngham put together a pick-up crew of men off the wharves, and on 1 May
1777 *Surprise*, mounting ten guns and carrying a crew of about
one hundred men, hoisted sail and put out into the Channel.
As soon as she cleared the roadstead, Conyngham ordered the
Continental colors raised and brought *Surprise* onto a tack that

carried her in the direction of the River Meuse, where he intended to lie in wait. Within a week he had captured the brig *Joseph* and the Harwich packet *Prince of Orange*. He sent them both into Dunkirk and then came about to go there himself.[28]

Conyngham's decision to send his prizes to Dunkirk and then go there himself was, in the words of the French foreign minister, the Comte de Vergennes, "stupid."[29] Lambert Wickes had already pricked the British in the south. Now this was considerably more than they could stand, and no amount of carefully phrased diplomatic language could explain it away. The French did remind the British that because they could not fortify Dunkirk, they were limited in what they could do to prevent ships from entering or leaving. Nevertheless, it was obvious that what was lacking at Dunkirk was spirit, not guns. The pressure from Whitehall was irresistible. Both prizes were confiscated by the French and returned. *Surprise* was detained and later sold while Conyngham was ordered to send his commission to Versailles for examination. It must have been a bitter disappointment for Conyngham to see his spoils whisked away, but it could have been much worse, for Lord Stormont was demanding this "pirate" be turned over so that he could be tried in England, an almost certain introduction to the gallows. He was held for a brief time by the French, but through the intercession of the commissioners he was presently released.

Within a few days Conyngham was back with his old friend Hodge looking for another ship. This time they bought something a little bit larger—a cutter named *Greyhound*, which, according to the resident British spies, had earned her name as "one of the best sailers known."[30] As a portent of what her mission would be, Conyngham named her *Revenge*. With Hodge's assistance he outfitted his new command with fourteen carriage guns and twenty-two swivels. When asked what he intended with her, he replied that she was a smuggler. That pretense had barely worked once, and it was a little bit too much, no matter how credulous the French were or wanted to be, to expect it to work again. Few smugglers carried that many guns along with a crew of 106 men. On orders from Versailles, de Guichard, the French commandant at Dunkirk, moved to prevent *Revenge* from sailing. Franklin and his associates were determined that *Revenge* would sail, and they went to see their friends at Versailles, trying to move levers to free *Revenge*. It was difficult but they succeeded, and the ship was released on the express condition that Conyngham would not cruise against the British but would set sail directly for America.[31] Once again it is difficult to assess the seriousness with which this pledge was made and then accepted by the French. Of Conyngham, though, there can be little doubt, for he plainly had no intention of abiding by such a commitment.

A little after nine on Friday evening, 17 July 1777, *Revenge*, steering a northerly course, stole silently out of Dunkirk harbor. Four days at sea Conyngham found his first prey, the schooner *Happy Return*, which he burned right in sight of a British man-of-war. That was only the prelude to a voyage that turned out to be a rampage against shipping. Conyngham took his ship into the North Sea around the northern tip of Scotland and down into the Irish Sea and then back into the Atlantic, all the way capturing, burning and sinking enemy ships. At one point he even landed in Ireland at the small village of Kinehead. Although he came only to take on fresh water and do some minor repairs, his presence terrified the villagers and sent rumors flying. From there he struck south, finally putting in at the port of La Coruña near Cape Finisterre in the northwest corner of Spain. All together on this one voyage Gustavus Conyngham captured or destroyed at least twenty ships.[32]

A much pleased Silas Deane reported to Robert Morris that by his two cruises, the first in *Surprise* and now *Revenge*, Conyngham had "become the terror of all the eastern coast of England and Scotland."[33] A bit of hyperbole, perhaps, but Conyngham's escapades had alarmed the British, and they were determined to put a stop to these insults. Since diplomatic protests had proven ineffectual, Lord Weymouth, one of the British ministers, hinted rather strongly to Vergennes that unless the French took quick measures to restrain the Americans, he would order the Royal Navy to intercept the French fishing fleet then on its way home from the Grand Banks. That was an alarming threat and one the British were quite capable of delivering on if they were pushed. The point was made. Conyngham was out of reach in Spain but his friend Hodge was not, and the king ordered his arrest and confinement in the Bastille. This action was enough to satisfy Lord Stormont and Weymouth. The fishing fleet passed unmolested, but as soon as they were safe in port, Hodge was released. The French made their sympathies all too plain, and while it might be an exaggeration to say, as one historian does, that Conyngham's activities led inexorably to war between England and France, it is true that captains like him helped to exacerbate already existing wounds.[34]

By late summer 1777 the British had beefed up their patrols in home waters, and since Conyngham obviously could not again put into a French port, he decided to try his luck elsewhere. Using La Coruña, Bilbao and El Ferrol in northern Spain and Cádiz in the south as bases, he sailed out after British shipping. The Spanish, of course, were not at war with Britain, and the court at Madrid began to get the same kind of snarling protests from London that Versailles had long been accustomed to receiving. The Spanish were no more pro-American than were the French. The only thing that inclined either country to be sympathetic to the rebels was a common grudge against the British. In the case of the Spanish the outstanding and most sensitive issue was Gibraltar. Taken by the British in Queen Anne's War (Treaty of Utrecht, 1713), Gibraltar was the focal point of Anglo-Spanish diplomacy. All during the years of the Revolution the rock held its place as the polestar by which the Spaniards reckoned their diplomatic course. They often waffled on the other points and issues, frequently to curry British favor, but on this one issue they always remained firm; they wanted Gibraltar back.[35]

Within this unhappy diplomatic world Conyngham's activities provided an annoyance that the Spanish could well have done without. Nevertheless, there was little the government could or would do. Conyngham had become a hero in a David and Goliath drama. Sailing single-handedly against the might of the Royal Navy, he managed to capture the imagination of people all over Europe, including the Spanish. His popularity in Spain was attested to by an English officer at Cádiz who was aboard *Monarch*, one of the ships belonging to the Royal Navy's Mediterranean squadron, which was riding at anchor as *Revenge* came sailing by. Right under British noses Conyngham boldly hoisted his colors and fired a salute to the Spanish admiral which the admiral promptly returned. The exchange of honors was taken as an insult by the British, and to make matters worse, the local merchants decided that they would make *Monarch* wait for her provisions and supplies while they tended to the needs of *Revenge*.[36]

For several months Conyngham cruised the Atlantic from the Bay of Biscay to the Canaries, with an occasional foray into the Mediterranean. As usual the documents disagree, but a good estimate would be that he took somewhere in the neighborhood of twenty prizes while operating out of Spain.[37] Many were retaken, but those that did manage to get safely to port were sold by agents, and the money, after commissions and shares were deducted, was used to purchase arms and munitions or to support American diplomats in Europe.

As a sea raider Gustavus Conyngham had few peers, then or now, but despite his successes, problems were beginning to set in; chief among them was the decimation of his crew. In July he had left Dunkirk with a little over one hundred men, but by early 1778 many of them were gone. Some were victims of combat, others were captured while aboard a prize ship that was retaken, and some simply deserted. Replacements were hard to come by, and Conyngham could not be too choosy about seamen. The result was a hodgepodge collection of disorderly, truculent, greedy men, many of whom probably had never even seen America and did not know the Continental Congress from the Icelandic Althing. Conyngham had trouble controlling his motley crew, and before long they were complaining about getting shortchanged or not paid at all.

Conyngham himself was to blame for some of the troubles. In his cruising he had been a bit lax about the rights of neutrals, and at least one captured vessel had been ordered released by the Spanish authorities.[38] The final straw came on 31 May 1778. On that day, according to Conyngham's account, *Revenge* sighted a merchantman that turned out to be the ship *Henrica Sophia*, a bona fide neutral flying the Swedish flag. Conyngham wanted to let her go, but his men, hungry for a prize, had other ideas, and over their captain's objections they insisted on taking her.[39] She was *Revenge*'s last prize in European waters.

The Spanish court was ready for a change of heart, and this blatant violation of neutrality provided a convenient opportunity for them to close down Conyngham's operation. On 1 September, under pressure from the local authorities, he took leave of Spain and headed west for Martinique, where he reported to William Bingham at Saint Pierre. For three months he cruised in and out of the Leeward and Windward islands. As usual he was successful and took at least five prizes, slightly off his previous record, but the waters here were alive with enemy warships, which made hunting more difficult and dangerous.

Conyngham seemed to lead a charmed life. He had been cruising in *Revenge* for eighteen months, and in that time he had taken at least twenty-seven prizes and burned or sunk thirty-three more.[40] It was a phenomenal record and might have been even better if the Congress had let well enough alone, but early in January 1779 the Marine Committee, acting on a number of complaints they had received about Conyngham's conduct, ordered the captain to appear before them in Philadelphia.[41]

The most serious charge was that Conyngham had not paid certain members of his crew. The justice of the claim was difficult to assess, so Congress began an investigation into *Revenge*'s accounts. They soon discovered that Conyngham was a far better captain than bookkeeper. The accounts, the ones that they could find, were in a sorry mess. Out of fairness to Conyngham it should be pointed out that he had been sending in prizes from Dunkirk to Cádiz to Saint Pierre and several ports in between where they had often been sold, because of possible violations of international law, in a rather shady fashion. It was not a situation conducive to careful record keeping, and those accounts that did exist were generally somewhere abroad, and it would take months and sometimes years for them to arrive in Philadelphia.

Justly or not, the captain was wide open to accusations of wrongdoing, and it did not help that ever since his days aboard *Surprise* he had been closely associated with Silas Deane. It was through Deane and his friend Hodge that he had managed to get *Revenge*. From the very beginning some of Deane's enemies, Arthur Lee being the most vocal, suspected that he had used his position to mix his own money and interest in *Revenge*. That was only a small part of Deane's activities, and in the fall of 1777 he had been recalled by Congress, ostensibly to report on the status of negotiations, but in fact, as he himself knew, to answer charges of profiteering and chicanery that were being bandied about in Congress. The controversy, eventually resulting in Deane's dismissal, consumed Congress during the summer and fall of 1778, and even when Conyngham arrived at Philadelphia in February 1779, the affair was still the talk of the town, and inevitably Conyngham got caught in the back eddy.[42] Conyngham's association with Deane did not enhance his position, nor did the fact that the chairman of the Marine Committee was Richard Henry Lee, Arthur's oldest brother. Sloppy bookkeeping, allegations of wrongdoing, politics—all added up to such a confusing state of affairs that Congress could see only one way out: sell *Revenge* and wash their hands of the whole business.[43]

By order of Congress *Revenge* was sold at public auction. The high bidder was none other than Cunningham and Nesbit, the same firm for which Gustavus Conyngham had sailed aboard *Charming Peggy* four years earlier. His ship sold out from under him and with no prospect of another Continental command, Conyngham quickly accepted the invitation to become captain of the privateer *Revenge*.

As a privateer *Revenge* had an inglorious career. In April she was captured by the frigate *Galatea* and carried into New York. Conyngham, instead of being treated as a legitimate prisoner of war, was slapped into irons and charged with piracy. The British claimed that three years earlier he had sailed *Surprise* without a commission and was therefore a pirate.[44] Sadly, Conyngham could not prove otherwise, since the commission which he did indeed have while sailing *Surprise* was the one that had been surrendered to the French, and it had not been seen since. The British were deaf to American protests and finally relented only when Congress ordered a British officer confined to chains until Conyngham was treated properly.[45] He was shipped back to England and put into Mill Prison, from which, after three unsuccessful attempts, he finally escaped in November 1779. He made it to the Texel, where he met John Paul Jones, who was then the commander of *Alliance*. *Alliance* carried him to La Coruña, where he took passage for America on board the privateer *Tartar*. For a man who had been so fortunate during his earlier career Conyngham certainly seemed to be running afoul of bad luck now. On 17 March 1780 *Tartar* was captured, and Conyngham was soon back among his friends in Mill Prison. For a year he was kept in prison. His wife, Anne, peppered Congress with petitions urging them to arrange his release. When that proved futile, she went to France to carry on her struggle for the release of a man she had seen for only two months out of the last six years. She arrived only a short time before her husband, who finally walked through the gates of Mill Prison in June 1781.[46] Together they left France and returned home to Philadelphia, and for the rest of the war Gustavus Conyngham remained ashore, joining the growing ranks of unemployed Continental captains.

It is a pity that Gustavus Conyngham has never been afforded the high place in American naval history he deserves. Next to John Paul Jones, he was the Continental navy's most successful captain, having captured or destroyed at least thirty-three vessels with ships considerably smaller than Jones's *Alfred, Ranger, Bonhomme Richard,* or *Alliance.* This undeserved neglect and near anonymity springs from two causes. The first is that all his activities in European waters took place before the French alliance and were therefore illegal and clandestine. The only party that had anything to gain by publishing them was the British. Neither the French nor the Americans were anxious for the world to know about Gustavus Conyngham.

The other reason for his low profile has to do with Conyngham himself. On the quarterdeck he was a man almost without peer, an aggressive and blustering commander. But ashore he was a different man. He could handle rabble in the forecastle, but he was stymied by the subtle and sometimes devious machinations of shore-side politicians. Unlike John Paul Jones, he was not an especially articulate or clever man and he had difficulty presenting his case, and in contrast to the chevalier, in the postwar years he did not sail off to Europe for a career as a sailor of fortune but was content to remain in his home, dabbling in business and politics until he died in 1819. By then many people had forgotten that this old man was once feared far and wide as the "Dunkirk Pirate."

Conyngham's departure to the South brought a temporary lull to northern European waters which lasted until Paul Jones's arrival aboard *Ranger* in the winter of 1777. During the intervening months other Continental captains did put into French ports, but for the most part they came not to fight but to pick up supplies. As far as the commissioners and the

French government were concerned, that was just fine since neither was in a mood to go again through the kind of hubbub that Conyngham had caused. For the time being, at least until France made up her mind to openly join the Americans in an alliance, it was going to be difficult for Continental captains to operate in the confused wake left by Conyngham.

Among those who came during this time was Captain John Young of the Continental sloop *Independence*. After a forty-five day passage from Philadelphia he came up the Loire on 24 September 1777 and disposed of a couple of prizes he had taken en route. From late September until early March *Independence* and her crew remained in France. The reason for such a long stay in port when so much needed to be done is not clear. It might well have been that Young did not think he could make it through the British patrols alone and was waiting for a propitious moment or a heavy escort. A more likely explanation is that he was simply waiting for the commissioners to get their dispatches together and those gentlemen delayed, hoping to have great news to send. At any rate the time in port was not spent in complete idleness. Young was never pleased with the way *Independence* handled as a sloop, and while at Nantes he put his men to work converting her to a brig.

Early in December Young and his men were joined by Paul Jones, who dropped anchor in *Ranger*. Jones left his ship at Paimboef, the deep-water port for Nantes, and rode up to the town, where he joined Young to tell him about his grand plans. Young would have loved to join Jones, but his orders were to carry dispatches, not to spend time cruising. On 13 February Young, stretching his orders a bit, sailed with *Ranger* along the coast of Brittany up to Quiberon Bay, where the two American ships were saluted by the French admiral LaMotte Piquet on 14 and 15 February. This was not, as Jones in his typical cocky fashion later claimed, the first time a Continental ship had been saluted by the French; however, it was the first time since the signing of the secret treaty of alliance, on 6 February 1778, that these honors had been exchanged. At Quiberon Young asked and was granted permission to join LaMotte Piquet's fleet, which was readying for sea bound for the West Indies. On 25 February the fleet, including Young, got under way. At the Azores he parted company, and *Independence* headed for America. Along the North Carolina coast he decided to make for Ocracoke Inlet. *Independence* never made it over the bar. Thanks to an incompetent pilot, she was stuck fast and had to be abandoned before she was battered to pieces. The crew made it ashore, and Young went on to Philadelphia to make his report to Congress.[47]

Following closely in Young's wake came the frigate *Raleigh* with Captain Thomas Thompson and her consort, the old veteran *Alfred* under Captain Elisha Hinman. They put in at the port of Lorient in what one crew member called "sham distress."[48] They had just finished the outward leg of a voyage during which they had encountered part of the British Windward Islands fleet. Despite some sloppy and timid ship handling, they managed to take several prizes, and so when they arrived in France, they were able to raise enough money to meet nearly all their own expenses. That was a pleasant turn of events, and the commissioners wasted no time in letting the people back in Philadelphia know how pleased they were at this unusual development. Since the Marine Committee had told Thompson and Hinman to put themselves at the disposal of the commissioners, it was now up to Franklin and the others to find useful employment for them. The treaty with France was still two months in the future, so the Americans at Paris decided that whatever *Raleigh* and *Alfred* were going to do had best be done outside European waters. The commissioners suggested that they sail home by way of West Africa and the Caribbean, and on 29 December the two vessels dropped down to the open sea and headed south.[49] It was a smooth and relatively uneventful voyage until 9 March, when they spotted two sloops belonging to the Royal Navy, *Adriane* and *Ceres*. Despite their superiority in metal, the Americans showed themselves, as they often did, inferior in seamanship. *Raleigh* and *Alfred* were so far apart that they were of no help to each other, which allowed the two British to gang up on *Alfred.* She had to strike or be sunk, while *Raleigh* barely had time to flee.[50]

Since Conyngham's departure no one else had yet shown the kind of pluck that had made him so famous. This was about to change, for John Paul Jones was now at Nantes getting his *Ranger* ready to sail. It was while he was in that port early in February that he heard the long-awaited news of the Franco-American treaty. Unlike his predecessors, he now would be free of all the legal fetters and able to enjoy full and open French aid as he stood out to harass the British.

Chapter Eight

The War at Sea:
The European Theater
Post Alliance

Jones's arrival, along with the announcement of the grand news of an official Franco-American alliance, opens the most famous, if not the most important, chapter in the story of the Continental navy. Jones came aboard *Ranger* but intended to stay with her only as long as it took him to get to the yard in Holland where he planned to take command of the beautiful new frigate being built there for the American commissioners.[1] He was full of hope, cocky and brazen as usual.[2] In what must go down as one of the most unctuous letters ever to come from his busy pen, he wrote to the Marine Committee shortly after he arrived in France that it was his "heart's first and favorite wish to be employed in Active and enterprising Services" and that the honor done him by the Congress caused him to be full of "Sentiments of Gratitude which I shall carry with me to my Grave." He seems to have enjoyed playing with the pen as much as with a brace of pistols, and his arrival in Louis XVI's France inspired him to conclude by telling the men in Philadelphia that their approval meant more to him than all "the Empty Pagentry which Kings ever did or Can bestow."[3] He was nearly as good an actor and penman as seaman.

A visit to Franklin dampened the captain's enthusiasm a bit, for the old man told him that matters had not proceeded as far as he wished in either Holland or Versailles. The French were dragging their feet and could not be rushed in this affair. Franklin told Jones to be patient and in the meantime to make himself at home as his guest in Paris. What he did not tell his young friend was that he had spent months nudging and gently tugging at the French to bring them into the American camp. With painstaking effort he had carefully erected a very delicate structure that had yet to be finished, and under no circumstances would he risk it by making indecorous demands on behalf of Captain Jones.

Although Jones wished mightily to be at sea, his sojourn in Paris was anything but unpleasant. Young, good-looking, clever and witty, Jones fell right in with Parisian society and sampled all the fruits of the salon, including the wife of Franklin's landlord, Le Ray de Chaumont, with whom he struck up an intimate relationship. For several weeks he traipsed about Paris, wiling away his evenings entertaining the ladies and the days plying their husbands in hopes of finding a suitable command. Franklin, despite his charm and feigned simplicity, could not persuade the French that Captain Jones ought to have a ship, and on 16 January Jones was officially given the bad news. For the time being there would be no fine new frigate to command. He would have to make do with *Ranger* and "proceed with her . . . distressing the enemies of the United States."[4]

Disappointed that he had lost the grand prize but confident that he could show his mettle with *Ranger*, Jones packed up and set off back to Nantes to ready *Ranger* for sea. His orders were open-ended enough so that he could do almost anything as long as it annoyed the British and did not violate any neutral rights and kept him away from France for a few weeks.[5] The orders were signed by Franklin and Deane but not by Arthur Lee. The very next day Lee wrote to Jones explaining why he had not signed. He said that he approved of the orders in general but felt compelled to dissent on the section that involved disposition of prizes. He did not agree with the list of agents suggested by his two colleagues and thought that others ought to be given a chance at the business. Jones paid little mind to Lee. Increasingly Lee had become the odd man out in the delegation, and Jones probably just regarded this display as another example of the interminable bickering going on among the commissioners.[6]

For two weeks Jones was all over *Ranger*, checking her hull, which had just been careened, and taking a close look at the mainmast, which had been restepped farther aft. Victuals were stored below in the hold while gunpowder and shot were laid carefully down in the magazine deep in the bowels of the ship. With a clean bottom, new rig and a reasonably happy crew that had just been paid, *Ranger* sailed out of the Loire on 13 February 1778 in company with the Continental sloop *Independence*, bound together north toward Quiberon Bay.[7]

Over the next two months Jones accomplished very little. He spent some time cruising off the Brittany coast in weather so foul that it tested his seamanship and *Ranger*'s seaworthiness. The former was skillful as usual but the latter was found lacking, so at Brest, where Jones spent most of March, *Ranger* had her masts taken out and completely restepped, sails were cut and altered and ballast was shifted to improve the trim. All this, of course, was done in plain view and even with the cooperation of the French, who by this time had secretly cemented their alliance with the Americans and were preparing to go over the precipice into war.[8] On 20 March Franklin, Deane and Lee were officially received by the king, while back in Brest Jones was feting and being feted by the French navy. On 7 April the order went out from Versailles that all American warships were to be welcomed and assisted in French ports. To demonstrate French hospitality, three days later Lieutenant General Le Comte d'Orvilliers ordered the frigate *Fortunée* and her tender to accompany *Ranger* out of

Brest and stay with her long enough to be sure she got safely past the British patrols.[9]

With *Fortunée* leading the way, Jones put out to sea and then bade farewell to his escort and headed north toward the Irish Sea and the west coast of England. Along with the Hudson Bay fleet, the Greenland fisheries and the whalers off Brazil, the west coast of England was a target long urged by the commissioners. Remote and undefended, it was, according to Deane and Franklin, an area where the Continental navy could strike and deal a heavy military and psychological blow to the British. Quite independent of the commissioners, Jones had come to much the same conclusion; indeed, it had been the very thought of such an expedition that had drawn the captain to France.

Four days out of Brest *Ranger* took her first prize, a small brig bound to Galloway. She was laden with flaxseed and was not worth a great deal, so Jones took the crew aboard *Ranger* —they could be useful in a prisoner exchange—and then sent her to the bottom. *Ranger* continued northward into Saint George's channel, where three days later, on 17 April, they fell in with a fair-sized ship of three hundred tons, *Lord Chatham*, loaded with a variety of merchandise including some good English porter. This one was a keeper. A prize crew was transferred and she was sent into Brest.[10]

After dispatching *Chatham*, Jones picked up his bearings, and once again *Ranger* plowed north through the chilly but clear spring night. The next morning, off the northern tip of the Isle of Man, *Ranger* met her first enemy man-of-war. It was *Hussar*, a lightly armed revenue cutter. She was no match for *Ranger*, and her captain, after firing a few parting shots, decided to make a run for it. *Ranger* took up the chase and set out after her. The American ship was faster and with a better wind she might have caught her prey, but the English captain, whose experience in chasing smugglers had taught him every rock and cove in the area, tacked in closer to shore than Jones dared to go, and Jones had to give up the chase, allowing *Hussar* to speed away.

Jones decided for the time being to stay where he was and prowl the northern Irish Sea. On 19 April he took a small coaster with oats bound for Irvine. She was not worth wasting a prize crew on, so after putting her men below with the other prisoners, Jones ordered her scuttled. The next day he found another coaster, this one in ballast, so she too was sunk. Except for the brush with *Hussar*, the cruise had been exceptionally dull, but from the crew of the second coaster Jones picked up some information that he knew would enliven his business. According to his intelligence, H.M.S. *Drake*, a twenty-gun sloop of war, was only a short distance away peacefully riding at anchor in Belfast lough, her captain blissfully unaware of Jones's arrival. Intrigued with the idea of taking one of His Majesty's ships, Jones told his men that they should sail directly into the lough and let fly with some broadsides. His crew, nervous at best, mutinous at worst, objected to the bully-boy approach. To allay their fears, Jones worked out a more subtle plan. *Ranger* would keep her gun ports closed and sail slowly into the lough, trying to appear a peaceful merchantman. She would pass across *Drake*'s bow, come around to the windward side, drop anchor and open fire. Then, while the British were reeling from the broadside, *Ranger* would grapple and board. It was a good plan, but it went awry because *Ranger*'s anchor got fouled in one of the catheads and the quartermaster in charge of the anchor detail could not move fast enough to free it. As a result *Ranger* overshot, and the men, sure that they had been discovered, braced for a broadside. None came. *Drake*'s sleepy crew never knew what almost hit them, and *Ranger* was able to slip by and get back out to sea before anyone was the wiser. Jones was lucky, but still he had accomplished little. He was disappointed and his crew was restless. They had signed on for money, and the few paltry prizes sent in so far, once divided, would hardly give them a good fling ashore.

It was probably at this juncture that Jones decided to follow through on a plan that had been in his mind since he had left Portsmouth. He was determined to bring the Revolution right to the British doorstep by landing and raiding. It would be a first for the Continental navy and a heavy blow for the British.

The target was Whitehaven, a small port along the west coast of England, directly across the Irish Sea from Belfast. For Jones it made sense to go to Whitehaven, not because it had any particular strategic value—it did not—but because it was a port he had sailed out of as a boy and he knew it well.

Under the cover of darkness he planned to slip into the harbor, land, spike the guns and then set afire as many ships as possible before getting away. Nothing seemed to go right. Far outside the harbor *Ranger* was becalmed and had to lower her boats into the water a good three hours' row from Whitehaven. By the time the men made it to the harbor, they were tired from their stint at the oars and many were in a sullen mood. There was not much in the way of prize money to be gained from burning and sinking vessels in port, so at least to get some fun out of their brief stay ashore, some of the crewmen, ignoring orders to the contrary, went into the local tavern and drank up a storm while Jones and a gang of loyal men took care of the guns and set fire to a few ships. By dawn the boats were pulling back to *Ranger*, leaving behind some smoldering ships and a panicked populace. Despite the daring, very little actual damage was done—altogether the estimate was less than £1200—but psychologically the effect was astounding. Wickes and Conyngham had already shown that the British trident was a bit rusty, but Jones made some think that it had rotted away entirely. For the first time in more than one hundred years a British port had actually come under close attack by an enemy.

From Whitehaven *Ranger* bore north across the Solway Firth toward Saint Mary's Isle in Kirkcudbright Bay. Jones was determined to land again, but this time, instead of burning and sinking, kidnapping was on his mind. He was going to carry away the Earl of Selkirk, a minor Scottish peer, and hold him in exchange for American seamen in British prisons. It was not a very sound scheme. Selkirk was such a small fish that in all likelihood the government would never have exchanged many prisoners for him, but Jones, at heart a romantic, thought they would. As for the men aboard *Ranger*, their interest was cash, and if Selkirk was as great a lord as Jones made him out to be, there would be plenty of loot at the manor to fill their sea bags.

By mid-morning of the twenty-third *Ranger* was under shortened sail off the entrance to Kirkcudbright Bay. Jones ordered the ship's cutter into the water, and with the captain himself sitting in the stern she moved quickly toward shore. With him were David Cullam, the master, Lieutenant Samuel Wallingford, a marine officer, and a dozen sailors armed to the teeth. They scrambled ashore and moved up the hill toward the manor house. On the way they met an elderly gardener who took them for a press gang on the lookout for "volunteers." Brandishing pistols and cutlasses, they looked ferocious enough to be just that, and as soon as word got around that there was a gang in the area, every young man in the neighborhood took to hiding. That was all the better for the Americans. As they approached the house, Jones heard some disturbing news. His Lordship was not at home; he was "taking the waters at Buxton in Derbyshire."[11] *Hussar*'s escape, *Drake*'s blind fortune and now Selkirk's absence. It was the third piece of bad luck in six days. If he left here as empty-handed as he had departed Whitehaven, his crew would be sure to mutiny, so he decided to allow them to take the family silver. Gallant as usual, Jones told his men that they were not to barge into the house nor were they to molest Lady Selkirk. There was no violence, the plate was taken and Jones, somewhat ashamed at this bit of looting, returned to *Ranger*. Later after a good deal of reflection Jones wrote a very long letter to Lady Selkirk extolling her courage and virtue while decrying the necessities of war which had compelled him to do what he had done. He even offered to make amends for what happened on Saint Mary's Isle and bought the Selkirk plate himself so he might return it. At first His Lordship refused, insisting that the silver would only be accepted if it came by official act of Congress. That, of course, was impossible, and however hard-headed Selkirk might have been, he was still a Scot, and after he had time to think the matter over, he decided to accept Jones's offer, and the silver remains today on Saint Mary's Isle.[12]

Ranger departed Kirkcudbright Bay and jogged along the Scottish coast across the mouth of the North Channel and ended up where she had been six days before, at Belfast lough. This time *Drake* was awake and under sail on her way out of the lough to take a look at the stranger. *Ranger* was approaching bow on, so it was impossible to see her row of gun ports or her by now rather well-known black hull and bright yellow topsides. To some she might have appeared to be a merchantman making her way toward port, but under the circumstances only a fool and Captain Burden, commander of *Drake*, could make such an assumption. He knew *Ranger* was about, and surely as he eyed this vessel through his glass, he must have suspected her sharp bow and rakish appearance to be something more than just another peaceful, lumbering trader. Burden called on *Ranger* to identify herself. The stars and stripes went up briskly and Jones hollered back, "The American Continental Ship *Ranger.*" At the same time he brought *Ranger* hard over at ninety degrees, crossed *Drake*'s bow and raked her fore and aft. It was downhill from there for Burden and his crew. Sixty-five minutes after the opening salvo the captain and his lieutenant were dead, the master was in command and *Drake* was a shambles. Quarter was asked and *Drake* became *Ranger*'s prize. After spending a day repairing her, Jones appointed his lieutenant, Thomas Simpson, a man for whom he had little respect or fondness, to be prize master. Together they sailed around the north of Ireland out into the Atlantic, always keeping a careful watch. Jones tried to take another prize, the brig *Patience*, and he chased her until he discovered she was a neutral. Before he took off after her, though, he ordered Simpson to follow him. The lieutenant did not understand the order, so when Jones veered off, Simpson held to his course bound for Ushant. A few days later when Jones caught up with Simpson, he went aboard *Drake*, rebuked the lieutenant for his conduct and, without waiting for an explanation, brusquely ordered Simpson removed from command and placed under arrest. It was a poor and unjust way to treat a fellow officer. The fact was Jones's order had not been understood aboard *Drake* by either Simpson or anyone else, and Jones's conduct toward the lieutenant was resented by the crew, who knew the story and took Simpson's side.[13]

If Jones expected a hero's welcome when he got back to France, he was sorely mistaken. As far as the commissioners were concerned, all the good news—the captured merchant-men, *Drake*, Whitehaven, Saint Mary's Isle, and a red-faced Royal Navy—was barely enough to balance out the grief thrust upon them by an arrogant captain who had arrested his lieutenant, lost the favor of his crew and was now presenting them with bills they could not pay and prisoners they could not care for. Jones was up to his ears in problems.

When he presented some bills to Franklin, he was told that they could not be honored because they had not gone through proper channels.[14] Arthur Lee, who had been nursing a grudge against Jones anyway because he thought he was a Deane man, took the opportunity to compare what was happening now to the awful mess that had been created as a result of the confused affairs of Conyngham's *Revenge*.[15] John Adams, the most recent arrival on the European scene, shared Lee's dislike of the captain and noted in his *Autobiography* that "Jones had been so elevated by his success in taking Prizes and especially by the Glory of capturing the *Drake* that he had acted a very high handed and presumptuous part upon many Occasions, which gave us a great deal of trouble from several Sources."[16]

Adams was probably right. John Paul Jones was not an easy man to get along with, and arrogance became his trademark. Nevertheless, whatever his shortcomings, the American cause would have been better served if more leaders had possessed them.

If hubris was his flaw, persistence was his strength. John Paul Jones had come to France for a frigate, and in all his dealings with the commissioners and the French he hewed to that line. On 1 June he finally got some good news when Franklin wrote him that the forty-gun frigate building at Amsterdam, *Indien,* might well be his.[17] That helped to balance a bit of bad news the captain received two days later when he was ordered to release Lieutenant Simpson.[18] Jones never gave up trying to get Simpson court-martialed and cashiered, and months afterward he was still urging unsuccessfully the convening of a court to hear the charges.[19] His concern with Simpson, however, was only peripheral to his main interest, getting *Indien,* and for that purpose, at Franklin's invitation, Jones packed his baggage and moved to Paris so that he might be closer to the springs of power where his fate would be decided. In the meantime *Ranger* was turned over to Simpson, who cast off on 21 August bound for Portsmouth, New Hampshire. Her departure left Jones beached but unworried since he was sure *Indien* would be his.

Through a succession of events involving politics, diplomacy and personal grudges, Jones did not get *Indien.*[20] For the rest of 1778 and somewhat into the early months of 1779 he was an unemployed and somewhat unhappy captain searching for a command.[21] At Franklin's invitation he looked at a number of prizes brought to port with an eye toward converting them to warships, but none seemed suited for what he had in mind and he rejected every one of them. After one such fruitless inspection tour he wrote to Chaumont, in words that would go ringing through time, "I wish to have no Connection with any ship that does not sail fast, for I intend to go in harm's way."[22]

It was on a later trip, this one to Lorient, that Jones saw an old East Indiaman, *Le Duc de Duras,* built in 1766. He probably did not like her very much, but by this time almost anything would have been better than sitting on the beach. He took *Le Duc* and renamed her *Bonhomme Richard* in honor of his friend Franklin.

Along with the midnight ride of Paul Revere, Benedict Arnold's treason and Washington crossing the Delaware, the story of John Paul Jones and *Bonhomme Richard* is probably one of the best known of the entire American Revolution. With Jones carefully scrutinizing every detail, she was fitted out as a warship. Sartine, the French minister of marine, paid all the bills, and when finished, *Richard* mounted twenty-eight twelve-pounders on the gun deck, six or eight nine-pounders on the forecastle and six eighteen-pounders in the gun room just below the main battery. Although the eighteen-pounders were theoretically quite formidable, in fact they were practically useless because they were mounted so low that in the slightest sea their ports had to be kept closed.

Instead of sending *Richard* out to cruise alone, as *Ranger* had, this time Jones and the commissioners organized a squadron, for they were considering the possibility of sending ships along the very weakly defended western shore of England and Scotland. The cities of Glasgow and Liverpool had been singled out as potential targets. A naval squadron carrying a small landing force aboard could easily take these towns and hold them long enough either to pillage them or to get ransom money for them. It would be a fitting retribution for what the English had done to towns like Falmouth and Norfolk on the American coast, and it would help offset the recent American reverses in Georgia. Jones favored it, and Franklin was enthusiastic. The French too, now that they were openly at war, thought it was promising not only as an operation in itself but also as a diversionary tactic to draw the British away from the Channel, which the French and Spanish were then making plans to cross in the most ambitious invasion attempt since the Armada. Ever since the humiliation of 1763 the French had been toying with the idea of a cross-Channel invasion. By the spring of 1779 the idea had begun to take substantive shape, as thousands of soldiers and tons of equipment were secretly assembled along the coasts of Brittany and Normandy while back in Paris and Madrid the French and Spanish high commands were laying plans for joint army and navy operations.

The Americans were kept completely in the dark and were unaware that the new French interest in their proposal was in any way connected to a far wider and more important venture. Maurepas, Vergennes and Sartine thought that Jones's raid would be a useful side show to throw the British a bit off balance.[23]

A young war hero just returned from America, the Marquis de Lafayette, was chosen to command the landing forces aboard Jones's squadron. He had arrived aboard the frigate *Alliance*, exuberant, restless and eager for a new opportunity to display his military skill. Money loomed as an obstacle, just as it always did. The total cost was estimated at one million francs. But in the face of Franklin's well-known powers of persuasion and Lafayette's connections at the French court, even that problem faded away. The squadron assembled at Lorient. The flagship was Jones's *Richard*. *Alliance*, the new frigate from America, joined him under the command of Pierre Landais, a French officer with good American connections. To this pair of Continental vessels were attached three French navy ships: the frigate *Pallas*, a brig, *Vengeance*, and the cutter *Le Cerf*. If all went as Jones and Lafayette planned, this squadron would be joined by transports with fifteen hundred men (about three regiments) which under the heaviest cloak of secrecy possible would depart Lorient and descend upon either Glasgow or Liverpool.[24]

To avoid any possible squabbling over command—a very real risk when dealing with two such proud and irascible individuals as Jones and Lafayette—Franklin made it perfectly clear to his commodore that the marquis, due to his rank as a major general, was the senior officer but that Jones for all intents and purposes would be commander at sea while Lafayette would command ashore. In a letter that is worth quoting at length Franklin gave his instructions to Jones:

> It has been observed that joint Expeditions of Land and Sea Forces often miscarry, thro Jealousies and Misunderstandings between the Officers of the different Corps. This must happen,

where there are little minds, actuated more by personal Views of Profit or Honour to themselves, than by the warm and sincere Desire of Good to their Country. Knowing you both as I do and your just manner of thinking on these occasions I am confident nothing of the kind can happen between you; and that it is unnecessary for me to recommend to either of you that Condescension, mutual Good Will and Harmony which contribute so much to Success in such Undertakings.

I look upon this Expedition as an Introduction only to greater Trusts, and more extensive Commands, and as a Kind of Trial of both your Abilities and of your Fitness in Temper and Disposition for acting in Concert with others. I flatter myself therefore that nothing will happen that may give Impressions to the Disadvantage of either of you, when greater Affairs shall come under Consideration. As this is understood to be an American Expedition, under the Congress's Commission and Colours, the Marquis, who is a Major-General in that Service, has of course the Step in Point of Rank, and he must have the Command of the Land Forces which are committed by the King to his Care; But the Command of the Ships will be entirely in you: in which I am persuaded that, whatever Authority his Rank might in strickness give him, he will not have the least Desire to interfere with you. There is Honour enough to be got for both of you, if the expedition is conducted with a prudent unanimity. The Circumstance is indeed a little Unusual; for there is not only a Junction of Land and Sea Forces but there is also a Junction of Frenchmen and American, which increases the Difficulty of maintaining a good Understanding. A cool, prudent Conduct in the chiefs is, therefore, the more necessary; and I trust neither of you will in that respect be deficient.[25]

Appended to the letter were specific instructions for Jones. The actual target selection would be left up to Lafayette; after landing the troops, Jones was to stand by and under no circumstances was he to leave the area; prisoners were to be treated humanely and held for exchange; towns might be burned but only after a reasonable time had been allowed for the evacuation of women and children.

It was a grand scheme, and with some good planning and a lot of luck they might have been able to carry it off, but unfortunately they were never given the chance. For some reason—probably because they wanted to husband their soldiers for the upcoming invasion—the French had a change of heart and decided not to support the raid. To his great dismay Lafayette learned in early May that the expedition was not to be and instead he was being posted to command a regiment of the king's dragoons. As for the ground invasion itself, after much waiting accompanied by a good deal of bickering, the French and Spanish fleets managed to rendezvous. Together during July and August they sailed along the southern coasts of England trying to draw the British fleet out to do battle. The fleet quite wisely refused a general engagement, and all the allies accomplished was to have their ships ravaged by scurvy and fever so that by the end of the summer they had barely enough men to limp back to port. It was one of the greatest fiascos of the entire war.[26]

Lafayette's departure left Jones with five ships ready for sea but no soldiers and nowhere to go. Having expended so much effort in gearing up, Jones was determined to make use of his squadron. The French agreed, and for the time being the ships were kept together, although they were given the rather prosaic and unexciting task of convoy duty. Playing shepherd to a flock of merchantmen was not much to Jones's liking, and he yearned for greater things. His chance came early in July when he got new orders from Sartine countersigned by Franklin. Jones was told to take his squadron on a clockwise cruise up the west coast of Ireland, across the top via the Orkneys to the North Sea and down the English coast, winding up at the Texel in Holland. His mission: commerce raiding.

Jones was not enthusiastic. The great objective on his mind was a landing, and there was no mention of that in the new orders. As far as Jones was concerned, Sartine's letter had all the grandeur and imagination of a bill of lading. Since Franklin's signature appeared on the orders, Jones thought that perhaps he could approach the commissioner and ask him to make some changes. At times Jones, and the other American captains as well, seemed to think that Benjamin Franklin had nothing else to do but to attend to their wants and desires, when in fact he was deluged with all kinds of responsibilities. The old man was sick to death of being bothered by these men whose business he was ignorant of in the first place, who cost him a great deal of money and about whom he really cared very little except inasmuch as they brought him prisoners he could exchange and goods he could sell.[27]

Rather bluntly Franklin told Jones that the French had "the best right to direct" since they were paying the bills.[28] Lest Jones think that this was not final enough and that there was still a possibility of Franklin's using his influence with Sartine to get the plans changed, he told Jones, "When a thing has been once considered and determin'd on in Council, they do not care to resume the Consideration of it, having much Business on hand, and there is not now time to obtain a Reconsideration."[29]

To sweeten the bitterness a bit, Franklin did hint that the reason Sartine designated the Texel as a finishing point was so Jones's squadron could meet and escort *Indien* from that port, where for some months she had been under British blockade. Implied in this, of course, was that if Jones freed her he might get to command her. With that brass ring Jones was ready to be off on his cruise round the isles.

Late in the afternoon of 14 August 1779 the commodore and his squadron rendezvoused at Isle de Croix, just off Lorient. Jones counted seven ships: the original five plus two new additions, the privateers *Monsieur* and *Granville*. It took nearly ten days to cover the short distance from Isle de Croix to Mizzen Head. Along the way he lost the rascally *Monsieur* (*Granville* would follow in only a few days) when her captain, a typical privateersman, simply decided that he no longer wished to be subject to the commodore and went to seek his fortune elsewhere. The five remaining stayed together and held to their course and went up along the rugged west coast of Ireland. After nearly two weeks at sea they had only taken three prizes, none of them of much consequence. On the evening of the twenty-third *Richard* lay becalmed not far offshore with an incoming tide. In order to keep her from going aground, Jones ordered his barge out to tow her to sea. It was a natural situation that had some very unnatural results. What happened is best related in Jones's own words.

> Soon after sunset the villains who towed the ship cut the tow rope and decamped with my barge. Sundry shots were fired to bring them to without effect; in the meantime the master of Bon homme Richard, without orderes, manned one of the ships boats and with four soldiers pursued the barge, in order to stop the deserters. The evening was clear and serene, but the zeal of that officer, Mr. Cutting Lunt, induced him to pursue too far, and a fog which came on soon afterwards prevented the boats from rejoining the ship, although I caused signal guns to be frequently fired. The fog and calm continued the next day till toward evening. In the afternoon Capt. Landais came on board the Bon homme Richard and behaved towards me with great disrespect, affirming in the most indelicate manner and language that I had lost my boats and people through my imprudence in sending boats to take a prize. . . . He told me he was determined to follow his own opinion in chasing when and where he thought proper and in every other matter that concerned the service.[30]

In this instance at least, Landais was as good as his word, and for the rest of the cruise he did pretty much as he pleased, separating from Jones at his own whim and rejoining whenever it suited his fancy.

When the fog cleared, the cutter *Cerf* was sent in to look for the lost boat. She lost sight of Jones and then was hit with a sudden gale that sprang her mainmast, leaving her with no choice but to turn south and strike for home. Adding to the grief and diminution of the squadron was *Pallas*, which somehow during all this confusion had damaged her rudder and had to be left behind to make repairs. *Richard* with her lone consort *Vengeance* bade a temporary farewell to *Pallas* and resumed her northerly course.

On 1 September off Cape Wrath *Alliance* hove into sight with a prize. The next morning *Pallas* caught up, and for two days the squadron, now numbering four, cruised between the Orkney and Shetland islands, taking about six prizes. On the third, as the squadron rounded the northern tip of Scotland and began to come down the east coast, *Alliance* took off again. At this point Jones hoisted a signal ordering the captains of *Pallas* and *Vengeance* to come aboard the flagship for a conference. They entered the commodore's cabin and found him standing over his charts of the North Sea with his eye fixed on the Firth of Forth and the town of Leith which lay at its head. One glance at the commodore, and the captains did not have to be told what he had in mind. He wanted to raid Leith. It took some persuading on Jones's part, but after he dangled the possibility of getting a £200,000 ransom for the town, the captains consented. They entered the firth and against a strong breeze worked their way to windward toward Leith. Time was of the essence, and Jones had already lost a good deal of it in conferring with his captains; now this contrary wind added to the delay. On the sixteenth they were spotted from the fortress at Edinburgh and sent that town and nearby Leith into a complete panic. Despite the alarm, the attack could still be carried off if the squadron moved quickly before troops and artillery assembled. Jones was so close, but then disaster struck; a fierce gale hit and drove them east down the firth and out to sea. By the time it cleared, the whole countryside was up in arms, and all that Jones had time to do was get away.

On 23 September *Richard*, *Alliance* (rejoining again), *Pallas* and *Vengeance* were off the English coast near Flamborough Head. They had been at sea for more than five weeks on a cruise that had taken them more than fifteen hundred nautical miles, but so far it had been an expedition more touted for its promise than its accomplishments. Prizes had been taken, but others—Wickes and Conyngham, for example—had done just as well with fewer ships and men. Jones had managed to alarm the folk on shore, but aside from whatever value that kind of psychological trauma had, there was little that he had actually accomplished. There had been no landing, no raid, no ransom, and certainly no glorious victories. All this was much on Jones's mind as he cruised along the Yorkshire coast. Prospects did not look too good, when from a captured pilot he learned that the Baltic fleet was due to pass by. That news held out the alluring possibility of striking a single decisive blow that could recoup the whole voyage. Jones decided to keep in the area for as long as possible so that he might intercept and destroy the convoy.

At about three o'clock in the afternoon of the twenty-third the lookout identified a fleet of forty-one sail north-northeast of *Richard* and bearing in her direction. It was, of course, just what Jones had been looking for—the British Baltic fleet on its way home with a valuable cargo of naval stores, the sinews of the Royal Navy.

The appearance of the American squadron was not a surprise to Captain Richard Pearson, the convoy commander and captain of the powerful forty-four-gun frigate *Serapis*, for both he and Captain Thomas Piercy, captain of the other smaller escort vessel, *Countess of Scarborough*, had been warned that the Americans were in the area. Pearson signaled the convoy to run for cover. With signal guns booming and sheets and canvas snapping, they came about onto a northerly tack, scurrying to the safety of the guns at Scarborough Castle. In the meantime Pearson and Piercy crowded on sail and came down to stand between the fleeing merchantmen and Jones.

The wind was so light that it took two hours for the opponents to close. *Serapis* and *Scarborough*, outnumbered and outgunned if the Americans fought in decent order, never flinched and came straight on. About six o'clock Jones signaled his captains to form a line of battle. The three Frenchmen ignored the command, and *Richard* squared off against *Serapis* alone. The odds were in the enemy's favor, and Jones knew it. *Serapis* was newer, faster and more heavily armed than the old *Richard,* most of whose armament was either light or antique.

Jones brought his ship up on the weather port quarter of *Serapis.* Midshipman Nathaniel Fanning, in *Richard*'s foretop with his detail of sharpshooters, had a bird's-eye view from his precarious position aloft. It was, according to Fanning, a clear cool evening with practically no wind and the sea as smooth as glass.[31] In the moments before battle, as the two wooden fortresses slid gracefully toward each other, there was great commotion aboard. Sailors and marines with practiced, disciplined rhythm moved to their battle stations. Over the din of voices could be heard the thump of wooden wheels on the decks and the creak of tackle as guns were drawn back to be loaded. When they were less than one hundred yards apart, everything was silent. Gunners with matches lit took their places near the touchholes and waited for the command. From the deck of the *Serapis* Pearson was sizing up *Richard* and called out for her to identify herself. Jones, trying to buy time so he could get closer, was flying the Union Jack, so he told his master, Samuel Stacy, to answer Pearson, *"Princess Royal."* To that Pearson asked, "Where from?" Silence followed. Pearson, an experienced captain and certainly no fool, realized that he had a tartar on his hands, and as soon as he saw the Union Jack come fluttering down and the Stars and Stripes go up, he ordered open fire. Jones fired simultaneously and the battle was on. Among the first casualties in the melee were two of Jones's ancient eighteen-pounders. They exploded, killing at least a dozen men.

With her heavier guns and greater maneuverability, *Serapis* had only to keep her station a hundred yards or so from *Richard* and batter her to pieces. Jones decided that the only way to win or even just survive was to grapple and board and fight it out hand to hand. In this deadly ballet Jones and Pearson showed themselves to be seamen of the first order. *Richard* came about and tried to cross the "T," that is, shoot across *Serapis* and rake her stem to stern. She almost made it, but before she could clear, the tip of *Serapis*'s bowsprit got tangled in *Richard*'s aft section and fouled her mizzenmast. Caught together, the ships pivoted clockwise, *Richard* coming around a bit faster, so that within a few moments of their collision they were locked gun port to gun port. It was a stroke of luck for Jones and doom for Pearson.

For more than two hours they lay together slugging it out. *Vengeance* kept away at a safe distance and was never engaged, while *Pallas* had her hands full with *Countess of Scarborough*. The only one who approached was Landais, who came up, circled and fired a few random shots into *Richard*! He was either a fool or a knave, and the evidence is stronger for the latter than the former.[32]

Like a dazed boxer, *Richard* clung to *Serapis*. She had five feet of water in her hold and more coming in. She was mortally wounded, and it was only a matter of time before she would go down. *Serapis*, on the other hand, was in no danger of sinking, but her mainmast was tottering and the rest of the rigging was not much better. By eighteenth-century standards the carnage was awesome. After more than three hours of battle nearly half the men on *Richard* and *Serapis* were either dead or wounded. Amid the tumult and sprawled bodies it is a wonder that anyone had the strength to continue. Finally Pearson, even though in a strict sense neither his ship nor his crew had been bested, struck. With *Richard* in imminent danger of sinking, Jones took his prize and signaled his squadron to make for the Texel. *Pallas*, her prize *Countess of Scarborough*, *Vengeance*, *Alliance* and *Richard*, low in the water but still afloat, sailed east. For two days and nights the crew aboard *Richard* worked the pumps and tried to plug holes in a desperate attempt to keep her afloat. It was hopeless and Jones had to order abandon ship. At eleven in the morning on 25 September *Bonhomme Richard* slid beneath the waves.

As soon as the squadron came to rest at the Texel, Jones went ashore to hasten the disposal of prizes and to politick for a new command. The former business was a mess as usual, and for years afterward petitions and memorials flowed into Congress from crewmen seeking what they claimed to be their rightful shares. Not until 1848 did Congress once and for all put an end to this interminable business by voting a cash award to the survivors and heirs.[33]

As for another command, Jones did get *Alliance* but then lost her to that madman Landais. The ship *Ariel*, on loan from the French, was given to him as a consolation prize. He took her from Lorient to Philadelphia, where after some delay he was given command of the seventy-four-gun ship building at Portsmouth, New Hampshire, *America*. He went there and watched her shape up with all the enthusiasm of a young man about to get his first car. What happened, of course, was that Jones got to stand on the quarterdeck only long enough to participate in a change-of-command ceremony by which the ship was turned over as a gift to the French navy.[34] The ceremony in New Hampshire marked the end of John Paul Jones's career in the American navy. It was a career that had peaked with *Ranger* and *Richard* and thereafter had been pretty much anticlimactic. He left America, journeyed back to Europe and eventually wound up as a rear admiral in the Russian Black Sea fleet, an honor which he could well have done without and which caused him nothing but anguish and anxiety. As soon as he could, he came back to Paris, where he died alone in his apartment on 18 July 1792, only twelve days beyond his forty-fifth birthday. His body was wrapped in a plain white shroud, no uniform and no medals (they had been sold at auction), and was then sealed in a lead coffin filled with alcohol and lowered into a grave at a small Protestant cemetery just outside Paris. More than one hundred years later, in a spasm of naval enthusiasm, the former assistant secretary of the navy and now president, Theodore Roosevelt, ordered Jones's body brought to America. According him all the honor of a great national hero, the navy brought Jones across the Atlantic on board the cruiser U.S.S. *Brooklyn* and finally placed him in a marble sarcophagus at the United States Naval Academy, where he remains today.[35]

Jones's cruise around the British Isles, like those of his predecessors Wickes and Conyngham, was meteoric, that is, a brilliant flash and then nothing. It could have been followed up, but no one seemed to have the heart for it. Franklin wondered if it was all worth while as he kept trying to dig himself out of the pile of business brought on him by prizes, fitting out, prisoners and so forth. Besides, he was too strapped for money himself to think of giving any assistance. The French, who had been paying most of the bills, had the money but they were occupied elsewhere. Their own navy needed attention so that it could do battle with the British.

The important action for the Continental navy in Europe was over. In the remaining years of the war other American warships did, of course, venture overseas but not to stay or cruise. Their job was to ferry men and supplies back and forth across the Atlantic. But even these humdrum missions were few and far between.[36] By 1780 most of the American fleet was either destroyed, bottled up or in British hands. *Alliance* under John Barry made three trips to France, one in March 1781 and the others in January and October 1782. The last American warship to put into France during the war was *General Washington*, a swift privateer purchased for Congress by Robert Morris for use as a packet and put under the command of young Joshua Barney. She arrived at Lorient late in October 1782 with dispatches for Franklin and departed for home early the following January.

Chapter Nine

The Freshwater Fleet

It is probably safe to say that the Congress's saltwater navy did not have any significant effect on the overall outcome of the Revolution. If in a contrafactual exercise we designated the navy a variable and removed it, the chances of the war's ending with a different winner would be slim. But what might be said of the deep-water navy cannot be applied to its freshwater counterpart that operated in the remote areas of upstate New York and Vermont along the Hudson River–Lake Champlain corridor. Here an American fleet played a vital role in what was perhaps the most important campaign of the Revolution; in fact, this naval action among the mountains was the only battle fought by Americans that Alfred Thayer Mahan thought worthy of including in his *Major Operations of the Navies in the War of American Independence.*

Lake Champlain was the largest and most important link in a long chain of waterways extending from New York City to Quebec. It was by way of this route in 1609 that Samuel de Champlain came south to discover his lake, and for more than two hundred years afterward French, Indians, British and Americans were still using it as their favorite north-south invasion route. The trek begins at the village of Sorel, about thirty miles downstream from Montreal, where the Richelieu debouches into the Saint Lawrence.[1] The Richelieu is naviga-

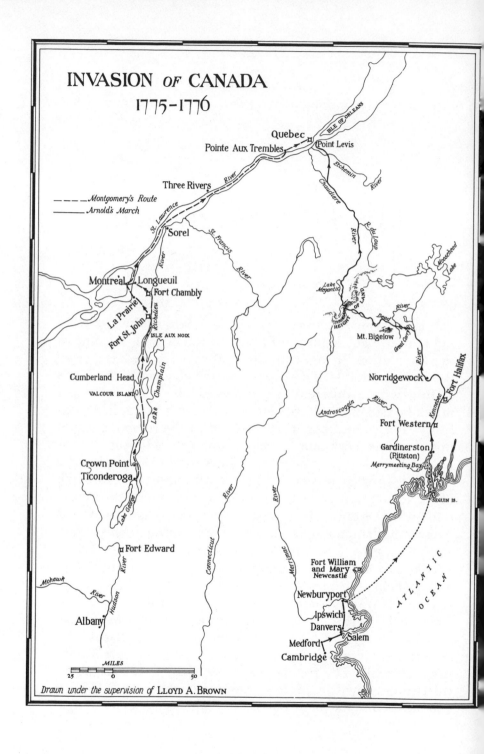

INVASION *OF* CANADA
1775-1776

- - - - - *Montgomery's Route*
———— *Arnold's March*

Quebec

ISLE OF ORLEANS

Pointe Aux Trembles

Point Levis

Etchemin River

Three Rivers

St. Lawrence River

Chaudière River

Sorel

St. Francis River

du Loup River

Montreal Longueuil

Lake Megantic

Fort Chambly

La Prairie

HEIGHT OF LAND

river

Dead

Fort St. John

Richelieu River

ISLE AUX NOIX

Mt. Bigelow

Great Carr y

River

Cumberland Head

VALCOUR ISLAND

Lake Champlain

Norridgewock

Fort Halifax

Kennebec

Androscoggin River

Fort Western

Crown Point

Ticonderoga

Lake George

Gardinerston
(Pittston)
Merrymeeting Bay

SEGUIN IS.

Fort Edward

Connecticut River

River

Merrimac River

Fort William
and Mary
Newcastle

ATLANTIC OCEAN

Mohawk River

Hudson River

Newburyport

Ipswich

Albany

Danvers

Salem

Medford

Cambridge

MILES
25   0   50

Drawn under the supervision of LLOYD A. BROWN

ble by small vessels for about twenty-five miles to a place called Fort Chambly. At Chambly the traveler begins a twelve-mile portage past falls and rapids over to Fort Saint Johns. At Saint Johns the river becomes navigable again and can be followed down to Champlain about twenty miles due south.

The lake itself looks like a giant salamander hunkered down between long rows of green rolling hills. Its head points to the north and the Saint Lawrence, while its tail swishes down past Lake George, almost hitting the Hudson. From tip to tip it is about 125 miles, and across the belly at the widest 12 miles. At a very narrow point where the tail seems to join the body stands Fort Ticonderoga, a star-shaped fortress begun by the French in 1755 and captured by the British in the French and Indian War. Past the fort and to the south the lake trends in a narrow, fairly shallow stretch of water all the way to the village of Skenesborough some twenty miles below.

In the spring of 1775 Fort Ticonderoga was only a remnant of its former self. No longer standing guard against French and Indian invaders, it had become a hollow shell with a corporals guard whose main function was to greet travelers and stand as a reminder of the empire. Since there were no roads on either side of the lake, all travel was water borne. Despite its shabby appearance, Ticonderoga was a vital and strategically important post.

In the aftermath of Lexington and Concord, as the British dominoes began to go down one by one, Ticonderoga stood alone ready to be taken by a minimal effort. Geography alone was sufficient reason for the Americans to want the fort, but there was another and more immediate need it could fulfill as well. Behind its high stone walls were several dozen cannon and mortars that, if captured, could be of critical importance for American resistance. In Connecticut a band of men gathered at Hartford and marched north to join up with Ethan Allen and his Green Mountain Boys and attack Ticonderoga. At the same time and quite independent of them, Benedict Arnold was commissioned a colonel by the Massachusetts

Committee of Safety and told to go on the same mission.

Arnold was thirty-four years old, an experienced business-man, sea captain and soldier. He stood about five feet nine inches tall and had the build of a middleweight wrestler and the stamina of a professional athlete. He was not a particu-larly handsome man. He had a swarthy complexion, black hair, a sharp nose and a distinctive jaw. His physical strength and vigor helped to make him a powerful and forceful figure and one of the best combat commanders (on both sides) in the entire Revolution.

He left Cambridge and joined up with Allen. After a brief squabble over who should command, with Arnold losing, the Americans entered the fort in the predawn hours of 10 May. Allen stormed the stairs to the commandant's quarters, where a surprised captain with his waistcoat and coat on but still holding his pants in his hands, was told to surrender, "In the name of the Great Jehovah and the Continental Congress."[2]

While Allen secured Ticonderoga, a detachment of thirty men under Captain Samuel Herrick managed to capture the village of Skenesborough, including the town father Major Philip Skene himself, without firing a shot.[3] Down at the waterfront, tied up to a dock, was a prize almost as valuable as the cannon at Ticonderoga—a small schooner belonging to Skene. Herrick went aboard, renamed her *Liberty* and or-dered her brought up to the fort.[4]

Liberty's arrival at Ticonderoga on the thirteenth helped to avert, at least temporarily, a showdown between Arnold and Allen. Never very happy with his ambiguous position under Allen and especially resentful at having been cheated out of command, Arnold was brooding as he watched with con-tempt the undisciplined and raucous behavior of the Green Mountain Boys.[5] The schooner offered him a sort of safety valve, a chance to get off on his own. He was an experienced seaman and could rightfully claim that he ought to be given command of the vessel so that he could use her to carry the American momentum onto other parts of the lake, especially to the northern end and up the Richelieu to the outpost at

Saint Johns. Since Crown Point, a small fort on the west shore about ten miles north of Ticonderoga, had fallen on the twelfth, Saint Johns was the only important point on the lake left in British hands. It was an inviting target made even more tempting by reports it had storehouses full of supplies and an armed sloop in the river, which aside from *Liberty* was the only other vessel of force on the lake. If Arnold could take these, Champlain would be an American lake.

Arnold took the matter up with Allen, who agreed that they should move quickly. On the fourteenth Arnold set out with *Liberty*, accompanied by two bateaux full of soldiers who trailed behind.[6] Their first day out a northerly breeze, common for that time of year on the lake, prevented them from going any farther than Crown Point. The next day the wind still held from the north, so Arnold, after climbing aboard a bateau himself, ordered the bateaux to row ahead and let *Liberty* join them later as best she could. While the schooner tacked back and forth in nearly parallel lines, Arnold and his soldiers strained on the oars to make some distance against a strong head wind. After a day of that agony "a fair gale" came up from the south, and *Liberty* sped up the lake, easily overtaking the bateaux. Arnold went back aboard and made sail for Saint Johns. Not more than thirty miles below the post they were becalmed. Again Arnold ordered the bateaux alongside. The soldiers scrambled down into the boats, and with the colonel sitting in the stern of the lead bateau, they pulled north. They rowed all night until they came up to within a half mile of their objective. In silence and with oars muffled as best they could, they slid into a small creek just off the river and below the fort. At dawn Arnold sent a scout forward while he and the rest waited with the boats and tried unsuccessfully to beat off attacks by hordes of gnats and mosquitoes. The scout reported all clear. The Americans moved rapidly and the garrison was taken completely unaware. The inventory of loot included fourteen prisoners, two brass field pieces and nine small boats, five of which were burned. The greatest prize of all, though, was the king's sloop, about seventy tons and mounting two six-pounders. She was taken and renamed *Enterprise*.[7] The Americans went about their business quickly, loaded their vessels, including the sloop, and with a strong northerly breeze—once their adversary, now a friend—practically flew back down the lake to Crown Point and thence to Ticonderoga. To keep control of the lake, Arnold immediately began to fix up his vessels.[8] He mounted extra carriage guns and swivels and scoured through the companies at Crown Point and Ticonderoga looking for experienced sailors, gunners and carpenters, all the while keeping up a barrage of letters to his superiors requesting more men and supplies. Benedict Arnold, a sailor turned soldier, was back in his own element and he liked it.

The quick succession of events on the lake had caught the British off guard, but within a few days they had regrouped and begun to make their own moves. Four hundred regulars advanced up the Richelieu and occupied Saint Johns. Their arrival sent rumors flying that they were only the forward guard of a much larger force poised to sweep all the way back to Ticonderoga.[9] Hearing that news, a nervous Continental Congress, acting on the basis of the most recent information rather than a deliberate weighing of evidence, resolved that the forts on the lake should be immediately abandoned and the American forces withdrawn to an east-west line anchored along the southern end of Lake George.[10] It was an outrageous decision. Arnold and Allen, for once agreeing on something, protested vehemently, while the legislatures of New York and the New England states reminded the Congress in no uncertain terms that such a precipitous withdrawal would leave their states wide open to British attack.[11] Under pressure, Congress did a complete about-face, and instead of ordering a retreat on 27 June, they resolved that Saint Johns should be retaken, along with Montreal and any other part of Canada "which may have a tendency to promote the peace and security of these Colonies."[12]

The most immediate and knottiest problem facing the

Americans, though, was not the British—that threat had been exaggerated—but rather who was to command the American forces on the lake. As so often happened in the Revolution, officers arriving on the scene had the same rank and bore commissions from different states. Who was the senior officer? Later in the war, as the command structure had a chance to develop, many of these wrinkles would be worked out, although even then the army continued to have its problems, but for the time being at Champlain and elsewhere the general policy was majority rule. Whoever brought the most troops would command.

Arnold held his commission from the Massachusetts Provincial Congress. Since Ethan Allen had been voted out of command of the Green Mountain Boys late in May, Arnold had become the *de facto* commander on the lake.[13] In the meantime, quite unbeknownst to him, Massachusetts was trying to pass the buck for Ticonderoga to Connecticut. Colonel Joseph Henshaw had been sent to Hartford to see if the Connecticut authorities would send men and supplies to the lake. If they agreed, then Henshaw was to order Arnold back to Cambridge and let the Connecticut people take charge.[14] Connecticut agreed but somehow Henshaw never got the message through to Arnold. So when Colonel Benjamin Hinman arrived with one thousand Connecticut troops and asked him to turn over command, Arnold flatly refused, whereupon he was summarily dismissed. Bested ashore, Arnold continued the farce one step further by taking *Enterprise* and *Liberty* out into the lake while he went below to his cabin and sulked. When a committee rowed out and came on board to talk with the colonel, they were forced to stand at the point of bayonets. The next day, after tempers had cooled a bit, Arnold packed his belongings, bid a rancorous good-bye and rode off to Cambridge.[15]

Major General Philip Schuyler, the newly appointed commander of the Northern Department, within whose jurisdiction Champlain lay, breathed a sigh of relief when Arnold left. He certainly had enough problems on his hands without worrying about internecine warfare within his own ranks. Schuyler was a slow, methodical and plodding man who now found himself, as a result of the congressional resolution on 27 June, responsible for leading an invasion of Canada. He ordered bateaux built so that troops could be carried up the lake, while in the meantime *Enterprise* and *Liberty* sailed north to reconnoiter.[16] By late July Schuyler had determined that Saint Johns had to be taken if the lake was to be thoroughly secured in anticipation of use as an invasion route north into Canada. Speed was essential, for intelligence sources reported that the British had moved men and supplies up the Richelieu and were working feverishly at the fort to launch two vessels, each mounting sixteen to eighteen twenty-four-pounders. Against such a powerful force the American squadron would not stand a chance. The only hope was to prevent them from ever getting onto the lake.[17]

On 6 August Schuyler informed the president of Congress that within the month he would lead his troops against Saint Johns. He had, he assured Hancock, sacrificed everything so that he could complete enough bateaux to ferry his men and supplies up the lake. This meant, of course, that every useful item down to the last nail and scrap of timber that he could lay his hands on went into the boats. He had given hardly a thought to building anything larger, and so *Enterprise* and *Liberty* remained the sole American vessels of any strength on the lake.

Philip Schuyler was a reasonably intelligent and well-meaning, wealthy New Yorker who owed his position to politics. Unfortunately for him and the American cause, he was psychologically and physically unsuited for command. Never very energetic (he was chronically ill), Schuyler seemed always in a quandary over what to do; he was the Warren Harding of the Revolution. For guidance he turned to the Congress, which was a futile exercise since they were not even sure what was going on in upstate New York and were therefore hardly in a position to give advice. He was a man in over his head, and as his health deteriorated, he became even less effective and more vacillating.

Schuyler's second in command, Brigadier General Richard Montgomery, was everything the old man was not. A born leader, tall and ramrod straight, he even looked the part. He was eager, exuberant and chomping at the bit to invade Canada. The ominous news from Saint Johns that the two British vessels were nearly finished convinced him that he could not wait for Schuyler to make up his mind, and in mid-August, while his commander was in Albany, he ordered his troops to take up a blocking position at Isle Aux Noix on the Richelieu between Saint Johns and the lake. There they would at least be able to prevent the British from getting onto the lake. On 4 September Schuyler caught up with his army but then, because of ill health, withdrew back to Ticonderoga, leaving Montgomery in charge.[18]

Montgomery did his job well. He wasted no time in gathering up his forces and quickly advanced on Saint Johns. The fort was too strong for an assault, so the Americans made camp and prepared for a lengthy siege. It was a long, dull process, and the mere fact that Montgomery could keep his ragamuffin men together is a credit to his ability. Sporadic artillery duels enlivened the camp a bit, but in general the men settled down into a tedious routine in which the main concerns were food and finding a dry place to spread a blanket. On 19 October the British post at Chambly, farther down the river toward the Saint Lawrence, fell. Saint Johns was now completely cut off and isolated, with no line of resupply. On 2 November, after holding out for a month and a half, the British commander asked for terms. The following day the entire garrison, six hundred regulars, marched out in front of the Americans and grounded their arms.[19] It was the greatest victory yet in the Revolution.

Montgomery, eager to get under way again, tarried at the fort only long enough to move the prisoners to the rear and take an inventory. It was an impressive list of loot, including the usual soldierly accouterments along with a considerable number of artillery pieces and a large quantity of naval stores, cables, sails, pitch, tar and rigging. Most exciting of all, though, was the capture of the recently finished schooner *Royal Savage*, already in the water, and a sloop still on the stocks but nearly ready for launching. The addition of these vessels doubled the strength of the American squadron on Lake Champlain. *Royal Savage*, along with any supplies Montgomery felt he did not need, was sent back to Ticonderoga while the general, at the head of his victorious army, broke camp and marched north toward Montreal.

The ordeal the Americans went through in Canada that winter of 1775–76 belongs to the annals of military rather than naval history, but a brief sketch is necessary in order to understand what happened on Champlain afterward. Montgomery easily reached Montreal, and the city fell without resistance on 13 November. Meanwhile to the east another American force, under the command of Benedict Arnold, was tearing its way through the rugged Maine wilderness in an effort to reach Quebec.[20] The two forces, Montgomery from the south and Arnold from the east, planned to meet at the gates of Quebec and reduce that fortress to American control. The operation was marked by a bold but misguided strategy. Just getting through the forests and swamps of Maine proved to be an arduous task, and so by the time his force reached Point Levis, opposite Quebec City, on 9 November, Arnold could muster only 675 men, about half the number of men he had left Cambridge with two months before.[21] Quite wisely he decided not to assault; even with ten times the number of men he had, going up against an eagle's nest like Quebec would have been suicide. He stayed beyond cannon range and made camp within sight of the town on the Plains of Abraham. Behind their thick stone walls the British, under the command of the extraordinarily able Guy Carleton, settled down in relative comfort, secure in the knowledge that all they had to do was wait out the spring, when a relief force was sure to arrive.

On 2 December Montgomery came down from Montreal.

He brought with him only three hundred men. That was a disappointment, but as partial recompense he did deliver a large quantity of artillery and heavy clothing, which was well received by men whose tents, lean-tos and tattered clothing were being put to the test by a biting arctic wind. As the days shortened and the weather turned to a wintery hell, the besiegers suffered far more than the besieged. American enlistments would run out at the end of the month, but with the prospects so dismal and gloomy men were already leaving, and each morning report showed more gone and fewer fit for service. As Arnold watched his army fading away, he knew that by the first of the year he might well be standing outside the walls alone. The only hope was a quick assault. Since a frontal attack on Quebec with fewer than a thousand men was sheer suicide, Arnold and Montgomery decided that the best, indeed the only, hope was a night attack launched first at the old town at the foot of the fortress and then up and over the steep cliffs through the gates and into the upper town. In the predawn hours of 31 December, during a fierce blizzard that they hoped would mask their movements, Arnold and Montgomery moved the army into position. It was an American calamity, and before it was over, Arnold lay with a ball in his leg, Montgomery was dead and the army was in despair.[22]

After the repulse, the siege went on and the Americans even managed to increase their numbers to about two thousand. Nevertheless, from the American standpoint the situation was hopeless. It was an open secret that as soon as the ice left the Saint Lawrence, the British would come up in force with men and ships to deliver the city. On 1 May Major General John Thomas arrived from Massachusetts to take command. Arnold had been promoted to brigadier general and evacuated to Montreal. Five days after taking command Thomas heard the inevitable; a British fleet had been sighted coming toward Quebec. He now had to lead a defeated and demoralized army in retreat. He tried, but the army, harassed by Carleton and decimated by smallpox, quickly became a mob running for their lives. Thomas reached Montreal but within a month he was dead from smallpox.[23] The "retreat" did not stop at Montreal. General John Sullivan from New Hampshire took over from Thomas, and he ordered Arnold to take command of the rear guard while the army tried to get itself together and move south in an orderly fashion. The two of them together halted the mob and turned it back into an army.

Despite the precarious and vulnerable position of the Americans, Carleton showed no desire to strike for the jugular. The opening of the Saint Lawrence had brought him thousands of troops, and among them was the erstwhile playwright and colonel of the Queen's Dragoons, General John Burgoyne. By quick action Carleton could have captured or destroyed most of the American army, but he deliberately choose a more cautious course that allowed Sullivan and Arnold time to escape.[24]

As of mid-June Saint Johns was the only important post still in American hands, and even it was in imminent danger. On the ninth Arnold and his rear guard arrived at the fort and found everything "in the greatest confusion."[25] The engineer who was supposed to be digging fortifications was a "perfect sot," and not a spade of earth had been turned. With such a poor position in the face of so powerful an enemy, Arnold had no choice but to order evacuation. He sent his carpenters over to the nearby shipyard to number the timbers of the vessel still in frame so that she could be dismantled and shipped off for reassembly elsewhere. Bateaux were brought up, and while the healthy stood guard, sick and wounded soldiers were loaded aboard to be taken down to Crown Point. Almost as the redcoats were breaking through the woods, the last boat load got off, fell down to the Isle Aux Noix and thence across the lake to Crown Point.[26]

It had been a costly invasion. Five thousand American soldiers had been left behind in Canada as either casualties or prisoners. Of those who got away, fully three thousand were wounded or sick and unfit for service. The remainder of the army, perhaps five thousand men, were ragged, whipped and demoralized.[27] From Crown Point the view was not a pleasant one. Between the Americans and Carleton were a hundred miles of open lake down which the British would have to come if they intended to move south. For the time being all that stood between the two armies, one eaten up by disease and defeat, the other carrying the momentum of victory, were three small schooners, *Liberty, Enterprise* and *Royal Savage*. These vessels and their commodore, Jacobus Wynkoop, held sway on the lake, but how long they could maintain that supremacy was an open question.[28] It depended upon how quickly the British could put together a squadron and how effectively the Americans responded.

Schuyler just did not seem to know what to do. As early as October 1775, when things were going well for his army, he had asked Congress if they wanted him to prepare timber for ship construction on the lake. If they did, he would have to see to the cutting of roads immediately so that when the ground froze, his men would be ready to fell the trees and drag them down to the water. The severe winter in northern New York made it impossible for shipwrights to work outside, but the ice and hard ground made an ideal surface to move bulky timber over. If they moved quickly, enough timber could be stockpiled so that as soon as the weather broke in the spring, the shipwrights could get to work.[29] Congress responded to the general's request in their usual fashion; they appointed a committee to visit the area and make a determination. More time was wasted and not a single mention made about the urgency of building craft for lake service.[30]

Winter came early in 1775, and before mid-November the ground was covered with snow, and ice was forming on the lake. Schuyler ordered sleds built to lug timber and, if need be, to carry cannon and supplies north for Montgomery. On 28 November the congressional committee arrived to give what assistance they could—mostly advice and second guessing.

As the weather worsened, Schuyler's problems multiplied,

especially the logistical ones. It was up to him to get arms, food and clothing from the rear areas in New York and New England up to the front lines in Canada. The usual route was up the Hudson as far as Fort Edward, from there over to Wood Creek by portage, then down to Skenesborough and out onto the lake. The overland portion was the most difficult part of the trip. Between Fort Edward and Wood Creek there were forests, swamps and a narrow, usually muddy path that some called a road. At almost any point along the line there could be trouble and there usually was.

Through the winter Schuyler limped along forwarding supplies as best and as fast as he was able. Timber was also collected for the construction of bateaux. Whatever thought had been given to the building of larger vessels for the lake service had to be shunted aside for the moment since the immediate need was to provide boats to get men and supplies up north. Schuyler asked Congress, the state and anyone else who would listen to send him carpenters, shipwrights and sailors, along with oakum, sails and every other naval item that he did not have. By mid-April the ice was nearly gone, and yards at Skenesborough and Ticonderoga were turning out bateaux, made of green wood and very leaky, at the rate of four per day. From a short-term tactical point it is hard to fault Schuyler for allocating all his resources to bateau building; after all, without them there could be no invasion or retreat across the lake. Nevertheless, his devotion to them at the expense of larger vessels was a strategic error for which the Americans would eventually pay dearly. Once they had done their job of ferrying men and supplies, the bateaux were just so many oversized, unarmed rowboats. In the face of an enemy armed with anything heavier than a musket, they would be matchsticks in a matter of minutes. To defend the lake the Americans needed a well-organized flotilla made up of sizable vessels.

Schuyler had a vague inkling of the problem but little appreciation of its immediacy and magnitude. Not until late

January did he get around to asking the Congress for a naval commander on the lake. His choice for the job was Major William Douglass, a Connecticut officer who had served on the lake under Montgomery but had then come back and was now somewhere in the vicinity of Albany. Schuyler suggested his old friend Jacobus Wynkoop, a crusty and stubborn Dutchman from Albany, as second in command.[31] Congress agreed but left it up to the New York Provincial Congress to find and notify Douglass and Wynkoop.

One was bad and the other was worse. When notified by the provincial congress, Douglass hemmed, hawed and dodged. Wynkoop, on the instructions of the provincial congress, even went personally to Douglass in March to solicit some kind of firm answer. Douglass told Wynkoop he might accept but only if his health permitted and in any case he could not get to it for at least two months.[32] Annoyed by Douglass's cavalier and evasive attitude, the provincial congress tried to lay it on the line so they could get a straight yes or no answer. The men in New York were edgy; after all, it would not be long before the weather turned warm and the lake would be open for navigation. Unless someone grabbed the tiller and moved quickly to fit the vessels and recruit sailors, the Americans would be in a very tenuous position should the British move south. For whatever the reason, probably because he was dickering for a better command, Douglass just sat on his hands. Wynkoop, a man who was most often full of himself, always thought that the command should have been his anyway. He watched Douglass's antics with nothing but contempt, and finally in an angry tone he told the provincial congress that he was not going to serve under anyone as casual and indolent as William Douglass. The men in New York could wait no longer. They told Wynkoop to take charge, recruit sailors and report to General Schuyler.[33] Douglass made no protest about being pushed aside, and a short time later he was appointed to command a Connecticut battalion. It was apparently the post he had been waiting for, and in contrast to his previous conduct he moved quickly to accept it, but his twiddling had cost the Americans two months of precious time.

Wynkoop, the brevet commodore, wasted no time in getting started. He gathered a group of sailors, mostly men from the Hudson River trade, and marched north to Ticonderoga, where, according to Schuyler's orders, he was to put the vessels into "the best Condition possible for immediate service."[34] If anyone still considered Douglass to be the commodore and Wynkoop simply a fill-in, the Dutchman took pains to let his superiors know how he felt on that score. He told Schuyler and anyone else who inquired that he would be commodore or he would not serve. At the head of his company of sailors Wynkoop left Albany and headed upriver and across the portage to Fort George, at the southern tip of Lake George. There he and his men saw a whirlwind of activity as carpenters, shipwrights and caulkers were working feverishly to finish dozens of bateaux needed to carry men and supplies up the lake to Ticonderoga. They took passage on some of the new bateaux to the head of Lake George, and finally after a short portage they arrived at Ticonderoga on 10 May. At the fort Wynkoop surveyed his tiny squadron and found that they had come through the winter in pretty good shape. After the usual scraping, painting, caulking and some rerigging aloft, they were ready by the end of the month to begin cruising on the lake.

With the question of command on the lake settled at least for the moment, Philip Schuyler could now turn his thoughts to the immensely difficult problem of logistics. Although the distances were not great, the terrain, consisting of forests and swamps, and the bulky nature of the supplies made transport tremendously difficult. Items such as nails, oakum, lead and gunpowder were very heavy, and moving them in awkward hogsheads over mushy ground and in crude, sluggish wagons was a labor worthy of Hercules. As if Schuyler did not have enough problems just finding and moving the goods, the Continental Congress ordered him to begin a system of internal improvements to smooth the flow of troops and supplies north:

> Resolved—That General Schuyler be directed to make a good waggon road from Fort Edward to Cheshire's; to clear Wood creek, and to construct a lock at Skenesborough, so as to have a continued navigation for batteaus from Cheshire's into Lake Champlain; . . . to order skilful persons to survey and take the level of the waters falling into Hudson's river near Fort Edward, and those which fall into Wood creek and interlock with the former.[35]

Congress also indicated to the general that he ought to build armed vessels for the lake. The best place to do that was down at Skenesborough, where in the years before the war Philip Skene had operated a small sawmill and yard. The apparatus and buildings were still there, although they were in need of some repair. Schuyler ordered the facility brought into good working order so that the construction of armed boats could begin as soon as possible. Specifically, what Schuyler had in mind was the building of gundalows (sometimes referred to as gondolas) and galleys.

Gundalows were small vessels, fifty to sixty feet on the keel, with open flush deck, flat bottom and shoal draft. They were a common sight on rivers and were most often used to transport bulky deck cargoes such as lumber and grain. They had only one mast, stepped amidship with a single square sail. When armed, they generally carried a heavy gun in the bow and a couple of smaller pieces of ordnance in the waist. As sailers they left a lot to be desired. Their shoal draft made them difficult to handle, and in an opposing current or the slightest head wind they had to depend on sweeps. But if shoal draft was a disadvantage out on the open lake, it was an operational advantage closer to shore and in among the islands of Champlain. This advantage and the belief that gundalows could be built quickly with a minimum of expertise

(187)

encouraged Schuyler and the Congress to depend on them.[36]

The second type of vessel Schuyler ordered laid down at Skenesborough was the galley. Galleys were about half again as large as gundalows and carried more ordnance of a lighter caliber and a crew of eighty men. They had two masts, a fore and a main, both lateen rigged. Unlike the gundalows, they had a round bottom, which meant they took more water but sailed better, and a raised quarterdeck. Along the bulwarks they were pierced for anywhere from ten to twelve guns.[37]

Schuyler's decision to opt for small, relatively easy to build boats was made necessary, he thought, by the press of time, the scarcity of trained men and inadequate stores. It would have been a serious gamble for him if he had ventured to build larger vessels, and Major General Philip Schuyler was a man who never took more risks than absolutely necessary. By the time other men with more experience and different ideas arrived, it was too late and the American naval force on Champlain was irrevocably committed to a dependence on small craft. From one point of view small craft were an advantage; their shallow draft and light displacement made it easy to maneuver them with sweeps whenever the wind failed or came from the wrong direction. In combat, though, where it really counted, the Americans came up short, for no matter how many additions they made, their fleet was still just a collection of puny boats. What counted was not the number of boats but the weight of the metal being thrown and the skill of those doing the throwing.

Skenesborough began to hum with activity. The general himself went to the site so that he could set the men to work and get a firsthand view of the operation.[38] His personal secretary, Captain Richard Varick, was sent out to scour the countryside and try to beg, borrow or steal everything from nails to sails. Schuyler, an old man being run ragged with problems, had been only a few days at Skenesborough when he heard distressing news from another part of his command. The Tories living along the Mohawk River west of Albany were arming and threatening the peace. Unless the general moved quickly with a show of force to bridle them, he could well end up with his entire rear area in disarray. In some haste Schuyler left Skenesborough and headed back to Albany.

The work at the yard proceeded at a crawl. It took nearly three weeks to get the first gundalow into the water, and despite Schuyler's pushing, there was no sign that the pace would pick up very much. Workmen, especially those who knew anything about galleys or gundalows, were in short supply. An appeal for assistance was sent down to General Washington in New York City but he had his own pressing needs and was husbanding all the men and talent he could find. Farther up the river at Poughkeepsie there were trained men and a fair amount of naval stores, but they were pledged to the frigates building there and for the time being could not be spared.[39]

New Hampshire, Massachusetts, Connecticut and Rhode Island had shipwrights and carpenters, but many of them were busy with Continental ships and privateers. Despite the difficulties, skilled men had to be recruited if the lake was to be held. But how could men be persuaded to sacrifice the comforts and security of home to journey more than one hundred miles inland to a remote and isolated spot where they were expected to build a navy?

The universal recruiter and most effective enticement available was proffered—money. The Marine Committee of the Congress was instructed to offer thirty-four and two-thirds dollars per month for shipwrights who would go to Champlain. In addition the shipwrights were to be given one month's pay in advance; receive one and one-half rations per day, including a half pint of rum; two-thirds of their pay could go to anyone they designated; for every twenty miles of travel they received one day's pay; and finally all this would commence as soon as they left home. It was a generous offer and meant that shipwrights on Champlain were more highly paid than anywhere else in America; in fact, aside from Esek Hopkins, they were paid more than any enlisted man or officer in the entire Continental navy.

The allurement worked, and men from New England, New York and as far away as Pennsylvania began arriving to lend a hand. They were broken into gangs of twenty-five men, each responsible for the building of a single vessel.[40] Toward the end of July there were probably as many as three to five hundred men living and working at Skenesborough. The village was crammed with carpenters, shipwrights, woodsmen, soldiers and sailors, and just keeping order became a heavy task in itself as this backwater community began to look and behave like a frontier logging camp. To his credit Schuyler had anticipated some of these problems and had given rather detailed orders on how the yard was to be run. The commander at Skenesborough, Colonel Hermanus Schuyler, the former assistant deputy commissary general of the Northern Department, was told:

> Take a list of all the people employed under your Direction, distinguishing the Carpenters from the Ax-men, and those from the Teamsters, and discharge such as may be unfit for Service either by Disease Drunkenness or Laziness, and keep an exact Cheque Book, and call over the Names of every person at Sunrise before they got to Work.
>
> You must provide a Master Sawyer for the Mill & the sawing must go on by Night as well as by Day and that the Sawyers may not play Tricks count the Logs on the Log-Way at Sunset, and again at Sunrise in the Morning and then you will be able to know if the Sawyers have done their duty.[41]

A company of fifty men arrived from Philadelphia under the command of Captain Thomas Casdrop, who brought with him not only some experienced men but also an interesting idea. For several months he had been busy down on the Delaware with similar kinds of small boats and had come to the conclusion that gundalows should be armed with a heavy gun amidships mounted on a movable skid so that it could be brought to bear in any direction without having to bring the boat around.[42] It was an idea that might have proved useful, but Schuyler did not show the least interest and nothing more was heard of it.

Any improvement that might have been made in the American position on the lake because of the activity at Skenesborough was overshadowed by the rapidly deteriorating military situation. For the army things were bad and growing worse. The invasion force, or what was left of it, had retired to Crown Point, but this post was in such a decrepit condition and the men were so sick and weak that a council of war was already pondering evacuation. On the lake Wynkoop and his squadron had become something of a joke. The schooners were at Ticonderoga most of the time waiting for work to be done, while the sloop had shown herself to be such a poor sailer that she could not even get clear of the dock unless an almost perfect wind was blowing. About once every two weeks the bare shell of a gundalow arrived from Skenesborough to be fitted out and armed. The production rate was slow, less than half of what General Schuyler had promised, but it really did not matter because when the gundalows arrived at the fort there were no guns or rigging for them.

It was a wretched and precarious situation. From the north reports were filtering in that the British were busy at Saint Johns building a fleet and gathering an army. It was the eleventh hour and the Americans seemed to be foundering. What they needed even more than sails and guns was leadership.

Chapter Ten

Valcour Island

It was a glum Congress that kept hearing reports of death, defeat, disease and retreat from the Northern Department. The New England delegates, who had never liked Schuyler anyway because he was a Yorker, were now even more eager for the general's removal.[1] That they could not get, but they did manage to persuade a majority of their fellow members at least to appoint a new commander for the army in Canada. The choice was Horatio Gates.[2]

Gates was the son of the duke of Leeds's housekeeper, and via that upstairs connection he grew to know and covet the good life. He never did quite rise to the social heights he thought he deserved, but that did not stop him from becoming a "ruddy-faced . . . snob . . . with a repellant personality."[3] He entered the British army, and through a combination of competence and device, he rose rapidly through the ranks and retired as a major in 1765. After leaving the army, he settled in America, and in 1772, with the help of his neighbor and friend George Washington, he bought some land and took up the life of a gentleman farmer in Virginia. When the war came, Gates, sensing his destiny, took sides with the rebels and followed Washington to become the commander in chief's adjutant general.[4] He performed well in that job, and with the support of his chief and others, especially the New Englanders, he was posted to Canada.

According to Congress, he was replacing the late General Thomas as commander of the American army in Canada, but by the time he arrived in Albany, the army was no longer in Canada and it was an open question of just what General Gates commanded. He apparently held to the belief that Congress's charge entitled him to all of Schuyler's command. That was an assumption not shared by the New York general, and within a few days of his arrival Gates had his first row with Schuyler.[5] The issue was a picayune one and not even worth recounting, but it sparked a roaring battle between the two generals over who was in charge. Only Congress could answer that, and on 8 July they decided in favor of Schuyler. Lest Gates be too offended, they told him of their high regard for his "Resolution and Magnanimity" and assured him that it was their fervent hope that he would remain in the Northern Department to assist Schuyler and cultivate "harmony."[6]

In the meantime, while the two generals were savaging each other, matters had grown worse on the lake. On 7 July a council of war was held at Crown Point. Since the precipitous withdrawal from Canada, Crown Point was the most northerly position still in American hands, and the question to be decided at the council was whether to hold on or withdraw to a more southerly line at Ticonderoga. Schuyler presided, and joining him were Gates, Benedict Arnold, John Sullivan and Frederick William, Baron de Woedtke, a young Prussian officer in the American service.[7] After surveying the situation—a decaying fortress defended by a pathetic army—the council decided that Crown Point had to be abandoned and the troops withdrawn to a more defensible line anchored by Ticonderoga.[8] The abandonment of Crown Point left only a fragile wooden barrier of small vessels between Ticonderoga and the British. If they did not hold them, all was lost, for it was common knowledge that the army encamped at the fort was in such a wretched and edgy condition that the mere

sight of scarlet uniforms would send them into headlong retreat.

The council realized the peril, and to quash any rumors
that by giving up Crown Point they intended to give up the
lake, they further resolved at their meeting to take "Effectual
Measures" for securing Champlain by building more "Gun-
dolas, Row Gallies, [and] Armed Batteaus." Of all the general
officers present, the only one with any experience on the
water was Arnold, and he let that fact be known. Gates had
faith in him, and he was by far the most logical choice for the
assignment. For nearly two weeks after the conference Arnold stayed at Crown Point, but then at Gates's urging he
came down to Ticonderoga to take on closer supervision of
naval preparations. Officially he was just a brigade commander, but Gates left no doubt about where he expected his
brigadier to devote his time. Wynkoop, according to Gates,
had failed both as a commander (he had barely gotten his
boats past the dock) and as a builder (the shipwrights were a
lazy lot and in his fecklessness the old Dutchman had not
bothered to push them).[9] Gates hoped that an infusion of
Arnold's skill and energy would get the shipwrights moving.
Indeed, under Wynkoop the fleet had actually grown weaker
because he had allowed guns to be removed from the schooners so that they had become nothing more than "Floating
Waggons." As for the gundalows and galleys for which so
much had been promised, only a very few of them were off
the stocks, and those that were had yet to be fully rigged and
armed.[10]

Arnold blew into Ticonderoga like a gale, stirred up the
men there and then he went off down to Skenesborough,
arriving on the twenty-third. The heat of this place alone was
enough to discourage him. Sunk down between the hills amid
a fetid marsh, in the hot July sun Skenesborough had turned
into an "ante-room of hell." Under the circumstances the
shipwrights and carpenters were doing their best, but there
were just too few of them, too much heat and too much to do.
Arnold stayed only a few days, long enough to give some

direction on how he wanted the gundalows and galleys built, and then he shuttled back to Ticonderoga.

All the galleys, gundalows, sloops and schooners in the world would not be able to hold Champlain if somehow Arnold could not find able men to man them. He went through the ranks of the northern army searching for men who could hand, reef and steer, but all who would step forward were a paltry seventy. There were more, many more, who were experienced sailors, but they held back, knowing that service on the lake was bound to be dangerous and no matter how uncomfortable they were at Ticonderoga they were a lot better off behind stone walls than sailing on the open lake aboard some leaky makeshift craft. The pickings on the lake were so poor that there was not even an offer of prize money, and the only reward for those who signed up was the usual monthly pay.[11] Washington was approached and asked if he would lend some men, but with General Howe breathing down his neck, he was short himself and could not spare a soul.[12] Later toward the end of August he did relent a bit and allowed some recruiting for the lake out of a recently arrived Connecticut regiment.[13] Nevertheless, seamen were scarce up north, and when the American fleet finally put out onto the lake, they went manned by a lot of green hands who were treading a deck for the first time in their lives.

Arnold went roaring about Ticonderoga scrutinizing every detail on his vessels: stepping the masts, securing ballast, bending sails, placing the guns and a dozen other key operations. By early August, thanks to his efforts and those of the men he drove, the Americans had two schooners, a sloop and four gundalows on the lake and standing by at Crown Point awaiting orders.

Although Arnold was pleased that the work at Skenesborough and Ticonderoga was proceeding, there were other things that troubled him. For example, he knew very little about what was going on at the other end of the lake. He was a blind man rushing headlong to meet an enemy about whom he knew very little. In this case ignorance was probably a blessing, for if he and more likely the men under him had known what Herculean efforts were going on at Saint Johns, they might have become so discouraged as to retreat before the battle even began.

Unlike Philip Schuyler, Guy Carleton had from the very start cast a keen eye on Champlain and recognized the strategic importance of having a fleet on that lake. It was the key to controlling the entire northern sector, and as early as July 1775, even as he was withdrawing under American pressure toward Quebec, Carleton was writing to Admiral Graves in Boston asking for shipwrights and seamen so that he could immediately begin work preparing a fleet to regain control of the lake and "drive out the Rebels."[14]

Carleton was by no means alone in his concern for the lake, and all during the winter naval and military staffs in England were busy formulating plans for campaign 1776, plans that included a counterattack and invasion into New York via Champlain. The operation would require building a fleet on the lake, and that was exactly what the ministry planned. From their dockyard stores the Admiralty drew enough materials to build two sloops and bateaux. There was no need to requisition timber and planking since that was available in Canada, but everything else had to be shipped across. About a dozen gunboats, each thirty-seven feet on the keel, twelve feet on the beam, open decked and rigged with a lug sail, were built and then "knocked down" and stowed aboard transports bound for Quebec.[15] The British lacked for nothing, and tons of matériel were loaded aboard transports ready to sail with the relief fleet. Time was their chief enemy, and the Admiralty had to move quickly. Unless Canada was retaken in time to launch the invasion, that is, before the cold weather set in, everything would be delayed at least a year. Such a delay would bring with it a slew of military and political complications that the ministry preferred not to contemplate.

In order to check the situation on the Saint Lawrence, the Admiralty decided to send out an advance guard to be sure that their fleet, when it finally did advance up the river, would not run across an American force. They gave the mission to Charles Douglas, captain of H.M.S. *Isis*. Douglas sailed in mid-February, *Isis*'s hold crammed with extra guns and supplies and the forecastle filled to overflowing with two companies of troops being sent as reinforcements.[16] Accompanying him were the frigate *Surprise* and the sloop *Martin*. Close on, following only a few days behind, was a small convoy of transports under the escort of Captain Skiffington Lutwidge aboard the sloop *Triton*.

A winter crossing of the North Atlantic is a cold, wet and dangerous affair. Douglas, Lutwidge and the rest were lucky to make it without any loss. When they finally reached the Gulf of Saint Lawrence in early April, they found an awesome sight to greet them—a huge and seemingly endless ice floe. For days *Isis* lay trapped in a frozen vise. Slowly the ice began to break up, and *Isis* could move again. Having escaped being crushed like an egg, she now faced another threat; ice floes were coming at her. Men were sent over the side to fix fenders to protect the hull, while others were stationed up forward and along the side with pikes and boat hooks to try to deflect hunks of ice as best they could. Douglas all the while was gingerly moving his ship up the river toward Quebec. On 6 May *Isis*, *Surprise* and *Martin*, after three weeks of dodging river ice, dropped anchor in safe water off Quebec City. From the fortress Carleton saluted them, and two days later they were joined by *Triton* and her convoy of five.

The city was saved. The Americans, hearing of Douglas's arrival, had beat a hasty retreat two days earlier. The river below the city was spotted with ships; some, which had spent the winter there, were busy repairing leaking hulls and tattered rigging. Others, like *Isis* and her companions, were unloading stores and preparing to give chase to the enemy.[17] Douglas, since he was the senior naval officer present, fell heir to the command of the whole river, and he hoisted the commodore's pennant aboard *Isis*.[18]

The new commodore, Charles Douglas, was the kind of

naval officer whom contemporaries referred to as one of "Fortune's favorites." He was the seventh son of an earl whose fecundity guaranteed that Charles would never inherit either the title or the fortune. But his name alone guaranteed a position almost anywhere, and the young Douglas choose to cast his lot with the Royal Navy. He entered the service in 1746 and thereafter had his ticket punched in a series of posts as he steadily climbed up the command ladder. Blood lines and connections alone would probably have ensured Douglas of flag rank someday, but happily he was one of those rare individuals in whom genealogy and competence were combined. Over the next few months he displayed imagination, organization and a considerable talent for selecting men who could get jobs done. On top of those accomplishments he exhibited one of the rarest gifts of all for an eighteenth-century naval officer—an ability to get along with generals. When the Canadian campaign of 1776 came to a close, the reputation of Charles Douglas shone like a beacon, and for his conspicuous conduct in June 1777 he was named a baronet.[19]

Douglas stepped quickly to his business. He lightened his frigates as much as possible so that he could send them upriver in pursuit of the retreating Americans. At Quebec City the schooner *Maria*, which the invaders had been using on the river, was retaken and put under the command of Lieutenant John Starke. Mounted with six six-pounders and manned with seamen from *Lizard*, one of the ships in the river, she became Carleton's flagship and he went aboard to pursue his quarry up the river.[20] Accompanying *Maria* was another rebel prize, the schooner *Brunswick*, under the command of a young naval lieutenant, Edward Longcroft. She was manned and victualed entirely from *Isis*. They carried the general as far as Chambly at the foot of the rapids, but that was the end of the line; no vessel of any draft could make it through the white water. Twelve miles of shallow and rock-strewn water lay between Chambly and Saint Johns. Carleton, of course, pushed ahead on land with his army, but when they reached Saint Johns, they had gone as far as they could go without a fleet. It was up to Douglas and the Royal Navy to overcome this obstacle.

Two alternatives were possible. The first was simply to do, only better, what the Americans were doing down at Skenesborough and Ticonderoga—build a fleet of small boats from scratch. The second and more daring course was somehow to bridge the land barrier behind them and bring ships from the Saint Lawrence to Saint Johns.

The first choice was really a trap, and Charles Douglas was astute enough to recognize and avoid it. Building a whole new fleet would take months, and he had to be ready to sail by the end of summer. And more importantly he knew, even if the Americans did not, that whatever the multiplication of small boats, they could never be a match for a few large ones. He needed big ships and he needed them quickly. Douglas decided, in consultation with his officers and Carleton, that they would indeed build vessels at Saint Johns but at the same time they would transport warships across the portage.

The first two candidates for the trip were the schooners *Maria* and *Carleton*, the latter apparently having been brought over in pieces for just this purpose from a dockyard in England. A quick survey of the Richelieu convinced the British that it was impossible to float the vessels by. Even if they were stripped bare and lashed with camels (airtight containers such as barrels attached to provide added buoyancy), they would still draw too much water. The only way was to haul them out of the water and cart them overland.

Afloat, the two schooners were graceful and quick, but out of the water they looked and behaved like great beached whales, ponderous, awkward, and practically immobile. *Maria* was hauled out first. Her captain, John Starke, saw to it that she was stripped of everything possible: masts, rigging, guns, furniture, ballast and stores. Block and tackle were rigged, and slowly she edged her way up from the water as men and animals tugged on the lines. As she moved onto the road, other men walked ahead, placing rollers under the keel to ease the passage. As long as the weather was dry, everything went well, but as soon as the first shower hit, the road turned into muck and men were slipping and sliding in the mud. Under those conditions *Maria*, despite her nakedness, was still too heavy, so Starke ordered her planking taken down to the beams' ends. That seemed to do it, and once again men, sweating and swearing in the hot August sun, singing some melancholy chantey, heaved on the lines as the schooner made her way down the road and toward deep water. *Carleton* came over in the same fashion, and so too did a captured gundalow, *Loyal Convert*, along with twenty gunboats, although their much smaller size made the journey easier.

The biggest ship came last: *Inflexible*. She was a 180-ton vessel that had been on the stocks at Quebec. Carleton asked Douglas if she could be brought over too. The ship was twice the size of the schooners, but fortunately she was still in frame and only a few strakes of planking had been put in place. Douglas thought it could be done, and he sent for one of his best men to do the job—Lieutenant John Schank, captain of the armed ship *Canceaux*.

Schank had a reputation not only as a good naval officer but also as a clever mechanic. In some spare moments before the war he had invented a rig with a series of pulleys that allowed him to raise or lower his cot without getting up. For that, the men in the fleet had nicknamed him "Old Purchase."[21]

Schank sent *Canceaux*'s carpenter over to the yard where *Inflexible* stood and told him to break her down into pieces, number them so they could be quickly reassembled and then hoist them into longboats for the trip to Chambly and thence overland to Saint Johns. While that was going on, Schank himself took *Canceaux* to Chambly, where everything aboard her, including the crew, was transferred to Saint Johns for duty with *Inflexible*. Schank was appointed to command the ship, but until she was ready, he was to remain at Saint Johns as superintendent of the yard. It was up to him and his very able assistant, Lieutenant William Twiss of the Royal Engineers, to get everything ready for the coming battle.[22] All during the summer and even into early fall the farmers along the Saint Lawrence from Quebec to Chambly could stand in their fields and look out across the valley to watch strings of longboats rowed gracefully up the river carrying men, supplies and pieces of the "jigsaw navy."

At the yard in Saint Johns Schank and Twiss were going straight out, stopping only long enough to get a few hours' sleep when it was too dark for anything else. Unlike the Americans at the other end of the lake, Schank had an abundance of skilled labor and naval supplies. Hundreds of carpenters, riggers, sail makers and caulkers had been sent down, along with most of the sailors from the ships still up in the Saint Lawrence. Schank had everything he needed except time. As he moved about the yard watching the construction and assembly of the boats, Schank got an idea. Lake service demanded shallow-draft vessels, but building to that specification meant sacrificing weatherliness. His solution was a centerboard, a device that could be raised or lowered from the keel according to the depth of the water and the direction of the wind. It was a good idea—one very common in modern sailboats—but at the time it was new, and whether British, American or any other nationality, sailors are a conservative bunch and the response to his suggestion was similar to the one Casdrop got in Skenesborough when he talked about a pivoting gun skid. It ranged from outright hostility to "ho-hum."[23]

About mid-August *Maria* was back in the water, and by the end of the month *Carleton*, *Loyal Convert* and most of the gunboats had joined her. *Inflexible* took longer. Her keel was laid at Saint Johns on 7 September. So that she would draw less water than originally planned, Schank ordered her lengthened eight or nine feet. All of this, of course, took time, but within the remarkable space of only twenty-eight days *Inflexible*, 180 plus tons, mounting eighteen guns, was in the water and ready for service. She went in on 4 October, and Commodore Douglas was there to watch "with unspeakable joy" as the lake squadron, armed and manned, prepared to sortie out.[24]

Lieutenant Thomas Pringle, lately of the armed ship *Lord Howe,* was given command of the squadron. As it sailed, the squadron consisted of four reassembled "knock-downs": the schooners *Maria,* mounting fourteen six-pounders, commanded by Lieutenant John Starke, and *Carleton,* with twelve six-pounders, under Lieutenant James Dacres; the ship *Inflexible,* mounting eighteen twelve-pounders; and the gundalow *Loyal Convert,* with seven nine-pounders, under Lieutenant Edward Longcroft. Accompanying these four was the one major vessel built entirely at Saint Johns, the radeau *Thunderer,* carrying a hefty armament of six twenty-four-pounders, six twelves and two howitzers.* Following along behind and on the flanks of the squadron were twenty gunboats, each with a brass field piece and some with howitzers, four longboats with carriage guns and twenty-four unarmed longboats laden with provisions.[25]

By every measure Douglas and his men had accomplished one of the epic feats of the Revolution. They had built, armed and manned a fleet in less than ninety days. Pringle hoisted his flag aboard *Maria* where General Carleton joined him, and on 4 October they left Saint Johns and stood down toward Isle la Motte.

At the other end of the lake things had not gone quite so well. It was not so much that the commanders were not competent; certainly Arnold was as good an officer as Douglas or Pringle, if not better. Rather, it was a woeful tale of no supplies and too few men. Arnold was his usual self, poking his nose everywhere, questioning, ordering and criticizing. It did not seem to bother him that his authority to do all this was at best vague and at worst nonexistent; after all, he was only a brigade commander, not the commodore of the lake. But his

---

*Radeaus were large, flat-bottomed sailing scows that could carry a number of different types of rigs: schooner, brig, sloop and so forth. *Thunderer* was ship rigged. Generally this type of vessel was acceptable in smooth water with a favorable breeze, but it could make almost no headway to windward and had to be moved by sweeps. *Thunderer* was an unusually large radeau.

compulsive nature would not let him sit idly by when something needed to be done that he thought he could do. Inevitably, of course, his enthusiasm and aggressiveness were going to put him on a collision course with that proud, aging and incompetent Dutchman, Jacobus Wynkoop.

Wynkoop might have been Schuyler's friend, but that counted for little as far as Gates and Arnold were concerned, and they looked upon the commodore as just another navigational obstacle on the lake. On 7 August Gates told Arnold to go down to Crown Point and take command of all American vessels on the lake.[26] Arnold arrived to take over his new command on 15 August, and within forty-eight hours he and Wynkoop were at loggerheads. Wynkoop had been appointed by Schuyler, and he flatly refused to recognize anyone sent to replace him unless he had been sent by the same or higher authority.[27] Perhaps Wynkoop was right, but under the circumstances he should have had enough sense to give way. He did not. On the afternoon of 17 August Arnold sent two schooners out of Crown Point and down the lake to cover the withdrawal of a party of oar makers who were along the shore cutting wood and in danger of being cut off by advance parties of Canadians and Indians. The schooners had barely cleared their moorings when Wynkoop, aboard *Royal Savage*, fired a shot across their bows and ordered them to come to. Then he demanded to know by what authority they were sailing.[28] Their response that they were under General Arnold's orders neither pleased nor satisfied Wynkoop. Arnold finally managed to bring Wynkoop to heel, but not before he reported the incident to Gates. Gates was furious. He sent Wynkoop packing off to Albany and forwarded Schuyler a stinging letter asking that the ex-commodore be immediately cashiered. Wynkoop did not really deserve that; even Arnold had said that Wynkoop repented his action. For Schuyler it was enough to just get him out of sight. He kept him off the lakes and gave him a billet at Ticonderoga.[29] No one else challenged Arnold's authority, and with Wynkoop out of the way the general had undisputed command of the fleet.

By the end of August the force at Crown Point consisted of the schooners *Royal Savage*, mounting four six-pounders and eight four-pounders, commanded by Captain David Hawley, a Connecticut officer, and *Revenge*, with four four-pounders and four two-pounders, under Captain Seaman. The sloop *Enterprise*, mounting twelve four-pounders, under Captain Dickson (or Dickinson), was also there, while a fourth vessel, the schooner *Liberty*, mounting four four-pounders and four two-pounders, commanded by Captain Premiere, was on the lake but not at Crown Point. Of the four only *Revenge* had been built by the Americans; the others had all been captured. Moored with them were seven Skenesborough gundalows, *Boston*, *New Haven*, *Providence*, *New York*, *Connecticut*, *Spitfire* and *Philadelphia*, each carrying identical armament—one twelve-pounder at the bow and two nines in the waist.[30]

On 24 August the Americans got under way bound north from Crown Point on their way to find the enemy. They were going to probe, harass and, if need be, block any British movement toward the south.[31] Their first day out a tremendous northeaster hit, and the open gundalows, with their fairly low freeboard, had a terrible time of it. Of course, it did not help that so many of the men had never sailed before, let alone run through so violent a storm. *Spitfire* almost went under, but somehow she and all the others managed to survive. When the storm cleared, the wind came around from the south, and with this fair breeze the fleet sailed down the lake past Isle la Motte all the way to Windmill Point, deep in enemy territory where the Richelieu begins. On 6 September two additional Skenesborough products joined up, the galley *Lee*, with one twelve-pounder, one nine-pounder and four four-pounders, under Captain Davis, and the gundalow *Jersey*, with the same armament as the others, under Captain Grimes.[32] Arnold ordered his force to come on a line stretching across the river from Windmill Point to the western shore so that they could block any Britisher who might try a run for the lake. Men from the fleet were sent ashore to cut small saplings and branches that could be fixed as fascines above the bulwarks of the gundalows as screens against small-arms fire. One boat-load of Arnold's men that pulled ashore was welcomed by a party of howling Indians who pursued them into the water, killing three and wounding six others.[33]

On the night of 7 September Arnold heard and saw movement ashore. It was the sound of men digging, accompanied by the occasional clanking noise of metal striking against metal. He rightly guessed that it could be only one thing—soldiers setting up an artillery battery. Keeping in mind the old naval adage "A ship is a fool to fight a fort," Arnold decided to withdraw. He moved his boats about eight miles back down the lake to Isle la Motte. Here he could still draw his fleet up on a line to block any advance and at the same time stay beyond effective range of any shore batteries.[34]

For nearly two weeks Arnold kept to this anchorage off the island. Each day more intelligence arrived—spies, deserters and prisoners were all carefully interrogated—and gradually a full picture of what was going on in Saint Johns began to come into focus.[35] From the information now at hand Arnold knew that it would not be long before the British came out to attack. He ordered a sharp lookout kept, and picket boats were posted to give some advance warning. The men spent most of their days in battle drill, manning the guns and repelling boarders. Because of a shortage of powder they never got to fire the cannon, but that did not prevent Arnold from constantly keeping at them to look sharp and move quickly. What little ammunition they did have was mostly of the ball variety, and for the kind of close ship-to-ship action Arnold anticipated, he wanted grape and chain shot, the former a very effective antipersonnel weapon and the latter useful for tearing rigging and sails aloft. He sent to Ticonderoga for some, but Gates was as short as the commodore and he could not give what he did not have. Arnold needed more men too; he was already short-handed, and the men he did have were green lads who were lucky to know port from starboard. And what about those galleys that were building at Skenesborough, he asked Gates; where were they and how soon would they join him?[36]

Since he had to face a superior force, Arnold decided that he would make the enemy come to him so that he could at least choose the place if not the time of battle. On the nineteenth he withdrew his fleet again; this time they sailed ten miles farther south to Bay Saint Amand along the west shore.[37] That was a good anchorage, but after scouting around, Arnold found one he thought was even better, a few miles to the south at Valcour Island, and on the twenty-third he took his fleet to an anchorage there. His intention was to wait at the island for the additional galleys. If the enemy should arrive before the galleys did, he told Gates, he would withdraw without fighting.[38] Within a couple of days the squadron was reinforced by the addition of three more galleys: *Trumbull*, with Captain Edward Wigglesworth, *Washington*, commanded by David Waterbury, and *Congress*, which Arnold himself went on board.[39] Each of the galleys carried ten guns: one eighteen-pounder, one twelve, two nines and six sixes. The Americans would now stand and fight.

Valcour Island is a pretty piece of land that lies a little less than a mile off the west shore of Champlain. It is about three miles long and two wide. Unlike so many of the other islands in the lake, Valcour is not a low, uninhabitable swampland but rather a mostly pine-covered highland with a small bluff on the west shore overlooking the mainland. Arnold could not have found a better place to hide, for the highlands masked any view from the open lake.

Arnold brought his fleet to between the island and the mainland midway down the shore. They were on a crescent-shaped line with the hollow facing south. There were fifteen vessels: two schooners, a sloop, four galleys and eight gundalows, altogether carrying eight hundred men and mounting enough guns to fire 703 pounds of iron in a discharge.[40] The flagship *Congress* was smack in the middle of the line. Waterbury commanded the right wing aboard *Washington*, and Wigglesworth the left from aboard *Trumbull*.

From a tactical perspective the position was a good one. The enemy would first have to find Arnold and then figure out a way to engage him. If they spotted him in time and decided to come in from the north, they would have to thread their way through a shallow and rocky passage that was sure to hang up a good many of their vessels. On the other hand, if they passed by the island and then tried to come up to Arnold, they would have to beat to windward against the prevailing northerlies—something that the square-riggers like *Inflexible* and *Thunderer* would be hard put to do. The one disadvantage the position had was that it offered no easy route of escape. If the British did approach from the south, the Americans, in order to escape, would have to find some way to break through the British ships. All these factors weighed heavily on his mind as Arnold waited.

Having debouched out of the Richelieu on 4 October, Pringle kept his fleet near the river for a week. They checked rigging, shifted ballast and drilled. Pringle had five good-sized vessels, each manned by Royal Navy veterans out of the ships on the Saint Lawrence. All together these vessels could throw more than 1300 pounds of metal, nearly twice the American capability. On the tenth the British came into the open lake, and without taking the slightest precautions, with no scouts or advance guards, they took a fresh northerly breeze and came scudding down the lake with *Maria* leading the way.[41]

As they came around Cumberland Head, five miles north of Valcour, Arnold's lookouts spotted them and gave the warning. Waterbury wanted to up anchor and head for mid-lake where, he told Arnold, they could fight a running retreat. Waterbury was a brave and good soldier, but his advice was foolish. In the open lake the British would have the windward position and could easily overtake the Americans. They would also be able to bring nearly every gun they had to bear on the fleeing Americans. Arnold listened to the advice, but he knew that in his present position the British would have to beat up to him and even then could only engage him piecemeal. Arnold elected to wait.

Pringle came head on right past the island. As soon as the lookouts saw the rebels, Pringle signaled his captains to come about and engage. Because of the wind, those in the van had a hard time of it, and for a long time the only vessels that could get close enough to fire effectively were the schooner *Carleton* and the gunboats, which were brought up under oars. *Carleton* took a terrible beating; nearly every American gun was trained on her, with Arnold himself doing the honors of aiming and firing from *Congress.* For nearly five hours the schooner bore the brunt of the fire while the rest of the squadron struggled without success to come up to her rescue. Dacres rigged a spring on his cable so that he could keep his vessel broadside to the Americans. Holed everywhere, taking water, her rigging in shreds and her cable cut by a lucky American shot, *Carleton* swung around head to the wind. In this perilous position she was raked fore and aft. By now Dacres was wounded and lying unconscious below. Edward Pellew, a nineteen-year-old midshipman, took over. He climbed out onto the bowsprit (the widow maker, as it is sometimes so aptly called) and tried to back the jib so that the vessel would come onto a starboard tack. It did not work. Finally two boats came up from *Maria.* Pellew, still perched out on the bowsprit, threw a line to one of the boats, and *Carleton* was towed to safety.[42] For most of the afternoon she had been under fire; half of her crew were either dead or wounded, and she had three feet of water in her hold, with more coming in.

The whole engagement had lasted about six hours, from eleven in the morning to five in the afternoon, when the British decided to withdraw and await the next day. The Americans had not gotten away unscathed. The schooner *Royal Savage* had fallen off to leeward and run aground. Under heavy fire her crew had had no choice but to abandon her, whereupon she was boarded by men from *Maria,* set afire and destroyed. The other American casualty of the afternoon was the gundalow *Philadelphia,* which had taken several shots between wind and water and finally went down shortly after dark.[43]

The night brought relief. The British withdrew to an east-west line about seven hundred yards to the south of the Americans. In the morning, they thought, they could move in and finish the job. Arnold had two choices. He could stay and fight—but with three-quarters of his ammunition gone, that would be suicide—or he could try to slip by the British and escape. Had Pringle been more alert, the latter choice could easily have become as suicidal as the former. However, he had a tendency to underestimate the enemy, and he would have to suffer the embarrassing consequences. Arnold determined that trying an escape was worth the gamble. About seven in the evening *Trumbull* hoisted sail and began to glide slowly and silently through the darkness around the west end of the British line. The others in the squadron fell into line, each with a single lantern hung aft with blinders on the sides so that only those directly astern could see it. A fog crept in, cutting the visibility even further, and within a few hours the whole fleet was past. Once they were beyond hearing, the men broke out the sweeps and pulled for all they were worth while others worked the pumps. At first light a wind came up out of the south. It was too much to buck, and neither the Americans nor their surprised pursuers could make any headway. At Schuyler's Island, five miles below Valcour, *Providence, New York* and *Jersey* were found to be taking so much water that they had to be abandoned. Arnold stayed there only long enough to transfer some gear and mend *Washington*'s sail. The Americans rowed all the rest of that day and through the night. The next morning, 13 October, the wind shifted again and started to blow out of the northeast. By the time the American fleet reached the narrows of the lake at Split Rock, the enemy had drawn alongside them. Arnold described it best.

The *Washington* and *Congress* were in a Rear, the rest of our Fleet were a Head. . . . The *Washington* galley was in such a shattered Condition and had so many Men killed and wounded she struck to the Enemy after receiving a few Broadsides. We were then attacked in the *Congress* Galley by a Ship mounting twelve Eighteen Pounders, a Schooner of fourteen sixes and one of twelve Sixes, two under our Stern and one on our Broadside within Musquet shot. They kept up an incessant Fire on us for about five Glasses with Round and Grape Shot, which we returned as briskly—The Sails Rigging and Hull of the *Congress* was shattered and torn in Pieces, the first Lieutenant and 3 men killed, when to prevent her falling into the Enemy's hands, who had seven Sail around me, I ran her ashore in a small Creek ten Miles from Crown Point on the East Side when after saving our small Arms, I set her on Fire with four Gondolas, with whose Crews I reached Crown Point thro the Woods that Evening, and very luckily escaped the Savages who way laid the Road in two Hours after we passed. At 4 OClock Yesterday Morning I reached this place [Ticonderoga] exceedingly fatigued and unwell having been without Sleep or Refreshment for near three days.[44]

When the losses were tallied, all the Americans had left were two galleys, two schooners, a gundalow and a sloop. Eighty men were wounded or dead and another 110 were prisoners. Crown Point was untenable, and as soon as the British hove into sight, the Americans put it to the torch and withdrew to Ticonderoga, their last stronghold on the lake.

At Ticonderoga Arnold, Gates and the recently arrived Arthur St. Clair awaited the British assault. It did not come. The struggle for the lake had cost the British weeks of precious time, and in Carleton's judgment it was now too late to begin a land campaign.[45] He withdrew back up the lake and went into winter quarters at Saint Johns. Arnold had lost the battle, but in doing so he had exacted a price—one year—and in that time the Americans were able to gather enough men and matériel so that the following October they would be able to meet and defeat the British at Saratoga—a victory rightly referred to as the turning point of the Revolution. That triumph, second only to Yorktown, was made possible by the gallant and heroic conduct of Benedict Arnold and his fresh-water navy.

Chapter Eleven

The Ships in the Fleet

It is easy to be querulous and point out all the shortcomings of the Congress and the navy, insolvency and committee-itis being only the most glaring and debilitating. But to dwell on these without appreciating the magnitude of the project attempted or the significant accomplishments actually made is to do an injustice, for despite their medley of mistakes and difficulties, the Congress did manage to build a navy.

During eight trying years of war the Continental navy had under its command—counting everything that floated, from the smallest lake galley to the short-lived ship of the line, *America*—in the neighborhood of one hundred vessels mounting over thirteen hundred guns. They were of all sizes, shapes and descriptions, from the conventional rigs such as schooners, sloops, ships, brigs and brigantines to the more specialized galleys and gundalows and finally to the exotic Arab Xebec.[1]

The schooner rig and its naval advantages have already been discussed in relation to Washington's fleet. If we include the general's seven, there were at least seventeen of this type of vessel sailing under Continental colors. Only one was actually built for the navy—the schooner *Mercury*, launched by John Peck in Plymouth, Massachusetts. All the others were either captured or bought. Outside Massachusetts Bay they seem to have been used mainly as packet and dispatch vessels. That certainly was the intended purpose of Peck's *Mercury*, for she was described by the Navy Board of the Eastern District as being lightly built and very fast but of little use in a fight.[2]

There were even fewer sloop-rigged vessels in the navy than schooners. In all there were probably about fourteen, of which only two were laid down for the Continent: *Active* at Marshfield, Massachusetts, and *Baltimore* in the town of the same name. The term *sloop* itself can at times be confusing and vague. In naval parlance it was generally used in reference to armament rather than rig. A sloop of war in the British navy could be almost any ship-rigged vessel that carried less than twenty-four guns on one deck. However, in the civilian world of the eighteenth century the term referred to a particular type of rig, namely, a vessel with a single mast, a gaff mainsail, headsails and quite often a square topsail and course. From descriptions of the armament carried and the craft themselves, it seems that many of the Continental sloops were so called because of their rig and were therefore relatively small single-masted vessels. Like their close relative the schooner, sloops were better at running than fighting, and the bulk of their work consisted in patrolling coastal waters or scurrying abroad as dispatch boats.

Ship-rigged vessels were larger than schooners and sloops, but there were fewer of them in the Continental service. Of the ten that sailed for the Continent, only three were actually built under contract for the Congress: *Ranger*, of John Paul Jones fame, at Portsmouth, New Hampshire; *Saratoga*, at Philadelphia; and *Indien*, at Amsterdam, Holland. The rest, like so many of the other vessels that made up the American roster, were either purchased, chartered or captured. Although the term *ship* is used to denote almost anything from a rowboat to an aircraft carrier, it does nevertheless have a very specific reference. Technically, it is a three-masted vessel square-rigged on each mast, fore, main and mizzen. Since ships were larger than schooners and sloops, they could carry more and heavier guns and therefore were better able to go about the business of a warship, finding, engaging and destroying the enemy. Under a capable and aggressive commander they could acquit themselves well, as Jones on *Ranger* and Nicholas Biddle on *Saratoga* so ably demonstrated.[3]

Falling in after ships in terms of their numbers in the Continental fleet were the brigs and brigantines, one dozen of them. No vessels of either of these rigs were built expressly for the Congress; they were all obtained from other sources. In appearance they were generally smaller than ships, having only two masts instead of three. The brigs were square-rigged on both their fore and main, while the brigantines were square-rigged on only the fore, with their main carrying a fore and aft configuration. *Andrew Doria*, part of Hopkins's fleet, was a brig, and *Washington*, Captain Sion Martindale's command out of Plymouth, was rigged as a brigantine.

The remainder of the American force, excluding frigates, which will be discussed later, consisted of a wide variety of rigs, most of which were rather specialized. For close inshore work in harbors and coastal waters as well as Lake Champlain, gundalows and galleys were popular.

To wrap up this inventory of vessels of less than frigate size, we need to mention four cutters, two xebecs and a ketch. The cutters were small, single-masted vessels usually equipped with headsails, square topsail and lower course and a good-sized gaff mainsail. In appearance and service they were quite like the sloops. Lightly armed, they served as dispatch and pilot boats. None of them were built directly for the Continental service; they all ended up there by purchase.

The most exotic but relatively unimportant vessels in the navy were the xebecs *Champion* and *Repulse*. Both were loaned to the Congress by the Pennsylvania State Navy for service on the Delaware River and Bay. It would be interesting to know who designed them or where they came from because they were so unusual. All of the other types of rigs seen in the American navy were rather common and abundant in both the merchant marine and the Royal Navy, but not so with the xebecs. They were of Arab origin, three-masted with lateen sails and a hull characterized by a large overhang at both the bow and stern. They only mounted eight guns so they could not have been very large, and considering their area of operation they must have been of shallow draft with a high degree of maneuverability.

Finally there was a ketch, *Mercury.* She was the only one in the entire navy. Built under contract in Philadelphia by Wharton and Humphreys, she, like the schooner of the same name, saw service as a packet boat. This being the case, it seems certain that she was rigged not as a naval bomb ketch —that is, with a square-rigged mainmast stepped almost amidships and a mizzen with square sails and a spanker—but rather as a regular ketch with a square-rigged mainmast and a mizzen with a fore and aft sail (gaff, lateen or sprit).[4]

Taken together all of these vessels—sloops, schooners, brigs, brigantines, gundalows, galleys, cutters, xebecs and ketch—comprised about three-fourths of the whole number of ships in the American navy. But these were tatterdemalions, and despite their impressive numbers they were never the most important part of the fleet. That honor was left to the Continental frigates.

During the era of the American Revolution the term *frigate* was used to designate a three-masted, ship-rigged warship that carried her main armament on a single gun deck. The number of guns varied from twenty-four to thirty-six, although these figures may be misleading since quite often a warship would actually carry more guns than her official rate.[5]

In European navies frigates were employed as auxiliaries and reconnaissance vessels for the main battle fleet, stationed to relay signals between distant elements of the fleet or to screen and maintain contact with the enemy. In the American navy they performed none of these functions since the Congress had no capital ships at sea for them to serve. For reasons of strategy as well as economics, the men in Philadelphia had always been dubious about the usefulness of large ships; yet if the American force was to be a true navy and in any way pose a threat to the British, then it had to be composed of something larger and more powerful than the waterbugs already mentioned. Frigate-sized vessels seemed a convenient compromise, and pride if nothing else moved the Congress to build them.

Building a fleet of frigates was no mean chore, and by adopting this course of action the Congress brought upon themselves an avalanche of problems. Relying on frigates meant that they would have to undertake a major construction program, for while smaller types of vessels were available for purchase or hire in almost every major American port, frigates were so large and specialized that they had no real counterpart in the merchant service. They would have to be built from the keel up. Altogether at one time or another during the war the Americans had twenty-three frigates at various stages of existence, from pure thought to physical completion. Of that number only nineteen ever actually made it into the service, the remaining four either having fallen into other hands or never having existed at all. The famous first thirteen were authorized by Congress in December 1775. An additional five, along with some other vessels, were directed to be built by an act of 20 November 1776, and in January 1777 two more were ordered.[6] The frigates built in Holland and the two purchased in France were handled in a separate fashion.

Burdened down with a host of other problems the Congress hardly ever dallied long over naval matters. Although they authorized the construction of some forty-six vessels during the war, they never went further than simply to designate the type of vessel ordered and the state wherein it was to be built. The rest was left to the Marine Committee, which meant that for the first thirteen frigates the committee would have to carry on two very important jobs simultaneously. They would have to settle upon proper designs and at the same time find builders to execute them.

The latter task was disposed of in a simple and straightforward fashion, albeit somewhat casually. The member of the Marine Committee from the state where a vessel was to be built was allowed to select people there who would be responsible for the construction. In three New England states this meant that one man would handle the job: New Hampshire's John Langdon, a merchant and shipowner; Massachusetts's Thomas Cushing, a political chum of John Hancock; and Connecticut's Barnabas Deane, brother of the ubiquitous Silas.[7] Elsewhere the work was lodged with committees. In Rhode Island, for example, Stephen Hopkins selected twelve men and in Pennsylvania, where the operation was particularly complex because four frigates were being built, an elaborate maze of committees was erected to oversee the job.[8] Once selected, these local agencies, whether one man or several, had to pick a builder. There were no sealed bids or volumes of specifications to comply with; that sort of paraphernalia was alien to eighteenth-century naval contracting. The local agents were expected to appoint men whose experience and reputation would ensure speedy and competent construction. Not infrequently this meant awarding the contract to a relative or friend who they hoped was reliable. After selecting the builder the agents were expected to keep a watch on the business and dispense money as they received it from Congress. For their trouble they were paid a five percent commission.[9] Since the agents were ofttimes businessmen who were not necessarily well versed in the technical aspects of ship construction, Congress authorized the appointment of experienced shipwrights who in the name of Congress would oversee the day-to-day work at the yard. These men, superintendents as they were called, were to guard against any faulty or shoddy workmanship and to see to it that the Congress got the best ships in the shortest possible time.

Langdon decided to depend upon three Portsmouth gentlemen, James Hackett, Stephen Paul and James Hill, to build his frigate and he appointed a well-known local captain, Thomas Thompson, to superintend their work.[10] Since Boston was occupied, the Massachusetts agent, Thomas Cushing, had to go almost to the New Hampshire border to find a secure site for his frigates, at Newburyport on the Merrimack about thirty miles north of Boston. There he contracted for two frigates, one to be built by the brothers Stephen and Ralph Cross and the other in the nearby yard of Jonathan Greenleaf. The superintendents were John Avery and John Odid.[11]

Stephen Hopkins thought to divide up the work of building the two frigates in his state among a committee of twelve men. Despite the biblical overtones it was a political move in a state where politics counted for everything; and if the critics are right Hopkins's handiwork soon turned into a thieves' banquet. After enduring a torrent of criticism resonating from Providence to Philadelphia, the dozen gentlemen finally abdicated in favor of one man, Daniel Tillinghast. He had charge of the final stages of construction of the thirty-two in the yards of Benjamin Talman and of the twenty-eight at Sylvester Bower's, both in Providence.[12] Upon launching they were, in the words of Robert Morris, a man who would have reason to know, "the two worst frigates. . . ."[13]

The always zealous and sometimes venal Silas Deane appointed his brother Barnabas to act as the Connecticut agent. Captain John Cotton of Middletown, a man who had "followed the Sea from his infancy . . . ," was given the contract to build the twenty-eight assigned to Connecticut.[14]

The remaining seven frigates were to be laid down in yards south of New England: two in New York, four in Pennsylvania and one in Maryland. In New York the situation is somewhat unclear but apparently Francis Lewis, the New York member of the Marine Committee, selected a committee of four to act as agents in that state. At any rate, the job itself was done in the yard of Lancaster Burling at Poughkeepsie on the Hudson where a twenty-eight and a twenty-four were built, the former under the superintendency of Samuel Tudor and the latter under the watchful care of Augustus Lawrence.[15]

As noted, the laying down and building of the four frigates in Pennsylvania, two thirty-twos, a twenty-eight and a twenty-four, was shrouded in a heavy overlay of committees. One of the thirty-twos was built by three brothers, Manuel, Jehu and Benjamin Eyre, at Kensington, a section within present-day Philadelphia. A twenty-eight was built in the same area by Grice and Company while the other thirty-two and the twenty-four were both launched in the Southwick neighborhood of Philadelphia by Wharton and Humphreys and Warwick Coats respectively.[16]

South of the Mason-Dixon line there was only one frigate built, a twenty-eight laid down in the yard of Captain George Wells at Fells Point about one mile below Baltimore. Jesse Hollingsworth was the superintendent and he was responsible to a committee of four appointed by Samuel Chase, the Maryland delegate on the Marine Committee.[17]

By early January 1776 the machinery for building the frigates was set up. The agents were ready and the contractors were standing by waiting for instructions. Naturally they knew, in general terms at least, what was expected of them, that is, the type of vessel to be built and the number of guns she would carry, but beyond that they were left pretty much in the dark and had to await the pleasure of the Marine Committee.

The committee fully intended to provide proper designs for the frigates. Their plan was to have only one common design for each of the classes, twenty-fours, twenty-eights and thirty-twos. These plans would be drawn in Philadelphia under their scrutiny and then sent to the various builders. By centralizing the drafting procedures the committee hoped to produce three sets of uniformly high-quality designs that could then be used, under the watchful care of agents and superintendents, to fashion effective fighting ships. It was a good thought and might have worked in more normal times, but the pressures and exigencies of war interceded to produce a system quite different from and far more hectic than the one originally envisioned.

To prepare the three basic designs the committee turned to a twenty-four-year-old Quaker, Joshua Humphreys.[18] He was a skipper's son but his taste had run to design rather than command. His father was captain of the legendary Philadelphia privateer *Hero*, the scourge of the French in the Seven Years War. She had been built by a friend of Captain Humphreys, James Penrose, and in 1765 young Joshua went to work as an apprentice in Penrose's yard. Penrose died in 1771 and the youthful, inexperienced but highly competent Humphreys took over direction of the business. Three years later he entered into partnership with his cousin John Wharton, a local ship chandler and close friend of Robert Morris. Wharton's business acumen and connections coupled with Humphrey's skill made this partnership into one of the most successful shipbuilding enterprises in early America.

It was in the yard of Humphreys and Wharton that the tender-sided merchantmen *Alfred, Columbus, Andrew Doria* and *Providence* had been converted to warships to join Hopkins's fleet. The committee, fully satisfied with the yard's performance on that job, quite naturally turned to them again for help in designing the frigates. It is probably safe to say that neither Humphreys nor Wharton had ever before designed a warship. They certainly had never built one.

As a result, it is quite likely that for the twenty-four class they modeled their ship on one that already existed. According to a vote of the committee, probably at Humphreys's or Wharton's suggestion, it was decided that the twenty-fours were to "be of the Same dimensions as the *Hero* Privateer built in the City of Philadelphia in the last war."[19] This was, of course, the same privateer that had gone out of the Penrose yard, and there can be little doubt that Humphreys probably still had the plans on file or could quickly redraft them from memory.

It is not so easy to determine the origin of the two larger classes of twenty-eights and thirty-twos, although in the case of the latter the committee seems to have been influenced by the design of the Royal Navy's thirty-six-gun frigate

Pallas.[20] Marion V. Brewington, writing in 1948, made a strong case that the design of all the frigates authorized in December 1775 came off the board of Joshua Humphreys. However, in 1949 Howard Chapelle questioned Brewington's assertion and, without resolving the issue, simply pointed out that there was contrary evidence to suggest that Humphreys was not the designer.[21]

While it is difficult, if not impossible, to ascribe the designs with any certainty to any particular person, it does seem tolerably well established that the drafts presented to the committee did come from the firm of Humphreys and Wharton. Given the way in which the Marine Committee was accustomed to work, that is, relying on friends and relatives, and recognizing the fact that whatever their merits this firm had more political influence than any of their competitors, the conclusion seems inescapable that the designs had to come from Wharton, Humphreys or someone in their employ. Thirty-one days after Congress resolved to build the frigates, Joshua Humphreys laid the drafts before the committee. With apparently no discussion or objection the committee approved them and ordered copies made and distributed to the builders.

What then followed proves that Faulkner was right when he said that "history resides in small things closely notched —a lock on a courthouse door, one plank from a whorehouse door, one family."[22] The Marine Committee and the naval architects, whoever they might have been, saw their carefully worked designs temporarily laid aside because they were too large to send by regular mail. No one had given the slightest thought to how to get these bulky and cumbersome drawings, five feet long and two feet wide, out to the builders. It was no problem sending them down the street to the builders in Philadelphia, and a courier could easily carry them the eighty miles to Baltimore. Sending them northward, however, caused some delay, and for at least ten days they sat on a shelf collecting dust while a means was sought to get them to New York and New England. Finally on 13 February the drawings for New Hampshire and Massachusetts got off with Colonel John Bull, who was traveling north to Cambridge with the Continental payroll.[23] In the meantime, as the drafts were lying idly by in Philadelphia, the impatient Yankee shipbuilders were becoming increasingly eager to lay timber and begin construction. In New Hampshire and Rhode Island the contractors became so weary of waiting that they decided to go ahead on their own initiative without the Philadelphia drafts.

Fortunately for Langdon, at Portsmouth there was a fairly well-known shipbuilder, William Hackett, who was able to supply him with a design for a thirty-two-gun frigate. While Hackett was lofting the frigate, Langdon signed on nearly one hundred men at his yard and prepared to go to work using Hackett's design. As he reflected on what he had done, Langdon thought that perhaps he had been a bit brash, and fearful that his enterprise and zeal might not be appreciated in Philadelphia, he wrote to his chum Josiah Bartlett, the New Hampshire delegate on the Marine Committee, obliquely asking for reassurance that he could do what he was already doing. Bartlett's reply eased his mind when he told him that he was "fully authorised to Build the Ship to be Built in New Hampshire and finish her fit for Sea."[24] More confident now, Langdon pressed ahead and told Bartlett in his usual blunt and sometimes truculent manner, "dont Cramp my Genius and the ship shall be Launched soon."[25] The plans eventually arrived in Portsmouth about 27 February, but by that time it was too late, and Langdon's frigate went down the ways in May, a thirty-two-gun frigate designed and built in New Hampshire. Her hull differed from the Philadelphia plan, and in fact it more closely resembled that of an English frigate than an American. She had a round bow, her tumble home amidships was greater than the one the Continental plan called for, and the quarterdeck and forecastle had less rise to them than the American version.[26]

Where Langdon was blunt and assertive, Thomas Cushing, the Massachusetts agent, was timorous and wary. His predicament was the same as Langdon's, but unlike his neighbor to the north, he was not daring enough to move ahead on his own account. As early as mid-January he was engaged in informal conversation with the Cross brothers and Greenleaf, but not until 1 March, when he had the designs well in hand, did he actually sign a contract.[27] Although Cushing would not let Cross and Greenleaf begin framing until they had the Philadelphia plans, he left matters entirely in their hands once the drafts were delivered. As a result, the twenty-four slid into the water looking pretty much as she ought, but the thirty-two came off wider and deeper than her sisters. Cushing either did not notice or did not care.

At Narragansett Bay the parceling out of authority among a twelve-man committee divided responsibility but did not dilute ardor in driving forward to the business at hand. Convinced that a good Providence shipwright could match anything coming out of Philadelphia, the Frigate Committee on 10 January 1776 appointed Sylvester Bowers to "make a Draught of the Large ship as soon as may be."[28] Bowers drew a plan for the large ship, a thirty-two, and probably for the smaller twenty-eight as well. The committee gathered materials and the work got under way. While things began to move in Providence, two of the committee members traveled to Philadelphia to meet with the Marine Committee. After a short visit they arrived back in Providence the evening of 18 February, carrying with them sixty thousand dollars and the Philadelphia drafts. By that time the hulls were already framed and there was little that could be done to alter them to conform with the newly arrived plans. However, the local committee did agree that the upper works of the thirty-two and the twenty-eight would follow the Continental plan.

On the Connecticut River John Cotton was readying to build his twenty-eight. He was no less eager than Langdon, Cushing or the Rhode Island committee to get under way, but the weather was not cooperating. It had been relatively mild in Connecticut during January and February, with above-freezing temperatures and not much snow. But a lot of rain had turned roads into rivers of mud and swelled streams to near flood stage. There were more swamps than highways, and not even the heaviest teams of oxen could drag timber to the yard if they were belly deep in mud. By the end of February Cotton was still not ready. Framing finally got under way in March, and by that time, of course, the official drafts were in his hands. So from keel to truck the Connecticut twenty-eight shaped up all Humphreys.[29]

As for the design of the two frigates built at Poughkeepsie on the Hudson, a twenty-eight and a twenty-four, it is difficult to come to any firm conclusion. No plans exist of the vessels, and both barely had time to get their bottoms wet before they were destroyed to avoid capture. Nevertheless, given the late start at construction, it seems safe to assume that the men at the yards had the Philadelphia plans in their possession before they began work and that therefore these frigates were built along the approved lines.

Once the builders had worked out their problem of getting a design, they could then begin. They had an enormous task facing them, but at first most were optimistic and very few appreciated what lay before them. They were expected to build in a few months thirteen ships at seven different ports with a total tonnage equal to more than one-quarter of the entire tonnage launched in all the colonies during the last year of peace.[30] These were large vessels. The smallest, the twenty-fours, went over five hundred tons, while the twenty-eights and the thirty-twos had burdens of over six hundred and seven hundred tons each. In more than 160 years of American shipbuilding very few ships of this size had ever slid down the ways. Hundreds of tons of iron would be needed, hundreds of thousands of feet of timber, miles of rigging and acres of canvas.

To some of those involved it became a race to see who would be first to complete their vessel. Hancock felt the competitive spirit, and he urged Cushing to "exert every nerve [and] spare no expense" so that Massachusetts could land the prize.[31] In Philadelphia the men in charge asked their subordinates to put forward their "utmost exertions . . . so that

Pennsylvania may produce four Ships, superior in Quality of less cost [and] with more expedition than the Neighboring Colonies engaged in the same business."[32] Elsewhere the zeal might not have been as great, but the goal remained the same —get the frigates to sea. This was the common theme, but there were noticeable local variations.

As soon as a construction site had been selected, usually at an already functioning yard, although in the case of New York it was necessary to start from scratch, the most immediate task was to assemble timber. The thirty-twos, for example, required at least a thousand tons of timber, and even that impressive amount could probably be revised upward by forty percent because of heavy wastage.[33] Often the builders had to scour the countryside for adequate supplies. The Rhode Islanders went up the Taunton River into southern Massachusetts searching out timber. From Newburyport vessels sailed to the Kennebec River and Penobscot Bay to load timber. In Pennsylvania the ax men had to tramp so far inland that they needed troops to protect them from Indian war parties. Advertisements appeared in local newspapers promising cash for delivery of oak and pine and occasionally for other types of wood as well; for example, in Rhode Island thirty tons of locust were sought for tree nails (trunnels).

At the yard the timber came under the experienced eye of the master shipwright, who checked it closely for quality and shape and kept a sharp watch for certain peculiarly formed pieces that could be used for special purposes. For example, large curved timbers known as knees, ten to twelve feet on the outside curve and twenty to thirty inches thick, were needed to brace the deck where it joined the inside of the hull. More large pieces were needed for other parts of the frame, such as the keel, deck beams and futtocks, which were curved timbers scarfed together to form the ribs. All these had to be cut and shaped by handsaw, ax and adze.

The sheer size of some of these timbers caused difficulties because the workmen were not accustomed to such a scale and the facilities at the various yards were often put to a strain to accommodate them. The worst job was in the saw pits where the huge oak and pine logs were cut into long beams and planks for the hull and deck. The men in the bottom of the pits had to stand underneath pulling down on the saw as they walked under the log. They must have bellowed a litany of curses trying to work in a swirl of blinding sawdust that stopped nostrils and irritated throats.

In other parts of the yard men were busy preparing the stocks that would cradle the hull and hold it upright until slid into the water. They had to be careful to build the stocks on ground solid enough to support the weight yet close enough to the water for launching. Another factor equally important was the incline to the water. It had to be just right. If it was too steep, the builders would run the risk of knocking the blocks out and watching their creation charge wildly into the water. If the slope was not sufficient, the builders would suffer the embarrassment of watching the ship slide, stop and then hang there like a helpless beached whale.

Once the timber was ready and the stocks prepared, the frigate was set to be framed up. Parts of the frame would be assembled on the ground, and when the carpenters were ready, the cry would go out to "frame up." At the call others in the yard would leave their own work and hurry over to lend a hand setting up these heavy and bulky pieces. In some communities where patriotism and pride ran especially high, the event became a festive occasion, and even people outside the yard would respond to the call for help. In Kensington, just outside Philadelphia, where one of the twenty-eights was being built in the yard of Grice and Company, people often gathered after dinner in the warm spring evenings to assist in getting the deck beams into place.[34]

With the skeletal structure up, the frigate next needed to be fleshed out with a hull and decks. Planking was one of the most demanding and important aspects of the whole construction process. Lengths of oak plank sometimes four inches thick were brought from the saw pit. They first had to be secured to the frame with thousands of tree nails fashioned from oak, locust or some other hard, durable wood. Some-times two feet long, the tree nails were driven into holes through the planks and into the frame. The only metal used was iron caps temporarily placed over the head of the tree nail to prevent it from splitting as it was hammered in. The planks were joined end to end to form a continuous line from stem to stern called a strake. Just above the waterline an extra layer of planking, the wale, was laid to give greater longitudinal strength along the hull and to provide additional support for the gun deck and the heavy burden it would bear. As the strakes were snugged together, caulkers tended to the seams, filling them with oakum (tarred robe fibers) and then paying them over with hot pitch or tallow. When the area beneath the waterline had been planked and caulked, water would be pumped into the hull so that men on the outside could watch for leaks.

As the hull took shape, other men were busy with the decks. Since decks did not have to do constant battle with salt water, they could be built of cheaper and softer pine. The principal deck was the main or gun deck. It ran aft from under the quarterdeck all the way forward up under the forecastle. On it were mounted the guns. Unlike America's later and more famous frigates of the 1790s, such as *Constitution*, with her double tier of guns, these Revolutionary vessels mounted all their cannon on a single deck. For most of its length the gun deck was open, but rising up about six feet at either end were the quarterdeck and forecastle. Down below in the hold beneath the upper decks there was space for stowing extra equipment, victuals, cargo and, in the most protected spot possible, a magazine for ammunition. It was cramped quarters between decks, only about five and a half feet of head room, no place for tall men. The decks themselves were laid out in planks twenty to forty feet long, three inches thick and nearly a foot wide. They were cambered and sealed but left unpainted. At the edge of the deck the hull continued upward for about six feet to form the bulwark. It was through this wooden wall that the gun ports were cut.

Hull caulked and sealed, decks in place, the frigate was ready for some of the fine work. The bulwarks and quarter gallery needed a coat of paint and a figurehead might be added. Depending upon how quickly the other craftsmen completed their jobs, the painters and woodcarvers might do their work while the frigate rested in the stocks, or else it could be done while she lay in the water beside a wharf.

Generally, striking colors were used for the exterior around the bulwarks and stern. Not pure white, though, for that tended to yellow with age. It seems that the most popular colors were yellow and black. *Hancock*, for example, went about as gaily attired as the man for whom she was named. The stern was painted black and yellow and the quarter gallery was entirely yellow. Gun ports were not singled out for special attention but rather were painted to blend in with the bulwarks. At sea no commander wanted to advertise the fact that his vessel was a warship. If at a distance his bulwarks did not appear to have the telltale gun ports, he would have a better chance of drawing close to skittish merchantmen and more lightly armed warships without scaring them away.

The color and profile of a vessel helped to identify her at sea almost as much as the name on her stern. Another signature that could be equally revealing was the figurehead on the bow. Carved with great pride and care by local craftsmen, these wooden sculptures came to represent one of the high points of American folk art. The figure did not necessarily have to depict the name of the vessel. One of Cushing's frigates, for example, which was named *Boston*, had on her bow "An Indian Head with a bow and arrow in the hand, painted white, red and yellow."[35]

The two most famous figureheads in the navy, however, did symbolize their namesakes. These were sported by *Hancock* and the seventy-four-gun ship *America. Hancock*, as might be expected, had a man dressed in "yellow breeches, white stockings, blue coat with yellow button holes, small cocked hat with yellow lace." She was fancy on the stern as well, with a carved rattlesnake and the inscription "Don't Tread on

Me."[36] The other figurehead, on *America*, was described by her commander John Paul Jones: "The right arm raised with the forefinger pointing to heaven as appealing to that high tribunal for the justice of the American cause. On the left arm was a buckler with a blue ground and thirteen stars. The legs and feet of the figure were covered here and there with wreaths of smoke to represent the dangers and difficulties of war." Jones also noted proudly the appointments on the stern.

> On the stern under the windows of the great cabin appeared two large figures in bas relief, representing Tyranny and Oppression, bound and biting the ground, with the cap of liberty on a pole above their heads. On the back part of the starboard quarter gallery was a large figure of Neptune and on the larboard gallery a fine figure of Mars. Over the window of the great cabin the part of the stern was a large medallion on which was a figure representing Wisdom surrounded by danger with the bird of Athens overhead.[37]

Hidden among the mass of figures itemizing the cost of each of the Continental vessels was an entry headed "entertainment." This was the cost of feting the spectators and workmen on launching day. In Rhode Island fifty dollars per frigate was considered adequate, while the more extravagant New Yorkers thought at least one hundred dollars per launching was more to their liking.[38] Whatever the cost, everywhere the event was an occasion for public jubilation and self-congratulations. Langdon, writing in a Portsmouth newspaper about the launching of his frigate, commented on the "diligence and care [and] harmony" that prevailed in his yard during the building. According to him, these Stakhanovite workers of eighteenth-century America exerted themselves to the utmost, never grumbling or complaining, so that they could complete "this noble fabrick."[39] A bit of Revolutionary rhetoric to be sure, but nevertheless a measure of the great joy and pride that went with these vessels as they slid into the water, there to stand not only as powerful warships and examples of American craftsmanship but as patriotic symbols as well.

If launching could be festive, it was also perilous; after all, once the blocks were knocked out, there were several hundred tons of timber loose, headed into the water. During the launching of the thirteen frigates there were several incidents involving injury and damage. The two at Newburyport got stuck on the ways, and when the large Providence frigate slid into the water, she went out of control and smashed into the dock. In New Hampshire Langdon made meticulous preparations for his launching lest anything go wrong. He even went so far as to order troops to the yard to hold back the crowd. It paid off, and he prided himself on the smoothness of the proceedings: "I dont know of one Man of having even his Finger hurt in Launching, we were very regular the whole Yard guarded, to keep people off, strict Silence, orders properly timed, and well Executed, about three Minutes to her Anchor from the time she run."[40]

Once the ship was safely down the ways and riding high in the harbor or snug against a dock, the spectators and workmen could toast the event. The menu varied, but the table set at the Crosses' yard in Newburyport could not have been unusual. Ordinary New England rum was not good enough for the event, so fifty gallons of West Indian rum along with a quarter cask of wine and a hamper of ale or beer were ordered. To complement the liquor Cross also bought a firkin of ham, another of tongue and a third of corned beef.[41] It must have been a grand and delicious feast.

Part of any launching ceremony is, of course, the naming of the vessel. In the case of the frigates, as well as the other Continental ships, the selection of names was left to Congress. On 6 June 1776 they agreed on thirteen names for the frigates but left the individual assignments to the Marine Committee.[42]

The choice of names by the Congress provides a glimpse at the emerging panoply of American heroes. Three of the frigates were named after fallen American patriots: *Warren*, after General Joseph Warren, killed at Bunker Hill; *Montgomery*, at Poughkeepsie, after Brigadier General Richard Montgomery, one of the casualties in the invasion of Canada; and *Randolph*, in Pennsylvania, for the late Peyton Randolph, first president of the Continental Congress. Three more of the warships were named to honor living American patriots: *Washington*, in Pennsylvania, for the commander in chief; *Hancock*, for the presiding president of the Continental Congress and chairman of the Marine Committee; and *Trumbull*, in Connecticut, for the aged patriot governor of the state, Jonathan Trumbull. Two of the remaining six were named after Englishmen: *Raleigh*, Langdon's frigate, for that courtier, historian, explorer and soldier of fortune, and *Effingham*, being built in Pennsylvania, to honor the earl of that name who had defended American rights in Parliament. The other frigate building at New York was christened *Congress*. The remaining four took their names from American geography: *Virginia*, at Baltimore; *Delaware*, on that river in Pennsylvania; *Providence*, in that town; and *Boston*, in Newburyport.

Not one of the frigates was built within the expected time period; in fact, not one of them even saw service before 1777. The late arrival of the plans got them off to a bad start, and the difficulties in finding men and materials hampered their progress all along the way. The first to get her bottom wet was *Warren*, on 15 May 1776, and the last to get into the water was *Congress*, in late November of the same year. But even when the frigates were afloat, they were still a long way from being ready for sea. Until they were outfitted and rigged, they were only helpless hulks about as mobile and dangerous as a turtle on its back.

The first thing to be done was to step the masts. The frigate was hauled next to a wharf where a high derrick was set up. Gangs of men tugging and pulling on lines run through a series of blocks would lift the sticks on board and lower them down until their heel was fixed on the keel. The lower mainmast on the frigates was generally about eighty feet from top to bottom and capped with a topmast about fifty feet high that in turn had a topgallant in the range of thirty feet. The fore and mizzenmasts had a similar configuration, lower, top and topgallant, but on a smaller scale.

It was quite a chore locating, cutting and transporting these giants. The only builders who seemed to have no difficulty were Cushing and Langdon, but that was to be expected since both of them lived in an area that before the war had made a good living at exporting masts. Elsewhere builders were not so fortunate. In Pennsylvania they had to press pretty far inland to find trees large enough for the frigates in the Delaware. At Poughkeepsie Tudor and Lawrence called on William Duer, a local timber merchant. Duer was, of course, the same man who later became deeply involved in some highly questionable speculation and ended his colorful career in disgrace and bankruptcy. At this time, though, he was honestly exerting himself and he was shamefully treated for his efforts. He supplied the masts in good time but then had to wait five years to be paid.[43]

At Providence, where things seemed to go wrong with frightening regularity, Sylvester Bowers had to find three sets of masts for his two frigates. The first two sets were rafted down the Taunton River from southern Massachusetts. The extra set would not have been needed at all if the workers had been more careful on the job; they snapped the foremast and sprung the mainmast while trying to haul *Warren* over on her side to tend to the bottom. When that happened, the frigate committee had to look about for another set and the only one who could help them was Langdon. It must have caused some red faces when the Rhode Islanders explained to him why they needed another set. Langdon, perhaps inwardly chuckling to himself, supplied the masts without comment.

Thrusting up from the deck like lonely, limbless sentinels, these sticks still had to be crossed with yards, draped with rigging and sheeted with canvas before they could be of any use to the ship. Nearly a dozen yards would cross the masts, and they ranged in size, in the case of *Randolph*, from a main yard seventy-two feet tip to tip to a topgallant only thirty-six feet from tip to tip. Up forward sizable pieces would be secured to form the bowsprit, and aft a gaff was fixed to the mizzen.

To handle and secure all this paraphernalia, miles of rigging were needed on each of the ships. For men who had never worked on vessels this large before, the rigging requirements of the frigates must have seemed staggering. The frigates needed miles of cordage for standing and running rigging as well as extra large cables for their anchors. Large supplies of hemp and men to work it were needed in the local ropewalks that were expected to produce these unprecedented quantities of footage. For the most part the rope makers met their demands, except in the case of the exceptionally large anchor cables. The large frigates needed a fifteen-inch cable six hundred feet long. Very few, if any, cables of this size had ever been produced in America, and for ropemakers in Boston, Providence, and Philadelphia, it was a new and difficult task to turn them out.

After the masts were stepped and the rigging was in place, the ship's propulsion system was still only two-thirds ready. The final touch was left to the sail makers, who were responsible for sewing literally dozens of different sails to be hoisted aloft. The sails were made of either heavy canvas or a lighter duck material. The latter was preferred, but it had to be imported and was therefore scarcer and more expensive.

In the water with her rigging in place and the sails bent, the frigate had all the appearance of a warship but not the sting. Her gun ports were still empty. She had yet to be armed.

Chapter Twelve

Thirteen Beautiful Frigates —Almost

When it actually came to building ships, none of the states had enough resources of their own; at one time or another they all had to depend to some extent upon a neighbor for assistance. To say that such aid was always rendered cheerfully and without question would be to put a gloss of conviviality and cooperation on an aspect of the Revolution that is more characterized by coolness and suspicion. The thirteen states were just learning to be independent, and it would be many years before they would be able to work in full harmony with one another. Theirs was a fragile coalition based on the threat of a common enemy, and its vitality ebbed and flowed according to the proximity of the king's forces. The project of building a navy, like all the ventures of the war, put this association to the test and in the process revealed the underlying tensions and discord.

Iron was the most difficult item to procure for the frigates, and the quest for it clearly revealed some of the problems of interdependence. Americans had never seen ships devour iron as these frigates did. Taken together they ate up more than fourteen hundred tons of the stuff.* By eighteenth-

---

*This is a deliberately conservative figure. It assumes that all the guns were of the short variety and does not count any guns that might have been aboard the two

century American standards it was an impressive amount, almost equal to the entire export production of Pennsylvania, the iron-making center of North America.[1] The iron furnaces in the states had sufficient capacity to produce what was needed; nevertheless, the Continental navy had great difficulty in getting iron. The explanation for this apparent paradox lies first with certain characteristics of the industry itself and secondly in the logistical problems of Revolutionary America.

Eighteenth-century iron manufacturing was a capital-intensive industry, as it is in the twentieth century; that is, it required an inordinately large amount of money for the construction of facilities. This alone would have restricted the number of forges, but a further resource requirement had the additional effect of concentrating their number in certain geographical locations. They had to be close to sources of ore, fuel and water power. Only certain parts of the country had this happy conjunction of money and natural resources: eastern Pennsylvania, parts of New Jersey and southeastern Massachusetts. Such concentration of the industry created severe problems of distribution, especially in the critical situation brought on by the war, when unprecedented quantities of iron had to be shipped to seven different locations. Even in the best of times delivery would have been difficult, but in wartime, with the enemy prowling the usual sea routes, the hazards increased geometrically. Making and shipping iron were not the only problems. The iron masters were not al-

---

frigates destroyed in the Hudson or the three in the Delaware, nor does it take into account the twenty-five to thirty tons of shot each ship carried. For ballast a figure of ten percent of the total tonnage has been used. The weight for the guns is as follows:

18 pound cannon	2700 pounds
12 " "	2900 "
9 " "	2600 "
6 " "	1900 "
4 " "	1200 "

"Pound" refers to the weight of the shot fired by the cannon.

ways willing to supply the navy, for the navy was only one
of several customers bidding for iron. Everyone wanted
heavy metal for cannon. Urgent demands were being made
by the army and by privateersmen, and not infrequently naval agents found themselves out-talked and out-maneuvered
by forge owners who preferred a privateersman's hard cash
in hand to the Congress's promised largesse.

Most of the iron that eventually found its way aboard the
Continental vessels was left in raw bar form to be stowed
deep in the hull as ballast. There it was called kentledge, and
its job was to act as a counterweight to the natural tendency
of the vessel to heel to leeward so that she might sail on a more
even keel and move efficiently and quickly through the water.
A lightly ballasted vessel is unstable or tender in rough
weather and drifts and bobs like a cork, while one too heavily
ballasted or with her weight not properly balanced moves
with all the agility of a mastodon. Either situation was obviously unsafe, especially for warships, and could wreak havoc
in battle. Exchanging broadsides in a seaway, an unstable
warship might well find her lee gun ports under water and
her windward ones pointing helplessly in the air. The approach of an enemy at such a time could prove to be unfortunate if not fatal.

American builders would use almost any heavy substance
they could find for ballast, including gravel, stone and sometimes even water, but by far they preferred to use bars of pig
iron. Iron took up less room and was easier to handle and stow
—an important consideration when it became necessary, as it
often did, to shift ballast at sea. Complaints of faulty ballast
were frequent, and it is possible that some ships went down
because they carried too little weight in the hold to compen-
sate for topside guns and a heavy sparring. On an average the
ships in the Continental navy probably carried about ten
percent of their total displacement in ballast. That was a
moderate load compared to the nearly eighty percent that
modern racing boats require.[2]

The pig iron in the hold was the raw material from which the cannons topside were made, but between that unfinished bulk down below and those ministers of death above was a long, laborious and costly process. If the builders thought they had trouble getting ballast, they soon realized that that had been only the prelude to their battle for cannon.

In armament, as in design, the Marine Committee's wish was for uniformity. The celebrated Philadelphia scientist David Rittenhouse was asked by the committee to prepare a plan for the guns. As soon as the design was ready, they intended to give it to local Pennsylvania forges where all the guns would be cast and then shipped out to the frigates. Each class of frigates would mount identical batteries. The thirty-twos would have twenty-six twelve-pounders and six six-pounders; the twenty-eights would have twenty-six twelve-pounders and two six-pounders, and the smallest class of twenty-fours would be armed with twenty-four nine-pounders.[3] The plan made good sense. If the armament of the vessels was standardized, all the equipment needed to operate the guns, including shot, sponges, rammers, wads and tackle, could be the same size. Such a system would be a boon to production and supply and at the same time help make training gun crews more efficient. If the plan worked, everything, men included, would be interchangeable.

Like so many other golden ideas before the committee, this one soon turned to dross. The committee's reliance on the Pennsylvania producers proved to be ill founded. The iron makers in Pennsylvania and virtually everywhere else in America were inexperienced in cannon founding, and before they could launch into any kind of production, they had to solve a plethora of technical problems. It did not take them long to discover that casting guns was a complex and difficult task. The business did not permit mistakes and required high standards of quality control. A flawed cannon fired on board ship would burst, hurling deadly fragments of hot iron and burning powder that could cause heavier casualties than a broadside from a seventy-four.[4] No wonder captains took personal responsibility for proving* their guns and often rejected what they saw as unfit for service.[5] Through trial and error most of the technical problems were solved, but it took time, and while iron masters were discarding inferior metal or cracked castings, the frigates were nearing completion. By the spring it was certain that the furnaces of Pennsylvania would never be able to supply all the ships even if they worked day and night. Only the ships in Philadelphia and possibly Baltimore could look to the committee for guns; the others would have to fend for themselves.

This was disturbing news to the New England agents, Langdon, Cushing, Tillinghast and Deane. The iron resources of their region were meager compared to Pennsylvania. The largest furnace in the Northeast was the Hope furnace, located near the Pawtuxet River in Scituate, Rhode Island. It was part of the business empire of the Browns of Providence and had been in operation since 1765.[6] Other than Hope there were only two sizable furnaces in New England, one at Salisbury, in the northwest corner of Connecticut, and the other at Abington, Massachusetts, fifteen miles southeast of Boston.[7] Apparently there was no important furnace at all in New Hampshire.

The owners at all three were willing to supply cannon for the Congress, but first they each had to solve their common technical problem. Their furnaces were equipped only to produce low-grade pig iron and would require the installation of more sophisticated apparatus before they would be able to turn out the higher grade metal needed for cannon. The Browns and the owners of the Salisbury works moved quickly to convert their facilities to meet the demand, and it was not long before they were turning out guns for their customers. At Abington, though, the situation was far less promising. The owner, Aaron Hobart, slogged along at a

---

*"Proving" a gun usually meant firing it with an extra charge of powder and double shot.

snail's pace. Poor Cushing, who was depending on him for guns, bombarded the iron master with letters urging him on. It did little good, and Cushing soon discovered he had about as much chance of getting cannon out of Abington as he did out of Philadelphia. The next place to look was the Massachusetts General Court.

The general court was willing to work a deal. They were being inundated with complaints about British activity in Massachusetts Bay, especially that of the frigate H.M.S. *Milford*. Cushing was told that if the Marine Committee would agree to use at least one of the frigates under construction to rid the bay of this nuisance, the general court would do its best to find cannon for the frigates out of local stock.[8] The bargain was made, and by order of the general court it was resolved that they would "afford him every . . . assistance in their power," providing, of course, that in addition to clearing the bay Congress also agreed to reimburse the state for any expenses and to return the guns if the frigate left Massachusetts waters.[9] As far as the Marine Committee was concerned, Cushing's deal left a lot to be desired. Massachusetts was holding her cannon hostage so that the frigate would never leave, but what could they do? By early fall Cushing could happily report that he had received most of the guns and that the rest, along with powder and shot, were on their way. He anticipated some good sport as soon as his frigates got to sea, and the people along the North Shore who were long tired of hearing the tocsins ringing looked forward to the battle.[10]

Cushing would soon taste some bitter disappointment; nevertheless, as things stood in the summer and fall of 1776, he did have good reason to be riding high. His neighbor to the north, Langdon, was not so fortunate. His euphoria at *Raleigh*'s launching had quickly faded after he realized that he did not have a single gun for the ship and that there was precious little hope of obtaining any. New Hampshire did not have a single furnace capable of casting cannon for his frigate. At first he thought, as did nearly everyone, that the Pennsylvania forges would supply his needs. That was futile. Even later in the war when the forges were operating and Langdon needed cannon for other ships, he discovered that guns, like all supplies, were distributed according to rules of proximity. Local markets would be satisfied first, and only then would goods begin to move down the line to other areas. At the current rate of production there was no likelihood of that happening very soon; even so, Portsmouth was at the farthest end of the line.

William Whipple, a New Hampshire delegate and important member of the Marine Committee, suggested that Langdon look to Connecticut or Rhode Island for help. The former was of little use; the Salisbury furnace was working long hours supplying local needs, and anything left over was carted off to New York for the frigates there.[11] That left only one furnace, the Browns' at Scituate, Rhode Island. The Brown brothers, Nicholas and John, were astute businessmen who over the years had amassed a sizable fortune from commerce and manufacturing; the Hope furnace was only one of their many investments. The war brought them more good fortune, for between Salisbury's commitment to Connecticut and New York on the one hand and Aaron Hobart's lethargy on the other, the Hope works had a virtual monopoly on cannon founding in New England. It was to these gentlemen that John Langdon had to turn.

As businessmen the Browns were eager to turn a profit, but how far they would go to do it is an open question. Certainly in their dealings with Langdon, as their biographer has pointed out, they showed some inclination at trying to squeeze out a few extra dollars.[12] The testy Langdon would have none of it and let loose a broadside that rocked the Rhode Island Frigate Committee and sent waves out of Portsmouth that rolled all the way to Philadelphia.

It began early in June 1776 when Langdon, tired to death of trying to find cannon by correspondence, decided to go in person to Providence. Whenever he had suggested to the Rhode Islanders that they should sell him some of their can-

non, they had always told him that they could not because
their frigates were nearly ready for sea and would be needing
the guns. So when Langdon got to the dock and saw the ships
for the first time, he was much disturbed. Instead of two
frigates nearly finished, as had been reported to him and the
Congress, he found ships that in his judgment were not more
than two-thirds completed. What particularly annoyed him
was that sitting on the dock alongside the unfinished hulls
were two full sets of guns waiting to be shipped on board.
Were the Rhode Islanders hoarding the guns? Langdon
thought so, and if anyone doubted him, he was willing to
"produce Thousands of Witnesses" to attest to what he had
seen.[13]

The Rhode Islanders stalled, but Langdon would not be put
off. He made a second and even a third trip to Providence,
each time coming back to Portsmouth empty-handed and
more angry than when he left. He wrote to Josiah Bartlett,
another New Hampshire delegate in Philadelphia, about the
"false information" being circulated to keep the cannon from
him. He even passed some strong hints that in his opinion the
Rhode Islanders by their selfish conduct were damaging the
whole war effort.[14]

Right in the middle of this intensifying storm sat the
Browns, the Krupps of Providence, who at this point were
not only the chief suppliers but also key members of the
Rhode Island Frigate Committee. Late in August Nicholas
Brown told Langdon that the hearth at his furnace had col-
lapsed and that between repairs and casting time it would be
at the very least fifty-five days before *Raleigh* could expect any
cannon from that quarter. The news strengthened Langdon
in his determination to have the guns already cast. Once more
he rode to Providence.

He received a restrained reception, for by now the Rhode
Island committee had seen quite enough of this New Hampshire "shop keeper." Langdon cared little for what they
thought, and he was persistent in his determination to have
the guns. Under the circumstances there was not much the

committee could do, so they offered him the cannon, but only on certain conditions—conditions so restrictive and insulting as to make it impossible for a man with Langdon's ego to accept.

The guns would be delivered up to him if he signed a contract with the Browns pledging to pay for the cost of replacements within fifty days at the rate of £100 per ton.[15] That was an enormous sum, since less than a year before costs were only one-third as much.[16] Langdon protested but he agreed to the "unheard of sum." With that unpleasantness over, he excused himself from the committee and went to sign the contract. When the paper was laid before him, he was stunned. The Browns would not recognize his authority as an agent of the Congress and demanded that he personally guarantee the full amount, about £4000. Furthermore, they wanted one-half of the money down in cash. It was bad enough that he had to pay what he thought was an extraordinary price, but under no circumstances would Langdon suffer the Rhode Islanders to question his authority and integrity. He left Providence in a foul temper and without the cannon. Back home he wrote another of his acerbic letters, and for perhaps the first time in American history a demand was made for a congressional investigation of a war contractor.

Langdon was not the only one concerned about what was going on. In Braintree Abigail Adams, John's sprightly and observant partner, told her husband that the Portsmouth ship had lain idle for six weeks because she lacked guns. It was, according to Mrs. Adams, an unpleasant situation made all the more sorry because, while *Raleigh* lay unarmed, "Private Adventurers" had no trouble getting guns. These reports from Braintree and Portsmouth reached Congress along with other rumors suggesting that supplies in Providence intended for the frigates were being sold privately. It was all very disconcerting, especially to the Rhode Island delegate William Ellery, who was being called upon by his colleagues to supply answers to their embarrassing questions. Ellery claimed ignorance and asked Governor Cooke if he would provide some explanation to refute these charges. Cooke never responded to the request.

This was the first of many instances in the history of the Continental navy when allegations of wrongdoing were hurled about, agent charging agent, the Marine Committee blasting away at someone while officers bickered among themselves. It was not at all uncommon, when the navy came up in conversation, to hear people talk of hoarding, profiteering, stealing, incompetence and cowardice.

The Marine Committee, dismayed at the internecine sniping going on in New England, ordered Langdon back to Providence and at the same time told the Frigate Committee in no uncertain terms that they were to deliver up to him immediately the cannon in question. Moreover, they announced to the committee they were sending a personal representative, Captain Nathaniel Falconer of Philadelphia, to view the frigates and report back.[17]

The captain's orders were terse and pointed. Upon arriving in Providence, he was immediately to inspect the two ships in question and take an inventory of all stores and materials. If necessary he was warranted to require the assistance of "all persons employed in the building or fitting of said Frigates." Falconer made his inspection trip, but before he returned, the Marine Committee had received other intelligence that gave them reason to regret their rush to judgment against the Rhode Islanders. According to the new information, *Warren* and *Providence* were far from being in the state described by Langdon but were rather afloat, armed and ready for sea. It gave the committee pause, and with some chagrin they rescinded their order to deliver up the cannon.[18]

Had Langdon deliberately misled the Marine Committee into believing the Rhode Island frigates were not ready so that he could have the guns for himself? Probably not. There is nothing in his career either before or after this imbroglio to suggest that he was ever anything but an honest and patriotic man. In his haste and inexperience he had underestimated the ability of Bowers and his workmen to hurry the job. When he saw the two frigates in the summer, he thought it would take far longer to finish them than it actually did. That error, coupled with his own waspish nature and the Browns' curious behavior, led him to his peremptory judgment against the Rhode Islanders.

It took almost another full year for Langdon to scrounge up enough cannon for his ship. In the end *Raleigh*'s ordnance was a hodgepodge of local donations, purchases and imported French guns. When there was so much work for *Raleigh* to do, her unemployment was a loss to the American effort and a great disappointment for Langdon and all the New Hampshire men who on that beautiful afternoon in May felt so much pride in watching her slide into the water.

At the other building sites there was less dissonance but no more expedition. For example, *Trumbull* took three years to get to sea. She was built in a reasonable length of time, but when she was brought down the Connecticut, she drew too much water and it was impossible to get her over the bar at the mouth of the river. It was a sad if not silly business, and it took two years, much scheming and practically the full-time attention of a member of the navy board at Boston, John Deshon, before the builders finally stripped her bare and lashed empty barrels to the hull. With the added buoyancy she cleared the bar and was brought around to New London in August 1779, where she remained for another nine months awaiting guns and fittings.[19]

The collapse of the centralized plan for guns, like the previous failure in uniform ship design, meant that the contractors were thrown back on their own resources and had to make decisions about ordnance based solely on what they could get their hands on. In most cases they tried to follow as nearly as possible the congressional plan. The only frigate that made a radical departure from these norms was *Warren*. She carried eighteen-pounders, cast by the Browns, and was the only frigate in the American navy to carry guns that large. The difficulty in getting guns pointed up an additional problem for the navy. In their chronic state of unreadiness the American frigates presented an inviting target to the enemy. Lying dockside or swinging at anchor, unarmed and unmanned, they were sitting ducks for a quick thrust by red-coated raiders. To guard against this, the Marine Committee continually sought the assistance of local authorities and General Washington in posting troops. As far as the general was concerned, such requests were a great annoyance. In his opinion the navy was useful only when it supported the land operations of his army, and inasmuch as it distracted the attention of the Congress from his concerns, he was critical of it.[20] Relations between him and the navy were always correct and sometimes friendly, especially when agents of the Marine Committee and later the Board of Admiralty sent gifts of wine, fresh fruits, and on one occasion a live sea turtle, all captured by the Continental navy.[21] Nevertheless, it seems apparent from his attitude that Washington was never fully convinced that the Continental navy was worth the bother.

Skeptical from the first, he became openly angry in 1777 when the Marine Committee asked him to supply troops for the protection of the unfinished frigates lying in the Delaware. During the winter of 1776–77, when it seemed obvious that with good weather in the spring General Howe would advance on Philadelphia, the Marine Committee tried to get the frigates out of the Delaware to a place of greater safety. The Congress itself had fled to Baltimore in December, and there was some talk about bringing the frigates around to that town. *Randolph* did manage to get out, but the other three— *Effingham, Washington* and *Delaware*—were stranded at the capital.[22]

Washington, who was busy fighting a losing battle to save the city, could see no sense in using his men to defend ships. On no less than five occasions he suggested—he could not order, since he had no authority over the navy—that they be scuttled. The Marine Committee was reluctant. Under a similar British threat on the Hudson, they had just put *Congress* and *Montgomery* to the torch and they had little heart for doing the same on the Delaware. Their foot dragging would prove costly.[23]

As expected, Howe took the city in September. Two months later the Royal Navy broke through the river defenses and came upon the American ships. *Delaware*, under the command of Captain Charles Alexander, was armed and therefore could fight, but the battle was all too brief. She could not escape, ran aground and struck. The other two frigates got a temporary reprieve and sailed upstream to an area near Bordentown, New Jersey, where the Marine Committee thought they would be safe. Washington was not so sure and he warned that they were still prime targets for attack. Hopeful to the last, the committee resisted Washington's pressure all through the winter of 1777–78, but in May, just as the general had feared, a British party penetrated the American lines and burned *Washington* and *Effingham*.[24]

Not one of the original thirteen frigates lasted long enough in the American service to see Yorktown. Three—*Congress, Montgomery* and *Warren*—were destroyed to avoid capture. The first two were destroyed even before they got to sea, and the last was one of the suicides on the ill-fated Penobscot expedition.

Seven of the frigates, more than half of the entire fleet, were surrendered to the enemy. *Virginia* was taken when she tried to run the blockade off the Chesapeake capes. *Boston* and *Providence* were turned over when Charleston capitulated. *Raleigh* and *Hancock* and *Trumbull* were taken at sea. Ironically, *Trumbull*, the last of the thirteen, was captured at sea by the British frigate *Iris*, the former Continental frigate *Hancock*, which had been the first of the thirteen to be captured. The last of the group to be accounted for is *Randolph*, and she, of course, had the saddest fate of all when she blew up battling *Yarmouth*.

Although the number thirteen carried an almost mystical quality, the Congress was by no means satisfied with it when it came to the navy. After the authorization of December 1775 an irresistible pressure grew to expand, and in November 1776 Congress voted additional ships. Considering the agony that they had been through over the first thirteen, of which none had yet seen deep water, it seems hard to believe that they could have had such incredible pretensions. The new act called for:

In New Hampshire	1 ship of 74 guns.
In Massachusetts Bay	1 ditto of 74 ditto and 1 ditto of 36 ditto.
In Pennsylvania,	1 ditto of 74 ditto
	1 brig of 18 guns and a packet-boat.
In Virginia,	2 frigates of 36 ditto each.
In Maryland,	2 ditto of 36 ditto each.[25]

This act was an expanded version of 1775, but it met with measurably less success. Only one of the five thirty-six-gun frigates was ever completed—*Alliance,* built under the direction of Hancock's friend Cushing in the yard of John and William Hackett of Salisbury, Massachusetts. Some work was apparently begun on the ships in Virginia but it was not much, and the two in Maryland never moved beyond just being a resolution.[26] Two months later, on 23 January 1777, a grievous omission in the resolution was rectified when Connecticut was awarded two frigates, *Bourbon,* built at Chatham, and *Confederacy,* at Norwich. *Confederacy* got to sea in the spring of 1779. She was captured two years later and ended her career as H.M.S. *Confederate. Bourbon,* on the other hand, was not even laid down until 1779. She took four years to build, and by the time she was finished, the war was over and so she was sold.

Rounding out the frigates in the American service were three obtained abroad. *Deane,* later renamed *Hague,* was built in Nantes, France, and brought to America in 1778. *Deane* was one of the few American warships to survive the war, and she was placed out of commission in 1783. *Pallas* was a frigate in the French navy turned over to the Congress in 1779 and returned after the war. Finally there was _Queen of France_, an old lady purchased by the American commissioners in Paris. She was scuttled by the Americans at Charleston in 1780.[27] Despite their fate, the frigates that got to sea did at least bring a few moments of brief glory to the American navy, and in some measure they did help partially to balance out the trauma and woe they caused in building. No such consolation, however small, awaited the Americans in the case of the seventy-four-gun ships authorized in the act of November 1776.

Only one of the three, _America_, was ever actually built. She was one of an intended fleet of eleven seventy-four-gun ships of the line. Three would be built in America, and eight would either be purchased or chartered from the French. The eight from the French never materialized; the one in Pennsylvania was probably never even lofted; and the Massachusetts seventy-four was framed but then abandoned and left to rot. That left only the one in New Hampshire, and as usual John Langdon was in charge. _America_ was laid down in his yard in May 1777 by James Hackett.[28]

As always Langdon had things well in hand. In the spring of 1777 his yard on Badger Island out in the middle of the Piscataqua was running along smoothly, and he was preparing to launch his second Continental ship, _Ranger_. She was one of the finest vessels ever built for the Continental navy and was described by one English captain who felt her bite as "Hake built and Hollow Counter'd." On 14 June 1777 this sleek vessel was given by the Congress to John Paul Jones, who sailed her on some of the most exciting exploits of the entire war.

As Jones went aboard his new command and bade farewell to Portsmouth, Langdon was just getting _America_ under way. With _Raleigh_ and _Ranger_ to his credit, he was now ready to embark on the biggest shipbuilding project ever attempted in an American yard.

Right from the start the omens augured ill, and before long

the dream turned into an interminable nightmare. The project gulped money with a ravenous appetite, and by early March 1778 the Marine Committee in an unwonted moment of austerity ordered a moratorium while they caught their breath and reevaluated the whole situation. The pause provided an opportunity for some members to raise objections, which had been discussed earlier but overridden, about the usefulness of the seventy-four. In their more chastened mood Congress listened to such men as Henry Laurens, William Ellery and William Whipple, who pointed out how difficult it would be to man such vessels even if they could be finished. A seventy-four would take at least a six-hundred-man crew, the equivalent of more than a regiment, to say nothing of provisions, powder, shot and other matériel.[29]

In a quandary about how to proceed, Congress listened attentively to the suggestion of a dashing young French naval officer newly arrived from Paris, Captain Pierre Landais. Later in the war Landais of course showed himself to be a mad scoundrel, but in the spring of 1778 he had some sound advice for a Congress much in need of it. He recommended that the seventy-four be cut down to two decks, eliminating the raised quarterdeck and forecastle deck. Razed to this configuration, she would then carry two batteries: one of twenty-eight twenty-four-pounders and the other of twenty-eight eighteen-pounders. *America* would be a super frigate giving as good a fight as a seventy-four but would be much faster and easier to man.[30]

Congress was in a mood to accept anything French, and the Marine Committee was eager to get something going again in Portsmouth. It was decided to adopt the Landais plan, and orders to that effect were sent to the Navy Board of the Eastern Department and to John Langdon. Both were unimpressed. Construction had been proceeding so slowly that the reducing of *America* was a moot question since she had not gone much beyond framing. With or without the Landais design, the project was in irons.[31] In July 1779 the Marine Committee as a last resort decided to rely on the well-known persuasiveness of Benjamin Franklin, and they forwarded to him a shopping list for their ship to be filled in France that contained everything "from a Brass Cannon to a Shoe-buckle." The list itemized enough material to fit out and arm eight frigates and a seventy-four. It was a bit much to ask even for a man of Franklin's known abilities, and it is not al-together certain that he ever even seriously pressed the issue in the French court.[32]

Predictably, the Marine Committee never let go of the dream, and in December they ordered Langdon to complete his ship on the original design even though, as they admitted to him, there was "great difficulty . . . in furnishing you with a fund sufficient for carrying out the work." They offered no explanation for the change back to the seventy-four.[33]

In January 1780, after nearly three years of work, the Navy Board of the Eastern Department gave the Board of Admiralty a progress report. It was not very heartening. To finish the job they needed more than half a million dollars, seven hundred tons of timber and a work force of 120 men. The board was only able to supply dribs and drabs, and the whole business just limped along. To provide funds John Bradford in Boston was allowed to sell a few dozen hogsheads of rum and sugar which had accumulated in his warehouse as part of the Continental share of prizes. That money did not last long. In July the pressure was on again, this time at least to get the hull launched. The board reckoned that if they had something in the water, perhaps the commander of the French fleet recently arrived in Rhode Island might be persuaded to part with some of his stores to finish the job. It was only another faint hope. By the time the chill November winds swept into Portsmouth, *America* was still high and dry, and once more work on her had come to a complete halt. Hopeless was the only way the Board of Admiralty could describe the project, and they suggested that Congress sound out the French min-ister concerning a possible sale of the ship to the French navy so that she might not be a total loss. The response was negative; the French had no interest in buying a half-finished hull.[34]

At any point Congress might well have decided to cut its losses and simply abandon the whole dismal business, but pride dictated that *America* be finished. On 23 June 1781, with the war all but over, Congress ordered Robert Morris, who had taken charge of naval affairs from the defunct Board of Admiralty, to finish the ship. Three days later, to underline their determination in this matter, they named John Paul Jones to command her. It was the biggest command in the navy, and Jones may well have anticipated promotion to flag rank. Whatever his expectations, he hurried to Portsmouth to take charge.[35]

The work at Portsmouth did not please him. He was by nature a man of action, impatient with delay and made cranky by long stays ashore. Never a very amiable or politic man, he also had great difficulty getting along with Langdon. Both were aristocrats, one on the quarterdeck, the other in the town. They were too much alike, proud and haughty, and a clash was inevitable. Jones, America's greatest naval hero, flew into a rage when Langdon, described by Jones as "a man who was bred in a shop and hath been a voyage or two at sea under a nurse," had the temerity to assert that he knew as well as the chevalier "how to fit out, govern, and fight a ship of war!"[36] For a man who had probably wrung more salt water out of the seat of his pants than Langdon had ever sailed over, this was too much, and the wonder is not that *America* finally did get launched but that these two gentlemen did not assault each other in the process. On 5 November 1782 the Continental navy's first and only ship of the line slid down the ways under the watchful eyes of Jones and Langdon.

The occasion was robbed of much of its joy by the knowledge that this ship would never see service under the American flag. She had been made a gift to the French. Some months earlier the French ship of the line *Le Magnifique* had run aground and broken up in Boston harbor. She had stayed afloat long enough to be stripped, and most of her fittings, including cannon, had been used to complete *America*. As a gesture of thanks for their aid during the war and to replace *Le Magnifique*, Congress gave *America* to the French. It was probably just as well; it is hard to imagine what the Americans could have done with this white elephant, for they had neither the money to equip nor the men to man her. Furthermore, why should they bother? The war was over. Accordingly, after getting her to a safe anchorage, Jones welcomed Captain de Vaisseau de Macarty Macteigne aboard to induct *America* into the Royal French Navy.[37]

The naval construction acts of 1775, 1776 and 1777 account for twenty-five vessels. Although these were by far the most important ships, there were at least twenty-one others authorized by Congress at various times. Some were built, such as the *Mercury* packet, but others obviously were not. In addition, Congress continued to add to its fleet by purchase. Much of this *ad hoc* buying was done at the discretion of the local agents who had the opportunity to buy prizes brought into their ports.[38]

Congress plowed through mountainous seas to get ships launched, fitted and armed, but having done that, they could look forward only to brief spans of fair weather before these same vessels would be back in port to be refitted and repaired. Damage by enemy fire was only part of the problem. The main culprits were rot and barnacles. The first was a silent but deadly enemy, often making its presence known only when it was too late. Such was the case with *Randolph* when she was caught in a gale off the Carolinas. All her topmasts, as well as the bowsprit, were carried away because they were so rotten they could not take the strain. Proper seasoning of the timber could have retarded rot, but that took time and American builders rushed into construction with green wood. The American ships that ended up in foreign navies, either French or British, were often put out of service ahead of their time because they were so enfeebled by rot. Guarding against and repairing damage from rot was an expensive and time-consuming task. *Alliance*, for example, one of the best frigates in the navy, was described as being "old" when she had been in the service less than five years, and she leaked so badly that no one wished to put to sea in her.

Almost as important as a sound hull was a clean bottom. Whenever a vessel was in port, microscopic marine organisms such as barnacles, algae, hydroids and sea sprites attached themselves to the underside of the hull. The worst offenders were the barnacles, tiny animals covered with a hard shell. When the ship began moving again, they died, but in the process they left behind their shells, intact and firmly fixed to the hull. Before long several tons of these fellows were hitching a ride on the hull, slowing the vessel down and reducing her maneuverability, sometimes by as much as fifty percent.[39] The problem was particularly acute in warm seas where barnacles thrived. When Nicholas Biddle was commanding *Randolph* in the tepid waters around South Carolina, he discovered that her bottom became so foul that it was necessary to careen after every voyage. Fortunately for the American navy, most of their ships kept to higher latitudes, and scraping every six months or so was adequate. Even this moderate maintenance schedule was hard to keep. There was not a single dry dock available to the American navy, and so the scraping could only be done in the time-honored fashion of careening or heaving down. First of all the guns, stores and ballast had to be removed. All the topgallants and topmasts were taken down, along with all the yards. Next every gun port, hawsehole and any other opening had to be closed and made watertight. Planks were nailed to the deck in a lattice-like configuration to provide footing when the vessel went over on her side.

After the ship had been stripped and anchored fore and aft, protector tackle was secured to the high side to support the masts. Openings caulked and masts braced, heavy tackle was then secured to the masthead and rove through blocks ashore. With the crew walking round a capstan, the vessel was brought over until she lay almost on her side, with her hull in the air. Men using either staging or rafts could then work to clean and repair, and when one side was clean, the same procedure was used to clean the other. It was a major undertaking, costly in terms of time and money, and if done carelessly, it could be dangerous. Masts were often sprung, and hulls, improperly sealed, filled with water.

One bit of preventive action that could be taken was to sheathe the hull with copper plate. This warded off toredo worms that could bore through the hull and it delayed fouling. Vessels with their hulls covered were able to keep station longer, and with clean bottoms they were considerably faster. Only one American warship, *Alliance*, was sheathed; the others, because of lack of funds, had only conventional bottoms.

Coppering was seen to be such an advantage that, although the British had not sheathed many of their ships before the war, once the French navy became an active participant, they quickly realized the strategic value of being able to keep more and faster ships on station for longer periods of time. As a result, in 1778 the Royal Navy began a crash program so that "within six weeks twenty ships were coppered and before the war was over it had been applied to every ship fit for service."[40]

Certainly the entire naval program of the Continental Congress, stretching over some eight years and involving building more than three dozen ships as well as maintaining an even larger number, had a considerable economic impact on the wartime economy. Because of the paucity of hard economic data, appraisals of the effect cannot be precisely determined. Nevertheless, certain general observations seem valid.

The first is that hundreds of men who might otherwise have been unemployed because of the disruption of American trade were kept busy building ships for the Congress. If John Langdon's operation is any indication, it seems reasonable to estimate that each frigate required a work force of about a hundred men. This figure includes only men in the yard, and to it must be added ax men in the forests who felled the timber, teamsters who had to transport it and, of course, all the men involved in manufacturing items used to outfit the ship: cannon, instruments, cordage and so forth. There can be little doubt that the activity associated with building the Continental ships of war helped stimulate the economies of places like Portsmouth, Newburyport, Plymouth and Philadelphia.[41]

Beyond launching, there was the business of maintenance and provision. In this regard no place surpassed Boston, and all during the war Continental vessels put in there more than anywhere else to seek markets for their prizes and take on large quantities of food and equipment, all supplied by local victuallers and chandlers. Other ports, such as Philadelphia, Providence and Baltimore, did their share as well, but they envied Boston's preeminent position. There seems to be no question that the American Revolution helped to spur American business, and the Continental navy did its share.

Chapter Thirteen

On the Quarterdeck

The more Congress fretted over their ships, the more acutely aware they became that navies are like machines and, no matter how finely made, their ultimate fate depends upon the motion given them by men. The real success of a navy depends upon one proposition: that good men command its ships.

Eighteenth-century naval commanders were a special breed of men. In the Royal Navy, to which the Americans looked for guidance in almost all matters, a ship's captain was not simply above his men; he was on a different plane entirely. His cabin, always spacious even in the most cramped vessel, was aft in the special world of the quarterdeck, a realm reserved only for officers. When he came on deck, the whole windward side was cleared for his promenade. He gave his orders crisply and expected, and usually received, instant obedience. In almost every respect his word was the law, backed by hard discipline meted out to the slow and recalcitrant. Such power was awesome, and in the hands of weak or sinister men it could be corrupted into inhumane brutality, but such examples were rare. In fact most captains were stern but decent men who used their positions to turn their crews of unruly derelicts, criminals and seamen into well-drilled teams that turned to smartly in every crisis. This was the type of man the Continental Congress hoped to find to command its ships.[1]

It is nearly impossible to determine how many captains and officers the Continental navy needed; any figure would depend upon how many ships were actually in service at any one time, and that remains something of a mystery. What is certain, though, is that after 1776, no matter how many officers were needed, Congress always had an embarrassing surplus. That had not always been the case. Earlier, when the Naval Committee was readying Hopkins's fleet, they had run into some difficulty recruiting men, but then the only ships they could offer were cranky, tender-sided merchantmen. Later, of course, there were thirteen grand frigates building, and the thought of commanding one of those beauties was enough to swamp the Congress with applications from men who dreamed of sailing in a sea of glory. Quite often the applications came to Congress via the good offices of a member who, in addition to his other duties, acted as a sponsor and lobbied for his nominee.

All together, including marine officers who also served aboard ship, Congress commissioned about 340 men, a rather high figure since at no time were there more than 3000 seamen and marines on duty and the result was an officer-to-enlisted-man ratio of 1:10.[2] This surfeit of officers amid a thinning fleet meant a high rate of unemployment. With rare exceptions, only half of the officers were actually on duty at any one time during the war. The beaching of so many men was a source of constant irritation to both Congress and the navy. Some of them spent a good deal of their time scrambling for the few commands available and caring little about whom they stepped on, while others simply gave up, returned home and went privateering. With such a crowded establishment, Congress tended to assign too many officers to its vessels, and this also sparked discontent, especially when it came time to divide the profits of a cruise.[3]

The reason for the existence of such a large number of supernumerary officers can best be laid to Congress's congenital incapacity to say no when it might mean offending a state, coupled with the illusion that there would soon be ships enough for everyone. They frequently commissioned men for ships that were barely off the drawing boards, and when the construction dragged on, or worse was abandoned, Congress found itself with more officers than berths.

All officers held their commissions, as they do today, by an act of Congress. In most cases this meant that they had been recommended to the attention of the Naval Committee, Marine Committee or the Board of Admiralty, which had then submitted their name to the Congress. In most cases the commissioning process worked rather smoothly, and Congress generally followed the advice of its subordinates. Whatever battles were fought were apparently waged outside Congress. A potentially serious problem that was settled quite early in the war was the question of who had authority to commission. Was Congress the exclusive agent or could others appoint men to the commissioned ranks? The question arose when the gentlemen of the Rhode Island Frigate Committee apparently took it upon themselves to appoint officers to *Warren*. The Congress quite rightly took exception to this and quickly informed the Rhode Islanders that they would brook no interference in an area that was exclusively theirs. Later, times and distance would make it necessary for Congress to forward blank commissions to agents in the field to be filled in locally, but even in these instances it was made clear that these appointments were temporary until Congress officially passed on them.[4]

Although the Marine Committee were quick to claim their authority, they were not so eager to exercise it. The chill months of early 1776 dragged on as they met and met again in their room above the City Tavern with little to show for their time except some pleasant moments of conviviality amid the smoke and rounds of port. It was Hancock who was to chair the meetings, but he was often absent, and even when his body was there, his mind was elsewhere. As president of the Congress, he was concerned with far more weighty matters, and although some members murmured that he should resign from the committee, no one dared suggest it publicly, and for the time they muddled on, talking about but not commissioning officers.

Indirection was not the only reason for inaction. The committee was in a holding pattern awaiting developments on several fronts. One had to do with Commodore Hopkins and his peripatetic fleet that no one had yet heard from. They were sailing under orders from the defunct Naval Committee and were cruising somewhere to the southward. It would be inappropriate for the committee to make any appointments until they had a chance to hear the results of that operation and judge the performance of the officers. After all, Hopkins's senior officers had a good claim to the new commands. A second factor encouraging delay was the uncertain and unfinished state of the frigates themselves. There was no urgency to appoint men for ships that were not yet in the water. The third factor, and one that involved more than just the Marine Committee and the Congress, was the total uncertainty of the times. No one knew what the spring might bring. It had been a desultory winter marked by a standoff in Boston and inaction elsewhere. Many congressmen hoped that somehow the spring would bring a resolution to the problems and that events had not gone too far for some sort of reconciliation. Reasoned arguments, a victory or a defeat, a minister's or king's change of heart—any of these might well mean an end to the business before it really began. Time would destroy these hopes, but for the moment patience seemed more prudent than action.

Spring brought new life to the Revolution. The British made their inglorious departure from Boston, and Washington, buoyed with confidence, moved his army toward New York and, he hoped, even greater victories. The Marine Committee also stirred itself. Early in April they reported out a new form of commissions, and a couple of weeks later they recommended to Congress four appointments.[5] Two of them were of relatively minor importance: William Hallock to command *Hornet* and Charles Alexander to *Wasp*. The others, though, were major commands: the two frigates in Massachusetts. For these posts the committee endorsed Isaac Cazneau, a friend of Hancock's, along with the most famous of Washington's schooner captains, John Manley.

On the other commands that were going to open up, the Congress was silent. For the next two months the committee sat and deliberated over them as each day's mail brought in additional letters, applications and recommendations attesting to the virtues of one particular officer or another.[6] Technically, of course, all thirteen committee members were responsible for recommending proper persons to Congress, but in fact, as had already been shown with Cazneau and Manley, the real work was done by the men from the state where the frigate was being fitted out. It seems to have been understood from the very outset that each frigate would be commanded by a man from the state where she was built. The committee member involved had to consult with the folks back home to find someone qualified and acceptable to them who would also be amenable to the committee and Congress. After considerable jockeying and weighing of qualifications, both naval and political, the committee selected nine more names to present to Congress. There was no problem; the full body approved and designated the men by state, leaving the actual assignment by ship to the Marine Committee.[7]

During the summer, as other posts became available, additional commanders were appointed, and by the early fall of 1776 the Continental navy had at least twenty-four captains on its rolls. Some were inherited from Hopkins's old flotilla, including the commodore himself; others, such as James Nicholson and Charles Alexander, were recruited out of the state navies; and still more came straight out of privateering or the merchant marine. No matter by what route they came, they were all made captains in the Continental navy, and that caused some problems. Ordinarily when a group of officers hold the same title, rank is determined by seniority, but neither Congress nor the Marine Committee had ever stated this, and in a previous resolution they had in fact said, although in a somewhat vague manner, that rank would be settled at a later time.[8] This uncertainty among such a group of rank-happy men as the Continental captains caused considerable uneasiness, but amid the pressure of other business Congress put off determining rank for another time.

In regard to the man who outranked all the captains, or at least thought he did, Commodore Hopkins, the Marine Committee faced a particularly sticky problem. The old Naval Committee had appointed him commander in chief of the fleet, but it was not altogether clear exactly what they meant by that title. Did they intend that he be commander in chief of the navy, as Washington was of the army? The most reasonable explanation seems to be that they intended him to be commander in chief only of the fleet then fitting out in the Delaware. The subsequent accretions to the fleet were never brought under his command, and at no time did he exercise the kind of broad authority enjoyed by Washington. At any rate, the commodore, whether or not he was commander in chief of the entire navy, was by the summer of 1776 an embarrassment to the Marine Committee and an albatross that they could well do without. The Marine Committee's difficulty with Hopkins helps to explain why, despite pressure from many quarters, they never appointed anyone to flag rank. After Hopkins the Continental navy had no commodores or admirals.[9]

Through the summer of 1776, as Washington was busy digging in around New York, the Marine Committee continued their deliberations and appointments—with the strict understanding that at a later date they would decide on rank. By October Washington had been lucky enough to escape from New York, and he and General Howe were dancing through New Jersey. In the meantime the committee had finally drawn up a list of officers according to rank.

The list carried the names of twenty-six men—twenty-four captains and two lieutenants—who were then in actual command of vessels. Whatever the criteria the committee used in its arrangement—and many have been suggested—one thing is certain; politics was every bit as important as merit.[10]

The number-one captain was James Nicholson, commander of the frigate *Virginia*, building at Baltimore. Nicholson, a member of a prominent Maryland family, had been the senior officer in the Maryland state navy, and since he was a southerner, his appointment gave a nice balance to the Yankee commander in chief. Further down the list, though, New England interest remained strong, and the three men following Nicholson were all northerners: John Manley of *Hancock*, a Bostonian; Hector McNeill of *Boston*,[11] from the same town; and Dudley Saltonstall, commander of *Trumbull* and a native of Connecticut. Manley and McNeill were new to the Continental navy, but Saltonstall was a veteran, and for him being ranked fourth was a comedown. He was originally commissioned in December 1775 and had served under Esek Hopkins as second in command; now he was fourth. His demotion and replacement by Nicholson were an offering to the southerners in Congress. Saltonstall could not have been pleased at this turn of events, but there was little he could do. His influence on the Marine Committee had peaked nearly a year before when his brother-in-law, the tireless Silas Deane, secured him his command under Hopkins. Since that time the fortunes of both men had been on the wane. Deane had not been reelected to the Congress, and in April he left America to take up his duties as one of the American representatives in Paris. With his patron gone and his own reputation under something of a cloud, Saltonstall did not stand a chance, and he was lucky to be ranked fourth.

On down the list the story was predictable. John Paul Jones, a young man whose chief handicaps were an acerbic pen and a lack of political friends, found himself moved from his place as fifth in Hopkins's fleet to number eighteen in the new establishment. It was a slight he did not forget.[12] The captains ranking highest were those in command of the frigates. The one exception to this was Lambert Wickes *(Reprisal)*, number eleven. He was the only captain in the top fourteen without a frigate.

Having once gone through the hassle of sorting out and ranking their captains, the Marine Committee resolved that from 10 October forward any additional captains would be ranked in accordance with the date of their commission. At least twenty-one more men were so ranked.[13]

If the Americans had been able to increase or even just preserve their fleet, they might well have avoided the single most divisive issue in the navy—command. The Continental navy probably reached its peak in terms of number of ships actually in service sometime late in 1777 or early in 1778; thereafter it was a matter of steady decline, despite some additions. As the fleet thinned, beached captains looked covetously on the commands of junior officers as well as on any new ships coming down the ways. Buttressed by the seniority rule, some felt fully justified in insisting that they be granted the best commands regardless of who might be displaced. It was a system plagued with squabbles.

One such tempest arose over the command of the famous sloop of war *Ranger*. By all accounts she was a beautiful vessel, and a good deal of credit for her design and construction must go to John Roche, a captain in the West Indian trade and a close friend of John Langdon. Roche had arrived in America shortly after the outbreak of war. He offered his services to Washington and had been appointed a lieutenant on board the schooner *Lynch*.[14] Early in the fall he left the general's fleet, and armed with introductions from Langdon to all the right people, including Sam Adams and Richard Henry Lee, he traveled to Philadelphia. He personally went before the Marine Committee and laid out a design "calculated for a Vessel of War a fast sailer and of strong Construction to carry Eighteen six Pounders and about 120 men."[15] The committee liked the plan, and work was begun in the yard of James Hackett, the same man who had built *Raleigh*. Although he held no official title, Roche was employed by Congress and hovered about the vessel giving advice and assistance as he could, apparently expecting that when she was launched, he would be named to command her.[16] It was not an unreasonable expectation. Congress was vague on the matter, but it is quite likely that when Roche rode up to Portsmouth from Philadelphia, he carried with him some kind of informal assurance that he would get the job. It is certain that back in New Hampshire his friend Langdon did nothing to persuade him otherwise. That was the fall of 1776; the spring of 1777 told a different story.

In March the indefatigable John Paul Jones arrived in Philadelphia looking for a new command. He certainly deserved it, for he had shown himself to be a brave and energetic officer while serving under Hopkins and later in his own independent commands on board *Providence* and *Alfred*. He arrived in Philadelphia from Rhode Island, where he was to have commanded a fleet, but circumstances had kept the ships bottled up. Jones, tired of sitting idly by, had decided to come in person to the Congress to see if there was not other more exciting and useful employment available. He spent at least a month lobbying for a new command. Finally in April he packed his bags and headed north to Boston with one of the "strangest set of orders ever received by a captain of the navy."[17] He was told to go aboard *Amphitrite*, a French armed merchant ship recently arrived at Portsmouth. She was bound to France by way of Charleston. According to the instructions, he was to sail on the ship, "appearing or acting on suitable occasions as the Commander."[18] Those "occasions" were to be whenever there was a chance to take a prize, and if that happened, as the Marine Committee hoped it would, the proceeds would be split three ways: one-third to Jones and his Continental men, one-third to the French and one-third to the Congress. The orders concluded by telling Jones that when he arrived in France, he was to present himself to the American commissioners and through their good offices get a vessel of his own to sail and raid around the British Isles. The Marine Committee had concocted a fantastic scheme, and the marvel is that a man with Jones's experience would ever have considered it. We can only conclude that his eagerness to get to France so that he could have his own command overrode his good judgment. But if Jones was temporarily blinded to the folly of the venture, the French captain of *Amphitrite* was not. He took a glum view of the business and refused to have any truck with Jones and his men.[19]

It was a strange way to hand out commands, and Jones probably was not too concerned over this setback; after all, at best he would only have been half a captain on board a foreign ship. Still, he wanted to get to France. His orders stated that he could "command any Ship in the service."[20] Why not *Ranger?* To be sure, Roche considered himself to be the captain, but that was an assumption on his part, and he had no documentation to back it up. Furthermore, there were allegations floating around that Roche had been involved in some shady business deals, and the Massachusetts General Court had described him as "a person of Doubtful character." The charge remains unproved; nevertheless, its utterance only served to lower Roche's stock in Congress. Jones, on the other hand, had a good claim. His career so far spoke for itself, and in addition he was, by the resolve of 10 October 1776, eighteenth on the list of captains, where Roche's name did not even appear. On 14 June 1777 Congress resolved "that Captain Roach be suspended," which was strange, since they had never appointed him to anything. In the next breath they appointed Jones to command *Ranger*.[21] The decision to appoint Jones cannot be faulted, but the method left much to be desired. Roche's nebulous status, the silly scheme with *Amphitrite*, the removal of an officer whom they never had appointed—all made the committee look bad. Roche was certainly embittered, and he took a high place on what was becoming a long list of captains irritated at the way in which Congress and the Marine Committee granted commands.

Although the Marine Committee moved clumsily through the *Ranger* affair, at least in the end the results redounded to the credit of the Continental navy, for no one questions John Paul Jones's place in the pantheon of American naval heros. But Jones was unique and serendipity is rare. The other captains, and there were many of them, who felt jilted or scorned caused just as much trouble, but unhappily their bickering and caterwauling seemed to be inversely proportional to their abilities.

One captain, Daniel Waters from Malden, Massachusetts, was offered command of the brigantine *Resistance*. He replied in a huff that such a small vessel was beneath his dignity. Equally annoyed, the committee told him that they would overlook his flippancy this time but if he acted like that again they would dismiss him. A short time later he was commanding the Continental sloop *General Gates* on a cruise to the West Indies, where he spent public monies for his own business. When his accounts were challenged, Waters left the Continental service, sailed for a while in the Massachusetts state navy and finally ended up the war as a privateersman commanding the captured British sloop of war *Thorn*. In command of her and out of the Continental service, he went on, in the words of the *Boston Gazette*, to "glorious combat."[22]

Waters was picky over what he would command. If instead of *Resistance* he had been offered the frigates *Trumbull* or *Confederacy*, then building in Connecticut, he probably would have been falling over himself to accept. But they could never be his; like their sister frigates, they were choice political plums that only the senior and most influential captains could hope to have. *Trumbull* was originally given to Dudley Saltonstall, but she took so long to finish that the captain grew impatient waiting for her and left her to take command of *Warren*. In his absence Elisha Hinman, former captain of *Cabot* and *Alfred* and number twenty on the 10 October list, took over the yeoman's task of watching the frigate put together. It was Hinman who saw *Trumbull* through her final stages and got her rigged and fitted. The Navy Board of the Eastern Department was impressed with his diligence and hard work, and in recognition of his efforts they practically promised him permanent command of the frigate. Unfortunately, that was a promise they could not deliver on, for although they had authority to appoint captains to ships of twenty guns or less, they had absolutely no power to appoint a commander to *Trumbull* or any other frigate in the navy. There must have been grimaces and red faces in Boston when the Marine Committee announced that James Nicholson would be the *Trumbull's* new captain. Not only was he a southerner coming north to a Yankee port, guaranteeing under the best of circumstances a cool reception, but his entire career in the navy had amounted to nothing more than losing his first command, *Virginia*, without firing a shot. The navy board in Boston was not pleased, to say nothing of Hinman.[23]

Nicholson, after a delay of several months, got his ship to sea bound for the Delaware and Philadelphia. It was during this voyage that *Trumbull* had her famous encounter with *Watt*.[24] Once at anchor, Nicholson, a man whose ambition quite often surpassed his talent, cast an envious eye in the direction of the nearby *Confederacy*, a larger vessel and, according to him, a command more in keeping with his senior status in the navy. Despite the fact that the frigate was already under the command of the Connecticut Yankee Seth Harding, Nicholson petitioned the Board of Admiralty to remove Harding and appoint him in his stead. The board, because of difficulties they had had with Harding, entertained no great fondness for him and probably welcomed the opportunity to be rid of him. They approved the request, but when it came onto the floor of Congress, it was another story. Harding was a Connecticut man. If they pushed him summarily aside, that would mean that twice in less than a year Connecticut men would have fallen victim to the whim of James Nicholson. Congress had no intention of permitting that and shunted the request aside.

Every time one of these squalls died down, Congress and the Marine Committee sighed with relief and hoped that they had seen the last of the carping captains. Once a captain assumed his command, so the expectation ran, the normal relationship between naval and civilian authority would be one of mutual respect and cooperation. For the Continental navy, as for the Continental army, that expectation for placidity was not borne out. The normal relationship turned out to be one of tension, most often subdued but occasionally erupting into an intense and glaring confrontation. The potential for collision between civilian and uniformed authority was greater with the navy than with the army. At least in the army there was a competent and respected commander in chief who, along with his staff, not only performed the usual military functions but played an important political role as well. Washington acted as a buffer between the Congress on one side and the army on the other. Through his extraordinary prestige and influence in both camps he was able to ameliorate differences and absorb problems that, if left to fester and come out into the open, would have created grave difficulties between the Congress and the military.

The navy had no Washington. Hopkins was a pale imitation who had lost most of his power long before he was dismissed. That left only the captains, fiercely independent prima donnas who often acted with more belligerence toward their civilian superiors than toward the British navy. Technically all of them were under civilian jurisdictions, Congress at the top and beneath it the Marine Committee (later the Board of Admiralty) and the local boards in the Middle District and the Eastern District or for ships in European waters the commissioners in Paris. Despite the infrastructure the officers played politics, bypassing the local authorities when it suited their needs and going directly to the Congress. This tended to weaken an already fragile chain of command, and the inevitable erosion of authority led to some toe-to-toe confrontations between civilian and naval authorities. Usually a gentle rebuke, a congressional resolution or a strongly worded letter would serve to rein in a stubborn officer. If these methods failed, the ultimate weapon would be brought to bear, a court-martial.

The convening of a court-martial is an extraordinary event

and is never done lightly. No matter what the outcome, guilty or innocent, the person under charges emerges with a blemish on his record that can never be erased. To ensure that justice was done and to forestall any needless trials, the Congress generally insisted that the local naval authorities conduct a preliminary inquiry before summoning a court. If the investigation turned up probable cause, a court would be called to hear the evidence. If, as sometimes happened, an individual demanded a court-martial in order to clear his name, the preliminary inquiry would not be conducted.

The rules and regulations of the navy set out numerous offenses for which an individual might be tried. There was nothing unusual in the list, and for the most part it followed rather closely the regulations of the British navy. The regulations also stipulated the composition of the board: three captains and three first lieutenants from the naval ranks along with an equal number of the same ranks from the marines. The senior naval captain would act as president of the board. The boards were obviously overstaffed, and as the war took its toll of the navy, it became increasingly difficult, in fact in some cases impossible, to find enough officers to make up a full court.[25] As a result, some men of the Continental navy were spared a well-deserved trial for the lack of a quorum.

From the spring of 1776 through 1780 at least seven Continental captains were hauled before a court-martial. Only one of those, John Manley, was acquitted. On the remaining six, five were dismissed outright and one, Abraham Whipple, was found guilty of poor judgment but allowed to remain in the service.[26]

Every trial was a newsworthy event, but one in particular stands out—that of Pierre Landais, the Captain Queeg of the Continental navy.[27] Landais, a former captain in the French navy, arrived in Philadelphia in 1777 armed with letters of recommendation from Silas Deane. He soon became a favorite of the two Adamses and Richard Henry Lee, and before long the ambitious Frenchman was up to his neck in congressional politics. Although the evidence remains unclear, at least one historian, Samuel Eliot Morison, maintains that the Adamses and Lee saw in Landais an opportunity to create a naval Lafayette to counter the growing reputation of John Paul Jones.[28] At any rate, the Massachusetts-Virginia axis swung into action, and amid a surge of pro-French sympathy rising out of the recently completed Franco-American alliance, Pierre Landais was given command of the new frigate building at Salisbury.[29] As a tribute to the French, she was named *Alliance*. After launching, she was brought around to Boston, and on 14 January 1779 she fell down the harbor past the Castle and set sail bound for France. It was not a happy voyage. Four days out of Brest there was a mutiny aboard, and when John Adams saw Landais ashore, he described the captain as being

> . . . jealous of every Thing, jealous of every Body, of all his officers, all his Passengers; he knows not how to treat his officers, nor his passengers, nor any Body else. Silence, Reserve, and a forbidding Air will never gain the Hearts neither by Affection nor by Veneration of our Americans. There is in this man an Inactivity and an Indecisiveness that will ruin him. He is bewildered—an absent bewildered man—an embarassed Mind.[30]

Rather damning testimony from a man who should have been inclined to favor the captain.

In an example of shameful inactivity, Landais kept *Alliance* at anchor in Brest for the next six months. It was a great annoyance to the navy board at Boston that the pride of the American fleet should be lying idly in a foreign port swinging to and fro with each change of the tide. To them it was inexcusable, and they took the opportunity to vent their spleen against all the officers of the navy, describing them as men who "either Dont know their duty or shamefully contempt and neglect it."[31]

Finally in late summer 1779 *Alliance* left her safe anchorage and joined the squadron under the command of John Paul

Jones for their cruise around the British Isles. This was the venture that climaxed off Flamborough Head with immortality for Jones and infamy for Landais. Following that battle and the loss of his own ship, Jones was given *Alliance*. However, for the next few months she lay idle at Lorient and later at Saint Louis while her new captain absented himself to seek the more pleasant surroundings of the Parisian salons where coiffured women and aping gentlemen fawned over the famous new thirty-two-year-old chevalier. While Jones was occupied in the pursuit of pleasure, the seemingly tireless Landais was politicking to get back his old command. In June 1780 his efforts bore fruit, and with only token opposition from Jones, Pierre Landais again became captain of *Alliance*, a most undeserved command. Not long after, *Alliance* weighed anchor and set out on "one of the maddest crossings of the Atlantic ever made."[32] Once at sea, Landais displayed unparalleled incompetence bordering on insanity. Before the first day had passed, *Alliance*'s brig had its first guest, Captain Matthew Parke, the senior marine captain in the Continental navy, who was locked up because he refused to take a blanket oath swearing to obey the captain in all circumstances. Off to a bad start, the voyage grew steadily worse as the brig became more crowded. Seamen and officers were not the only ones to suffer from Landais's intemperate behavior. Arthur Lee, one of Landais's patrons and a passenger aboard *Alliance*, was treated to a tongue-lashing when he complained about the quality of the drinking water, and then, as if to add insult to injury, the captain threatened him with a carving knife at dinner when he neglected to defer to him in passing the meat. Enough was enough, and with Lee, an old hand at conspiracies, leading them, the officers and passengers confronted the captain and demanded he relinquish his command. He had no alternative but to surrender. Though bloodless, it was still mutiny, and when *Alliance* arrived in Boston, the navy board officially suspended Landais and launched an immediate inquiry. When the startling news was announced in Philadelphia, the Board of Admiralty reacted with unwonted speed and ordered Captain John Barry to go immediately to Boston and take command so that *Alliance* could get to sea again quickly. Accompanying him was William Ellery, a member of the board, who was to report on this extraordinary occurrence.

It was a messy situation and one particulary embarrassing to those members of Congress who had so warmly supported Landais before. The case became something of a public spectacle. Landais continued to disgrace himself and had to be physically dragged from his cabin aboard *Alliance*. This time he had no friends to save him from a trial and a court-martial was summoned. Sam Adams, now back in Massachusetts, stood by him, but in the face of overwhelming evidence the court found him guilty and dismissed him from the service. Losing in one arena, Landais tried another and filed petitions and memorials with Congress and made public appeals via newspapers. Congress was not impressed and the public was little interested. The navy was well rid of Pierre Landais. His departure signaled the last time a captain in the Continental navy would be hauled before a court-martial. It was a fitting climax to those unhappy moments when Continental naval officers had to sit in judgment of their peers.

While some captains failed in their duty and were court-martialed, most performed adequately or at least well enough to avoid public censure and discipline, and a few were even outstanding. To assess their performance, good or bad, it is necessary to appreciate that those officers, like officers in all wars and every service, were called upon to play the dual role of leader and teacher. For the Continental naval officer these roles were set out partly in the rules and regulations, partly in orders from the Marine Committee and Board of Admiralty and partly in the traditions and customs of the sea.

In all their conduct, whether at sea or on shore, the captains, according to the regulations, were to provide examples of "honor and virtue." They were to see that religious observances were held at least twice daily and a sermon delivered on Sunday. There can be no doubt that John Adams was quite serious when he wrote this section into the Regulations, and as a good Puritan, he fully expected the captains to keep their men as free from vice and sin as possible. It would have been easier for Canute to hold back the tide, and these rules were probably the most violated ordinances between the Ten Commandments and the Volstead Act. Nevertheless, the captains may be forgiven for not being more rigorous in exercising their men in moral calisthenics; after all, they were not divines but naval officers charged with engaging and destroying the enemy. To that end they needed to instruct and lead their men.

It was not easy. First of all, the captains themselves came to the navy with little or no experience. To be sure, they were all seasoned mariners, but with one or two exceptions, and even those are not significant, none had any naval experience. The burden of having neophytes on the quarterdeck as well as before the mast was eased somewhat by the lack of technological complications in the eighteenth-century navy. The difference between a merchant ship and a warship was not nearly so great then as it is today. In appearance, construction and rigging they were virtually the same, except that the warship was generally larger, more heavily armed and perhaps more sturdily built. The biggest difference dividing merchant ships and warships was not so much in physical aspects as in the training and discipline of their crews. Aboard a merchant vessel crews were small—thirty men would be a large number—and the distance separating the captain and his men, both physical and psychological, was not all that great. He and his mates were accessible, and in many cases they might well have been neighbors ashore. This degree of familiarity did not mean that it was a democratic world aboard ship, for the captain's word was law and no polls or votes were taken. On the other hand, everyone had signed on freely, and all wanted essentially the same things: to avoid danger, have a safe voyage and make a good profit.

The situation was quite otherwise aboard a man-of-war. Its mission was not to avoid danger but actually to seek it out, to

meet with and destroy the enemy. It was a business wherein
the victory went not only to the biggest guns but also to the
best crews. It was up to the boatswain and his mates working
under the first lieutenant to see that the men were drilled,
disciplined and rehearsed so that they were the best. With
experienced officers and a willing crew, a man-of-war became
like a large professional team with everyone sure of his job
and able to respond automatically, no matter what the situation. That was the ideal, but, of course, only rarely if ever did
the British or the American navy reach that plateau since in
both navies the enlisted ranks were filled with either men
overtly pressed and dragged aboard or war prisoners who
were given the damnable choice of rotting in prison or facing
death afloat. With such unwilling men, training and discipline became a heavy chore. The British overcame the problem with brutal discipline administered by an experienced
cadre of commissioned and noncommissioned officers. The
Continental navy could rely on neither terror nor experience.

The rules and regulations of the American navy were not
nearly as harsh as the British. The traditions of the American
merchant marine worked against that sort of brutality, and
the rhetoric of the Revolution ran counter to it as well. For
example, men were enticed to desert the British with such
propaganda broadsides as

> May you soon be freed
> from the service of
> tyrants, become the glorious
> defenders of freedom and
> join the victorious Americans.[33]

Men who were told to fight for liberty did not always find it
easy to accept the arbitrary commands of their captain. On
one occasion John Paul Jones found himself with a mutiny on
his hands because a lieutenant "held up to the crew that being
Americans fighting for liberty the voice of the people should
be taken before the Captain's orders."[34]

Although the death penalty could be meted out by a court-martial in cases of mutiny and desertion during battle, there is no record of that sentence ever actually being carried out. On his own authority the captain could administer a maximum punishment of only twelve lashes. If a captain stepped outside the regulations, he quite often found himself facing an indignant crew salted with sea lawyers not afraid to take their complaint all the way to the Congress. Early in the war the crew of the sloop *Providence* complained of being beaten with sticks and ropes by their captain, John Hazard, while he drove them mercilessly night and day. Congress listened, and that charge along with others got Hazard thrown out of the navy.[35]

Rules and regulations, while absolutely essential to the well ordering of a ship, do not in themselves win battles. To do that, men must be not only well disciplined but also trained. Landsmen, merchant seamen, old men, young men—no matter how assorted or inexperienced the crew, the captain could depend upon his lieutenants and noncommissioned officers to whip them into shape in short order. Unlike ships today, those in the eighteenth century had no great scientific mysteries to be mastered. The propulsion system was sail, not a nuclear reactor; gunnery was a matter of pointing the cannon in the right direction and letting her go. The most complex operation aboard was navigation, but that was no concern of the enlisted men. Seamen took their boot camp on deck, aloft and in the forecastle under the rough tutelage of veteran noncommissioned officers.

If, as happened so many times in the Continental navy, a captain discovered he was cursed with a green crew and bad officers, he was in trouble the minute he left port. Barely trained, poorly led, his men showed little taste for fighting and sometimes would not fight at all. Mutinies were not uncommon. In addition to the one already mentioned, John Paul Jones faced down several other uprisings aboard his ships, while Captain John Manley, a man of like temperament, crushed a mutiny singlehandedly by brandishing his cutlass under the noses of some would-be mutineers. Jones and Manley could handle their men and showed that they were not to be trifled with, but there were other commanders who, because of different circumstances or weaknesses in their own character, were not so successful. James Nicholson lost *Trumbull* when his men would not fight. James Robinson, captain of the Continental schooner *Fly*, was dispossessed by his crew while at sea.[36] These were unnerving events and did nothing to endear the captains to Congress and simply served to reinforce the charges of cowardice and neglect that were being thrown in their direction. William Ellery was so disturbed by the conduct of the captains that he suggested executing some of them, a "little Bynging."[37] It was an outlandish suggestion and thankfully was never taken seriously.

If the Congress could bemoan the distressing lack of belligerency shown by their captains toward the English, they became equally distressed by the hostility these gentlemen showed toward one another. From the very beginning they had displayed untold capacity for criticizing one another. No organization, civilian or military, is immune from this sort of behavior, but at least in older and more stable structures there are generally a defined chain of command, established policies and a bureaucracy to absorb and cushion internal feuding. In the case of the Continental navy the chain of command was laced with cracks; policies, such as existed, were in embryo, and the bureaucracy was jibing about in a fog.

In this situation it was not unusual for grievances, sometimes very legitimate ones, to sink into personal invective and eventually wind up in the Congress, where all things became politicized. It was a sorry scene that was repeated over and over again. Commanders behaved like cowbirds, trying to further their own careers by pushing their colleagues' eggs out of the nest. Among the first to be drawn into the fray was the commander in chief himself, Esek Hopkins, who began his involvement as an accusor and ended up the accused.

He took the first step down the road to ruin shortly after returning from the Bahama expedition.[38] He knew that dissatisfaction over his conduct on that cruise, as well as over other actions of his, was rife in the Congress. In defense of himself he tried to lay the blame on his officers, who he said were so busy politicking to advance their own careers that they did not have enough time to pay attention to their duties. He had bitter words for every officer save one, his own son. The feeling was mutual, and his men lost no time in penning their own condemnations of the commander in chief.[39] The commodore was summoned to Philadelphia and hauled before Congress to answer the charges. To what extent the aging Hopkins was culpable is a point open to question. He certainly was not blameless for all that had gone wrong, but on the other side it was a bit unjust to heap all the sins of the navy on his head. At any rate, for several days Congress debated the conduct of the commodore. It was a censorious atmosphere and one in which John Adams, a defender of Hopkins, spied an "anti New England spirit which haunted Congress in many other of their proceeding."[40] On 16 August 1776 Congress officially censured Hopkins. He retained his command and title but lost nearly everyone's confidence. For seven more months he teetered, but in March 1777 Congress, after receiving another complaint against him, this one signed by every officer aboard his flagship, resolved that "Esek Hopkins be immediately and he is hereby suspended from his command in the American Navy."[41] After prolonging the agony for a year, Congress finally decided in January 1778 that they did not need Commodore Hopkins at all, and without any fanfare or even a vote of thanks he was "dismissed from the service of the United States."[42]

The Hopkins affair was the major battle fought in the internecine wars of the Continental navy, but there were many other skirmishes. When Manley and McNeill sailed together, they behaved "like the Jews and Samaritans" and would not even talk to each other.[43] James Nicholson, the senior officer after Hopkins's departure, spent a good deal of his time reminding everyone of his exalted rank and demanding that he be given the largest ship in the navy. A rather ineffectual commander, with no vessel under his command ever taking a prize, Nicholson was eaten up with jealousy at the success of others. He tried to wrest command of *Confederacy* from Seth Harding, conspired with John Barry to block the advancement of John Paul Jones and on one occasion conducted himself with such arrogance as to precipitate a crisis between the state of Maryland and Congress.[44]

Perhaps Nicholson's conduct was the most egregious, but it was a matter of degree rather than kind; every one of the captains was strong willed and independently minded. They accepted orders only begrudgingly. Those are not necessarily bad traits when coupled with intelligence, vigor and courage, and certainly they served the navy well in the cases of Nicholas Biddle, John Paul Jones and John Barry. But in lesser men, who unfortunately made up the bulk of the ranks, they were nothing but trouble and greatly hampered the already bedeviled Continental navy.

Chapter Fourteen

In the Forecastle

As irksome as their behavior was, the captains nevertheless did have the saving grace of coming forward in considerable numbers to serve. Congress never had any trouble finding men for the quarterdeck. Up forward it was a different story, and despite the fact that prewar America liked to boast of being the great nursery of seamen, its children soon ran off to other pursuits when it came time to enlist in the Continental navy. Even in New England, which was considered the storehouse of naval talent, there was considerable difficulty in finding men. At the request of Congress, surveys were taken early in the war that gave great promise of thousands of men being available for naval service.[1] Somehow those men never materialized, and despite estimates that there were thirty thousand deep-water sailors idle and available, the Continental navy was lucky if it enlisted ten percent of that number. If they were not in the navy, what happened to all those thousands of men who had made the American merchant marine one of the largest in the world?

Some, a very small number probably, gave up the sea entirely and absented themselves from the Revolution, becoming a silent and invisible minority. An equally small group might have become Loyalists. The great bulk of American sailors, though, were neither silent nor Loyalists. They were active participants in the war but not in the Continental navy.

A good number served in the army, especially in New England, where during the winter months of 1775 and 1776 there was very little activity at sea. Hundreds, perhaps thousands of sailors, temporarily idled by the war yet eager to strike at the British, enlisted in the army. In the spring of 1776 John Paul Jones, lamenting the prospect that American ships would "rot in the harbors for want of hands," advocated drafting seamen out of the army, where he estimated four to five thousand were enrolled.[2] Even after allowing for a certain amount of hyperbole in Jones's statement, it remains true that along the New England coast many states raised regiments that were more than slightly tinged with salt. Colonel, later General, John Glover's "Webfoot Regiment" from Marblehead is the most famous, but there were others, and every unit raised within a whiff of sea air was bound to have sailors marching with it.[3]

Enlisting seamen into the army was a misuse of talent, but when warm bodies were needed to fill thinning ranks, army recruiters were not too particular about such niceties. A more direct form of competition came from the state navies. Every one of the thirteen states, with the exception of New Jersey and Delaware, fitted out and armed their own fleets. They did not usually amount to much more than a few row galleys, although Virginia, Massachusetts and South Carolina had larger ships; nevertheless, no matter what their size, the fleets needed men to man them.[4] Initially the states operated on the assumption that there would be plenty of sailors, but as the supply dwindled and demand grew, that illusion faded and the states moved quickly to hoard and protect their vanishing sailors. In 1776 South Carolina, having rapidly exhausted its own pool of local seamen, sent Captain Robert Cochran on a foraging expedition north to recruit sailors for the Carolina navy. Cochran went to Pennsylvania, New York and the New England states. His arrival in Massachusetts worried Washington, lest he lose men from his schooner fleet to the warmer waters of the south.[5] The captain's activities also alarmed the Massachusetts Provincial Congress, who were already concerned over a loss of men from their seacoast battalions to other states and the Continental navy—men who, according to James Warren, were tempted away by "full wages and large bounties."[6] The bounty race was on, and soon Massachusetts, along with her sister states, was offering her own bounties, competing with the Congress as well as with the other states. Within a short time there were twelve navies (eleven state and the Continental) and fourteen armies (thirteen state and the Continental) competing in a wasteful and scandalous duplication of money and effort.

The Continental navy could easily have survived the leakage of men to the state navies and the army. Losing men to them was more of a piddling nuisance than a critical affair. The real problem was the rush of men to privateering. American ports swarmed with privateers. In all, more than two thousand vessels sailed under private ownership with Continental and state commissions. Massachusetts alone sent out nearly one thousand, with the towns of Boston, Salem and Marblehead leading the pack.[7] Regardless of whether privateering was an asset or a liability to the Revolutionary cause, one conclusion at least does seem inescapable; privateering occupied thousands of American sailors who might otherwise have signed on Continental vessels. Everyone got in on the action. Continental naval agents who were charged with protecting the interests of Congress quite often engaged in a bit of privateering. Nathaniel Shaw, for example, the agent at New London, owned and operated at least ten privateers.[8] Almost all the Continental captains at one time or another, during interludes between public commands, took up privateering. The result was an incredible mishmash of confused accounts and conflicts of interest in which the Continent quite often came out on the short end.

Seamen were lured into privateering by promises of instant wealth. In Wethersfield, along the Connecticut River, men were told that for an investment of a mere eight weeks at sea they could be set for the rest of their lives. Who could resist?

Enticed by promises of money and entranced by glorious stories of richly laden Indiamen sailing unescorted and ready to strike their flag at the mere sight of an open gun port, men stood in line to sign aboard. Stories of men made wealthy for the rest of their lives by a single voyage filled seaport taverns from Boston to Lorient. A ballad about the successful voyage of Abraham Whipple, a Continental captain, referred to him as a privateer, for who would have thought a navy officer could be so lucky? Most of the stories were not true, of course, and for every vessel that struck it rich there were dozens that failed. But that did not seem to matter, and no privateer ever went begging for hands.

It was an unequal contest in the enlistment war between the Continental navy and the privateers. Even after men signed the Continental articles, it was not unusual for them to be lured away by privateers, and time and time again captains and agents spoke bitterly about those men whose pursuit of Mammon blinded them to the public good.[9] The prospect of a short and lucrative voyage aboard a privateer outweighed any patriotic notion of serving aboard one of the Congress's warships, especially when such service would be for a longer period and might well involve a good deal of time spent in nonproductive enterprises such as ferrying supplies and diplomats to and from the West Indies and Europe.

Despite the difficulties, the Congress did put forth a solid effort to enlist volunteers. "Sons of Liberty" were asked to join Hopkins's fleet "to engage in the defence of the Liberties of America." They were expected to join up for one year, and for their troubles they would receive one-third of all prizes to be divided among the crew according to congressional resolution. The division would be by shares, with the largest portion going to the commander and the smallest to the lowly seaman. These shares were to be paid in addition to regular wages, which were fixed by Congress. Initially the wages were fairly generous. Able-bodied seamen were allotted eight dollars per month, a sum slightly larger than that received by their counterparts in the Royal Navy. Officers, on the other hand, were paid relatively less than their peers in the Royal service, a fact that rankled some and persuaded John Paul Jones to suggest cutting enlisted men's pay and increasing the officers'.[10]

As the romance and rhetoric wore off and victories turned into defeats, Congress tried new measures to make service more attractive. Increased bounties were offered, and sailors were given their pay in advance. The latter turned into more of a curse than a blessing, for it meant that the Congress would give twenty dollars the first month and then deduct it from the next month's pay. In some cases when the voyage was a complete failure, the men came home actually owing money. If a man was incapacitated, Congress promised to provide him or his widow with half pay for life. Most of the provisions Congress made for sailors were quite similar to those given soldiers, with one major exception. Sailors were never offered land. That was reasonable, Congress thought; soldiers never had a chance to share in a prize.[11]

To the Congress these were just and fair measures, and perhaps they were, but the difficulty was that the men in Philadelphia never seemed to understand quite what made a man go to sea. Wages and pensions meant very little. Eight dollars per month was a paltry sum, while pensions were for those who were injured, and what sailor went to sea expecting to be wounded or killed? Men did not sign on for wages and for pensions; they went to sea for plunder, booty and wealth. If Horatio Alger had been writing during the American Revolution, Ragged Dick might well have been a sailor who went to sea, fought bravely and helped capture a richly laden Indiaman, at the same time somehow managing to save the captain's daughter and marry her. The plot would have him then returning to shore-side life, buying a country estate and living out his days amid bucolic tranquillity, surrounded by his adoring grandchildren. That was the dream. It was hardly ever the reality.

Jones, astute as usual when it came to naval matters, offered a solution. If long enlistments (one year) were a handicap, get rid of them and let the men sign on and leave as they wished, just as the privateers did. Considering the high rate of desertion in the American navy, that came close to being a simple recognition of an already existing situation. Further, he suggested, why not give the seamen all the proceeds from their prizes instead of taking such large portions for the use of the Congress? "What is the Paltry emolument of two thirds of Prizes to the Finances of this Vast Continent?" Even if these changes could have been made, there still remained the fact, well known among sailors, that the ships of the Continental navy spent a good deal of their time on essential but unremunerative cruises. Jones could offer no remedy for that, short of giving up all semblance of a navy and devoting full time to commerce raiding. Congress listened, but only halfheartedly, and agreed to increase the crew's share of prizes from one-third to one-half for transports and from one-half to all for warships and privateers.[12]

To remedy the problem of finding sailors, Congress would have done well to pull out all the stops. It is a measure of their lack of commitment and tight-fisted attitude toward the navy that they never drew upon their most abundant resource to attract and reward the sailors of the Continental navy—land. Congress offered land bounties to nearly everyone: British deserters, Hessian mercenaries, Canadian refugees and, of course, American troops. Land was handed out with an abandon that would later return to haunt Congress, but their beneficence never reached sailors or officers in the navy. Moreover, when the war was over and Congress granted five years' pay to army officers, they neglected to include the navy. Left out of the land giveaway and denied extra pay, many seamen and officers of the navy spent a good deal of their time in the postwar years lobbying for compensation.[13]

Without much to offer, the navy recruiters found it tough going. The task of recruiting rested mainly on the shoulders of the captains. The system was not as blatant as in the marine corps or in the army, where in some cases it was actually made a condition of commissioning that the officer personally raise sufficient men for his command. Nevertheless, no one doubted for a moment that it was the captain's job to fill his crew.[14]

"Expensive as well as Troublesome" was the way one officer described recruiting. Expensive because quite often the captain himself had to travel far and wide to find men. Dudley Saltonstall crisscrossed Connecticut making his pitch. John B. Hopkins sent his bosun all the way to Springfield, Massachusetts, looking for men. Such traveling was a costly and arduous business. When the captains were lucky enough to come across men who might be willing to go, they discovered that their most persuasive argument was cash in advance, which meant laying out personal funds with the hope that Congress would reimburse later.[15]

When the recruiters went out, whether to Boston, Philadelphia or some backwater town, they surrounded themselves with all the pomp and splendor they could muster. If they had uniforms, this was the time to wear them. Broadsides were slapped up promising adventure, wealth and a chance to strike at hateful English tyranny. Then at some central location—a busy street corner, a crowded tavern or some public meeting place—the drummer would begin a roll as the recruiter called for men to come on board. A good tale or two, free rum and a few ballads drew the men around.

> All you that have bad masters,
> And cannot get your due,
> Come, come, my brave boys,
> And join with our ships crew.

It was a scene repeated a hundred times over in ports, inland towns and even in foreign places. The results were spotty and depended a good deal on the reputation of the captain. In some cases it would have been easier to sign men on for a cruise with the devil himself. Foreigners like Landais, for example, were shunned, and so too were men who had lost ships, had never captured a prize or who had a reputation for double-dealing with their men. Others like Jones and John Barry, who were known as good, although stern, commanders, had less trouble finding men.

By order of the Congress no bought or indentured servants could be enlisted, nor could an apprentice sign on without the consent of his master, and certainly army deserters were not to be welcomed. Nevertheless, recruiters were none too particular, and if a man said he wanted to go, no recruiter ever asked him why or where he had been. On occasion such questions could be embarrassing, as in 1779 when the French vice consul complained to the navy board at Boston that wounded French sailors from Admiral d'Estaing's fleet had deserted from the naval hospital in Roxbury and were signing on board the privateers and Continental cruisers in Boston harbor.[16] Old men and young men, felons and patriots, brave men and cowards, they all crowded into the forecastle and slung their hammocks side by side. In race and nationality they were polyglot crews; English, French, Dutch, Spanish, blacks and others all sailed in the Continental navy.[17]

The Congress would have preferred an all-volunteer navy, but that was never possible, and little by little they had to resort to some rough-and-ready methods of eighteenth-century conscription. The most time-honored and widely practiced way to grab men was the infamous press gang. The British, of course, were the most notorious in plying this trade, to the point where it is considered by some to be one of the underlying factors bringing on the Revolution.[18] The rapid expansion of the Royal Navy during the Revolution created a near insatiable demand for sailors. There were also losses at sea due to disease, desertion and to a lesser extent battle casualties, and so the Royal Navy undertook to press men; by the end of the war nearly eighty thousand men had been enrolled in that fashion. Over the years Anglophobic historians and novelists have succeeded in greatly exaggerating the violence and cruelty in the system. The "gang," commanded by a lieutenant accompanied by a boatswain's mate, was made up of trustworthy sailors who carryed belaying pins and cutlasses to discourage resistance. By law they were to take only sailors, leaving unmolested officers, boatswains and carpenters in the merchant marine. Nor were men involved in harvesting or fishermen to be bothered. "Gentlemen," whatever that word might mean, were also exempt. When faced by the gang, a seaman was given a choice. He could accept a bounty, "the King's shilling," and sign the articles. If he did, he would be listed on the rolls as a volunteer. The alternative was to reject the bounty and refuse to sign. In many instances this was the wisest course to follow because if the individual later fled the service and was caught, he could not be charged as a deserter. Undoubtedly, when hard put for men, an officer might be somewhat less than scrupulous and allow mistakes to slip by him in the interests of a full complement. Nevertheless, it does seem accurate to say that pressing was a well-accepted method of recruitment and was more often than not carried out in a legal and routine manner.[19]

In the years before Lexington and Concord Americans were loud in their protests against impressment. They felt it was being practiced illegally on their side of the Atlantic because an act of Parliament passed in the reign of Queen Anne specifically excluded the American colonies from impressment. The callous and in these cases illegal action on the part of Royal naval officers occasionally resulted in violence, and there were serious riots in several American seaports, including Boston and New York, over press-gang activities. However, when faced with the same manpower problems as the Royal Navy, albeit on a much smaller scale, many Americans gained a new appreciation for impressment, and in an ironic twist of fate Continental naval officers began to practice what they had once so vehemently opposed.

Virginia pressed men to serve in her state navy. The Massachusetts General Court issued a press in 1779 so that Captain Dudley Saltonstall might get enough men to take *Warren* on the Penobscot expedition. Captain John Young of *Saratoga* impressed men from Philadelphia in 1780 and for it was thrown in jail by the local authorities.[20] These were minor imbroglios, though. By far the best-known and most dramatic incident over impressment involved that lightning rod of misfortune, Captain James Nicholson. The episode had its beginning in the spring of 1777. Nicholson had received several dunning letters from the Marine Committee urging him to get his command, the frigate *Virginia*, out of Baltimore harbor, where she had been since launching, and out to sea. Ridiculed in the local press as "Captain Snug in the Harbor," Nicholson felt the pressure and scurried around looking for hands to fill his crew. The captain thought a good deal of himself and much less of the local authorities. Asserting that as a Continental officer he was beyond, indeed above, local jurisdiction, Nicholson proceeded to impress local seamen into *Virginia*'s crew. The governor of Maryland, Thomas Johnson, demanded that he release the men "instantly." According to Johnson, Nicholson was not only doing a great wrong to the men whisked away, but the activities of the press gang were also "injurious to the Town, in deterring people from going to Market there, for fear of being treated in the same manner."[21] Nicholson's response was not designed to smooth ruffled feathers. In a tone that can only be described as arrogant, he told Johnson that Congress supported him and he did not give a whit "for the Threats of any Council of Maryland." Besides, he added, the governor was becoming needlessly exercised over something that was going on every day in many other American ports, including Philadelphia.[22] This was an affront to both him and his state that Johnson could not ignore. He sent Nicholson's letter off to Congress for their response.

It caused quite a stir in Philadelphia and the affair quickly became a cause célèbre. On the floor of Congress the question was seen as going far beyond impressment. The issue at stake now was state versus Continental authority. The reaction of Congress was predictable. Made up as it was of representatives from fiercely independent states, jealous of their own power and highly suspicious of any encroachment by a central body, it came down strongly on the side of Governor Johnson. Nicholson was reprimanded for his conduct and the pressed men were released.[23]

Pressing was only one type of conscription practiced by the American navy. There were several others. Prisoners of war, for example, were attracted into the navy by being given the option of joining or rotting aboard a prison hulk or in some prison ashore. The Marine Committee made it a standing order to their commanders that whenever they took a prize they were to make this offer to the crew. Not surprisingly, it worked, and nearly every Continental crew was made up in part of British prisoners.[24] They were a sullen and troublesome lot, and the navy probably would have been better off if they had been locked away in a hulk or shore-side prison. Prone to mutiny but not prone to fight, they caused endless grief to commanders. Paul Jones found them to be a sinister influence on his crews, while James Nicholson lost his second command, *Trumbull*, to H.M.S. *Iris* because his crew of prisoners refused to come up from below and fight.[25]

Impressed men and prisoners made up the bulk of the unwilling aboard ship, but there were others in the forecastle who for one reason or another were there as something less than volunteers. Some were there as punishment. The army was always plagued with desertions, and in the summer of 1777 Washington tried a new corrective measure. Seven men who had tried to go over the hill were given one hundred lashes, and then by order of the commander in chief what was left of them was turned over to the navy for service aboard the Continental frigates. How effective this was in preventing desertion is uncertain, but throwing these men in among an already motley crew did nothing to raise the morale of the ship's company.[26]

That the navy would resort to these unsavory methods of recruitment is a mark of the depth of difficulties it had in getting men to serve. It had no choice but to take the drafted, the vanquished and the caught. Nor did it draw any color line; within the enlisted ranks of the navy, blacks as well as

Indians served. There was certainly nothing unusual in this since both, especially blacks, had long been a common sight in the American merchant marine. In the Chesapeake Bay blacks played a crucial role. Along the treacherous and poorly charted shores of the bay, black pilots had long navigated coastal vessels. As many a stranded or wrecked skipper learned, their expertise and experience were essential. The Virginia state navy had at least 140 blacks. In the Continental navy there is specific mention of blacks serving on board *Ranger*, *Lexington*, the frigate *Providence*, and undoubtedly there were many more whose names and services have gone unrecorded and unnoticed. Although a large number who served, especially those from the north, were free born, freedom was not a prerequisite for enlistment, and in the navy, as in the army, black slaves fought for American freedom.[27]

Whether black or white, volunteers or forced, American or one of a dozen other nationalities, these men, once aboard, were all part of the ship's company sharing a common weal and woe. It was not always pleasant, but then again not every commander was a Captain Bligh, nor was every voyage like *Two Years Before the Mast*. To be sure, the men up forward were part of the inarticulate, and their recollections and memories aboard ship have to a great extent been lost to the historian; nevertheless, there are no documented cases of brutality or flogging to death in the Continental navy.

Accommodations for the sailor consisted of a hammock swung on hooks between the guns in the forecastle. The space was divided so that each man had less than two feet, but since half the crew was always on watch, there was more than enough room. When not in use, the hammocks were rolled and stored topside in netting above the bulwarks. Anyone who has ever slept in one will testify how comfortable a hammock can be, and the sailor had far better sleeping accommodations, whatever drawbacks they might have, than the Continental soldier lying on the hard ground or on top of a vermin-infested straw mattress.

Rations were fixed by the naval regulations for each day of the week. It was a monotonous menu leaning heavily on beef, pork, potatoes and bread. Although the meals might not excite any palates, at least the sailor knew where his next one was coming from. To wash it down, each man got half a pint of rum per day and more when he was on extra duty or in battle. For the sick an additional allowance of a pint and a half of vinegar was made. In addition to the provisions carried aboard, all captains were ordered to keep fishing tackle ready so that whenever possible the crew's diet could be supplemented with fresh fish.[28]

For the Continental sailor the most feared and deadly enemy was neither the British nor the perils of the sea; it was disease. In eighteenth-century navies diseases took tolls far in excess of any battle. Silent and unseen, they worked with deadly efficiency to reduce a ship or an entire fleet to complete impotency. Fevers (most likely typhus), dysentery and scurvy were the chief culprits.[29] The Marine Committee were well aware of how fearsome these diseases were, and within the confines of eighteenth-century scientific knowledge they did everything they could to practice preventive medicine. The old adage "A clean ship is a healthy ship" was followed as closely as possible. The committee's orders to Captain Nicholas Biddle were typical.

> You should . . . insist that your officers do frequently see the Ship thoroughly and perfectly cleansed, aloft and below from Stem to Stern, burn Powder and wash with vinigar betwixt decks—order Hammocks all bedding bed cloths and Body Cloaths daily into the quarters or to be aired on Deck, make the people keep their persons cleanly and use exercise—give them as frequent changes of wholesome food as you can, fish when you can get it and fresh food in Port. Ventilate the Holds and between Decks constantly. In short cleanliness, exercise, fresh air and wholesome food will restore or preserve health more than medicine.[30]

It was good advice, and had it been followed more assiduously, there might have been a considerable reduction in mortality. Just how many American sailors succumbed to disease, or to any cause, for that matter, is uncertain. There was a naval hospital in Boston, but how many sailors were confined there and for what causes are not clear.

The records of the Royal Navy are quite exact on these points, and although the figures are many times what they would be for the Americans, the relative proportions are probably about the same. According to these statistics, the chances were fifty-fifty that if a sailor died, it was disease that did him in—scurvy, perhaps, a disease caused by a lack of vitamin C in which the victim suffers from softening and bleeding gums, loosened teeth, hemorrhaging and finally swollen limbs. Typhus, or ship fever as it was most often known, was another frequent visitor aboard. It was transmitted (unknown to eighteenth-century physicians) by body lice. Characteristically it came on very suddenly, with the patient's temperature skyrocketing and remaining high for several days. Another common disease at sea was dysentery, an intestinal infection that in most cases was probably contracted from putrid water or spoiled food. It caused gripping abdominal pains coupled with a near constant desire to evacuate the bowels. Unchecked, it led to rapid dehydration and death. These were the three most common and virulent killers, but depending on where the ship was sailing, there might be other more exotic but just as deadly diseases.

The odds were three to one that a sailor might die of an accident. Falling out of the rigging was among the most prevalent. Quite often the culprit was rum. With so much of it being swigged, it would not be at all unusual to have a tipsy sailor aloft.

A sailor's chance of dying from one of the perils of the sea, shipwreck or drowning, for example, was about eight to one. At the bottom of the list was enemy action. The odds on being killed at battle ran thirteen to one.[31]

By far the most common but least dangerous disease was

seasickness. With so many landlubbers on board, it was not unusual to see green-pallored men leaning precariously over the leeward rail. The surest remedy was time and experience, although Captain Charles Biddle found an equally effective one—exercise.

> Knowing that exercise is an excellent remedy for sea sickness, and wishing to make the young men on board learn to go aloft whenever the weather was fair I had the hand pump taken up to the head of the main top-mast and there lashed and every one of them that wanted a drink of water was obliged to go up, bring the pump down, and after they had taken a drink carry it up again. For the first five or six days many of them would come up on deck, look wistfully at the pump, but rather than go aloft would go down again. However they were soon reconciled to it and I believe it was a great service to them.[32]

Some of the disease aboard ship might have been better controlled if the navy had had some way to screen men coming into the service. But there were no provisions for physical examinations, and any compunctions officers might have had about taking men who might not be fit for service were overridden by the critical shortage of men. Undoubtedly many of the men who came aboard, especially those who had been turned out of jail, brought with them all kinds of contagious diseases that could decimate a ship's company.

Caring for these men when they were sick or wounded was the job of the ship's surgeon. It was a difficult and demanding calling for which a man needed all the knowledge and skill of his land-based colleagues, along with an extra measure of zeal and courage. Congress tried to ensure that only qualified men filled these positions and even provided for a very rudimentary system of examination. But given the lack of doctors and the inadequacy of their training, about all such a system could do was to reveal how poorly qualified most men were. Those who served in the navy were given the title surgeon and paid $21 1/8 per month. Only the larger and better-manned Continental ships enjoyed the luxury of a full-time surgeon, and most were lucky if they had on board a surgeon's mate or even someone who knew how to dress a wound.[33]

The surgeon's place of business was called the cockpit. It was usually in a relatively secure part of the ship as far away from battle as possible, which meant it had to be below decks, most likely in a dark and poorly ventilated place.

Victims of disease, no matter what it was, were likely to get a pretty standard treatment. Bleeding was the universal prescription on land and sea for everything from the sniffles to heart failure. Great reliance was placed on the bark which came from the cinchona tree and contained quinine. Other folk remedies might be tried as well, but in the end it came down to letting the disease take its course.

In battle the cockpit was turned into a noisy, bloody jangle of wounded and dying men. Burns from fires and guns, along with fragmentation wounds received from flying splinters of wood and metal, took the greatest toll. Infection was a near certainty, and injuries that with modern antiseptic treatment might be considered minor often turned gangrenous and fatal. Broken bones could be reset, but a serious compound fracture demanded immediate amputation. Anesthesia consisted of heavy doses of rum and brandy and, when available, opium.

Considering the unwilling way many came into the navy; the attraction of other pursuits, especially privateering, and the dangers of the profession itself, it is not surprising that when an opportunity arose, many American sailors decided that they would rather be elsewhere. Great numbers left legally as their enlistments expired. Others, though, disgruntled with Continental service, did not wait their full term and simply deserted. Often they could hardly be blamed. Long days of sitting idly in port and interminable delays in pay (the men of *Bonhomme Richard* were still waiting in 1783 for their share of prizes taken five years earlier) contributed to a feeling of frustration and envy, especially when sailors watched others around them getting rich off prizes.[34]

How many men actually deserted the navy is not certain. The available records from the early days of the war, 1775–76, indicate an average desertion rate approaching twenty-five percent. It is possible that this rate increased as the war went on. As high as this might seem, it needs to be judged in perspective. The ranks of the Continental army were constantly being thinned by desertion, and the Royal Navy lost over seventy-nine thousand men. Desertion was a common and chronic malaise that sapped the strength of armies and navies on both sides.[35]

Efforts to capture deserters ranged all the way from stopping and searching ships to offering rewards and advertising in newspapers. None of these methods proved very successful, and about the surest way for a captain to prevent desertion was to stay at sea and avoid coming into port for as long as possible. Repeatedly commanders were told to stay out until their supplies were gone. Even when they came in, they were advised to remain some distance from land. They dropped anchor in remote locations to avoid contact with privateers and make it more difficult for their men to jump ship. At Philadelphia it was Reedy Island in the Delaware. In Boston it was Nantasket Roads out beyond the Castle. Despite precautions, desertions continued; ingenious and desperate men always found a way to run.[36]

No discussion about sailors in the Revolution would be complete without mentioning the thousands who became prisoners of war. Their confinement and sufferings, real and imagined, were a tender topic during the Revolution, and even in the years following the war a good deal of emotion was still expended on the issue. Charges and countercharges of brutality and inhumane treatment were hurled back and forth. It was all prime grist for the propaganda mills but of dubious value to the historian.[37]

To the British, American prisoners of war were an embarrassment. Technically, since Britain did not recognize the existence of an American nation, they could not hold American prisoners of war. After all, war can only be officially waged against another nation. Not until more than six months after Yorktown did Parliament finally come around to enacting a law that "rebel Prisoners" could be lawfully held as prisoners of war. In the very early days of the war captured Americans were simply held illegally. To the legalistically minded British that was a doubtful proposition. It was certainly a direct violation of *habeas corpus*, and in the West Indies some American prisoners were being released on a writ of *habeas corpus*. This difficulty was overcome by parliamentary statutes passed in December 1776 and March 1777. These laws had the effect of temporarily suspending *habeas corpus* and allowed British magistrates to imprison Americans on probable cause and hold them at the pleasure of the king.[38]

Ordinarily in eighteenth-century warfare prisoners were a minor problem. No belligerent wanted to expend resources watching over them. It was uneconomical and a waste of trained manpower. What most often happened was that after a relatively short confinement prisoners were exchanged or ransomed via a formal arrangement between nations known as a cartel, but because of Britain's refusal to recognize or deal with the American Congress, no formal cartel could be arranged. Legal impediments notwithstanding, reason dictated that there had to be some kind of exchange, and in February 1776 Lord George Germain told General William Howe, the British commander in America, that he must find a "means of effecting [prisoner] exchange without the King's Dignity [and] Honor being committed or His Majesty's Name used in any Negociation."[39] In America a system of informal exchange was worked out between field commanders, and with some exceptions the exchange of captured soldiers was carried on reasonably well during the war.[40] Sadly, the same cannot be said for sailors. Once captured, American seamen could despair of exchange and look forward to little except rotting in jail. The principal reason for this situation, aside from the usual politics, bureaucracy and red tape, was that the Americans had very little to trade with. Precious few British seamen fell into American hands, and although Washington did have numbers of British soldiers under guard, he was generally not willing to exchange them for sailors but preferred to use them to get back soldiers for his army.[41]

For officers the problem was not nearly as bad. As gentlemen they were allowed to go on parole, which meant they were allowed to go free after giving their word not to take up arms again. In other cases officers, instead of being kept under close confinement, were granted leave to live and roam anywhere within the general proximity of the prison. Although these liberties were customary, there were some instances when American officers were treated in the opposite fashion. Captain Gustavus Conyngham, who had been a particularly sharp thorn in the British side for his exploits in the Channel, was clapped into irons and shackled as a common criminal. When word leaked out, the American authorities were furious, and to bargain for better treatment, they ordered three British officers in their hands to be treated in a similar fashion. Conyngham was soon freed of his bonds.

Seamen carried to England for confinement were generally taken to Mill or Forton prisons. Mill Prison was located on a promontory of land that jutted out into the sound between the towns of Plymouth and Plymouth Dock. Forton Prison, the other major facility in England, was situated about two miles outside the town of Portsmouth. Together these two probably held somewhere in the neighborhood of twenty-five hundred to three thousand American seamen during the course of the Revolution.[42]

At Forton, the prison that has been studied in greater depth, the death rate for the period June 1777 to November 1782 was 5.75 percent; that rate, not extraordinary in itself, is skewed upward as the result of a virulent epidemic of influenza that swept through the prison population in 1782, and the actual average is closer to 3 percent. Among Americans the mortality was considerably higher than 3 percent, not because of any perversity on the part of the British toward Americans but rather because of the long confinement without exchange.[43]

(297)

For the men perhaps the worst punishment of all was the pall of gloom and boredom that constantly hung over them. To amuse themselves and fill their time, the sailors were left to find their own devices. That usually meant gambling, brawling and playing games. Sometimes the more talented and industrious turned to carving wood, scrimshaw, or making model ships. They were allowed to buy books and write letters, and frequently, although forbidden, newspapers would pop up inside the cells. Rations in prison, while not exciting, were adequate and health care, albeit primitive, was usually provided; at Forton there was a hospital, and quarantining of the sick was standard procedure. The prisoners were assigned space in an open barracks. Officers at their own request were segregated from the enlisted men, and nationalities were usually kept divided. Within the walls the men moved about with a minimum of restriction and in general handled and governed their own affairs. The garrisons guarding the men were made up of local militia units and regulars unfit for combat duty.

A favorite way for the men to while away the hours was to huddle together and hatch escape plans. Thanks to the ingenuity of the prisoners and the laxity of their captors, escape was always a distinct and alluring possibility. Between 1777 and 1779, 112 out of 415 prisoners at Forton were able to flee. Many were recaptured, but with the help of sympathetic Englishmen who ran a kind of underground to the Continent and freedom, many made it. Tunneling under the walls through His Majesty's good earth, climbing over the wall and simple bribery, by force of a guinea, were the favorite means of departure.

As always, for the schemers there was money to be made. They turned escape and recapture into a tidy and profitable business. The crown had a standing reward of five pounds for escaped prisoners, so enterprising guards and prisoners connived to collect the money. With the guard's assistance the prisoner escaped. He was quickly and willingly recaptured and turned in for the reward, which the two partners would then secretly split.[44]

Aside from escape and exchange there was a third possibility for freedom open to American seamen. They could volunteer for service in the Royal Navy. To a remarkable degree American prisoners rejected that option and remained loyal to the cause of American independence.[45]

On the face of this evidence it seems quite apparent that Forton and Mill were "no Andersonvilles." Most of the horror and atrocity stories coming out of the prisons were the product of propaganda and Anglophobia. By eighteenth-century standards American prisoners received a reasonable level of humane treatment. Brutality and starvation were not British policy. Indeed, compared to the close quarters and harsh treatment these men endured while prisoners aboard ship, incarceration at Mill or Forton was a change for the better.

Given absolute power over other men, prison keepers often turned into tormenters. Such tendencies toward cruelty were checked to some extent in England by a concerned public. English reformers, ministers and politicians quite often interceded on behalf of the prisoners and helped secure better treatment for them. In America, on the other hand, such guardian angels were rare, and all the things said in mitigation for confinement in England did not apply. Seamen taken in American waters were confined on the British prison ships at Wallabout Bay, New York, where they lived and died surrounded by horrors that could have added a new circle to Dante's Inferno.

Because of the shortage of space to confine American seamen ashore, in the fall of 1776 the British began to moor hulks, decrepit, dismasted vessels, in Wallabout Bay, the present site of the Brooklyn Navy Yard. As the number of prisoners grew, more ships were added, and in April 1778 the most infamous member of this death fleet was towed to her mooring—*Jersey*, a former sixty-four-gun ship built in 1736. Hundreds, perhaps thousands, of Americans perished aboard this rotting hulk whose stench was so strong that she could only be approached from windward. Crammed between decks, with no space to move and little air to breathe, men lived on spoiled food and scummy water. Each morning the day began with a call from the deck, "Rebels turn out your dead." The bodies were taken ashore and buried in shallow graves just above high water, and so after a hurricane or winter storm it was not unusual to see the remains floating by on the tide. Twenty-five years after the war at least twenty hogsheads of human bones were gathered up from along the shores of Wallabout.[46]

That such a barbaric situation could and did exist stands as damning evidence against those who perpetrated it as well as those who stood idly by, condoning it with their silence. There was no one in New York to intervene on behalf of the Americans. Both Congress and Washington filed protests and threatened retaliation, but it was just so much bluster, and the Yankee seamen aboard *Jersey* and her sister hulks continued to live and die amid horrendous conditions.

Of course, Americans also kept naval prisoners, but there were never many of them. Those who did fall into American hands were encouraged to join the Continental navy, and many did. The Americans seemed to have better luck at enlisting British seamen than vice-versa. The ones who remained in confinement were often exchanged for American seamen via local cartels generally made with the British authorities at New York. There could have been more exchanges if the Congress had paid closer attention to the prisoner situation. However, they chose not to and left the problem of confining and maintaining prisoners to the states. Since the states had little money or interest in this business, they frequently ignored the problem, and hundreds, perhaps thousands, of British who might have been used for exchange were allowed to roam free and wander off.

Like their British counterparts, American officials found that for reasons of space and security, prison ships were useful places to store men. There were at least two prison ships in use by the Americans. Both were anchored at the mouth of the Thames River in New London. They were under the general supervision of the Navy Board of the Eastern Department, who worked through their agent at New London, Nathaniel Shaw. They were small ships, and it seems likely that no more than two hundred men were ever confined aboard them.[47] There was some talk about establishing two additional prison ships, one at Boston and the other at Portsmouth, but nothing more is known about them. Appropriately enough, one of the ships at New London was named *Retaliation*.

Conclusion

The summer of 1780 was a low period for John Adams, and he was more grumpy and reflective than usual. He was in Paris, sent by the Congress to assist in peace negotiations. The city itself was hardly to his Puritan tastes and his host, the French foreign minister, Vergennes, who thought the time not propitious for peace, was doing everything in his power to put off, delay and sidetrack this sober Yankee. With each passing day Adams grew to trust the French less. In his idle moments he thought about America, the Revolution and the navy. He had grown up within scent of the sea, in a part of the world where from any hilltop he could view the gray-blue Atlantic. That is where his love affair (if one can even use that term when talking about John Adams) with the sea had begun, and had he been a more physical person, it is not hard to imagine him striding a quarterdeck barking orders at a scampering crew. Perhaps those thoughts had passed his mind, but the hectoring demands of another kind of life kept him from fulfilling any such dream. Nevertheless, wherever he was and whatever he was doing, in his mind John Adams was never far from the sea. It was Adams who early in the Congress took the van and urged his colleagues to a naval effort; he singlehandedly wrote the rules and regulations for the navy; indeed, he never tired of meddling in the navy, and the navy was usually the better for it.

Now from his Parisian perch he thought about the navy and about the years that had gone by since its launching. The recollections saddened him, and from Paris he wrote to the president of Congress so that he might share his melancholy with him. Looking, he said, "over the long list of vessels belonging to the United States taken and destroyed, and recollecting the whole history of the rise and progress of our navy, it is very difficult to avoid tears."[1]

Adams was right. If all the glitter and glamor of a few exploits, especially those of John Paul Jones, are put aside, the story of the Continental navy reveals itself as a rather drab and unimportant sideshow of the Revolution. What can be said about a navy that in one way or another lost nearly every ship? At times the Americans managed to create the impression of great and glorious voyages, as when some of them sailed in British home waters, but once the propaganda fog cleared, a more sober assessment showed that there was a good deal of sound and fury but little real accomplishment. It is worth remembering that the most famous naval engagement between American and British ships, *Bonhomme Richard* versus *Serapis,* was a battle celebrated as a victory by both sides. *Serapis* went to the bottom but only after gallantly completing her mission. As an offensive force the Continental navy failed.[2]

The story from the defensive side is much the same. The navy could never adequately defend either the coast or shipping. One notable exception to this, and perhaps the greatest American achievement afloat, was the trading of space for time that Benedict Arnold orchestrated on Lake Champlain.

If the Continental navy had never existed, it is hard to see how the outcome of the Revolution could have been any different. But a citation of failures should not be read as a condemnation of effort, for the men of the navy were as brave and as patriotic as any who served the American cause. Some

of them were made wise by the experience, and a later genera-
tion of Americans, led ironically by that rotund president
from Braintree, would call upon them to defend the young
Republic at sea. In a few years a new navy rose almost phoe-
nixlike from the ashes of the Revolution and went on to the
glory and permanence that had always eluded the Continental navy.

Notes

CHAPTER ONE

1. J. G. B. Hutchins, *The American Maritime Industries and Public Policy, 1789–1914* (Cambridge, 1941), 134–40.

2. Albert S. Bolles, *Industrial History of the United States* (New York, 1881), 570; John H. Morrison, *History of New York Shipyards* (New York, 1909), 6; William B. Weeden, *Economic and Social History of New England* (Boston, 1891), I, 166, 252; Massachusetts Colonial Laws, 138–39; Massachusetts Acts and Resolves, I, 114.

3. Oliver M. Dickerson, *The Navigation Acts and the American Revolution* (Philadelphia, 1951), 32; Victor S. Clark, *History of Manufactures in the United States, 1607–1860* (Washington, 1916), I, 18.

4. Morrison, 9.

5. Wayland F. Dunaway, *A History of Pennsylvania* (New York, 1950), 232; Carl Bridenbaugh, *Cities in Revolt* (New York, 1964), 269.

6. Frederick M. Gutheim, *The Potomac* (New York, 1949), 87.

7. "State of the British Plantations in America in 1721" in E. B. O'Callaghan (ed.), *Documents Relative to the Colonial History of the State of New York* (Albany, 1853–87), V, 606–10; Richard L. Morton, *Colonial Virginia* (Chapel Hill, 1960), II, 824; Hugh Talmage Lefler and Albert Ray Newsome, *The History of a Southern State: North Carolina* (Chapel Hill, 1954), 93; George C. Rogers, Jr., *Charleston in the Age of the Pinckneys* (Norman, 1969), 15–16; David Duncan Wallace, *South Carolina: A Short History, 1520–1948* (Chapel Hill, 1951), 193; for examples of the difficulty encountered in building ships at Charleston, see Philip Hamer (ed.), *The Papers of Henry Laurens* (Columbia, 1968–), especially vols. II and III.

8. The most important Navigation Act in regard to shipping was the Act of 1651, which stipulated that all goods shipped in the empire were to be carried in British or American ships or in the ships of the producer.

9. Richard B. Morris, *Government and Labor in Early America* (New York, 1946), 225; John J. McCusker, "Sources of Investment Capital in the Colonial Philadelphia Shipping Industry," *Journal of Economic History*, XXXII (March, 1972), 147.

10. Ibid., 152.

11. The best discussion of the factors involved in selecting timber for shipbuilding is Robert G. Albion, *Forests and Sea Power: The Timber Problem of the Royal Navy* (Cambridge, 1926).

12. George F. Dow, *The Sailing Ships of New England* (Salem, 1928).

13. *Pennsylvania Gazette*, 24 June 1762.

14. Carl Bridenbaugh, *The Colonial Craftsman* (Chicago, 1971), 92.

15. Weeden, 576; Carl Bridenbaugh, *Cities in Revolt*, 271; Lyman H. Butterfield (ed.),

The Adams Papers: Diary and Autobiography of John Adams (Cambridge, 1961), II, 103. Shortly after the outbreak of the Revolution this ship was at Charleston, where it was proposed to make her into a fifty-gun man-of-war. The project was never carried through. Henry Laurens to John Laurens, 8 June 1775, in *NDAR*, I, 638.

16. James F. Shepherd and Gary M. Walton, *Shipping, Maritime Trade, and the Economic Development of Colonial North America* (Cambridge, 1972). "Weatherliness" refers to the ability of a vessel to sail close to the wind without drifting to leeward.

17. There seems little justification for claiming that the schooner was first designed in America. The schooner rig had long existed, and although American builders did greatly favor it and made improvements on the design, nevertheless they did not invent the style. Howard I. Chapelle, *The Search for Speed Under Sail, 1700–1855* (New York, 1967), 11.

18. Hutchins, 153.

19. To be properly seasoned, the timber had to stand for a considerable length of time to allow the watery sap to evaporate out of the log. Omitting or shortening this process, as many American yards did, meant that the wood would be far more susceptible to rapid deterioration. American reputations suffered from the use of green timber. The problem became even more acute when American timber was used in English shipyards. Timber arriving in England had in many cases already begun to rot because of the method of transportation. Having been floated down streams in the colonies, the wet timber was loaded into the hold where for six to eight weeks it would lie, steaming and rotting. It was not unusual for American timber to arrive in England covered with fungi and in the first stages of decay. Albion, 13–14. For a discussion on longevity, see Marshall Smelser and William I. Davisson, "The Longevity of Colonial Ships," *American Neptune*, XXXIII (January 1973), 16–19.

20. Eighteenth-century warships were rated according to the number of guns carried.

	GUNS	MEN
First-Rate	100	850–950
Second-Rate	98 or 90	750
Third-Rate	80, 74 or 64	720, 640, 490
Fourth-Rate	50	350
Fifth-Rate	44, 40, 38, 36 or 32	320, 300, 250, 215
Sixth-Rate	28, 24, 20	200–160

John Masefield, *Sea Life in Nelson's Time* (London, 1905), 11.

21. Jeremy Belknap, *History of New Hampshire* (Boston, 1791–92), III, 147; Ralph May, *Early Portsmouth History* (Boston, 1926), 200; G. H. Preble, *History of the Navy Yard at Portsmouth, New Hampshire* (Washington, 1892), 9.

22. Quoted in Joseph Malone, *Pine Trees and Politics: The Naval Stores and Forest Policy in Colonial New England, 1691–1775* (Seattle, 1964), 14.

23. Preble, 9.

24. The British naval commissioners were not the same as the Lords of Admiralty. The former were responsible for building and supplying vessels, while the latter oversaw the actual disposition and administration of the fleet. Daniel A. Baugh, *British Naval Administration in the Age of Walpole* (Princeton, 1965), 35.

25. Ibid., 256.

26. Ibid., 257.

27. Preble, 10–11.

28. Harry J. Carman (ed.), *American Husbandry* (Port Washington, 1964), 490, 496; Alexander Cluny, *The American Traveller . . .* (London, 1769), 121.

29. Quoted in Richard B. Morris, *Government and Labor*, 248.

30. Neil R. Stout, "Manning the Royal Navy in North America, 1763–1775," *American Neptune*, XXIII (1963), 174.

31. Bridenbaugh, *Cities in Revolt*, 115–16.

32. Jesse Lemisch, "Jack Tar in the Streets; Merchant Seamen in the Politics of Revolutionary America," *William and Mary Quarterly*, XXV (1968), 401.

33. William Falconer, *A New Universal Dictionary of the Marine* (London, 1815), 353.

34. C. W. Kendall, *Private Men of War* (London, 1931), 251.

35. Lawrence H. Gipson, *The Great War for the Empire: The Culmination, 1760–1763*, vol. VIII of *The British Empire Before the American Revolution* (New York, 1953), 68.

36. Herbert L. Osgood, *The American Colonies in the Eighteenth Century* (New York, 1924), I, 549; William R. Smith, *South Carolina as a Royal Province* (New York, 1903), 188.

37. Gardner W. Allen (ed.), "Captain Hector McNeill of the Continental Navy," *Proceedings* of the Massachusetts Historical Society; William B. Clark, *Captain Dauntless: The Story of Nicholas Biddle of the Continental Navy* (Baton Rouge, 1949), 38.

38. James T. Flexner, *George Washington: The Forge of Experience* (Boston, 1965), 30.

CHAPTER TWO

1. The story of Lexington and Concord is one of the best-known events in American history. It has been examined countless times by historians and celebrated by poets. The best historical investigation is Allen French, *Day of Concord and Lexington* (Boston, 1925).

2. Frank L. Mott, "The Newspaper Coverage of Lexington and Concord," *New England Quarterly*, XVII (1944), 489–505.

3. The engagement probably took place on 12 May; "Journal of His Majesty's Sloop *Falcon*," in *NDAR*, I, 322; *Massachusetts Spy*, 24 May 1775.

4. Machias is located at 44°43′N and 67°28′W.

5. *Margaretta* also appears in the records as *Margueritta*. She was a small schooner hired by Admiral Samuel Graves late in March 1775. Prior to going to Machias she had been employed as a dispatch vessel. "Narrative of Vice Admiral Samuel Graves," 30 March 1775, in *NDAR*, I, 163 (hereafter cited as "Narrative").

6. Graves to Gage, 26 May 1775, in ibid., 538.

7. "Pilot Nathaniel Godfrey's Report of Action Between the Schooner *Margueritta* and the Rebels at Machias June 11 1775," in ibid., 655–56. A detailed secondary account of the battle appears in Andrew M. Sherman, *Life of Captain Jeremiah O'Brien* (Morristown, 1902), 29–46.

8. Journal of the Massachusetts Provincial Congress, 26 June 1775, in Peter Force (ed.), *American Archives* (Washington, 1839), 4th ser., II, 1447.

9. Lieutenant John Knight to Graves, 10 August 1775, in *NDAR*, I, 1108.

10. Graves to Philip Stephens, 7 June 1775, in ibid., 622; *Diana* was aground in the area of present-day Chelsea Creek.

11. George A. Billias, *General John Glover and His Marblehead Mariners* (New York,

1960), 73. In a remarkable piece of maritime detective work Philip C. F. Smith and Russell W. Knight have thrown new light on *Hannah*. See Smith and Knight, "In Troubled Waters: The Elusive Schooner *Hannah*," *American Neptune Magazine*, XXX (1970), 86–116.

12. Washington to Nicholson Broughton, 2 September 1775, in John Fitzpatrick (ed.), *The Writings of George Washington from the Original Manuscript Sources, 1745–1799* (Washington, 1931), III, 467–69. Broughton's Christian name can be found under a variety of spellings.

13. Compared to large warships, small vessels always tended to be more crowded, and in *Hannah*'s case the situation was even more acute. James Henderson, *The Frigates* (New York, 1971), 20.

14. Broughton to Washington, 7 September 1775, in *NDAR*, II, 36.

15. Washington to Broughton, 2 September 1775, in Fitzpatrick, III, 467–69.

16. William Bell Clark, *George Washington's Navy* (Baton Rouge, 1960), 119–21. For examples of Washington's entreaties to his friends in Congress to act in this matter, see Washington to Richard Lee, 8 November 1775, and Washington to the President of Congress [John Hancock], 11 November 1775, in Fitzpatrick, IV, 75, 82.

17. Washington to John Langdon, 21 September 1775, in Fitzpatrick, III, 513–14.

18. General Orders, 22 September 1775, in ibid., 514–15.

19. Smith and Knight suggest the possibility that during this interlude *Hannah* might have been involved in ferrying Benedict Arnold's troops to Kennebec, where they would begin their extraordinary march to Quebec.

20. Captain John Collins to Vice Admiral Samuel Graves, 12 October 1775, in *NDAR*, II, 417–18; a good secondary account of this engagement is in Edwin M. Stone, *History of Beverly* . . . (Boston, 1843), 64–65.

21. Clark, 14.

22. Ibid., 19.

23. Moylan was a prominent Philadelphian who had been recommended to Washington by John Dickinson. He later became Washington's secretary. Frank Monaghan, "Stephen Moylan," in *DAB*, VII, 302–303.

24. Instructions to Colonel John Glover and Stephen Moylan, 4 October 1775, in Fitzpatrick, IV, 6–7.

25. Appraisal of the *Speedwell* and Appraisal of the *Eliza*, 10 October 1775, in ibid.

26. John Hancock to George Washington, 5 October 1775, PCC, item 12A (roll 23).

27. Ibid.

28. Washington to Hancock, 12 October 1775, in Fitzpatrick, IV, 23–24.

29. Washington to Broughton, 16 October 1775, in ibid., 33–34.

30. Moylan and Glover to Colonel Joseph Reed, 22 October 1775, in *NDAR*, II, 565.

31. Clark, 50–57.

32. Moylan to Colonel Joseph Reed, 2 January 1776, in William B. Reed, *Life and Correspondence of Joseph Reed* (Philadelphia, 1847), I, 138.

33. Reed to Captain Ephraim Bowen, Jr., 13 October 1775, in *NDAR*, II, 436–37.

34. Charter Agreement for the Armed Schooner *Harrison* of Washington's Fleet, 22 October 1775, in ibid., 572–73; Charter Party for the Armed Brig *Washington*, 3 November 1775, in ibid., 871.

35. Clark, 37.

36. Reed to Bowen, 20 October 1775, in *NDAR*, II, 537.

37. William Watson to Washington, 29 November 1775, in ibid., 1189–90.

38. Moylan to Reed, 2 January 1776, in ibid., III, 572; Carpenter's Survey of the Armed Brig *Washington*, 8 December 1775, in ibid., 10.

39. Washington to the President of Congress, 14 December 1775, in Fitzpatrick, IV, 162.

40. Captain William Coit to Major Samuel Blachley Webb, 7 November 1775, in *Reminiscences of General Samuel B. Webb of the Revolutionary Army, by His Son, J. Watson Webb* (New York, 1882), 155–56.

41. Washington to Reed, 20 November 1775, in Fitzpatrick, IV, 106.

42. Robert Peabody, "The Naval Career of Captain John Manley of Marblehead," Essex Institute Historical *Collections*, XLV (1909), 7.

43. Graves to Major General William Howe, 12 November 1775, in *NDAR*, II, 1000; "Narrative," 18 November 1775, in ibid., 1065.

44. Captain John Symons, H.M.S. *Cerberus*, to Graves, 26 November 1775, in ibid., 1247.

45. Peabody, 16.

46. Although there was other American naval activity in late 1775, the fleet in New England was the only one actually under Continental direction.

47. The orders to Graves were dated 6 July, but it took three months for him to receive them. "Narrative," 4 October 1775, in *NDAR*, II, 292. The exact legal nature of the hostilities was not specified until the king proclaimed the American colonies to be in open rebellion. The proclamation was issued on 23 August, but it did not reach America until 9 November.

48. Ibid.

49. Graves to Mowat, H.M. Armed Vessel *Canceaux*, 6 October 1775, in ibid., 324.

50. Letter from Rev. Jacob Bailey, 18 October 1775, in ibid., 500.

51. "Narrative," 26 November 1775, in ibid., 1143.

52. Commodore Colville to Cleveland, 10 April 1761, quoted in G. S. Graham, "The Naval Defense of British North America 1739–1763," Royal Historical Society *Transactions*, 4th ser., XXX (1948), 98.

53. Francis Hutcheson to Major General Frederick Haldimand, 25 January 1776, in *NDAR*, III, 995.

54. In dealing with the inadequacies of the Royal Navy during the early stages of the Revolution it has long been the practice to blame first Lord Sandwich, the first lord of the Admiralty, for dereliction of duty, and secondly Admiral Graves for ineptness. For a more balanced view that takes into account the difficulties under which both of these men toiled, see M. J. Williams, "The Naval Administration of the Fourth Earl of Sandwich 1771–82" (Ph.D. diss., Oxford University, 1962), and J. H. Broomfield, "Lord Sandwich at the Admiralty Board: Politics and the British Navy, 1771–1778," *Mariner's Mirror*, LI (1965), 7–17.

55. "Narrative," 30 December 1775, in *NDAR*, III, 300.

56. Washington to the President of Congress, 25 April 1776, in Fitzpatrick, IV, 515–17.

NOTES

CHAPTER THREE

1. An excellent discussion of this interdependence can be found in Herbert W. Richmond, *Statesmen and Seapower* (Oxford, 1946). A more cursory discussion is in Ernest M. Eller, "Sea Power in the American Revolution," United States Naval Institute *Proceedings*, LXII (June 1936), 777–89.

2. *JCC*, I, 13.

3. Edmund C. Burnett, *The Continental Congress* (New York, 1941), 33–59; Marshall Smelser, *The Winning of Independence* (Chicago, 1972), 21–42.

4. Diary entry, 26 October 1774, in L. H. Butterfield (ed.), *Diary and Autobiography of John Adams* (Cambridge, 1961), II, 157.

5. Diary entry, 28 October 1774, in ibid.

6. Burnett, 65–79.

7. *JCC*, II, 15, 68–70, 89, 91, 93, 209.

8. John Adams to Elbridge Gerry, 5 November 1775, in Charles Francis Adams (ed.), *The Works of John Adams* (Boston, 1851), IX, 362. A discussion of Adams's role in the development of an American navy can be found in Frederick H. Hayes, "John Adams and American Sea Power," *American Neptune Magazine*, XXV (1965), 35–45.

9. Robert L. Meriwether, "Christopher Gadsden," in *DAB*, IV, 82–83.

10. John Adams to Elbridge Gerry, 7 June 1775, in *NDAR*, I, 628–29.

11. A measure for arming vessels was presented in the provincial congress on 20 June but tabled; Journal of Provincial Congress of Massachusetts, 20 June 1775, in Peter Force (ed.), *American Archives*, 4th ser., II, 1426; James Warren to John Adams, 7 July 1775, in W. C. Ford (ed.), *Warren–Adams Letters* (Boston, 1917–25), I, 78.

12. Josiah Quincy to John Adams, 11 July 1775, in *NDAR*, I, 859.

13. James Warren to John Adams, 11 July 1775, in Ford, I, 82.

14. John Adams to James Warren, 6 July 1775, in ibid., 75; diary entry, 18 September 1775, in Butterfield, II, 176.

15. *JCC*, II, 189.

16. Carl Van Doren, *Benjamin Franklin* (New York, 1938), 533–34; John W. Jackson, *The Pennsylvania Navy, 1775–1781: The Defense of the Delaware* (New Brunswick, 1974), 10.

17. J. H. Trumbull and C. J. Hoardley (eds.), *The Public Records of the Colony of Connecticut, 1636–1776* (Hartford, 1850–90), XV, 100; John R. Bartlett (ed.), *Records of the Colony of Rhode Island and Providence Plantations in New England* (Providence, 1856–65), VII, 347.

18. South Carolina Council of Safety to Clement Lempriere, 24 July 1775, in *NDAR*, I, 965–66.

19. Benjamin Franklin to Silas Deane, 27 August 1775, in ibid, 1244.

20. John Adams to James Warren, 24 July 1775, in Ford, I, 88.

21. *JCC*, II, 240.

22. William G. Roelker and Clarkson A. Collins, "The British Patrol of Narragansett Bay (1774–1776) by H.M.S. *Rose* Captain James Wallace," *Rhode Island History*, VII–IX (1947–50), serialized.

23. Bartlett, VII, 368–69.

24. Elizabeth Cometti, "Depredations in Virginia During the Revolution," in Darrett Rutman (ed.), *The Old Dominion: Essays for Thomas Perkins Abernethy* (Charlottesville, 1964), 135–40.

25. Diary entry, 7 October 1775, in Butterfield, II, 198.

26. *JCC*, III, 281.

27. Ibid.

28. Ibid., III, 277.

29. Ibid., 278.

30. Ibid.

31. President of the Congress [John Hancock] to the Massachusetts Council, 5 October 1775, in PCC, item 12A, 9 (roll 23).

32. *JCC*, III, 293.

33. Ibid., 280.

34. Ibid., 281.

35. Washington to the President of Congress, 5 October 1775, in John C. Fitzpatrick (ed.), *The Writings of George Washington* (Washington, 1931–44), IV, 11–12.

36. *JCC*, III, 294.

37. Ibid.

38. John Adams to James Warren, 13 October 1775, in Ford, I, 139.

39. Ibid.

40. Julian P. Boyd, "Silas Deane: Death by a Kindly Teacher of Treason?" *William and Mary Quarterly*, 3d ser., XVI (October 1959), 530.

41. Silas Deane to Thomas Mumford, 15 October 1775, in W. C. Ford (ed.), *Correspondence and Journals of Samuel Blachley Webb* (New York, 1893–94), I, 107.

42. Ibid.

43. "Estimate for Fitting Out Warships for a Three Months Cruise 30 October 1775," in *NDAR*, II, 647–52.

44. Ibid.

45. *JCC*, III, 311.

46. Ibid.

47. Butterfield, III, 350.

48. Ibid.

49. *JCC*, III, 315.

50. Ibid.

51. Adams, III, 12.

52. Their report can be found in PCC, item 33, 3–62 (roll 40).

53. Isaac Greenwood, *Captain John Manley* (Boston, 1915), 10.

54. John Adams to James Warren, 5 November 1775, in Ford, *Warren–Adams Letters*, I, 175.

55. Adams, III, 11–12.

56. *JCC*, III, 378–87.

57. C. O. Paullin, *The Navy of the American Revolution* (Cleveland, 1906), 17

58. Frank Mevers, "Congress and the Navy: The Establishment and Administration of the American Revolutionary Navy" (Ph.D. diss., University of North Carolina, 1972), 29–40.

59. Naval Committee to Commodore Esek Hopkins, 5 January 1776, PCC, item 58, 239–40 (roll 71).

60. Carlos Hanks, "A Cruise for Gunpowder," United States Naval Institute *Proceedings*, LXV (1939), 324.

CHAPTER FOUR

1. The ensign was hoisted by the senior lieutenant on board *Alfred*, John Paul Jones. It was the Grand Union Flag, thirteen red and white stripes with the British Union in the upper canton adjacent to the halyard.

2. *JCC*, III, 420.

3. Ibid.

4. See 53–54.

5. *JCC*, III, 425–26.

6. Ibid. New Hampshire, *Raleigh*; Massachusetts Bay, *Hancock* and *Boston*: Rhode Island, *Warren* and *Providence*; Connecticut, *Trumbull*; New York, *Montgomery* and *Congress*; Pennsylvania, *Randolph, Washington, Effingham* and *Delaware*; Maryland, *Virginia*. Isaac J. Greenwood, *Captain John Manley* (Boston, 1915), xxvii.

7. *JCC*, III, 425–27. A piece of canvas is equal to approximately twelve yards. *The Oxford English Dictionary* (Oxford, 1933), VII, 835.

8. *JCC*, III, 428.

9. George Read to his wife, 15 December 1775, in William Read, *Life and Correspondence of George Read, A Signer of the Declaration of Independence* (Philadelphia, 1870), 117.

10. Daniel Baugh, *British Naval Administration in the Age of Walpole* (Princeton, 1965), 254–61.

11. Some of these problems are discussed in J. H. Broomfield, "Lord Sandwich at the Admiralty Board: Politics and the British Navy, 1771–1778," *Mariner's Mirror*, LI (February 1965), 7–17; William M. James, *The British Navy in Adversity: A Study of the War of Independence* (New York, 1926); David Syrett, *Shipping and the American War* (London, 1970).

12. For an indication of the problems the American government actually did undergo in reestablishing the navy during peacetime, see Marshall Smelser, *The Congress Founds the Navy, 1787–1798* (Notre Dame, 1959).

13. Among these sixty men there were thirty-one lawyers, fifteen merchants, nine public servants, four doctors and one teacher. Frank C. Mevers III, "Congress and the Navy: The Establishment and Administration of the American Revolutionary Navy by the Continental Congress, 1775–1784" (Ph.D. diss., University of North Carolina, 1972), 58–59.

14. William Fowler, *William Ellery: A Rhode Island Politico and Lord of Admiralty* (Metuchen, 1973), 40–41.

15. For examples of other men burdened by committee work, see Jennings B. Saunders, *Evolution of Executive Departments of the Continental Congress, 1774–1789* (Chapel Hill, 1935), 4n.

16. Joseph Pennell to Robert Morris, 25 May 1784, PCC, item 137, 655–57 (roll 150).

17. C. O. Paullin (ed.), *Out-Letters of the Continental Marine Committee and Board of Admiralty* (New York, 1914), II, 104–105.

18. For examples of the difficulties that occasionally arose between the agents and their superiors, see Marine Committee to Rhode Island Frigate Committee, 9 October 1776, in ibid., I, 21–22; Marine Committee to Nathaniel Shaw, Jr., 17 June 1777, in ibid., 138–39; Board of Admiralty to John Bradford, 19 May 1780, in ibid., II, 198.

19. John Bradford to the Board of Admiralty, 11 January 1780, PCC, item 137, 219 (roll 150).

20. Board of Admiralty to Congress, 21 July 1780, PCC, item 37, 268 (roll 44).

21. E. James Ferguson, *The Power of the Purse* (Chapel Hill, 1961), 44–46.

22. Anyone familiar with the chaotic state of Continental finances must realize the tenuousness of this estimate. It is based on Ferguson's estimates compared to the "General View of Receipts and Expenditures of Public Monies." PCC, item 137, 319, 337 (roll 150). This percentage figure is not far removed from the 1971 level of expenditure for the navy. See *Department of Defense Appropriations for 1971* (Washington, 1970), 857.

23. Joseph Pennell to Robert Morris, 16 September 1783, PCC, item 137, 142 (roll 150).

24. *JCC*, VI, 970.

25. Naval Committee to Virginia Convention, 5 January 1776, in *NDAR*, III, 640.

26. See 54.

27. *JCC*, VI, 946–47.

28. Mevers, 83–84.

29. Marine Committee to John Bradford, 21 March 1777, in Paullin, I, 84–85; John Adams to James Warren, 6 April 1777, in W. C. Ford (ed.), *Warren–Adams Letters* (Boston, 1917), I, 311; William Ellery to William Vernon, 26 February 1777, in "Papers of William Vernon and the Navy Board, 1776–1794," *Publications* of the Rhode Island Historical Society, VIII (1901), 204.

30. *JCC*, VII, 281.

31. William Whipple to John Langdon, 10 May 1777, in E. C. Burnett (ed.), *Letters of the Members of the Continental Congress* (Washington, 1928), II, 359.

32. Samuel Adams to Samuel Cooper, 6 May 1777, in ibid., 340.

33. Ibid.

34. *JCC*, VII, 331.

35. During 1778 and 1779 Vernon was almost always at the board. Warren was there somewhat less, preferring to spend time on his farm in Plymouth. Deshon was rarely at the board during this time and could most always be found at Norwich trying to get the frigate *Trumbull* to sea. Letter Book of the Navy Board of the Eastern Department, NYPL.

36. For a discussion of some of the board's activities, see 103–104.

37. See 140–142.

CHAPTER FIVE

1. John Jay to George Washington, 26 April 1779, in Edmund C. Burnett (ed.), *Letters of the Members of the Continental Congress* (Washington, 1928), IV, 176.

2. Ibid.

3. A brief discussion of the "Family Compact" can be found in Richard B. Morris, *The Peacemakers* (New York, 1965), 8–13.

4. Jennings B. Saunders, *Evolution of Executive Departments of the Continental Congress, 1774–1789* (Chapel Hill, 1935), 1–5.

5. *JCC*, IV, 1218. The salary of the navy commissioners was not left at $14,000; on 12 November 1779 a report of the Board of Treasury recommended that their salary be reduced to $12,000. It was adopted (*JCC*, XV, 1261) and indicates in what regard the board was held by Congress. Of the three boards created by Congress—Admiralty, Treasury and War—the members of the first were the lowest paid. The com-

missioners on the other two boards each received $14,000 annually (*JCC*, XV, 1206, 1261).

6. William Laird Clowes, *The Royal Navy, A History from the Earliest Time to the Present* (London, 1898), II, 229.

7. Marquis de Chastellux, *Travels in North America in the Years 1780, 1781 and 1782*, Howard C. Rice, trans. (Chapel Hill, 1963), I, 181.

8. Extract from the diary of William Ellery, *Pennsylvania Magazine of History and Biography*, XIII (1889), 252; William Ellery to Governor William Greene, 23 May 1780, in William Staples (ed.), *Rhode Island in the Continental Congress* (Providence, 1870), 289; for a description of the hardships endured by civil servants of the Congress, see Elizabeth Cometti, "Civil Servants of the Revolutionary Period," *Pennsylvania Magazine of History and Biography*, LXXX (1951), 159–69. William Whipple to Nathaniel Peabody, 27 December 1779, in Burnett, IV, 531n.

9. Report of Board of Admiralty on Continental Agents, 8 February 1780, PCC, item 37 (roll 44); Board of Admiralty to John Bradford, 11 April 1780, in Charles O. Paullin (ed.), *Out-Letters of the Continental Marine Committee and Board of Admiralty* (New York, 1914), II, 182–83; Board of Admiralty to Navy Board of the Eastern Department, 11 April 1780, in Paullin, II, 180–82; Board of Admiralty to John Langdon, 14 April 1780, in Paullin, II, 184–85; Board of Admiralty to Bradford, 30 June 1780, 11 July 1780, in Paullin, II, 216, 228–29; Report of Board of Admiralty, 19 September 1780, PCC, item 37, 317 (roll 44); Navy Board of the Middle Department to Board of Admiralty, 18 December 1780, PCC, item 37, 499; Board of Admiralty to Congress, 12 June 1781, PCC, item 37, 483.

10. Report of Board of Admiralty, 14 August 1780, PCC, item 37, 291 (roll 44); *JCC*, XVIII, 823.

11. See 248–49.

12. Thomas Shaw to Board of Admiralty, 13 January 1780, in Ernest E. Rogers (ed.), *Connecticut's Naval Office at New London During the American Revolution, Including the Mercantile Letter Book of Nathaniel Shaw, Jr.* (New London, 1933), 326.

13. See 101–20.

14. Gardner W. Allen, *A Naval History of the American Revolution* (Boston, 1913), 544.

15. Lynn Montross, *The Reluctant Rebels: The Story of the Continental Congress, 1774–1789.* (New York, 1950), 314–15.

16. Luzerne to the President of Congress, 25 July 1780, in Francis Wharton (ed.); *The Revolutionary Diplomatic Correspondence of the United States* (Washington, 1889), III, 881; A. T. Mahan, *The Influence of Seapower Upon History* (New York, 1957), 338.

17. William Fowler, *William Ellery: A Rhode Island Politico and Lord of Admiralty* (Metuchen, 1973), 64–66.

18. Board of Admiralty to Congress, 24 August 1780, PCC, item 37, 299 (roll 44).

19. Ibid.

20. Ibid.

21. Board of Admiralty to Captain James Nicholson, 29 August 1780, in Paullin II, 253–54.

22. Allen, 510.

23. Ibid.

24. William Ellery to Nathaniel Shaw, 18 September 1780, Nathaniel Shaw Collection, Yale University Library; Board of Admiralty to William Ellery, 9 September 1780, in Paullin, II, 265–66.

257

2122

2212

NOTES

25. *Dunlap's Pennsylvania Packet or General Advertiser,* 2 May 1781; William Bell Clark, *The First Saratoga* (Baton Rouge, 1953), 174.

26. William Ellery to William Vernon, 5 June 1781, "Papers of William Vernon and the Navy Board, 1776–1794," *Publications* of the Rhode Island Historical Society, VIII (1901), 272.

27. *JCC,* XX, 732, 756.

28. Ibid., XXI, 943; Stephen T. Powers, "The Decline and Extinction of American Naval Power, 1781–1789" (Ph.D. diss., University of Notre Dame, 1964), 20–21.

29. Morris's responsibilities are described in Sanders, 129–145; Clarence L. Ver Steeg, *Robert Morris Revolutionary Financier* (Philadelphia, 1954), 65–186. The original intent of Congress had been that Morris would only supervise the navy temporarily and that an agent of marine would be appointed as a permanent. In fact this never occurred, and Morris continued to preside over the liquidation of the navy.

30. Report of Committee to Whom was Referred the Letter of Mr. Smith, 2 July 1781, PCC, item 28, 133–34 (roll 35).

31. A General View of Receipts and Expenditures of Public Monies by Authority from the Superintendent of Finance, PCC, item 137, 337 (roll 150).

32. *DANFS,* I, 40.

33. Ibid., 146.

34. Ibid., II, 248.

35. Ibid., 302; III, 65.

36. Officers of *Alliance* to Captain John Barry, 25 August 1783, PCC, item 137 (roll 150); John Barry to Robert Morris, 26 August 1783, PCC, item 137 (roll 150).

37. Report of the Committee to Inspect Alliance to Robert Morris, 1 November 1783, PCC, item 137, 253, (roll 150). This figure was unrealistically low. *Alliance* had copper sheathing, and the committee had not pulled the sheathing to inspect. Quite likely if they had, they would have found much more rot, which would have considerably increased the repair costs.

38. *JCC,* 15 January 1784.

39. Robert Morris to the President of Congress, 19 March 1784, PCC, item 137, 483–84 (roll 150).

40. Powers, 240.

CHAPTER SIX

1. William Stinchcombe, *The American Revolution and the French Alliance* (Syracuse, 1969), 9; Samuel Flagg Bemis, *The Diplomacy of the American Revolution* (Bloomington, 1957, reprint of 1935 edition), 29–40; Orlando W. Stephenson, "The Supply of Gunpowder in 1776," *American Historical Review,* XXX (January 1925), 279–81.

2. J. Franklin Jameson, "St. Eustatius in the American Revolution," *American Historical Review,* VIII (July 1903), 686; Nathan Miller, *Sea of Glory: The Continental Navy Fights for Independence, 1775–1783* (New York, 1974), 199–201.

3. Quoted in Miller, 200.

4. The trade with Martinique was so busy and lucrative during the war that the American agent there, William Bingham, made enough money from commissions and privateering so that when he returned home to Philadelphia, he was well on his way to becoming the richest man in America; Robert C. Alberts, *The Golden*

Voyage: The Life and Times of William Bingham, 1752–1804 (Boston, 1969).

5. Robert Morris to President of Congress, 23 December 1776, PCC, item 137, appendix, 24–31 (roll 150); Marine Committee to Captain James Nicholson, 23 October 1777, in C. O. Paullin (ed.), *Out-Letters of the Continental Marine Committee and Board of Admiralty* (New York, 1914), I, 160–61.

6. Report of the Board of Admiralty to Congress, 1 February 1780, PCC, item 37, 170–80 (roll 44).

7. Robert Morris to John Paul Jones, 5 February 1777, PCC, item 168, 5–8 (roll 185).

8. Hopkins should not have made such unilateral changes in his orders without consulting the Naval Committee. He did so because he felt a cruise to New Providence Island would be more productive and less dangerous than an operation along the coast. He was especially interested in capturing the large quantities of gunpowder and supplies known to be on the island. John J. McCusker, "The American Invasion of Nassau in the Bahamas," *American Neptune Magazine*, XXV (July 1965), 194–95.

9. Clyde A. Metcalfe, *A History of the United States Marine Corps* (New York, 1939), 13–15.

10. Extract of a Letter from the Captain of Marines [Samuel Nicholas] on Board the Ship *Alfred*, Dated at New London, April 10, 1776, in *NDAR*, IV, 748.

11. John J. McCusker, *Alfred the First Continental Flagship, 1775–1778*, Smithsonian Studies in History and Technology, no. 20 (Washington, 1973), 5.

12. John Brown to Lord George Germain, 2 May 1776, *Pennsylvania Magazine of History and Biography*, XLIX (October 1925), 350.

13. Captain James Wallace to Vice Admiral Molyneux Shuldham, 10 April 1776, in Robert W. Neeser (ed.), *The Despatches of Molyneux Shuldham . . .* (New York, 1913), 178–79.

14. John Paul Jones to Robert Morris, 17 October 1776, in *NDAR*, VI, 1304.

15. Samuel Eliot Morison, *John Paul Jones, A Sailor's Biography* (Boston, 1959), 76. Jones never gave up the idea of capturing Saint Helena. In 1780 he tried to persuade the French foreign minister, Vergennes, to assist him in a preposterous scheme for taking the island. Ibid., 291–93.

16. Robert Morris to John Paul Jones, 5 February 1777, PCC, item 168, 5–8 (roll 185).

17. Morison, 76–85.

18. William Vernon and James Warren to the Marine Committee, 24 March 1779, Letter Book of the Navy Board of the Eastern Department, NYPL.

19. William Vernon, James Warren and John Deshon to the Marine Committee, 26 February 1779, ibid.

20. Marine Committee to Captain Joseph Olney, 10 February 1779, in Paullin, II, 41–47.

21. William Vernon and John Deshon to the Marine Committee, 13 March 1779, Letter Book of the Navy Board, NYPL.

22. William James Morgan, *Captains to the Northward: The New England Captains in the Continental Navy* (Barre, Massachusetts, 1959); William Vernon and James Warren to the Marine Committee, 28 April 1779, and Vernon and Warren to Captain John B. Hopkins, 7 May 1779, Letter Book of the Navy Board, NYPL; Marine Committee to Navy Board of the Eastern Department, 20 May 1779, in Paullin, II, 75.

23. Marine Committee to Captain Samuel Tucker, 2 June 1779, in Paullin, II, 81–82; Robert W. Neeser, *Statistical and Chronological History of the United States Navy, 1775–1907* (New York, 1970 reprint), 288.

24. Oscar Brand, *Songs of '76: A Folksinger's History of the Revolution* (New York, 1972), 120–21.

25. Gardner W. Allen, *A Naval History of the American Revolution* (New York, 1962 reprint), II, 403. The dispatch of the frigates to Charleston was in great measure due to the lobbying of the South Carolina delegate and former president of Congress, Henry Laurens. Henry Laurens to John Laurens, 21 September 1779, in Edmund C. Burnett (ed.), *Letters of the Members of the Continental Congress* (Washington, 1921–36), IV, 428–29.

26. Christopher Ward, *The War of the Revolution* (New York, 1952), II, 696–703; William B. Willcox, *Portrait of a General: Sir Henry Clinton in the War of Independence* (New York, 1964), 300–19.

27. Henry I. Shaw, Jr., "Penobscot Assault—1779," *Military Affairs*, XVII (Summer 1953); Samuel F. Batchelder, *The Life and Surprising Adventures of John Nutting, Cambridge Loyalist, and His Strange Connection with the Penobscot Expedition of 1779* (Cambridge, 1912); Allen, II, 419–38. For this section on Penobscot I am also indebted to Peter Elliott, whose senior honors thesis, "The Penobscot Expedition of 1779: A Campaign of Adversity," was of great help.

28. William D. Williamson, *The History of the State of Maine; from 1602 to 1820* (Glazier, 1832), II, 469.

29. William Vernon and James Warren to the Marine Committee, 30 June 1779, and Vernon and Warren to Jeremiah Powell, President of the Massachusetts Council, 30 June 1779, Letter Book of the Navy Board, NYPL.

30. Solomon Lovell to Dudley Saltonstall, 11 August 1779, in James P. Baxter (ed.), *Documentary History of the State of Maine* (Portland, 1913), 310–11.

31. Captain Dudley Saltonstall to Colonel John Brewer, undated, in George A. Wheeler, *History of Castine, Penobscot and Brooksville, Maine* (Bangor, 1875), 47.

32. *Providence Gazette*, 22 January 1780.

33. Penobscot remained in British possession until surrendered according to the terms of the Treaty of Paris, 1783. Richard B. Morris, *The Peacemakers, the Great Powers and American Independence* (New York, 1965), 363–64; Allen, II, 577.

34. James S. Biddle (ed.), *Autobiography of Charles Biddle, Vice President of the Supreme Executive Council of Pennsylvania, 1745–1821* (Philadelphia, 1883), 393; William B. Clark, *Captain Dauntless: The Story of Nicholas Biddle of the Continental Navy* (Baton Rouge, 1949).

35. In an ironic twist of fate it is possible that Biddle once served aboard *Yarmouth*; Biddle, 393.

36. Miller, 312–13.

37. Gilbert Saltonstall to Gordon Saltonstall, 14 June 1780 and 19 June 1780, *Records and Papers of the New London County Historical Society* (New London, 1890), Part IV, vol. I, 51, 54 (hereafter cited as *Records of New London Historical Society*). As usual casualty figures vary from source to source. These figures are taken from Neeser, II, 30. Apparently Nicholson and Coulthard followed different tactics. Nicholson elected to fire on the down roll and pound *Watt*'s hull; Coulthard, on the other hand,

preferred to fire on the up roll into the rigging. Nicholson's approach, in this instance at least, would destroy and sink the enemy, while Coulthard's would disable and preserve a prize.

38. Gilbert Saltonstall to Gordon Saltonstall, 19 June 1780, *Records of New London Historical Society*, part IV, vol. I, 54.

39. Gomer Williams, *History of the Liverpool Privateers* (Liverpool, 1897), 274.

40. *Pennsylvania Packet*, 27 September 1781; *Records of New London Historical Society*, part IV, vol. I, 56–58; George F. Emmons, *The Navy of the United States . . .* (Washington, 1853), 3.

41. Robert Purviance, *Narrative of Events Which Occurred in Baltimore Town during the Revolutionary War . . .* (Baltimore, 1849), 95; Miller, 210n.

42. Allen, II, 548–50.

43. Ibid., 550–54; Richard J. Purcell, "John Barry of the American Revolution," *Irish Quarterly Review*, XXIII (1934), 628–29.

CHAPTER SEVEN

1. *JCC*, 23 March 1776; the best account of Wickes's career is William Bell Clark, *Lambert Wickes, Sea Raider and Diplomat* (New Haven, 1932). The first American captures made abroad were probably those of a Newbury, Massachusetts, privateer captain, John Lee. Twelve days out of Bilbao, on 15 April 1776, he took an English brig. Thomas Cushing to John Hancock, 3 May 1776, in *NDAR*, IV, 1390.

2. "Copy of the Statement Made by Captain Lambert Wickes, Commanding Officer of the Ship *Reprisal*, St. Pierre," 28 July 1776, in *NDAR*, V, 1264–66.

3. *JCC*, V, 813–16, VI, 884; Samuel Flagg Bemis, *The Diplomacy of the American Revolution* (Bloomington, 1957), 47–49; Edmund C. Burnett, *The Continental Congress* (New York, 1964), 198–212.

4. Committee of Secret Correspondence to Captain Lambert Wickes, 24 October 1776, PCC, item 37, 95–98 (roll 44).

5. Carl Van Doren, *Benjamin Franklin* (New York, 1938), 564.

6. Benjamin Franklin to John Hancock, 8 December 1776, in Francis Wharton (ed.), *The Revolutionary Diplomatic Correspondence of the United States* (Washington, 1889), II, 221.

7. Lambert Wickes to Commissioners in Paris, 14 January 1777, in Edward E. Hale (ed.), *Franklin in France* (Boston 1887–88), I, 112.

8. *JCC*, 10 December 1776.

9. Benjamin Franklin to Samuel Nicholson, 26 January 1777, in Wharton, II, 254.

10. Clark, 12, 161–76; Helen Augur, *The Secret War of Independence* (New York, 1955), 169–74; Gardner W. Allen, *Naval History of the American Revolution*, I, 263, incorrectly identifies Hynson as Wickes's brother-in-law.

11. Clark, 126–27; Robert W. Neeser, *Statistical and Chronological History of the United States Navy, 1775–1907* (New York, 1970), II, 286–87.

12. Wickes to Commissioners in Paris, 26 February 1777, in Hale, I, 115; Comte de Vergennes to Commissioners in Paris, 16 July 1777, in Wharton, II, 364.

13. Wickes to Commissioners in Paris, 5 March 1777, in Hale, I, 117.

14. American Commissioners to the Committee of Foreign Affairs, 26 May, 1777, in Robert W. Neeser (ed.), *Letters and Papers Relative to the Cruises of Gustavus Conyngham*

a Captain of the Continental Navy, 1777–1779 (New York, 1915), 30–31; Arthur Lee to Schulenburg, 20 June 1777, and Schulenburg to Lee, 26 June 1777, in Wharton, II, 346, 350–51.

15. Allen, I, 267.

16. Wickes to Henry Johnson and Samuel Nicholson, 23 May 1777, PCC, Item 41, 7, 150 (roll 51).

17. "Fencing" their goods in this manner was costly for the Americans. Buyers knew the Americans were under pressure to be rid of their prizes quickly before the officials moved in, so they offered low prices. When France entered the war, prizes were sold at public auction and the prices went up accordingly.

18. Neeser, *Statistical History of the Navy*, II, 286–87; Memorial of Captain Samuel Nicholson to the Continental Congress, 17 June 1788, PCC, item 41, 7, 138 (roll 51); Allen, I, 269; Memorial of Captain Samuel Nicholson to the Continental Congress, 23 March 1787, PCC, item 41, 154 (roll 51).

19. Wickes to Commissioners in Paris, 28 June 1777, in Hale, I, 122–23.

20. Adam Anderson, *Anderson's Historical and Chronological Deduction of the Origin of Commerce . . .* (Dublin, 1790), IV, 267, VI, 591; Frederick Martin, *The History of Lloyd's and of Marine Insurance in Great Britain; With an Appendix Containing Statistics Relating to Marine Insurance* (London, 1876), 164–66. Some Englishmen thought that the success of the Americans was due to the fact that British naval officers shunned patrols in home water so that they could cruise along enemy trade routes where the loot was far more plentiful and promising. *The Remembrancer*, 4 July 1777.

21. Wickes to Commissioners in Paris, 12 August 1777, in Hale, I, 128; Clark, 339–48.

22. Conyngham kept the usual spelling of his name. His relatives anglicized it.

23. Attestation of Gustavus Conyngham, in Neeser, *Letters of Gustavus Conyngham*, 159.

24. D'Anglemont to Gabriel de Sartine, 14 January 1776, in *NDAR*, III, 507.

25. Certificate of Dr. Franklin re: Memorial of Gustavus Conyngham, 7 August 1782, PCC, item 41, 2, 154 (roll 48).

26. E. H. Jenkins, *A History of the French Navy* (London, 1973), 63, 129.

27. Henri Malo, "American Privateers at Dunkerque," *United States Naval Institute Proceedings*, XXXVII (1911), 934.

28. Neeser, *Letters of Gustavus Conyngham*, 1–2; Malo, 938.

29. Comte de Vergennes to the Marquis de Noailles, 31 May 1777, in Neeser, *Letters of Gustavus Conyngham*, 37–38.

30. *Remembrancer*, 26 June 1777, 173.

31. William Carmichael to Gustavus Conyngham, 15 July 1777, in Neeser, *Letters of Gustavus Conyngham*, 64–65; Carmichael was a secretary in the American delegation. Samuel Gwynn Coe, "William Carmichael," *DAB*, II, 497–98.

32. Neeser, *Statistical History*, II, 286–87.

33. Silas Deane to Robert Morris, 23 August 1777, in Neeser, *Letters of Gustavus Conyngham*, 97–98.

34. Lord Stormont to Lord Weymouth, 9 August 1777, in ibid., 83; ibid., xxxvii; Lenoir to the Comte de Vergennes, 11 August 1777, in ibid., 88; Amelot to the Comte de Vergennes, 24 September 1777, in ibid., 109.

35. Richard B. Morris, *The Peacemakers, The Great Powers and American Independence* (New York, 1965).

36. Extract of a letter from an officer on board the *Monarch*, lately arrived at

Portsmouth from her cruise; Neeser, *Letters of Gustavus Conyngham*, 127–28.

37. Neeser, *Statistical History*, 286–87; Neeser, *Letters of Gustavus Conyngham*, 152; *Boston Gazette*, 15 February 1779.

38. Silas Deane to Gustavus Conyngham, 21 January 1778, and American Commissioners to Conyngham, 19 April 1778, in Neeser, *Letters of Gustavus Conyngham*, 120–21, 125–26.

39. Nathan Miller, *Sea of Glory: The Continental Navy Fights for Independence* (New York, 1974), 299–300; Comte de Creutz to the Comte de Vergennes, 1 October 1778, in Neeser, *Letters of Gustavus Conyngham*, 138–39.

40. Neeser, *Letters of Gustavus Conyngham*, 152; Neeser, *Statistical History*, 286–87; Miller, 301.

41. *JCC*, XII, 1256.

42. The Deane controversy is a long and complex tale. It can best be followed in Burnett and in Morris.

43. Marine Committee to President Joseph Reed, 12 March 1779, in C. O. Paullin, *Out-Letters of the Continental Marine Committee and Board of Admiralty* (New York, 1914), II, 52; *JCC*, XIII, 307.

44. *Rivington's New York Royal Gazette*, 28 July 1779; Conyngham told the tale of his imprisonment in "Minutes from Gustavus Conyngham of His Treatment and Remarks," in Neeser, *Letters of Gustavus Conyngham*, 160–73.

45. Benjamin Franklin to LeBrun, 25 October 1779, in Neeser, *Letters of Gustavus Conyngham*, 189.

46. Franklin to Conyngham, 20 June 1781, in ibid., 203.

47. William B. Clark, *The First Saratoga: Being the Saga of John Young and His Sloop of War* (Baton Rouge, 1953), 15.

48. Captain Charles Bulkeley's Narrative of Personal Experiences in the War of the American Revolution from His original Manuscript, in Ernest Rogers (ed.), *Connecticut's Naval Office of New London During the War of the American Revolution* (New Haven, 1933), 126.

49. Benjamin Franklin, Silas Deane and Arthur Lee to Captains Thomas Thompson and Elisha Hinman, 25 November 1777, in Wharton, II, 428.

50. Allen, 301–304.

CHAPTER EIGHT

1. *Indien* was authorized by Congress and contracted for by the American commissioners in 1777; *DANFS*, III, 437.

2. Jones's departure for Europe had come quite suddenly. In his haste to get away, he had left behind him a good deal of unfinished paperwork; Esek Hopkins to John Hancock, 11 April 1777, in Alverda S. Beck (ed.), *The Letter Book of Esek Hopkins* (Providence, 1932), 141.

3. John Paul Jones to Marine Committee, 10 December 1777, PCC, item 58, 137 (roll 71).

4. Benjamin Franklin and Silas Deane to John Paul Jones, 16 January 1778, in Francis Wharton (ed.), *The Revolutionary Diplomatic Correspondence of the United States* (Washington, 1889), II, 471–72.

5. The part about staying out for a few weeks was probably put in so that the

commissioners could avoid any problems vis-à-vis disposal of prizes. Although by this time the Americans were assured that a treaty of alliance was in the making, they had not yet actually signed one, and in anticipation of that event they probably wished to avoid any unnecessary problems. Hence, Jones was told to stay away.

6. Arthur Lee to John Paul Jones, 17 January 1778, in Wharton, II, 473.

7. See 144–45.

8. Samuel Eliot Morison, *John Paul Jones* (Boston, 1959), 128–34.

9. Jonathan R. Dull, "The French Navy and American Independence; Naval Factors in French Diplomacy and War Strategy, 1774–1780" (Ph.D. diss., University of California, Berkeley, 1972), 203.

10. Robert W. Neeser, *Statistical and Chronological History of the United States Navy* (New York, 1970), II, 288–89.

11. Morison, 145; Phillips Russell, *John Paul Jones; Man of Action* (New York, 1927), 97.

12. Benjamin Franklin to John Paul Jones, 24 February 1779, in Wharton, III, 61.

13. Franklin to Jones, 3 June 1778, in ibid., II, 604–605; Lyman H. Butterfield (ed.), *The Adams Papers: Diary and Autobiography of John Adams* (Cambridge, 1961), IV, 165; Abraham Whipple to John Paul Jones, 19 August 1778, in Wharton, II, 597.

14. Franklin to Jones, 25 May 1778, in Wharton, II, 597.

15. Ibid., 612.

16. Butterfield, IV, 165.

17. Franklin to Jones, 1 June 1778, in Wharton, II, 599.

18. Franklin to Jones, 3 June 1778, in ibid., 604–605.

19. John Paul Jones to Abraham Whipple, 18 August 1778, in ibid., 689.

20. The Dutch, not wishing to risk their neutrality by turning *Indien* over to the Americans, sold her instead to the king of France. Later she was given to the Chevalier Luxembourg, who leased her to Commodore Alexander Gillon of the South Carolina state navy. She sailed for South Carolina, accomplished very little and was finally captured by the British in December 1782. *Indien/South Carolina* was the largest ship to fly American colors in the Revolution. Gardner W. Allen, *A Naval History of the American Revolution* (New York, 1962), II, 526–63.

21. John Paul Jones to [Commissioners in Paris?], 25 November 1778, PCC, item 168, 46 (roll 185).

22. Quoted in Morison, 182.

23. Louis Gottschalk, *Lafayette and the Close of the American Revolution* (Chicago, 1942) 9–16; E. H. Jenkins, *A History of the French Navy* (London, 1973), 158–59; Alfred T. Mahan, *The Major Operations of the Navies in the War of American Independence* (New York, 1969), 117–19; Alfred T. Patterson, *The Other Armada* (Manchester, England, 1960), *passim*.

24. Gottschalk, 10.

25. Benjamin Franklin to John Paul Jones, 27 April 1779, in Albert H. Smythe (ed.), *The Writings of Benjamin Franklin* (New York, 1907), VII, 296–98; the instructions, dated 26 April 1779, were enclosed with the letter.

26. Jenkins, 160–61; Mahan, 116–21.

27. William B. Clark, *Benjamin Franklin's Privateers: A Naval Epic of the American Revolution* (Baton Rouge, 1956), 15.

28. Benjamin Franklin to John Paul Jones, 8 July 1779, in Smythe, VII, 365.

29. Ibid.

30. Robert Charles Sands (ed.), *Life and Correspondence of John Paul Jones* . . . (New York, 1830), 166–68.

31. John S. Barnes (ed.), *Fanning's Narrative: Memoirs of Nathaniel Fanning* (New York, 1912).

32. For Landais's later career, see 266–69.

33. C. O. Paullin, *Diplomatic Negotiations of American Naval Officers, 1778–1883* (Baltimore, 1912), 41.

34. See 266–69.

35. Morison, 407–409.

36. For an example of this type of mission, see Marine Committee to Captain Seth Harding, 17 September 1779, in C. O. Paullin (ed.), *Out-Letters of the Continental Marine Committee and Board of Admiralty* (New York, 1914), II, 109–11; the Congress also felt that the few ships left could be of more value in home waters. Board of Admiralty to Benjamin Franklin, 28 March 1780, in Paullin, 174.

CHAPTER NINE

1. There is some confusion on eighteenth-century maps over the name of the river. In some instances it is referred to in its entirety as the Richelieu. On others the northern segment is called the Sorel and the southern Chambly. I shall refer to the whole river as the Richelieu.

2. Alas, this is probably another one of those memorable quotes from the Revolution that were never actually said. Christopher Ward, *The War of the American Revolution* (New York, 1952), 68, 439n.

3. Hugh Hastings (ed.), *The Public Papers of George Clinton, First Governor of New York, 1777–1795, 1801–1804* (New York, 1899–1914), I, 201n.

4. Journal kept by Eleazar Oswald on Lake Champlain, 11 May 1775, in *NDAR*, I, 312; Oswald later became Benedict Arnold's secretary on the march to Quebec.

5. Allen French, *The Taking of Ticonderoga in 1775* (Cambridge, 1928); Willard M. Wallace, *Traitorous Hero: The Life and Fortunes of Benedict Arnold* (New York, 1954), 43.

6. Bateaux were open flat-bottomed boats used for transporting men and supplies. Resembling the common rowboat, they varied in size, although in this instance, considering the number of troops being ferried, they must have been fairly large. Generally they were oar driven.

7. Benedict Arnold to the Massachusetts Committee of Safety, 19 May 1775, in *NDAR*, I, 364–66; Oswald's Journal, 23 May 1775, in *NDAR*, I 513.

8. Arnold very correctly saw that for the moment the Americans did not have enough troops to keep Saint Johns, which the British could easily reach. His plan was to keep control of the lake with his vessels until the army built up enough strength to push north. As usual Allen disagreed. In a premature move he tried to occupy Saint Johns but was easily and quickly evicted by a superior British force; Ward, 70.

9. Benedict Arnold to the Massachusetts Committee of Safety, 23 May 1775, in *NDAR*, I, 512–13.

10. *JCC*, II, 55–56.

11. Ethan Allen to the Continental Congress, 29 May 1775, in *NDAR*, I, 563–64; Colonel Benedict Arnold to the Committee of Safety of Massachusetts, 29 May 1775,

in *NDAR*, I, 562; Walter Spooner to Governor Jonathan Trumbull, 3 July 1775, in *NDAR*, I, 807–808.

12. *JCC*, II, 110.

13. Charles A. Jellison, *Ethan Allen Frontier Rebel* (Syracuse, 1969), 142.

14. Journal of the Provincial Congress of Massachusetts, 27 May 1775, in *NDAR*, I, 543.

15. Edward Mott to Governor Jonathan Trumbull, 6 July 1775, in ibid., 829–30.

16. Minutes of the Albany Committee of Correspondence, 14 July 1775, New York State Division of Archives and History, *Minutes of the Albany Committee of Correspondence, 1775–1778* (New York, 1923), I, 149; Phylip Schuyler to John Hancock, 27 July 1775, in *NDAR*, I, 988–89.

17. Journal kept on Board the Continental Schooner *Liberty*, 3 August 1775, in *NDAR*, I, 1055.

18. Examination of Peter Griffin, in ibid., 123; Philip Schuyler to John Hancock, 8 September 1775, in ibid., II, 43.

19. Capitulation Terms for the British Garrison at Saint Johns, 2 November 1775, in ibid., 846–48.

20. Kenneth Roberts, *March to Quebec* (Garden City, 1942); Justin Smith, *Arnold's March to Quebec* (New York, 1903); a fictionalized account of the march is found in Roberts, *Arundel* (Garden City, 1930).

21. A great aura surrounds this march, and lavish praise has often been heaped on Arnold for leading it. Historians have been a bit more skeptical and have pointed out that the heavy attrition was more a result of men simply turning back rather than dying along the trail (Ward, 450n). Commager and Morris, *The Spirit of Seventy-six* (New York, 1967), 192, point out that "one of the most wonderful things about it [i.e., the march] is that so many simple, hungry, sick, miserable men had time to keep journals."

22. Carleton captured 426 men and lost only 5 killed and 13 wounded. Ward, 195.

23. Edward E. Curtis, "John Thomas," in *DAB*, IX, 438.

24. Paul H. Smith, "Sir Guy Carleton, Soldier Statesman," in George A. Billias (ed.), *George Washington's Opponents* (New York, 1969), 122–23.

25. Benedict Arnold to John Sullivan, 10 June 1776, in *NDAR*, V, 443–44.

26. Gustave Lanctot, *Canada and the American Revolution* (Cambridge, 1967), 145.

27. Ward, 201.

28. *Enterprise* was commanded by Captain Dickenson, *Liberty* by Captain Premiere and *Royal Savage* by Captain Hanley.

29. Philip Schuyler to John Hancock, 21 October 1775, in *NDAR*, II, 553.

30. *JCC*, III, 317, 446–52.

31. Leonard W. Labaree, "William Douglass," in *DAB*, III, 403–404.

32. Minutes of the New York Committee of Safety, 18 March 1776, in *NDAR*, IV, 396.

33. Minutes of New York Committee, 13 April 1776, in ibid., 800.

34. Philip Schuyler to Commodore Jacobus Wynkoop, 7 May 1776, in ibid., 1440.

35. *JCC*, V, 450.

36. Howard I. Chapelle, *The History of American Sailing Ships* (New York, 1935), 53–54.

37. The galley *Washington*, built at Skenesborough, was of sufficient size that when captured by the British, she was rerigged as a brig; Chapelle, 557.

38. Philip Schuyler to General George Washington, 31 May 1776, in *NDAR*, V, 317.

39. Washington thought that Congress ought to release the men and supplies at Poughkeepsie for Champlain. George Washington to Philip Schuyler, 28 June 1776, in J. C. Fitzpatrick (ed.), *Writings of George Washington* (Washington, 1931), V, 188.

40. Philip Schuyler to the Officer Bringing Carpenters from Massachusetts and Connecticut, 4 July 1776, in *NDAR*, V, 915.

41. Philip Schuyler to Hermanus Schuyler, 7 June 1776, in ibid., 411.

42. George Washington to the President of Congress, 10 July 1776, in Fitzpatrick, V, 248n; John W. Jackson, *The Pennsylvania Navy, 1775–1781* (New Brunswick, 1974), 18.

CHAPTER TEN

1. The ill-feeling between Philip Schuyler and the New Englanders went back to the days before the war. Schuyler had been the land agent for his father-in-law, John Van Rensselaer, and in that capacity he came into frequent conflict with various New Englanders over the New Hampshire grants. Don R. Gerlach, *Philip Schuyler and the American Revolution in New York, 1733–1777* (Lincoln, 1964), 67.

2. *JCC*, V, 448.

3. Hoffman Nickerson, *The Turning Point of the Revolution* (Boston, 1928), 278–82.

4. *JCC*, II, 97.

5. John Adams, a member of Congress at the time, took special note of the Schuyler-Gates controversy and thought it had ramifications that went far beyond the Revolution; Charles Francis Adams (ed.), *The Works of John Adams, Second President of the United States . . .* (Boston, 1851), III, 46.

6. *JCC*, V, 526; President of Congress [John Hancock] to Horatio Gates, 8 July 1776, in Edmund C. Burnett (ed.), *Letters of the Members of the Continental Congress* (Washington, 1923), II, 3.

7. Resolves of a Council of War held at Crown Point, 7 July 1776, in *NDAR*, V, 961.

8. This decision was reasonable and unanimous; however, it precipitated quite a set-to. The field-grade officers in Schuyler's command publicly dissented on the evacuation, and even Washington thought the decision a bad one. He told Gates that "your relinquishing Crown Point is in its consequences a relinquishment of the Lakes." George Washington to Horatio Gates, 19 July 1776, in J. C. Fitzpatrick (ed.), *The Writings of George Washington from the Original Manuscript Sources, 1745–1799* (Washington, 1932), V, 302. Gates was furious at being second-guessed by both his commander in chief and his subordinates. In a controlled rage he responded to Washington on 29 July:

It would be to the last degree improper to order those troops to Crown Point, or even hither, until obliged by the most pressing emergency; as that would only be heaping one hospital upon another. Those troops, when they arrive, are all ordered to halt at Skenesborough. Everything about this army is infected with the pestilence the clothes, the blankets, the air, and the ground they walk upon. To put this evil from us, a general hospital is established at Fort George, where there are now between two and three thousand sick, and where every infected person is immediately sent. But, this care and caution have not effectually destroyed the disease here; it is not withstanding continually breaking out. . . . I must now take the liberty to Animadvert a little upon the unprecedented behaviour of the Members of Your Council to their Compeers in this Department. They sir, having every Ample Supply at Hand make no allowance for the Misfortunes and wants, of this Army, nor for the Delay and Difficulty that Attends the procuring everything Necessary here. Had we a Healthy Army, Four times the Number of the Enemy; Our Magazines full, Our Artillery Compleat. Stores of every kind in profuse Abundance with Vast and populous towns and country close at Hand, to Supply Our Wants, Your Excellency would hear no Complaints from this Army; and the Members of your Council, our Brethren and Compeers, would have as little reason then as they have now, to Censure the Conduct of those who are in Nothing inferior to themselves (Fitzpatrick, 303n).

9. Horatio Gates to Benedict Arnold, 13 July 1776, in *NDAR*, V, 1957.

10. Gates to John Hancock, 16 July 1776, in ibid., 1099–1101.

11. Benedict Arnold to Philip Schuyler, 24 July 1776, in ibid., 1197–98; Schuyler did authorize some additional pay for sailors but it seems to have had little effect. General Order of Major General Philip Schuyler, 23 July 1776, in ibid., 1186–87.

12. George Washington to Philip Schuyler, 7 August 1776, in Fitzpatrick, V, 384.

13. Washington to Schuyler, 24 August 1776, in ibid., 483.

14. Vice Admiral Samuel Graves to Philip Stephens, 26 September 1775, in *NDAR*, II, 210; the British were also concerned about building boats on Lake Ontario. Later the Americans too thought about construction on Ontario. Their efforts never got beyond a congressional resolution, while the British did build and man vessels on Ontario as well as Erie. Francis Legge to General Thomas Gage, 7 August 1775, in *NDAR*, I, 1080; *JCC*, V, 542; Daniel B. Reibel, "The British Navy on the Upper Great Lakes, 1760–1789," *Niagara Frontier*, XX (Autumn 1973), 72–75.

15. George Jackson to John Pownall, 9 January 1776, in *NDAR*, III, 490; Lords Commissioners, Admiralty, to Lord George Germain, 6 February 1776, in *NDAR*, IV, 890–91; Harrison Bird, *Navies in the Mountains* (New York, 1962), 187. A lug sail is rigged fore and aft and slung with about one-third of it forward of the mast. It was a very popular type of rig for small boats.

16. Lords Commissioners, Admiralty, to Captain Charles Douglas, 16 February 1776, in *NDAR*, IV, 912–14.

17. The actual make-up of the force in the river changed from day to day as ships arrived and departed. On 8 May 1776 Captain George Talbot of *Niger* counted *Isis*, *Lizard*, *Hunter*, *Magdalen*, *Lord Howe* and several transports. Journal of H.M.S. *Niger*, in *NDAR*, IV, 1455. On 6 July 1776 Vice Admiral Molyneux Shuldham reported that the following vessels of the Royal Navy were in the river: *Hunter*, *Magdalen*, *Gaspee*, *Lord Howe* and *Bute*. "Disposition of His Majesty's Ships and Vessels in North America Under the Command of Vice Admiral Molyneux Shuldham," in *NDAR*, V, 950.

18. Captain Charles Douglas to Philip Stephens, 15 May 1776, in *NDAR*, V, 100; his rank was later confirmed by the new commander on the North American Station Vice Admiral Richard Lord Howe; Howe to Douglas, 13 June 1776, in *NDAR*, V, 503.

19. Douglas continued in the service and went on to distinguish himself under Admiral Lord Rodney. He is reputed to have been the officer who urged Rodney at the critical moment to break the French line at the battle off Dominica, 12 April 1782. John Knox Laughton, "Sir Charles Douglas," in *DNB*, V, 1194–96; W. M. James, *The British Navy in Adversity* (London, 1926), 345.

20. "The Case of Lieutenant John Starke of His Majesty's Navy together with a

Short Sketch of the Operations of the War in Canada, in which he was employed during the years 1775, 1776 and 1777," National Maritime Museum, MSS 49/129. Portions of the narrative have been reprinted in *NDAR*.

21. Schank went on to a successful career, eventually reaching the rank of admiral; John Know Laughton, "John Schank," in *DNB*, XVII, 897–98.

22. Captain Charles Douglas to Philip Stephens, 23 July 1776, in *NDAR*, V, 1184; Robert H. Vetch, "William Twiss," in *DNB*, XIX, 1323–24.

23. Bird, 186.

24. Quoted in Cyril N. Parkinson, *Edward Pellew, Viscount Exmouth, Admiral of the Red* (London, 1934), 28–29.

25. Captain Charles Douglas to Philip Stephens, 21 October 1776, in *NDAR*, VI, 1343–44.

26. Horatio Gates to Benedict Arnold, 7 August 1776, in ibid., 95–96.

27. Jacobus Wynkoop to Horatio Gates, 17 August 1776, in ibid., 216–17. In the same letter he went on to say that in case he did leave the lake, he wanted to cash in on a promise made to him that he could have command of one of the frigates building at Poughkeepsie. This claim might well have had some basis in fact. On 4 May 1779, after two and a half years of effort, Wynkoop was awarded back pay in the same amount as that received by a captain of a Continental frigate. *JCC*, XIV, 544.

28. Benedict Arnold to Horatio Gates, 17 August 1776, in *NDAR*, VI, 216.

29. William Wynkoop, "The Wynkoop Family," *Collections* of the Bucks County Historical Society, III (1909), 160–61. For Wynkoop's side of the affair, see the Memorial of Jacobus Wynkoop, 27 August 1776, in Hugh Hastings (ed.), *The Public Papers of George Clinton, First Governor of New York, 1777–1795, 1801–1804* (Albany 1899–1914), I, 321–24.

30. It is often difficult to determine with any certainty exactly what vessels were present at any particular moment. Such a determination can usually be made for battles since there are always numerous reports to draw upon, but information on the in-between times is hazy. This can be especially irritating in a situation like the one on Champlain, where so many landsmen were involved. Quite often they would not use the name of a vessel but just refer to her by the rig and then do it incorrectly. Thus two sloops might really be a schooner and a sloop. How many times is *Inflexible* referred to as a frigate!

31. No one on the American side, including Arnold, knew for sure what the British were doing at Saint Johns. Schuyler was convinced that whatever it was, it was only a diversion and their main attack would come via Oswego and the Mohawk River. Gates disagreed and told Schuyler so, but until Arnold began feeding back reliable intelligence, it was anyone's guess where they would come from.

32. Howard Chapelle, *History of the American Sailing Navy* (New York, 1949), 106, refers to *Lee* as a cutter. A British report refers to her as a sloop; "A List of the Names & etc. of Rebel Vessels Taken By His Majesty's Fleet on Lake Champlain October 13th in the Year 1776," in *NDAR*, VI, 1245; *DANFS*, IV, 80–81, refers to her as a row galley.

33. Benedict Arnold to Horatio Gates, 7 September 1776, in *NDAR*, VI, 734.

34. Arnold to Gates, 8 September 1776, in ibid., 747.

35. Arnold to Gates, 16 September 1776, and Examination of Antoine Girard, undated, PCC, item 153 (roll 172).

36. Arnold to Gates, 18 September 1776, in *NDAR*, VI, 884.

37. By this time his fleet had been augmented by the arrival of the schooner *Liberty*. Apparently, though, her usual duty was that of a messenger and patrol boat between Arnold and Ticonderoga, so she did not remain long at Saint Amand. Arnold to Gates, 21 September 1776, in *NDAR*, VI, 925–26.

38. Arnold to Gates, September 1776, in ibid., 1032–33.

39. Gates to Arnold, 26 September 1776, in ibid., 1006; Arnold to Gates, 7 October 1776, in ibid., 1151–52.

40. Christopher Ward, *The War of the Revolution* (New York, 1952), 472n, suggests that the gundalow *Success* joined Arnold on the eleventh, bringing his fleet to sixteen. There does not seem to be sufficient evidence to support that suggestion.

41. Frederick F. Van de Water, *Lake Champlain and Lake George* (Indianapolis, 1946), 195.

42. One participant on the British side suggests that Dacres actually chose not to withdraw until "the General's own boat came on board with positive Orders to dissist." Diary of Joshua Pell, Jr., in *NDAR*, VI, 1198. That seems a bit romantic. Thirty-six years later (1812) James Dacres was commander of the frigate *Guerriere* during her famous battle with the American frigate *Constitution*.

43. The remains of *Philadelphia* were discovered and removed to the Smithsonian; L. F. Hagglund, "The Continental Gondola *Philadelphia*," *United States Naval Institute Proceedings*, LXII (May 1936), 665–69; Philip K. Lundeberg, *The Continental Gunboat Philadelphia and the Northern Campaign of 1776*, Smithsonian Publication 4651 (Washington, 1966), unpaged.

44. Benedict Arnold to Philip Schuyler, 15 October 1776, in *NDAR*, VI, 1275.

45. If Carleton had been willing to sail with less than overwhelming superiority, he could have left Saint Johns a month earlier. The rebuilding of *Inflexible* added a month to the preparation time. Carleton was always a cautious and thorough commander.

CHAPTER ELEVEN

1. For the number, type and description of the Continental vessels I have relied on: Gardner W. Allen, *A Naval History of the American Revolution* (New York, 1962), 2 vols; Howard Chapelle, *The History of the American Sailing Navy* (New York, 1949); Myron J. Smith, *Navies in the American Revolution* (Metuchen, 1973); United States Navy Department, *Dictionary of American Naval Fighting Ships* (Washington, 1959–). These authorities do not always agree on the specifications of each vessel, and where there are conflicts I have used my own best judgment to reach a determination.

2. William Vernon and James Warren to the Continental Marine Committee, 24 March 1779, Letter Book of the Navy Board of the Eastern Department, NYPL.

3. Samuel Eliot Morison, *John Paul Jones, A Sailor's Biography* (Boston, 1959); William B. Clark, *The First Saratoga* (Baton Rouge, 1953).

4. A bomb ketch was a vessel especially rigged to accommodate one or more mortars placed forward of the mainmast. They were generally used to bombard land fortifications. James Henderson, *Sloops and Brigs* (London, 1972), 19.

5. This discrepancy between the true and rated number of guns becomes far more prevalent with the introduction of the carronade in 1779. These were not always counted as guns and their omission caused some underrating. An excellent discus-

sion of the role of frigates in the Royal Navy during the Napoleonic Wars (with some information relevant to previous wars) can be found in James Henderson, *Frigates* (London, 1971).

6. *JCC*, VI, 970, VII, 55; only three of these seven were ever actually built.

7. Josiah Bartlett to the New Hampshire Committee of Safety, 21 December 1775, in *NDAR*, III, 197n; Thomas Cushing to John Hancock, 20 January 1776, in *NDAR*, III, 875; C. O. Paullin, *The Navy of the American Revolution* (Cleveland, 1906).

8. Edward Field (ed.), *State of Rhode Island and Providence Plantations at the End of the Century: A History* (Boston, 1902), II, 423–24; Commissioners For Building the Philadelphia Frigates to the Commissioners of Naval Stores, 9 January 1776, PCC, item 78, XXIV, 331–32 (roll 104).

9. Extract of a letter from Joseph Pennell, Commissioner for Accounts of the Marine Department, 25 May 1784, PCC, item 137, III, 655–57 (roll 150).

10. Chapelle, 67.

11. John J. Currier, *History of Newburyport, Massachusetts, 1764–1905* (Newburyport, 1906), I, 449.

12. M. V. Brewington, "The Design of Our First Frigates," *American Neptune Magazine*, VII (1948), 13.

13. Robert Morris to Commissioners in France, 21 December 1776, in Peter Force (ed.), *American Archives*, 5th ser. (Washington, 1853), III, 1335.

14. Silas Deane to Robert Morris, 2 April 1776, in *NDAR*, IV, 630.

15. Report of Board of Admiralty, 26 October 1780, PCC item 37, 337 (roll 44).

16. Brewington, 12.

17. Ibid., 14.

18. The story of the design of the frigates is told in considerable detail by both Brewington and Chapelle.

19. Vote of the Continental Marine Committee, 16 December 1775, in *NDAR*, III, 130.

20. Josiah Bartlett to John Langdon, 3 February 1776, in ibid., 1115.

21. To buttress his position, Chapelle notes that when the Rhode Islanders ran afoul of some technical problems during the construction, the Marine Committee sent Captain Nathaniel Falconer, not Joshua Humphreys, to investigate. However, this does not necessarily mean that Falconer had anything to do with the original drafting. He was one of the commissioners in Philadelphia responsible for building the frigates in the town, and it would have been quite logical to send him on a troubleshooting mission in an area where he had considerable experience.

22. Review of *American Disease: Origins of Narcotic Control* by Matthew P. Dumont, *Psychotherapy and Social Science Review*, VII (July 1973), 28.

23. George Washington to John Hancock, 26 February 1776, in John C. Fitzpatrick (ed.), *The Writings of George Washington from the Original Sources, 1774–1799* (Washington 1931–1944), IV, 350.

24. Josiah Bartlett to John Langdon, 13 February 1776, in *NDAR*, III, 1262.

25. John Langdon to Josiah Bartlett, 26 February 1776, *New England Historical and Genealogical Register*, XXX (1876), 310.

26. Chapelle, 69.

27. Contract for Construction of Two Continental Frigates at Newburyport, 1 March 1776, in *NDAR*, IV, 124–25.

28. Journal of the Committee Appointed to Build Two Continental Frigates in Rhode Island, 10 January 1776, in *NDAR*, III, 715.

29. John Cotton to Barnabas Deane, 27 February 1776, in *NDAR*, IV, 96.

30. J. G. B. Hutchins, *The American Maritime Industries and Public Policy 1789–1914* (Cambridge, 1941), 152.

31. John Hancock to Thomas Cushing, 6 March 1776, in *NDAR*, IV, 196–98.

32. Commissioners for Building the Philadelphia Frigates to the Commissioners of Naval Stores, 9 January 1776, PCC, item 78, XXIV, 332 (roll 104).

33. With merchant ships the rule of thumb was one ton of timber for every ton of carrying capacity. In the case of warships, because of their heavier construction the ratio was nearer 1.5:1. David R. MacGregor, *Fast Sailing Ships, Their Design and Construction, 1775–1875* (Lymington, England, 1973), 23.

34. Diary of Christopher Marshall, 11 April 1776, in *NDAR*, IV, 774.

35. Quoted in Chapelle, 77.

36. Pauline Pickney, *American Figureheads and Their Carvers* (Port Washington, 1969), 47.

37. Ibid., 48.

38. Journal of the Committee Appointed to Build Two Continental Frigates in Rhode Island, 15 May 1776, in *NDAR*, V, 103; Augustus Lawrence and Samuel Tudor to the New York Provincial Convention, 28 October 1776, in *NDAR*, VI, 1435.

39. *Freeman's Journal* (Portsmouth), 25 May 1776.

40. John Langdon to William Whipple, 27 May 1776, in *NDAR*, V, 264.

41. Stephen Cross to the Honorable Board of War, 13 July 1779, in Currier, 589.

42. This meant that four frigates went into the water nameless: the thirty-two at New Hampshire *(Raleigh)*, the twenty-four at Newburyport *(Boston)* and the two vessels at Providence, the twenty-eight *(Providence)* and the thirty-two *(Warren)*. Before they were named, the four frigates being built in Philadelphia were referred to by number. Brewington, page 12, suggests that this is the origin of the practice of numbering naval vessels.

43. Report of the Board of Admiralty, 26 October 1780, PCC, item 37, 337 (roll 44).

CHAPTER TWELVE

1. Arthur C. Bining, *Pennsylvania Iron Manufacture in the Eighteenth Century* (Harrisburg, 1938), 179. By the eve of the Revolution, Americans were producing one-seventh of the world's supply of iron. Under pressure from English iron interests, Parliament had attempted to put curbs on certain types of American production that competed with British products. Such legislative restrictions generally failed in their purpose.

2. In calculating the ballast cargo, stores and guns would also have to be included so that the entire load of the ship was distributed in such a fashion as to guarantee maximum stability. Howard I. Chapelle, *The Search for Speed Under Sail* (New York, 1967), 113.

3. M. V. Brewington, "American Naval Guns 1775–1785," *American Neptune Magazine*, III (January 1943), 12, (April, 1943), 148, 158.

4. On at least two occasions guns burst on American ships, both times causing

heavy casualties: the first on *Bonhomme Richard* while she was locked in her death grip with *Serapis* and the other on board *Saratoga* while she was firing a salute at Cape François. S. E. Morison, *John Paul Jones, A Sailor's Biography* (Boston, 1959), 229; William B. Clark, *The First Saratoga* (Baton Rouge, 1953), 134.

5. For examples of instances when officers refused to accept cannon they judged to be unfit, see William Vernon, James Warren and John Deshon to Messrs. Bowen, Brown, and Co., 30 October 1778, Vernon and Warren to Major Joshua Huntington, 6 November 1778, and Vernon, Warren and Deshon to Marine Committee, 18 August 1779, Letter Book of the Navy Board of the Eastern Department, NYPL; Board of Admiralty to John Deshon, 18 December 1779, in C. O. Paullin (ed.), *Out-Letters of the Continental Marine Committee and Board of Admiralty, August 1776–September 1780* (New York, 1914), II, 138–39.

6. James B. Hedges, *The Browns of Providence Plantations Colonial Years* (Cambridge, 1952), 124.

7. Louis F. Middlebrook, *History of Maritime Connecticut During the American Revolution, 1775–1783* (Salem, 1925), II, 10; Thomas Cushing to Robert Treat Paine, 18 March 1776, in *NDAR*, IV, 390. There might well have been some cannon cast elsewhere in New England, but their numbers were small and certainly not in sufficient quantity to supply the frigates.

8. William Knox to Colonel Henry Knox, 25 August 1776, in *NDAR*, VI, 298–99.

9. Acts and Resolves of the Massachusetts General Court, 13 September 1776. Five days later the court agreed to arm the other frigate as well, so both *Boston* and *Hancock* were armed out of local stores.

10. Thomas Cushing to the Continental Marine Committee, 7 October 1776, in *NDAR*, VI, 1146–47.

11. New York tried but failed to supply iron for her own frigates. At least one of the local furnaces that might have cast cannon was busy forging the great chain that would be strung across the Hudson to prevent passage upstream. Robert Erskine to George Clinton, 29 February 1776, in Hugh Hastings (ed.), *The Public Papers of George Clinton, First Governor of New York, 1777–1795, 1801–1804* (New York, 1899–1914), I, 225–26; Francis Lewis to the New York Committee of Safety, 27 December 1776, in E. C. Burnett (ed.), *Letters of the Members of the Continental Congress* (Washington, 1923), II, 192.

12. Hedges makes this suggestion, page 271. In fairness it should be noted that later in the war, when the Browns contracted to the Congress for additional cannon, they suffered all the evils of a depreciating currency. Hedges, 273.

13. John Langdon to William Whipple, 5 August 1776, in *NDAR*, VI, 56.

14. Langdon to Josiah Bartlett, 19 August 1776, in ibid., 229.

15. Langdon to Bartlett, 14 September 1776, in ibid., 815–16.

16. Hedges, 270.

17. Marine Committee to the Rhode Island Frigate Committee, 9 October 1776, and Marine Committee to Captain Nathaniel Falconer, 9 October 1776, in Paullin, I, 23–24, 24–25.

18. Marine Committee to the Rhode Island Frigate Committee, 13 October 1776, in ibid. It is not clear how this new, more accurate information was obtained. The committee only mentions receiving it via "several channels."

19. *Trumbull*'s travail can best be followed in the Letter Book of the Navy Board of the Eastern Department. For examples, see William Vernon and James Warren

to Captain John Cotton, 3 December 1778; Vernon to John Deshon, 12 April 1779 and 27 May 1779; Vernon, Warren and Deshon to Elisha Hinman, 18 August 1779.

20. George Washington to Joseph Reed, 14 January 1776, in John C. Fitzpatrick (ed.), *The Writings of George Washington from the Original Sources, 1745–1799* (Washington, 1931–44), IV, 240–41; Washington to John Day, 23 April 1779, in Fitzpatrick, XIV, 435.

21. Nathaniel Shaw to George Washington, 1 August 1776, in Ernest E. Rogers, *Connecticut's Naval Office at New London During the War of the American Revolution* (New London, 1933); Board of Admiralty to Washington, 6 May 1780, in Paullin, II, 190–91.

22. Robert Morris remained behind in Philadelphia and did his utmost to get the frigates to either safety or sea. Robert Morris to the President of Congress, 13 December 1776, 21 December 1776, 26 January 1777, in Letters and Reports from Robert Morris, PCC, 137 (roll 150).

23. George Washington to Commodore John Hazelwood, 25 October 1777 and 27 October 1777, Washington to Continental Navy Board, 27 October 1777, in Fitzpatrick, IX, 434, 445, 445–47, 447–48; Washington to Continental Navy Board, 9 November 1777, Washington to President of Congress, 10 November 1777, in Fitzpatrick, X, 30–31, 33.

24. James Biddle (ed.), *Autobiography of Charles Biddle, Vice President of the Supreme Executive Council of Pennsylvania, 1745–1821* (Philadelphia, 1883), 102; Samuel S. Smith, *Fight for the Delaware, 1777* (Monmouth Beach, 1970), 6–8; George Washington to Governor William Livingston, 12 May 1778, in Fitzpatrick (ed.), XI, 378–79; John W. Jackson, *The Pennsylvania Navy, 1775–1781: The Defense of the Delaware* (New Brunswick, 1974), 296.

25. *JCC*, VI, 970.

26. Marine Committee to Marine Agents in Maryland, 15 January 1777, in James C. Ballagh (ed.), *The Letters of Richard Henry Lee* (New York, 1911), I, 249–50.

27. The combat careers of those ships is told in more detail in Chapter 6.

28. Committee of Secret Correspondence to Silas Deane, 23 October 1776, in *NDAR*, VI, 1387–88.

29. Marine Committee to the Navy Board of the Eastern Department, 6 March 1778, in Paullin, I, 210–11; Henry Laurens to John Rutledge, 3 June 1778, in E. C. Burnett (ed.), *Letters of the Members of the Continental Congress* (Washington 1926), III, 273; William Ellery to William Vernon, 16 March 1778, "Papers of William Vernon and the Navy Board 1776–1794," *Publications of the Rhode Island Historical Society*. The amount of gunpowder required by a ship of this size was phenomenal. In a single broadside she would probably blow off more than three hundred pounds of powder or the equivalent of enough for several thousand musket rounds. In addition to the tons of powder down in her magazine, if she were well stocked, there would also be somewhere in the neighborhood of one hundred rounds of shot per gun

30. William Ellery to William Whipple, 31 May 1778, in Burnett, III, 269.

31. William Vernon and James Warren to Marine Committee, 18 May 1779 and 24 June 1779, Letter Book of the Navy Board of the Eastern Department, NYPL.

32. James Searle to R. H. Lee, 10 July 1779, in Burnett, IV, 310. In this same letter the Congress asked for enough supplies to equip an army of fifty thousand men; that was equally out of the question.

33. Board of Admiralty to John Langdon, 28 December 1779, in Paullin, II, 144–45.

34. "Estimate of Sundrys for the 74 Gun ship," in Reports of the Marine Committee and the Board of Admiralty, 1776–81, PCC, item 37, 217–18 (roll 44); Board of

Admiralty to Congress, 27 May 1780, PCC, item 37, 247–48 (roll 44); Board of Admiralty to John Langdon, 16 June 1780, and 21 July 1780, in Paullin, II, 210, 230–31; Board of Admiralty to President of Congress, 24 November 1780, PCC, item 37, 529 (roll 44).

35. Morison, 315.

36. Quoted in Lincoln Lorenz, *John Paul Jones, Fighter for Freedom and Glory* (Annapolis, 1948), 117.

37. Report of Committee appointed to Confer with Agent of Marine, 3 September 1782, PCC, item 28, 233 (roll 35); James Madison to Edmund Randolph, 10 September 1782, in Gaillard Hunt (ed.), *The Writings of James Madison* (New York, 1900), I, 231.

38. At least one prize that the navy board in Boston particularly desired was sold privately. The board thought the business had been conducted in a "strange way," but there was nothing they could do. Other vessels, not necessarily warships, were bought and used by agents. This practice is one of the reasons it is so difficult to arrive at any precise determination about how many vessels were in the Continental navy. Navy Board Eastern Department to Marine Committee, 29 September 1779 and 6 October 1779, PCC, item 37, 145–46, 147 (roll 44).

39. "Barnacles Are an Unsolved Problem," *Life*, X (April 28, 1941), 120–25.

40. Maurer Maurer, "Coppered Bottoms for the Royal Navy: A Factor in the Maritime War of 1778–1783," *Military Affairs*, XIV (April 1950), 58.

41. This, of course, is to say nothing about the economic impact associated with privateering, which must have been far greater. Nor does it take into account the business brought into American ports with the arrival of the French fleets.

CHAPTER THIRTEEN

1. James Henderson, *Sloops and Brigs* (Annapolis, 1972), 31–36; Michael Lewis, *The Navy of Britain* (London, 1948), 157–286; John Masefield, *Sea Life in Nelson's Time* (London, 1905), 51–84; Board of Admiralty to Congress, 26 July 1780, PCC, item 37, 281 (roll 44).

2. The estimate of three thousand seamen is given by C. O. Paullin, "The Conditions of the Continental Naval Service," *Proceedings* of the United States Naval Institute, XXXII (June 1906), 594. Paullin does not indicate whether his estimate includes officers. At any rate, to this author the figure three thousand seems generous. The ratio in the present American navy runs about 1:7. *Budget of the United States for the Fiscal Year 1975* (Washington, 1974), 265.

3. William Vernon and James Warren to the Marine Committee, 12 May 1779, in Letter Book of the Navy Board of the Eastern Department, NYPL. The principal complaint was that there were too many marine officers. The official complement of officers for a thirty-two-gun frigate in the Continental navy was: captain, three lieutenants, master, captain of marines, two lieutenants of marines and surgeon.

4. Journal of the Committee Appointed to Build Two Continental Frigates in Rhode Island, 30 April 1776 and 20 June 1776, in *NDAR*, IV, 1327–28, and V, 637; William Whipple to John Langdon, 22 June 1776, in *NDAR*, V, 683–84.

5. *JCC*, IV, 247–48, 293.

6. William Whipple to John Langdon, 20 April 1776, in Edmund C. Burnett (ed.), *Letters of the Members of the Continental Congress* (Washington, 1923), I, 428; Whipple to Langdon, 5 June 1776, in *NDAR*, V, 385; John Adams to Joseph Ward, 16 April 1776,

in *NDAR*, IV, 851; Richard Henry Lee to Samuel Purviance, 1 May 1776, in J. C. Ballagh (ed.), *Letters of Richard Henry Lee* (New York, 1911), I, 187.

7. *JCC*, V, 420–23.

8. Ibid., IV, 290; Joseph Hewes to Samuel Purviance, 25 June 1776, in *NDAR*, V, 737.

9. The first admiral in the American navy was David Farragut, appointed in 1862.

10. In order of rank the officers were:

James Nicholson *(Virginia)*
John Manley *(Hancock)*
Hector McNeill *(Boston)*
Dudley Saltonstall *(Trumbull)*
Nicholas Biddle *(Randolph)*
Thomas Thompson *(Raleigh)*
John Barry *(Effingham)*
Thomas Reed *(Washington)*
Thomas Grennell *(Congress)*
Charles Alexander *(Delaware)*
Lambert Wickes *(Reprisal)*
Abraham Whipple *(Providence)*
John Hopkins *(Warren)*
John Hodge *(Montgomery)*
William Hallock *(Lexington)*
Hoysted Hacker *(Hampden)*
Isaiah Robinson *(Andrew Doria)*
John Paul Jones *(Providence)*
James Josiah
Elisha Hinman *(Alfred)*
Joseph Olney *(Cabot)*
James Robinson *(Sachem)*
John Young *(Independence)*
Elisha Warner *(Fly)*
Lieut. (John) Baldwin *(Wasp)*
Lieut. (Thomas) Albertson *(Musquito)*

JCC, VI, 860. Less than five years later a congressional committee investigating the method by which this list was drawn up reported that they could not "fully ascertain the rule by which that arrangement was made." *JCC*, XX, 710–11. The captains who had served under Washington's command in Massachusetts Bay, excepting Manley, were completely excluded from the list. Marine Committee to Navy Board of the Eastern Department, 9 May 1778, in C. O. Paullin (ed.), *Out-Letters of the Continental Marine Committee and Board of Admiralty* (New York, 1914), 1, 242.

11. McNeill replaced Cazneau.

12. Jones seemingly never tired of trying to improve his rank; *JCC*, XX, 710–11; *JCC*, XXI, 900; Board of Admiralty Report, 28 March 1781, PCC, item 37, 363–72 (roll 44).

13. In appointing men to commands, the committee and later the Board of Admiralty tried to follow the rule of seniority "where merit is equal." Of course, merit was hardly ever equal, but for political reasons appointment by seniority was the least troublesome course to follow. Report of the Board of Admiralty, 13 November 1780, PCC, item 37, 521 (roll 44).

14. John Langdon to Josiah Bartlett, 13 August 1776, in *NDAR*, VI, 161–62.

15. Continental Marine Committee to John Langdon, 17 October 1776, in ibid., 1308.

16. During construction the vessel was called *Hampshire*. At launching the name was changed to *Ranger* in honor of Rogers' Rangers, a famous unit of the French and Indian War in which many Portsmouth men served.

17. Samuel Eliot Morison, *John Paul Jones, A Sailor's Biography* (Boston, 1959), 101.

18. Ibid.

19. Ibid. This was not the only instance of such a scheme. In February 1778, the Marine Committee ordered the Navy Board of the Eastern Department to try a similar operation with the French ship *Flamand*. Nothing came of it. Marine Committee to Navy Board of the Eastern Department, 23 February 1778, in Paullin, I, 202.

20. Marine Committee to John Paul Jones, 9 May 1777, in Paullin, I, 133.

21. *JCC*, VIII, 465.

22. Marine Committee to Navy Board of the Eastern Department, 30 May 1778, and 19 April 1779, in Paullin, I, 251, and II, 65; *Boston Gazette*, 21 February 1779.

23. William J. Morgan, *Captains to the Northward: The New England Captains in the Continental Navy* (Barre, 1959), 168; Navy Board of the Eastern Department to Elisha Hinman, 18 August 1779, in Letter Book of the Navy Board of the Eastern Department, NYPL; Navy Board to Marine Committee, 18 August 1779, in Letter Book, NYPL; William Vernon to John Deshon, 29 October 1779, in Letter Book, NYPL; Marine Committee to James Nicholson, 20 September 1779, in Paullin, II, 115–16.

24. See 119–21.

25. The diaspora is well indicated by the following status report presented to the Congress by the Board of Admiralty in June 1781, PCC, item 37, 473 (roll 44).

RANK	NAME	DATE OF COMMISSION	STATUS
1	James Nicholson	10 October 1776	In command of *Trumbull*
7	John Barry	10 October 1776	In command of *Alliance*
8	Thomas Reed	10 October 1776	In private service, Philadelphia
9	Thomas Grennell	10 October 1776	Unemployed, Connecticut
10	Charles Alexander	10 October 1776	Unemployed, Philadelphia
12	Abraham Whipple	10 October 1776	Unemployed, Providence, R.I.
14	John Hodge	10 October 1776	Unemployed, N.Y. State
16	Hoysted Hacker	10 October 1776	Lieut. on *Alliance*
18	J. P. Jones	10 October 1776	Appt. to *America*
19	James Josiah	10 October 1776	In private service, Philadelphia
20	Elisha Hinman	10 October 1776	Unemployed, Connecticut
22	James Robinson	10 October 1776	Unemployed, Philadelphia
23	John Young	10 October 1776	In command of *Saratoga*

James Nicholson	19 November 1776	In command of *Deane*
Samuel Nicholson	10 December 1776	At Boston
Henry Johnston	5 February 1777	In private service, Boston
John P. Rathbun	15 February 1777	In private service, Rhode Island
Samuel Tucker	15 March 1777	In private service, Boston
Daniel Waters	17 March 1777	In private service, Boston
John Greene	11 February 1778	In private service, Philadelphia
Seth Harding	23 September 1778	On parole, Connecticut
Silas Talbot	17 September 1779	In private service, Rhode Island

26. The records of the courts-martial are spotty, and indeed some are apparently not extant at all. The circumstances surrounding some of these trials is more fully discussed in Chapter 6.

27. Richard B. Morris, "The Revolution's Caine Mutiny," *American Heritage*, XI (April 1960), 10–13, 88–91.

28. Morison, 190.

29. As might be expected, the appointment of a Frenchman to such a choice command caused great resentment among American officers. The two lieutenants on *Alliance* both resigned in protest, and Captain John Manley, who thought he should have received the command, also made his displeasure known. Samuel Adams to James Warren, 27 July 1778, in Burnett, III, 353.

30. Lyman Butterfield (ed.), *The Adams Papers: Diary and Autobiography of John Adams* (Cambridge, 1961), II, 368.

31. William Vernon to Marine Committee, 5 August 1779, Letter Book of the Navy Board of the Eastern Department, NYPL.

32. Morison, 299.

33. To the Soldiers and Seamen Serving in the British Fleet and Army in America, 15 June 1775, in Peter Force (ed.), *American Archives*, 4th ser., II, 1004.

34. Richard B. Morris, *Government and Labor in Early America* (New York, 1946), 272.

35. Court-Martial of John Hazard Commander of the Sloop *Providence*, 8 May 1776, PCC, item 58, 263–65 (roll 71).

36. Board of Admiralty to Benjamin Franklin, 6 May 1780, in Paullin, II, 191. In both cases charges were never brought against the culprits.

37. This was a reference to the 1757 execution of the English admiral John Byng for neglect of duty. John Knox Laughton, "John Byng," in *DNB*, III, 572.

38. See Chapter 6 for details of the cruise.

39. Commodore Esek Hopkins to Stephen Hopkins, 8 June 1776, in *NDAR*, V, 424–26; John Hancock to George Washington, 14 June 1776, in *NDAR*, V, 531; John Hancock to Commodore Esek Hopkins, 14 June 1776, PCC, item 12A, IV, 175–77 (roll 23); Nicholas Biddle to Charles Biddle, 16 June 1776, in William B. Clark (ed.), "Letters

of Captain Nicholas Biddle," *Pennsylvania Magazine of History and Biography*, LXXIV (July 1956), 389.

40. Charles Francis Adams (ed.), *The Works of John Adams* (Boston, 1850–54), III, 65.

41. *JCC*, VII, 204.

42. Ibid., X, 13.

43. James Warren to John Adams, 23 March 1777, in W. C. Ford (ed.), *Warren–Adams Letters* (Boston, 1917), I, 304.

44. For a discussion of this crisis, see Chapter 14; James Nicholson to John Barry, 24 June 1781, in Naval History Society *Publications*, I (1911), 125–26.

CHAPTER FOURTEEN

1. John Adams to Elbridge Gerry, 5 November 1775, in Charles Francis Adams (ed.), *The Works of John Adams* (Boston, 1850–54), IX, 363–64; Journal of the Massachusetts House of Representatives, 11 December 1775, in *NDAR*, III, 50.

2. John Paul Jones to Joseph Hewes, 19 May 1776, in *NDAR*, V, 151.

3. Washington fully realized the great number of sailors in his army at Cambridge. On 10 November 1775 Congress resolved to raise two battalions of marines composed of men who were good seamen or so acquainted with maritime affairs as to be able to serve to advantage by sea when required. Washington protested that recruiting for these battalions would seriously weaken his army. Congress agreed and suspended the resolve. *JCC*, III, 334, 393; George Washington to John Hancock, 19 November 1775, in John C. Fitzpatrick (ed.), *Writings of George Washington* (Washington, 1931–44), IV, 99–102; George Billias, *John Glover and His Marblehead Mariners* (New York, 1960).

4. C. O. Paullin, "The Administration of Massachusetts and Virginia Navies of the American Revolution," United States Naval Institute *Proceedings*, XXXII (March 1906), 131–64. The same article is also in C. O. Paullin, *History of Naval Administration* (Annapolis, 1968), 55–88.

5. *JCC*, IV, 65; George Washington to President of Congress, 30 January 1776, in Fitzpatrick, IV, 290.

6. James Warren to John Adams, 2 June 1776, in W. C. Ford (ed.), *Warren–Adams Letters* (Boston 1917–25), I, 252.

7. C. F. Goodrich, "The Sailor in the Revolution," U.S. Naval Institute *Proceedings* (1897), 173. Privateering was authorized by the Congress on 23 March 1776. *JCC*, IV, 229–33. Because both the Congress and the states commissioned privateers, there quite often tended to be some confusion over the final authority. The question was resolved in favor of the Congress. Sidney G. Morse, "State or Continental Privateers?" *American Historical Review*, LII (October 1946), 68–74.

8. Ernest E. Rogers, *Connecticut's Naval Office at New London During the War of the American Revolution* (New Haven, 1933), 54.

9. The documents of the Revolution relating to naval affairs are replete with complaints about privateers. For examples, see Governor Thomas Johnson to Governor Patrick Henry, 29 April 1777, in William H. Browne et al. (eds.), *Archives of Maryland* (Baltimore 1883–), XVI, 223; Navy Board of the Eastern Department to Marine Committee, 9 December 1778, New York Public Library *Bulletin*, XXXVI (1932), 809; William Vernon to John Adams, 17 December 1778, "Papers of William

Vernon and the Navy Board," *Publications of the Rhode Island Historical Society*, VIII, 256; Report of the Board of Admiralty to Congress, 6 November 1780, PCC, item 37, 517 (roll 44).

10. *JCC*, III, 370–76, 378–87; "1776 Comparative State of Wages Between American Navy Officers and the Officers of English Frigates of 32 Guns," in *NDAR*, VI, 1476–77; John Paul Jones to Robert Morris, 17 October 1776, in *NDAR*, VI, 1302–1304.

11. Robert May and Ferdinand Moulton (comp.), *Army and Navy Pension Laws and Bounty Land Laws of the U.S., Including Sundry Resolutions of Congress From 1776–1852* (Washington, 1852), viii, xxviii, 1, 3–4, 6, 227–30.

12. John Paul Jones to Robert Morris, 17 October 1776, in *NDAR*, VI, 1302–1304; *JCC*, VI, 973.

13. Samuel Nicholson to the President of Congress, 14 July 1788, PCC, item 78, XVII, 401–402 (roll 100).

14. Journal of the Committee Appointed to Build Two Continental Frigates in Rhode Island, 20 June 1776, in *NDAR*, V, 637, 638.

15. Nicholas Brown to Stephen Hopkins, 22 January 1776, in *NDAR*, III, 571–75; William Vernon and John Deshon to Navy Board of the Middle Department, 13 March 1779, in Letter Book of the Navy Board of the Eastern Department, NYPL; William Vernon and James Warren to Marine Committee, 9 June 1779, in Letter Book, Eastern Department, NYPL.

16. William Vernon and John Deschon to deVabus, Vice Consul of France, 12 March 1770, in Letter Book, Eastern Department, NYPL.

17. *JCC*, IV, 54–57, 101–104; William Vernon and James Warren to General Horatio Gates, 29 March 1779, in Letter Book, Eastern Department, NYPL. Congress offered bounties to men who would bring in foreign sailors and actively encouraged recruiting abroad. *JCC*, IV, 289–91; Committee of Secret Correspondence to Captain Peter Parker, 10 July 1776, PCC, item 37, 11 (roll 44). One hundred years later foreign sailors still made up a conspicuous part of the navy. In the Mediterranean squadron of the late nineteenth century less than one-half of the sailors aboard navy ships were American born. Stephen B. Luce, "Training Ships," Naval Historical Foundation pamphlet (Washington, n.d.), 1.

18. Jesse Lemish, "Jack Tar in the Streets: Merchant Seamen in the Politics of Revolutionary America," *William and Mary Quarterly*, XXV (July 1968), 371–407; Neil R. Stout, "Manning the Royal Navy in North America, 1763–1775," *American Neptune Magazine*, XXIII (1963), 174.

19. Roland G. Usher, "Royal Navy Impressment During the American Revolution," *Mississippi Valley Historical Review*, XXXVII (March 1951), 677–79.

20. Elizabeth Cometti, "Impressment During the American Revolution," in the *Walter Clinton Jackson Essays in the Social Sciences* (Chapel Hill, 1942), 100. William Vernon and James Warren to Marine Committee, 14 July 1779, in Letter Book, Eastern Department, NYPL; *JCC*, XVIII, 1138–39.

21. Governor Thomas Johnson to James Nicholson, 24 April 1777, PCC, item 70, 195–96 (roll 84).

22. Nicholson to Johnson, 25 April 1777, ibid., 199.

23. Maryland State Council to Maryland Delegates in Congress, 26 April 1777, *Archives of Maryland*, XVI, 230; *JCC*, VII, 312; William Paca to the Governor and Council of Maryland, 24 May 1777, in Edmund C. Burnett (ed.), *Letters of the Members of the Continental Congress* (Washington, 1921–36), II, 371.

24. Prisoners were defined as "all persons taken in arms on board any prize." They were "to be taken care of by the supreme executive power in each Colony, to which they are brought, whether the prize be taken by vessel fitted out by the Continent, or by others." Expenses would be paid by Congress; *JCC*, IV, 370.

25. Goodrich, 477.

26. General Orders, 20 June 1777, 13 July 1777, 2 September 1777, in Fitzpatrick, VIII, 269, 401–402, and IX, 168.

27. Benjamin Quarles, *The Negro in the American Revolution*, (Chapel Hill, 1961), 83–92. In one rather strange incident a slave aboard *Lexington* petitioned the Pennsylvania Committee of Safety for his share of prize money. Petition of a Slave to the Pennsylvania Committee of Safety, 3 May 1776, in *NDAR*, IV, 1394.

28. Rules for the Regulation of the Navy of the United Colonies, *JCC*, III, 378–87.

29. Christopher Lloyd and Jack L. S. Coulter, *Medicine and the Navy, 1220–1900* (Edinburgh, 1957–63), III, 129. Smallpox could also be a problem. *Connecticut Gazette*, 12 April 1776; Sir Gilbert Blane, *Observations on the Diseases Incident to Seamen* (London, 1785).

30. Marine Committee to Captain Nicholas Biddle, 26 April 1777, in C.O. Paullin (ed.), *Out-Letters of the Continental Marine Committee and Board of Admiralty* (New York, 1914), I, 101–10.

31. James Henderson, *Sloops and Brigs, An Account of the Smallest Vessels of the Royal Navy During the Great Wars, 1793–1815* (Annapolis, 1972), 41.

32. James S. Biddle (ed.), *Autobiography of Charles Biddle, Vice-President of the Supreme Executive Council of Pennsylvania, 1745–1821* (Philadelphia, 1883), 113.

33. John Paul Jones's *Ranger* was lucky to have aboard a Harvard graduate as ship's surgeon, Dr. Ezra Green. *Diary of Ezra Green, M.D.* (Boston, 1875).

34. John Paul Jones to Robert Morris, 13 October 1783, PCC, item 137, III, 211 (roll 150).

35. Usher, 682–83.

36. Sailors who deserted or ran were listed with an *R* after their name. J. R. Hutchinson, *The Press-Gang, Afloat and Ashore* (New York, 1913), 151.

37. Benjamin Franklin once told David Hartley, an English politician and diplomat, that he had been instructed by Congress to gather reports of English barbarities to American prisoners and publish them in a school book illustrated with thirty-five engravings, every one of them depicting a "horrid fact." With such reading material generations of Americans would grow up "impressed with the enormity of British malice and wickedness." Charles K. Bolton, *The Private Soldier Under Washington* (New York, 1902), 189.

38. Olive Anderson, "The Treatment of Prisoners of War in Britain during the American War of Independence," London University Institute of Historical Research *Bulletin*, XXVII (May 1955), 66; Decisions of Edward Webley, Chief Justice of the Jamaica Supreme Court, 19 January 1776, 23 January 1776, 25 January 1776, 12 February 1776, in *NDAR*, III, 868, 948, 1242–43.

39. Lord George Germain to Major General William Howe, 1 February 1776, in *NDAR*, IV, 881.

40. Naturally there were some cases of friction. When Ethan Allen was captured he was shackled and kept in close confinement. This prompted Washington to warn Howe, "The Law of Retaliation is not only justifiable in the eyes of God, and Man, but absolutely a duty which in our present circumstances we owe to our relatives,

Friends and fellow Citizens." George Washington to General Howe, 18 December 1775, in Fitzpatrick, IV, 171.

41. George Washington to the President of Congress, 18 February 1782, in ibid., XXIV, 4–5; J. L. Banks, *David Sproat and Naval Prisoners in the War of the Revolution* (New York, 1909), 8.

42. John K. Alexander, "Forton Prison During the American Revolution," *Essex Institute Historical Collections* (1967), 369; William R. Lindsey, *Treatment of American Prisoners of War During the Revolution*, vol. XXII (Summer 1973) of *The Emporia State Research Studies* (Emporia, Kansas, 1973), 23–24; Louis F. Middlebrook, *History of Maritime Connecticut During the American Revolution* (Salem, 1925), II, 324.

43. Alexander, 380.

44. Ibid., 382.

45. Jesse Lemisch, "Listening to the Inarticulate: William Widgers Dream and the Loyalties of American Revolutionary Seamen in British Prisons," *Journal of Social History*, III (1969), 17–18.

46. *Memoirs of Andrew Sherburne: A Pensioner of the Navy of the Revolution* (Utica, 1828); Danske Dandridge, *American Prisoners of the Revolution* (Charlottesville, 1911), 237–49; Bolton, 187; David L. Sterling (ed.), "American Prisoners of War in New York: A Report by Elias Boudinot," *William and Mary Quarterly*, XIII (1956), 385; Jeanette E. Rattray, *Perils of the Port of New York Marine Disasters from Sandy Hook to Execution Rocks* (New York, 1973), 202–203. Even allowing for a certain amount of exaggeration in the above accounts, the fact remains that American seamen were treated in a brutal fashion.

47. Ernest E. Rogers, *Connecticut's Naval Office at New London During the War of the American Revolution* (New Haven, 1933), 44; Middlebrook, II, 118–19.

CONCLUSION

1. John Adams to the President of Congress, 6 July 1780, in Francis Wharton (ed.), *The Revolutionary Diplomatic Correspondence of the United States* (Washington, 1889), III, 833.

2. John J. McCusker, in *Alfred: The First Continental Flagship* (Washington, 1973), 8, takes a different view. "The fleets of deGrasse and d'Estaing sailed where they chose because the Royal Navy had other Concerns with which to contend. One of these was the Continental Navy of the United Colonies—potentially if not in fact, a serious challenge to Britain's ability to carry on a major war at sea." I disagree and can find little evidence to suggest that the Continental navy ever forced the British to divert any significant force to deal with a threat from this quarter.

Bibliography

Writing this bibliography turned out to be a far more arduous and soul-searching project than I could ever have imagined. The tendency I fear in this kind of process is to go to extremes. One course can lead to a skeletal list of sources that notes the obvious and simply cites the "standard works." In the opposite direction is the corpulent collection of everything the author ever read, from *Uncle Wiggley* to the most recently discovered manuscript. I have tried to tack between the two and hope the result below is a useful but by no means exhaustive list of materials consulted.

To begin with, the most helpful bibliographic aids were Robert G. Albion, *Naval and Maritime History: An Annotated Bibliography* (Mystic, 1972); Naval History Division, *United States Naval History: A Bibliography* (Washington, 1969) and *United States Naval History Sources in the Washington Area and Suggested Research Subjects* (Washington, 1970). Both Albion's and the Navy Department's bibliographies are general in nature. The premier bibliography for the naval history of the Revolution is Myron J. Smith, *Navies in the American Revolution* (Metuchen, 1973). This is the first volume in a series of five that together comprise an impressive bibliography of American naval history. For a general bibliography of the Revolution two good paperback sources are Library of Congress, *Periodical Literature on the American Revolution* (Washington, 1971), and John Shy, *The American Revolution* (Northbrook, 1973).

To familiarize myself with some of the technical aspects of the eighteenth-century maritime world, I relied very heavily on the works of Howard I. Chapelle, especially *The History of American Sailing Ships* (New York, 1935); *The History of the American Sailing Navy: The Ships and Their Development* (New York, 1949) and *The Search for Speed Under Sail* (New York, 1967). Other references included Jack Coggins, *Ships and Seamen of the American Revolution: Vessels, Crews, Weapons, Gear, Naval Tactics and Actions of the War for Independence* (Harrisburg, 1969). This is a very basic source, but it is richly illustrated and most informative. A contemporary dictionary was valuable: William Falconer, *A New Universal Dictionary of the Marine* (London, 1815). Another early source whose title is misleading since it actually deals with much more than it indicates is William Hutchinson, *A Treatise on Naval Architecture* (Annapolis, 1969, reprint of 1794 edition). Two short works by James Henderson were frequently used: *The Frigates* (New York, 1970) and *Sloops and Brigs* . . . (Annapolis, 1972).

There is need for an up-to-date scholarly account of America's maritime history. This is not to say that the older accounts are not well done and reliable. For America's maritime background I consulted: S. W. Bryant, *The Sea and the States: A Maritime History of the American People* (New York, 1947); Victor S. Clark, *History of Manufacturers in the United States, 1607–1860*, vol. I (Washington, 1916); J. G. B. Hutchins, *The American Maritime Industries and Public Policy, 1789–1914* (Cambridge, 1941); Richard B. Morris, *Government and Labor in Early America* (New York, 1946), and a new provocative book by James F. Shepherd and Gary M. Walton, *Shipping, Maritime Trade and the Economic Development of Colonial North America* (Cambridge, 1972).

Local and regional histories are another important source of information for maritime history. I found the following useful: Jeremy Belknap, *History of New Hampshire*, 3 vols. (Boston, 1791–92); John J. Currier, *History of Newburyport, Massachusetts, 1764–1905*, 2 vols. (Newburyport, 1906); George F. Dow, *The Sailing Ships of New England* (Salem, 1928); Joseph J. Malone, *Pine Trees and Politics: The Naval Stores and Forest Policy in Colonial New England, 1691–1775* (Seattle, 1964); Ralph May, *Early Portsmouth History* (Boston, 1926); Samuel E. Morison, *The Maritime History of Massachusetts* (New York, 1941); John H. Morrison, *History of New York Ship Yards* (New York, 1909); William B. Weeden, *Economic and Social History of New England*, 2 vols. (Boston, 1891).

The greatest source for raw data on almost any aspect of the Revolution is the Papers of the Continental Congress. The 204 rolls of microfilm comprising the PCC are a treasure trove that has yet to be fully exploited. For naval purposes I found the following items to be of special significance: item 12A, Letter Books of the Presidents of Congress, 1775–87; item 19, Reports of Committees on Applications of Individuals, 1776–89; item 28, Other Reports of Committees of Congress—on the Prisoners' Department, the Admiralty and Agent of Marine, the executive departments and other subjects, 1776–86; item 37, Reports of the Marine Committee and the Board of Admiralty, 1776–81; item 41, Memorials Addressed to Congress, 1776–88; item 58, Letters of John Hancock, and Miscellaneous Papers, 1774–85; item 69; Pennsylvania State Papers, 1775–91; item 70, Maryland and Delaware State Papers, 1775–89; item 78, Letters Addressed to Congress, 1775–89; item 90, Letters from William Bingham and Others, 1777–82; item 132, Transcripts of the Letters from John Paul Jones, 1778–80; item 137, Letters and Reports from Robert Morris, Superintendent of Finance and Agent of Marine, 1781–85, with an Appendix, 1776–78 and 1781–86; item 142, Accounts of the Register's Office, 1781–83; item 153, Letters from Major General Philip Schuyler, 1775–85; item 168, Letters and Papers of John Paul Jones, 1777–91; item 196, Ships' Bonds Required for Letters of Marque and Reprisal, 1776–83. Other very useful sources on film included Clifford Shipton's *Early American Imprints*; newspapers, including the *Freeman's Journal, Boston Gazette, Connecticut Gazette, Providence Gazette, Rivington's New York Royal Gazette, Pennsylvania Gazette, Pennsylvania Packet*, and the Letter Book of the Navy Board of the Eastern Department at the New York Public Library.

Printed primary source material for the Revolution abounds. One of the most recent collections to appear on the scene is the United States Naval History Division, *Naval Documents of the American Revolution* (Washington 1964–). At the time of this writing six volumes were in print. The original editor was the indefatigable William B. Clark; upon his death William J. Morgan became editor. The books are absolutely indispensable. A general collection is Peter Force (ed.), *American Archives . . . , 9 vols* (Washington, 1837–53). In trying to fathom the congressional point of view, I found the most useful collections to be: C. O. Paullin (ed.), *Out-Letters of the Continental Marine Committee and Board of Admiralty, 1776–1780*, 2 vols. (New York, 1914); Edmund C. Burnett (ed.), *Letters of the Members of the Continental Congress*, 8 vols. (Washington, 1921–36), and the invaluable W. C. Ford (ed.), *Journals of the Continental Congress, 1774–1789*, 34 vols. (Washington, 1904–12). For a diplomatic perspective the above are also useful, along with Francis Wharton (ed.), *The Revolutionary Diplomatic Correspondence of the United States*, 6 vols. (Washington, 1889).

The papers of private individuals are in good supply and have become even more abundant since World War II in some very expert editions. Among those men involved in the war the most valuable collections are: C. F. Adams (ed.), *The Works of John Adams* . . . , 10 vols. (Boston, 1850–56); Lyman H. Butterfield (ed.), *Adams Family Correspondence*, 2 vols. (Cambridge, 1963), and *The Adams Papers: Diary and Autobiography of John Adams*, 4 vols. (Cambridge, 1961); William B. Clark (ed.), "Letters of Nicholas Biddle," *Pennsylvania Magazine of History and Biography*, LXXIV (1950), 348–405; Hugh Hastings (ed.), *The Public Papers of George Clinton* . . . , 10 vols. (New York and Albany, 1899–1914); Robert W. Neeser (ed.), *Letters and Papers Relating to the Cruises of Gustavus Conyngham* (New York, 1915); John S. Barnes (ed.), *Fanning's Narrative; Memoirs of Nathaniel Fanning* (New York, 1912); Albert Smyth (ed.), *The Writings of Benjamin Franklin*, 10 vols. (London 1905–1907); Edward E. Hale and Edward E. Hale, Jr. (eds.), *Franklin in France*, 2 vols. (Boston, 1887); "Diary of Ezra Green," *New England Historical and Genealogical Register*, XXIX (1875), 13–24; Alverda Beck (ed.), *The Letter Book of Esek Hopkins* (Providence, 1932); Philip Hamer (ed.), *The Papers of Henry Laurens*, 3 vols. (Columbia, 1968–); James C. Ballagh (ed.), *The Letters of Richard Henry Lee*, 2 vols. (New York, 1911); William T. Read (ed.), *Life and Correspondence of George Read* . . . (Philadelphia, 1870); William B. Reed (ed.), *Life and Correspondence of Joseph Reed* (Philadelphia, 1847); R. W. Neeser (ed.), *The Despatches of Molyneux Shuldham, January—July 1776* (New York, 1913); "Papers of William Vernon and the Navy Board, 1776–1794," *Publications of the Rhode Island Historical Society*, VIII (1901), 197–277; Bernhard Knollenberg (ed.), *Correspondence of Governor Samuel Ward, May 1775–March 1776* (Providence, 1952); W. C. Ford (ed.), *Warren–Adams Letters*, 2 vols. (Boston, 1917–25); J. C. Fitzpatrick (ed.), *The Writings of George Washington* . . . , 39 vols. (Washington 1931–44); Fitzpatrick (ed.), *Correspondence and Journals of Samuel Blachley Webb*, 3 vols. (New York, 1893).

In the two hundred years since their Revolution began Americans have never tired of telling the story. The amount of secondary literature, articles and books on the period is astounding. The non-naval books of most use were John R. Alden, *The American Revolution* (New York, 1954); Samuel Flagg Bemis, *The Diplomacy of the American Revolution* (New York, 1935); Oscar Brand, *Songs of '76: A Folksinger's History of the Revolution* (New York, 1972); Edmund C. Burnett, *The Continental Congress* (New York, 1941); Robert A. East, *Business Enterprise in the American Revolutionary Era* (New York, 1938); E. James Ferguson, *The Power of the Purse: A History of American Public Finance, 1776–1790* (Chapel Hill, 1961); Allen French, *The First Year of the American Revolution* (Boston, 1934); Gustave Lanctot, *Canada and the American Revolution* (Cambridge, 1967); William R. Lindsey, *Treatment of American Prisoners of War During the Revolution*, vol. XXII of the *Emporia State Research Studies* (Emporia, Kansas, 1973); Charles Metzger, *The Prisoner in the American Revolution* (Chicago, 1971); Richard B. Morris, *The Peacemakers* (New York, 1965); Allan Nevins, *The American States During and After the Revolution, 1775–1789* (New York, 1924); Benjamin Quarles, *The Negro in the American Revolution* (Chapel Hill, 1961); Kenneth Roberts, *March to Quebec* (Garden City, 1942); Jennings B. Sanders, *Evolution of Executive Departments of the Continental Congress, 1774–1779* (Chapel Hill, 1935); Marshall Smelser, *The Winning of Independence* (Chicago, 1972); Justin H. Smith, *Our Struggle for the Fourteenth Colony*, 2 vols. (New York, 1907); William Stinchombe, *The American Revolution and the French Alliance*, and finally the best and most complete in this category, Christopher Ward, *The War of the Revolution*, 2 vols. (New York, 1952).

The participants in the Revolution, including naval officers, have not lacked biographers. John C. Miller, *Sam Adams, Pioneer in Propaganda* (Boston, 1936); Charles

Jellison, *Ethan Allen, Frontier Rebel* (Syracuse, 1969); Willard Wallace, *Traitorous Hero: The Life and Fortunes of Benedict Arnold* (New York, 1954); James S. Biddle (ed.), *Autobiography of Charles Biddle* . . . (Philadelphia, 1883); Robert C. Alberts, *The Golden Voyage: The Life and Times of William Bingham, 1752–1804* (Boston, 1969); James B. Hedges, *The Browns of Providence Plantation's Colonial Years* (Cambridge, 1952); William Fowler, *William Ellery: A Rhode Island Politico and Lord of Admiralty* (Metuchen, 1973); Carl Van Doren, *Benjamin Franklin* (New York, 1938); George A. Billias, *General John Glover and His Marblehead Mariners* (New York, 1960); Louis Gottschalk, *Lafayette and the Close of the American Revolution* (Chicago, 1942); Clarence L. Ver Steeg, *Robert Morris, Revolutionary Financier* (Philadelphia, 1945); Don R. Gerlach, *Philip Schuyler and the American Revolution in New York* (Lincoln, 1964); James T. Flexner, *George Washington, The Forge of Experience* (Boston, 1965) and *George Washington in the American Revolution* (Boston, 1968); Douglas S. Freeman, *George Washington, Leader of the Revolution* (New York, 1951).

American naval officers of the Revolution have been the subject of a good deal of biographical work but unfortunately the quantity belies the quality. Among those I used was Ralph Paine, *Joshua Barney, A Forgotten Hero of Blue Water* (New York, 1924). A number of biographies have appeared on John Barry, but a new one needs to be done. In the meantime the following are useful: Martin Griffin, *Commodore John Barry* (Philadelphia, 1903); Joseph Gurn, *Commodore John Barry* . . . (New York, 1939), and William Meany, *Commodore John Barry* . . . (New York, 1911). The late William B. Clark, who almost singlehandedly rescued the Continental navy from oblivion, contributed a small squadron of books, including *Captain Dauntless, The Story of Nicholas Biddle of the Continental Navy* (Baton Rouge, 1949); *The First Saratoga, Being the Saga of John Young and His Sloop-of-War* (Baton Rouge, 1953); *Gallant John Barry, 1745–1803: The Story of a Naval Hero of Two Wars* (New York, 1938); and *Lambert Wickes, Sea Raider and Diplomat* . . . (New Haven, 1932). Gustavus Conyngham, an important but little-known officer, last had a biographer in 1902, James Barnes, *With the Flag in the Channel* . . . (New York, 1902), while Seth Harding, another lesser known, has a biography by James L. Howard, *Seth Harding, Mariner* (New Haven, 1930). Despite his importance and the availability of material, there has been only one full-length biography of Esek Hopkins: Edward Field, *Esek Hopkins* . . . (Providence, 1898).

Perhaps the neglect of Hopkins and the other captains can be explained by the almost magical attraction of John Paul Jones. Smith lists no fewer than 137 entries, articles and books, for Jones. I found the best to be the outstanding biography by Samuel Eliot Morison, *John Paul Jones, A Sailor's Biography* (Boston, 1959), along with Lincoln Lorenz, *John Paul Jones, Fighter for Freedom and Glory* (Annapolis, 1943), and Alexander Mackenzie, *The Life of John Paul Jones*, 2 vols. (Boston, 1845). Isaac Greenwood's *Captain John Manley* . . . (Boston, 1915) is the only full-length treatment of that gentleman, but it can supplemented by William J. Morgan's well-done *Captains to the Northward: The New England Captains in the Continental Navy* (Barre, 1959).

To this list of full-length biographies should be added a number of extremely valuable, albeit brief, sketches by various authors, in Allen Johnson and Dumas Malone (eds.), *The Dictionary of American Biography*, 20 vols. (New York, 1930).

Anyone writing on the naval aspects of the Revolution must begin with the two classics, Gardner W. Allen, *A Naval History of the American Revolution*, 2 vols. (Boston, 1913), and Alfred T. Mahan, *Major Operations of the Navies in the War of Independence* (Boston, 1913). Mahan devotes most of his attention to the European navies. A very recent and well-written general account is Nathan Miller, *Sea of Glory* . . . (New York, 1974).

Other histories found useful include: Thomas Clarke, *Naval History of the United States, From the Commencement of the Revolutionary War to the Present Time* (Philadelphia, 1814); William B. Clark, *Ben Franklin's Privateers* (Baton Rouge, 1956) and *George Washington's Navy* (Baton Rouge, 1960); James Fenimore Cooper, *History of the Navy of the United States of America*, 2 vols. (Philadelphia, 1839); George F. Emmons, *The Navy of the United States, From the Commencement 1775 to 1853, With a Brief History of Each Vessel's Service and Fate* (Washington, 1853); Charles W. Goldsborough, *United States Naval Chronicle*, 2 vols. (Washington, 1824); John W. Jackson, *The Pennsylvania Navy, 1775–1781: The Defense of the Delaware*; Dudley W. Knox, *The Naval Genius of George Washington* (Boston, 1932); Edgar S. Maclay, *A History of the United States Navy from 1775 to 1901*, 3 vols. (New York, 1906–10); John J. McCusker, *Alfred, The First Continental Flagship, 1775–1778* (Washington, 1973); Robert W. Neeser, *Statistical and Chronological History of the United States Navy, 1775–1907*, 2 vols. (New York, 1909); C. O. Paullin, *The Navy of the American Revolution* . . . (Cleveland, 1906), and Fletcher Pratt, *The Navy* (New York, 1941).

Although my research dealt almost exclusively with the American navy, inevitably there was a need to examine the British. A good history of the British navy in the Revolution is very much wanted. Books I found relevant were: R. S. Allison, *Sea Diseases* (London, 1943); Daniel A. Baugh, *British Naval Administration in the Age of Walpole* (Princeton, 1965); Sir Gilbert Blane, *Observations on the Diseases Incident to Seamen* (London, 1785); William L. Cowes, *The Royal Navy: A History from the Earliest Times to the Present*, vols. III and IV (London, 1899); Sir Richard V. Hamilton, *Naval Administration* (London, 1896); J. R. Hutchinson, *The Press-Gang Afloat and Ashore* (New York, 1913); William M. James, *The British Navy in Adversity: A Study of the War of Independence* (New York, 1926); Michael Lewis, *The Navy of Britain* (London, 1948); Christopher Lloyd and Jack L. S. Coulter, *Medicine in the Navy, 1714–1815*, vol. III (London, 1961); John Masefield, *Sea Life in Nelson's Time* (London, 1905); Sir Herbert Richmond, *Statesmen and Seapower* (Oxford, 1946); David Syrett, *Shipping and the American War, 1775–1783* (London, 1970), and Gomer Williams, *History of the Liverpool Privateers* (Liverpool, 1897).

There is a bountiful supply of information about the Revolution at sea contained in various journals. In this regard the two most valuable sources are the *American Neptune Magazine* and the United States Naval Institute *Proceedings*. Beyond the numerous articles in those two preeminent maritime journals I also found useful: John K. Alexander, "Forton Prison During the American Revolution . . . ," *Essex Institute Historical Collections*, CIII (October 1967), 365–89; Olive Anderson, "The Treatment of Prisoners of War in Britain During the American War of Independence," London University Institute of Historical Research *Bulletin*, XXVII (May 1955), 63–83; Marion Balderston, "Lord Howe Clears the Delaware," *Pennsylvania Magazine of History and Biography*, XCVI (July 1972), 326–45; J. H. Broomfield, "Lord Sandwich at the Admiralty Board; Politics and the British Navy, 1771–1778," *Mariner's Mirror*, LI (February 1965), 7–17; Dora Mae Clark, "The Impressment of Seamen in the American Colonies," in *Essays in Colonial History Presented to Charles McLean Andrews* (Freeport, 1966), 198–224; Elizabeth Cometti, "Civil Servants of the Revolutionary Period," *Pennsylvania Magazine of History and Biography*, LXXV (1951), 159–69; Cometti, "Impressment During the American Revolution," in Vera Largent (ed.),

The Walter Clinton Jackson Essays . . . (Chapel Hill, 1942), 97–109; J. F. Jameson, "St. Eustatius in the Revolution," *American Historical Review*, VIII (July 1903), 683–708; Jesse Lemisch, "Jack Tar in the Streets: Merchant Seamen in the Politics of Revolutionary America," *William and Mary Quarterly*, 3d ser., XXV (July 1968), 371–407, and "Listening to the Inarticulate: William Widger's Dream and the Loyalties of American Revolutionary Seamen in British Prisons," *Social History*, III (1969), 1–29; Malcolm Lloyd, "The Taking of the Bahamas by the Continental Navy in 1776," *Pennsylvania Magazine of History and Biography*, XLIX (October 1925), 349–66; Maurer Maurer, "Coppered Bottoms for the Royal Navy: A Factor in the Maritime War of 1778–1783," *Military Affairs*, XIV (1950), 57–61; Richard B. Morris, "The Revolution's Caine Mutiny," *American Heritage*, XI (April 1960), 10–13, 88–91; Sidney G. Morse, "State or Continental Privateers?" *American Historical Review*, LII (October 1946), 68–73; Hugh F. Rankin, "The Naval Flag of the American Revolution," *William and Mary Quarterly*, 3d ser., XI (July 1954), 339–53; Daniel B. Reibel, "The British Navy on the Upper Great Lakes, 1760–1789," *Niagara Frontier*, XX (Autumn 1973), 66–75; Henry I. Shaw, "Penobscot Assault 1779," *Military Affairs*, XVII (Summer 1953), 83–94; Orlando W. Stephenson, "The Supply of Gunpowder in 1776," *American Historical Review*, XXX (January 1925), 271–81, and Roland G. Usher, "Royal Navy Impressment During the American Revolution," *Mississippi Valley Historical Review*, XXXVII (March 1951), 673–88.

One last resource also needs to be touched on—dissertations. I found four to be especially relevant: Jonathan R. Dull, "The French Navy and American Independence: Naval Factors in French Diplomacy and War Strategy, 1774–1780" (University of California, Berkeley, 1972); Frank C. Mevers III, "Congress and the Navy: The Establishment and Administration of the American Revolutionary Navy by the Continental Congress, 1775–1784" (University of North Carolina, Chapel Hill, 1972); Stephen T. Powers, "The Decline and Extinction of American Naval Power, 1781–1787" (University of Notre Dame, 1964), and M. J. Williams, "Naval Administration of the Fourth Earl of Sandwich, 1771–1782," (Oxford University, 1962).

Index

Boston, Mass., 3, 6, 9, 12, 14, 16–17, 19, 20, 21, 24, 31, 32, 34, 35, 36–38, 42, 47, 50, 59, 70, 74, 75, 87, 97, 103, 104, 108, 122, 196, 218, 233, 238, 244, 255, 259, 262, 270, 271, 272, 281, 282, 285, 286, 287, 295, 301
Boston (frigate), 9, 93, 107, 110, 228, 231, 246
Boston (gundalow), 204
Boston Gazette (newspaper), 266
Bounties, enlistment, 283
Bourbon (frigate), 87, 89, 247
Bowen, Captain Ephraim, Jr., 27
Bowers, Sylvester, 218, 223, 232
Boyne (70 gun ship), 32, 55
Bradford, John, 70, 75, 83, 84, 87, 250
Brazil, 152
Brest harbor, 151, 152
Brewer, Colonel John, 116
Brewington, Marion V., 221
Bridenbaugh, Carl, 6
Brigs and brigantines, 214. *See also* names of brigs and brigantines
Brittany, 133, 146–47, 151, 159
Brooklyn (cruiser), 169
Broughton, Captain Nicholson, 21–24, 25–27, 101
Brown, John, 240, 241, 242, 244
Brown, Nicholas, 240, 241, 242, 244
Browne, Governor Montfort, 97
Brunswick (schooner), 198
Bryan, George, 81
Bull, Colonel John, 222
Bunker Hill, 76, 231
Burden, Captain, 156
Burgoyne, General John, 102, 182
Burling, Lancaster, 218
Buzzards Bay, 17

Cabot (brig), 57, 58, 96, 98–99, 100, 101, 266
Cádiz harbor, 140, 141, 143
Calais, port of, 130, 131
Cambridge, Mass., 17, 21, 26, 31, 35, 37, 54, 174, 177, 180, 222
Camilla (sloop), 117
Canada, 50, 111, 127, 176, 178, 184, 192, 193, 196
invasion of, 180–83, 193, 198, 231
Canceaux (ship), 200
Canton, China, 90
Cape Anne, 23, 30
Cape Breton Island, 102
Cape Cod, 3, 17, 105
Cape Finisterre, 139
Cape Henlopen, 104
Cape Henry, 106
Cape May, 104, 105
Cape Wrath, 165
Captains and ship commands, 256–78
commissions and appointments, 257–67
conduct and discipline, 272–78
courts-martial, 268–72
mutinies and, 275–76
officers and rank, 261–63

relations with civilian authorities, 267–68
Carleton, General Guy, 180, 181, 182, 196, 198–200, 210
Carleton (schooner), 199, 201, 202, 208
Casco Bay (Portland, Me.), 34
Casdrop, Captain Thomas, 190–91, 201
Castle William (Boston Harbor), 12
Cazneau, Isaac, 260
Cerberus (frigate), 30
Ceres (sloop), 147
Cerf (cutter), 164
Champion (xebec), 214
Champlain, Lake. *See* Lake Champlain
Chapelle, Howard, 221
Charleston, S.C., 4, 86, 93, 110, 118, 119, 248, 264
Charlottetown, 26
Charming Peggy (vessel), 136, 144
Chase, Samuel, 49, 219
Chatham, Mass., 247
Chatham (ship), 36
Chaumont, 158
Chesapeake Bay, 35, 59, 60, 105, 290
Civil War, 110
Clinton, General Sir Henry, 110
Coats, Warwick, 219
Cochran, Captain Robert, 280–81
"Cockpit," 294
Coit, Captain William, 28–29, 31
Collier, George, 117
Collins, Captain John, 24
Columbus (warship), 57, 58, 96, 98, 100, 101, 108, 220
Commerce (sloop), 46
Committee of Safety (Massachusetts), 173–74
Committee of Secret Correspondence, 129
Concord, Mass., 16
Concord, Battle of, 16–17, 41, 173
Confederacy (frigate), 85, 87–88, 103, 104, 105, 107, 247, 266, 267, 278
Congress (frigate), 206, 208, 231, 246
"Congress" (mortar), 31
Connecticut, 44, 46, 51, 64, 76, 103, 173, 189, 217, 218, 223–24, 240, 262, 285
Connecticut (gundalow), 204
Connecticut River, 2, 223–24, 244, 281
Constitution (frigate), 227
Continental Association, 40
Continental Congress, 14–15, 39–90, 231, 245
convened, 39–41
Marine Committee, 61–78
reorganization and failure, 79–90
Naval Committee, 56–60
resolution of 18 July, 46
Rhode Island resolution, 47–53, 63
task of, 39
trade question, 47–48, 50
Washington and, 41, 51, 52, 57, 79

INDEX

Hackett, John, 247
Hackett, William, 222, 247
Hague (frigate), 89, 247
Halifax, N.S., 31, 37, 111, 112, 125
Hallock, Captain William, 96, 259–60
Hampden (state ship), 100, 101, 102, 113
Hancock, John, 16, 25, 47, 65, 178, 217, 224–25, 247, 258–59, 260
Hancock (frigate), 31, 93, 123, 124, 228, 231, 246, 262
Hancock (schooner), 25, 27, 31
Hannah (schooner), 7, 21–24, 90
Happy Return (schooner), 139
Harding, Captain Seth, 104, 267, 278
Harpers Ferry, Battle of (1862), 110
Harrison, Benjamin, 57
Harrison (schooner), 27, 28–29, 57
Hartford, Conn., 173, 177
Hawkins, Sir John, 66
Hawley, Captain David, 204
Hazard, Captain John, 96, 275
Henrica Sophia (ship), 142
Henshaw, Colonel Joseph, 177
Hero (privateer), 220
Herrick, Captain Samuel, 174
Hessians, 106, 284
Hewes, Joseph, 56
Hibernia (schooner), 106
Hill, James, 217–18
Hinman, Colonel Benjamin, 177
Hinman, Captain Elisha, 147, 266–67
Hispaniola, 100
Hoaglandt, Okey, 68–69
Hobart, Aaron, 238–39, 240
Hodge, William, 136–37, 138, 140, 143
Holland, 149, 150, 162, 213, 216
Hollingsworth, Jesse, 219
Hope furnace, 238, 240
Hopkins, Commodore Esek, 57, 60, 61, 73, 100–101, 107, 108, 118, 214, 220, 257, 259, 261, 262, 264, 268, 276–77, 282
  dismissed, 277
  Nassau attack (1776), 96–97, 99
  off Block Island, 97–99
Hopkins, Captain John B., 57–58, 96, 105, 285
Hopkins, Stephen, 47, 48, 49, 56, 57, 217, 218
Hornet (sloop), 60, 96, 260
House of Burgesses (Virginia), 39
Howe, Captain Tyringham, 97–98
Howe, General William, 37, 195, 245, 246, 261, 296
Hudson Bay, 101, 103, 118, 152
Hudson River, 2, 49, 171, 173, 184, 186, 218, 224
Humphreys, Joshua, 220, 221
Humphreys and Wharton (shipbuilders), 215, 219, 220–22
Hunter, Captain Robert, 30–31
Hussar (cutter), 152, 153, 155
Hynson, Captain Joseph, 131

Impressment, British policy of, 11, 12, 43, 286–89
Independence (sloop), 146, 147, 151
Indians, 41, 171, 205, 225, 290
Indien (frigate), 158, 163, 213
Inflexible (square-rigger), 200, 201, 202, 207
Intolerable Acts, 39
Ipswich, Mass., 3
Ireland, 133, 136, 139, 152, 153, 154, 156, 162, 164
Iris (frigate), 123, 124, 246
Irish Sea, 133, 134, 139, 152, 153, 154
Iron manufacturing, 234–36, 237
Isis (50 gun ship), 197, 198
Isle de Croix, 163
Isle of Man, 152
Isle la Motte, 204, 205
Isle Aux Noix, 179, 182

Jamaica, 77, 103
Jason (ship), 106
Jay, John, 79, 80
Jefferson, Thomas, 129
Jersey (gundalow), 204, 209
Jersey (prison ship), 299–300
Johnson, Captain Henry, 132–33
Johnson, Thomas, 288–89
Jones, Ichabod, 18–19
Jones, John Paul, 66, 95, 144, 145–48, 149–70, 213, 214, 229, 248, 251, 252, 262, 270–71, 274, 275, 276, 278, 280, 283–84, 286, 289, 303
  African plan (1776), 99–101
  Bonhomme Richard command, 158–59, 160, 164–68, 169
  death of, 169
  Franklin's instructions to, 160–61
  Kirkcudbright Bay raid, 154–56
  Nova Scotia attack, 102–3
  order to abandon ship, 168
  in Philadelphia, 264–66
  Ranger exploits, 149, 150–57, 158, 159, 169
  in Russia, 169
  sojourn in Paris, 149–50
Joseph (brig), 138

Katy (sloop), 46
Kennebec River, 2–3, 225
Kirkcudbright Bay, 154, 155–56
Knowles, Admiral Charles, 9
Knox, William, 111

La Coruña harbor, 139, 140, 144
Lafayette, Marquis de, 160–62
Lake Champlain, 171–80, 187, 214
  American squadron on, 171–80
  Canada invasion and, 180–83
  logistics problem, 186–87
  naval command, 183–85, 186
  at Valcour Island, 192–211
Lake George, 173, 176, 186
La Luzerne, Chevalier de, 85

(351)

INDEX